Communication
and the Natural World

Communication
and the Natural World

Judith Hendry
University of New Mexico

Strata Publishing, Inc.
State College, Pennsylvania

9 8 7 6 5 4 3 2 1

Communication and the Natural World

Published by:
Strata Publishing, Inc.
P.O. Box 1303
State College, PA 16804
USA
telephone: 1-814-234-8545
fax: 1-814-238-7222
web site: http://www.stratapub.com

Text and cover design by WhiteOak Creative.

Cover image and interior background image on part openers, chapter openers, text
boxes and page ii: Petroglyphs at sunset by Richard Berry/Axiom Photographic Agency/
Getty Images

Printed and bound by Edwards Brothers, Incorporated, on EB Recycled Opaque paper.

Credits and acknowledgments appear on page 294 and on this page by reference.

Library of Congress Cataloging-in-Publication Data

Hendry, Judith, date.
  Communication and the natural world / Judith Hendry.
     p. cm.
  Includes bibliographical references and index.
  ISBN 978-1-891136-24-5 (pbk. : alk. paper)
  1. Communication in the environmental sciences. 2. Mass media and the environment.
  I. Title.
  GE25.H46 2010
  333.72--dc22
                              2010009837

ISBN (13) 978-1-891136-24-5

To Doug for his sustaining encouragement and patience.

Brief Contents

Contents

Part V
Public Participation and Environmental Advocacy   217

Preface

Throughout my years of teaching courses in environmental communication, I have been repeatedly reminded that there is something particularly gratifying about teaching a subject that really matters. This statement is not meant to suggest that all those other courses taught in the august halls of academe don't matter. Rather, it is a reflection of my firm belief in the central premise of this book—that the ways we communicate about the natural world profoundly influence, and to a large extent determine, the ways we perceive and interact with it. The current state of environmental affairs, brought about by our fundamentally unsustainable human/nature relationship, makes the study of environmental communication one of the most relevant, timely, and important courses taught on college campuses today. As the Senegalese saying tells us: "In the end we conserve only what we love. We will love only what we understand. We will understand only what we are taught." There is a direct and discernable connection between what we, as educators, teach and what we, as a society, care about and protect.

This book is intended primarily as an introduction to the study of environmental communication for undergraduate students. It synthesizes multiple perspectives, theories, and research topics in language that I believe will be accessible to undergraduate communication majors, as well as to students in other majors who are not acquainted with the disciplinary assumptions of communication studies. It draws on the research of environmental communication scholars and on the work of writers across a wide range of disciplines and discourses.

It is my hope that this book will have relevance for students in courses that focus on the human side of the human/nature relationship, including courses that deal with sustainability studies, environmental politics, social movements, environmental ethics, and, of course, environmental communication.

Because of the inextricable link between social systems and natural systems, I believe this book also has relevance for the study of this relationship from the "nature" side of the human/nature interaction. For students of ecology, environmental science, earth systems science, and conservation biology, the integrative framework of science and society offers an expanded and critical lens through which to view and interpret our current environmental conditions.

Practitioners in activities such as environmental advocacy, resource management, public stakeholder processes, environmental dispute resolution, and collaborative decision-making may also find this book useful. It examines the nexus of communication theory and practice through multiple examples and case studies that bring to light many of the issues involved in the day-to-day practice of managing our symbolic and natural resources.

The multi-disciplinary nature of the inquiry into environmental communication, the diversity of epistemological lenses employed, and the expansive range of applications are a testament to the richness and relevance of environmental communication studies. In one way or another, whether we approach environmental issues from the science side or from the human side, as academics or as practitioners, we are all engaged in the essential business of communicating about the environment.

Features of the Book

This book takes as axiomatic the assumption that we have serious environmental problems that we need to understand and address. Written with the lay reader in mind, it establishes an environmental literacy baseline for students beginning their studies in environmental communication. In my own teaching, I have found that a fundamental understanding of humans' impact on the natural world is a necessary starting point if students are to take an informed and critical look at the role that communication plays in our current state of environmental affairs.

This book also summarizes the various environmental philosophies and perspectives that ground environmental thinking. The voices of environmentalism are far from monolithic. Although most people can agree with the premise that we have serious problems that we need to address, multiple and often conflicting voices compete to define the problems and how to address them. An awareness of the nuanced yet significant differences among the various perspectives gives students a framework for interpreting the often contentious cacophony of environmental voices. Students are advised to use discretion when applying philosophy to practice since the various perspectives are not mutually exclusive and the lines separating them are sometimes blurred or indistinguishable.

The book builds on this foundation of environmental issues and perspectives to present an extensive examination of the environmental rhetoric that permeates our everyday lives. Students are introduced to the multiple sites of meaning-making and the rhetorical forms that shape the discourses of environmental advocacy, politics and science, as well as the mass-mediated discourses of popular culture, green marketing, and news reporting. Throughout the book, students are directed in a study of how and why messages matter and of the critical role of environmental rhetoric in constructing the human/nature relationship.

Finally, the book introduces students to citizen involvement in environmental decision making and grassroots advocacy, which are discussed within the context of their historical, political, and legal frameworks. It examines the essential role of citizen advocacy and the tools that are available for those who take on the challenges and rewards of environmental activism in a democratic society.

Pedagogy

In writing this book, I have made several strategic choices to enhance its pedagogical utility. I have attempted to address the subject areas in language that is accessible to undergraduate students and practitioners outside of the academic setting, while still maintaining the academic integrity of the content. Many examples from historical and contemporary discourse are incorporated to clarify concepts and to make the book more engaging for the reader.

The *Connections* textboxes, interspersed throughout the chapters, connect theory to practice, ideas, and events, and augment the book's content by offering alternative perspectives or additional information. A broad range of topics, such as newsworthy environmental events, scientific theory, new green trends, and controversial perspectives, are introduced to heighten interest, broaden knowledge, and advance awareness of environmental communication at work in the world.

Photographs and other illustrations, also interspersed throughout the book, help bring to life the people, perspectives, and concepts discussed in the text. Some of these give faces to historic names and iconic figures, while others illustrate environmental communication in contemporary contexts and real-world settings. The captions extend the visual commentary represented in these images.

At the end of each chapter, you will find discussion questions and exercises geared to engage the student through application of issues and concepts, and to challenge the student to reach farther and learn more. These have been beta tested in my own classrooms, and I have found them to work well as discussion guides, group exercises, or graded assignments.

Recommended readings at the end of each chapter invite the student to go beyond the book and further explore the topics and ideas it presents. These lists direct students to original authors, groundbreaking work, and influential writers in the field of environmental communication, as well as to significant works of environmental writers from a diverse range of disciplines and research traditions.

An Appendix, *Additional Readings,* contains five classic environmental essays that are intended to familiarize students with some of the compelling and influential voices of the past. The authors of these works have inspired environmental thinking throughout the decades and remain relevant, thought-provoking, and timely today. The essays, referenced throughout the text, may serve as useful artifacts for analysis and classroom discussions.

A *Selected Bibliography* offers an extensive list of classical, popular, and scholarly works from which I have drawn information and inspiration, and that I believe may be useful to students who wish to continue their study of environmental issues and communication. Examples from this list are used throughout the text to highlight and clarify ideas and concepts, and to introduce students to many of the noteworthy writers and scholars in this multidisciplinary field of study.

An annotated *Timeline* of significant milestones of the modern environmental movement is also included at the end of the book. Though representing only a small part of our inheritance from those who have gone before us, the milestones listed on this timeline bring to light our debt of gratitude to all those whose toil and tears were the driving force behind the environmental movement and led to the environmental protections we enjoy today.

The reader will undoubtedly recognize the pro-environmental bias that permeates the book. As mentioned earlier, this book begins with the assumption that we have serious environmental problems that we need to address—an assumption that implies a need for action. Thus, what we do and what we teach as environmental communication scholars is inherently and inevitably normative and prescriptive. I believe that our ultimate concern as scholars in this field should be the pursuit of knowledge to advance changes in the conditions of society that have led to our sobering environmental realities. Throughout the book, students are challenged to learn more, to contribute to the conversation, and to take an active role in bringing about changes necessary for a more sustainable future.

Organization of the Book

The wide range of topics and areas of research covered in this book are organized into five parts. Part I, "Environmental Communication in a Changing World," introduces students to the study of environmental communication and its grounding assumptions.

Chapter 1, "Communication and the Environment," shows how symbols influence perceptions of reality and, by extension, how communication influences the ways we perceive and interact with the natural world.

Chapter 2, "Our Changing Environment," discusses many of the significant environmental problems we currently face. It is intended to give students a baseline of environmental literacy from which to begin their study of environmental communication.

Part II, "Environmental Worldviews," summarizes the major environmental perspectives that ground environmental thinking, policies, and practices.

Chapter 3, "Mainstream Environmental Perspectives," looks at stewardship, conservation, preservation, and sustainable development, as well as some of the significant historical and cultural influences that have led to mainstream anthropocentric assumptions about the human/nature relationship.

Chapter 4, "Radical Environmental Perspectives," examines challenges to the mainstream views that have emerged through the philosophical perspectives of deep ecology, social ecology, and ecofeminism. The chapter outlines the differences among these perspectives while cautioning the student against applying blanket categorizations to a particular person or group based on these philosophical distinctions.

Part III, "Rhetoric and the Environment," is designed to move students toward a critical awareness of the pervasiveness of environmental rhetoric in our everyday lives, as well as its profound impact on our perceptions, policies, and practices.

Chapter 5, "An Introduction to Environmental Rhetoric," discusses rhetorical functions and forms. It also introduces students to some of the major rhetorical figures, both historical and contemporary, that have contributed to this richly diverse area of inquiry.

Chapter 6, "Rhetoric of Polarization," examines polarizing rhetoric by way of case studies involving two influential groups that are poles apart in their philosophies concerning humans' place in the natural world—Earth First! and Wise Use.

Chapter 7, "Prophetic Rhetoric: Apocalyptic, Irreparable, Utopian, and Jeremiadic," examines forms of prophetic rhetoric that figure predominantly in messages we create and receive about the natural world.

Chapter 8, "Technical Rationality and the Rhetoric of Risk, Science, and Technology," looks at the roles of technical rationality and cultural rationality in discourse about environmental issues. It shows why technical rationality, even when grounded in the most compelling science, often fails to sway public opinion or translate into policy and practice.

Part IV, "Media, Popular Culture, and the Environment," exposes students to a number of sites of rhetoric production. The chapters in this section are designed to bring to light the pervasive influence of cultural messages and their implications for constructing humans' place in the natural world.

Chapter 9, "Environmental News Reporting," deals with one of the more conspicuous sites of meaning construction. This chapter examines some of the difficulties faced by those who are tasked with reporting complex, sound bite–defying environmental issues.

Chapter 10, "Green Advertising and the Green Consumer," deals with another conspicuous site of meaning construction. This chapter looks at the kinds of ads used in green marketing, the messages they send, and the inherent paradox of "green consumption."

Chapter 11, "Popular Culture and the Environment," explores some less obvious but profoundly influential sites of meaning construction, by way of a guided tour of selected popular culture sites that environmental communication scholars have examined. This chapter gives the student a glimpse of the power to create environmental realities that resides in the vast domain of popular culture.

Part V, "Public Participation and Environmental Advocacy," shifts the focus from citizens as consumers of environmental messages to citizens as activists and participants in the dynamic and ever-evolving environmental conversation.

Chapter 12, "Public Participation in Environmental Decision-Making," covers a broad range of topics. It discusses the National Environmental Policy Act of 1970, which created the mechanism for incorporating public participation in federal land use decisions. This chapter also highlights significant legislation that has enhanced access to information for citizen activists. Several case studies demonstrate the benefits of citizen participation in environmental decision-making, as well as some of the obstacles that often impede the effectiveness of that participation.

Chapter 13, "From the Ground Up: The Environmental Justice Movement," directs attention to ways in which those who are most impacted by environmental pollutants and degradation are silenced by the rhetorical disadvantages that accompany racial, social, economic, and political inequalities. It offers an extended look at the environmental justice movement, topics, and sites of concern, both in our own backyards and abroad. The chapter concludes with a look at the injustice of global warming and a call to consider the moral implications of a world where the poorest populations bear a disproportionate share of the costs.

In reading this book, students will examine a broad range of symbolic resources and environmental messages through multiple lenses. I look at these lenses as telescopic viewfinders like those stationed periodically in our national parks that, for a quarter, will frame and magnify a select portion of the panorama. Each perspective discussed in this book brings into focus that which might have been obscured, and presents a communication framework through which to view our complicated, inextricably intertwined, and manifestly broken human/nature relationship.

Acknowledgments

The true pleasure of writing this book has come from the subject matter handed to me by the scholars and writers in this rich, relevant, and exciting field of inquiry. It is with tremendous gratitude that I acknowledge my debt to all those academics and practitioners on whom I have drawn so extensively throughout this work. I also gratefully acknowledge the invaluable contribution of my students who have significantly influenced this work from its earliest inception and who have been my impetus, my inspiration, and my most adroit critics. I would also like to recognize the large and impressive jury of peer reviewers, many of whom I have the honor of knowing. Much of what you read in this book is a direct result of their insight, expertise, and enthusiasm for this emerging field of study. Among those who have contributed extensively to this book are James G. Cantrill, Northern Michigan University; Terence Check, College of Saint Benedict and Saint John's University; Catherine Collins, Willamette University; Stephen Depoe, University of Cincinnati; Jonathan Gray, Southern Illinois University; James Hasenauer, California State University, Northridge; Jeffrey Kassing, Arizona State University West; William Kinsella, North Carolina State University; Mark Meisner, State University of New York, Syracuse; Jennifer Peeples, Utah State University; Daniel J. Philippon, University of Minnesota; Emily Plec, Western Oregon University; Steven Schwarze, University of Montana; Susan Senecah, State University of New York, Syracuse; Stacey K. Sowards, University of Texas at El Paso; Jessica Thompson, Colorado State University; and Anne Marie Todd, San Jose State University.

I wish to express my profound appreciation and gratitude to my editor and publisher, Kathleen Domenig, whose patience, encouragement, astute analysis, and sterling insight have brought this book to publication and taught me so much. I also wish to thank Brian Henry, Strata's general manager, for his hard work and meticulous oversight of this project. Every page of the book has been refined and enhanced through their keen judgments and extraordinary efforts.

And finally, this book could never have come to fruition without the tireless support and enduring patience of my husband, Doug who, as in the timeless words of William Blake, can "see a world in a grain of sand." Time and time again, his confidence in me, his gentle persuasion, and his steadfast support smoothed the journey and kept me going.

Part I

Environmental Communication in a Changing World

Chapter 1

Communication and the Environment

In December of 1972, *Apollo 17* **astronauts** returned home from their mission with what would become, in the words of popular astronomer Carl Sagan, "the icon of our age."[1] The "blue marble," as it has come to be known, was the first clear photographic image of an illuminated face of the whole earth in all its colorful magnificence and rare beauty.[2] From this planetary perspective, the organic holism of a fragile unitary ecosystem was brought into focus. As President Jimmy Carter stated in an address at the 1978 Congressional Space Medal of Honors Ceremony, "We saw our own world as a single, delicate globe of swirling blue and white, green, brown. From the perspective of space, our planet has no national boundaries. It is very beautiful, but also very fragile. And it is the special responsibility of the human race to preserve it."[3]

Many believe that we have failed in our responsibility to preserve our global inheritance. In our unbridled pursuit of technological advancements and economic growth, progress has come at a high price. "Human beings and the natural world are on a collision course." So begins the document titled "Warning to Humanity" released November 1, 1992, by the Union of Concerned Scientists.[4] This document, signed by more than 1500 of the world's leading scientists, including 99 out of 196 living Nobel laureates, further states:

> No more than one or a few decades remain before the chance to avert
> the threats we now confront will be lost and the prospects for humanity
> immeasurably diminished. . . . A great change in the stewardship of the earth
> and the life on it is required, if vast human misery is to be avoided . . . .

While some may challenge this bleak and unforgiving portrait, the fact remains that human intervention has significantly altered our natural environment. If we are to avoid the apocalyptic prophesies of the "Warning to Humanity" we must find ways to live not only within, but as a part of, the natural world. To do this, we must radically alter the way we perceive the natural world and our place in it.

Environmental communication, as a field of inquiry, seeks to describe and understand the role that communication plays in establishing the meaning of nature and humans' relationship to the natural world, and to influence human action as it pertains to the natural environment. This is no easy task. Social, cultural, religious, political, and economic influences all intervene as complicating and restraining dynamics in creating the necessary changes. Yet, the way we communicate about our environment affects, and to a large degree determines, our perceptions, practices, and policies.

Environmentalism has relied primarily on the work of environmental scientists to solve our ecological problems. While scientists have played and will continue to play a vital role, the critical work of changing the way we view and subsequently treat the natural world is the challenge of environmental communicators. The first step toward this lofty end is understanding the role that communication plays in creating and maintaining humans' relationship to the natural world.

Assumptions Grounding the Study of Environmental Communication

Environmental communication is still a very new and evolving field of inquiry, with a wide range of research interests and methodologies. Attempting to characterize and define the common properties of the research or the parameters of the field is a formidable task. The following description of the assumptions and of the study of environmental communication encapsulate what I believe are the fundamental anchor points of this rich, relevant, and timely area of study.

Three assumptions ground environmental communication research. The first is that *we face serious global environmental problems that must be addressed.* Some will argue that things are not as bad as the prophets of gloom would have us believe; that throughout the eons, nature's remarkable resilience has withstood natural onslaughts far more destructive than anything humans could ever impose. Yet, as environmental writer Alan S. Miller suggests, "In a fashion qualitatively different from any preceding period, we have now created both a set of socioeconomic-environmental-ethical problems and a science and technology that together pose the real possibility of unimaginable chaos in the near-term future."[5]

Determining the degree of any given environmental problem—whether it is a "concern," a "crisis," or something in between—is not within the scope of our enquiries as environmental communication scholars. That important work is left to the ecologists, biologists, climatologists, and so forth. Most of the work of environmental communication scholars starts with the assumption that there are problems that must be addressed, and focuses on addressing, in some form or fashion, the second and third assumptions that ground the study of environmental communication.

Assumption number two is that *our environmental problems are not fundamentally problems of nature, but human problems (social, cultural, political, psychological) that stem from the way we view the natural world and our relationship to it.* While ecologists examine the "nature" side of the problem, we examine the "human" side of the problem. For example, in looking at oil drilling in the Arctic National Wildlife Refuge (ANWR), ecologists would address questions concerning such things as how environmental pollutants from drilling will impact the region's flora and fauna. Environmental communication scholars, on the other hand, would examine such things as media portrayals of polar bears or caribou, the stories a culture shares about polar bears and caribou, and how these stories, in turn, shape our views about whether these animals should be protected.

The third assumption follows logically from the two preceding premises: *the way we communicate about the natural world influences and, in large part, determines the values we ascribe to the natural world and the ways we subsequently treat it.* The ways in which we talk about nature, the words we use, the stories we tell, all act to guide our behaviors. Susan L. Senecah, an environmental communication scholar and one of the leaders in establishing environmental communication as a formal area of study within the communication discipline, offers a pertinent point when she asks, "one wonders what the fate of the [Grand] Canyon would have been had John Wesley Powell chosen to call it Hell's Canyon."[6] (Powell was the first person to run the Colorado River through the entire length of the canyon). The implications of Senecah's question reach far beyond the Grand Canyon. Our best hope of changing the current course of environmental destruction is to change the way we communicate about the natural world. It is my hope that this book will help you to articulate an informed, theoretically based, sound answer to Senecah's question at the end of this course of study.

Defining the Study of Environmental Communication

Having established the basic assumptions grounding the study of environmental communication, I offer the following description of the study of environmental communication: *The study of environmental communication examines the use of symbols to influence, construct, and maintain humans' relationship to the natural world.* Don't be misled by the brevity of this description. It is a broad, loaded statement containing several terms and phrases that require further explanation: "symbols," "influence and construction," "maintenance," and "humans' relationship to the natural world." Let's begin with that last phrase.

Humans' Relationship to the Natural World

The meaning of **humans' relationship to the natural world** may, at first glance, seem self-evident, but it is loaded with implications, beginning with the idea of the natural world. The term "nature" is deceptively slippery and highly problematic in several ways. What exactly is the natural world that environmentalists care about protecting and preserving? We tend to view the natural world as the "big out there"—a place or thing that is separate and distant from humans and their cultures. Yet, upon reflection, one quickly comes to the realization that this view of nature is problematic on both conceptual and practical levels.

Conceptually, the "big out there" view of nature is misleading in that nature, even the most distant and "untamed" wilderness, is inextricably tied to culture, politics, economics, religion, and any number of human institutions of influence and control. Humans have penetrated and left an indelible mark on every corner of the earth. Those few areas that are left "mostly untouched," in their "almost pristine" form, are that way because of policies put in place or because of resource management plans that have oxymoronically designated those areas to be "managed as wilderness" until such time as the policies or plans change. A standing joke among U.S. Forest Service employees is that prior to the 1964 Wilderness Act, only God could make a wilderness, but now only Congress can.[7]

Even what appears to be nature's most magnificently unalterable wildness, Niagara Falls for example, is a product of the interaction of culture and nature, as Anne Whiston Spirn, professor of Landscape Architecture, demonstrates:

> Niagara Falls is shaped by water flowing, rocks falling, and trees growing, by artists and tourists, by journalists and landscape architects, by engineers and workers who divert the water. Niagara is constructed through processes of non-human nature, through water use and treaties, through paintings and postcards, memory and myth. Even the most awesome landscapes are products of both nature and culture . . . .[8]

The misleading view of nature as remote and separate from humans has broad implications for the way we treat the natural world. Many environmental philosophers believe that the conceptual human/nature split has led to and perpetuated

Cave of the Winds or Rock of Ages. Niagara Falls, N. Y.

One more for the album

Figure 1.1
Niagara Falls Postcard

Niagara Falls, an icon of the natural sublime, has inspired poets, artist, and lovers, as well as commercial developers, since becoming a popular tourist attraction in the early 1800s. This postcard, postmarked in 1906, shows the footbridge that was built in 1848 to accommodate sightseers, just one example of the nature/culture interaction that has shaped the falls. By the middle of the nineteenth century, its natural beauty had become overshadowed by the vast number of industrial and commercial enterprises that had sprung up around the falls. Preservationists won a major victory in 1885 when legislation created the Niagara Reservation, New York's first state park. The Canadian province of Ontario established Victoria Niagara Falls Park that same year.

Illustrated Postal Card Co., New York/Leipzig

our current environmental crisis. Eco-theologian Thomas Berry observes that "a radical discontinuity between human and other-than-human" is the essential problem because the "other-than-human" is seen as "less than," having no rights, and thus vulnerable to exploitation. We have bestowed all of the rights on humans, Berry points out, yet "every being has rights to be recognized and revered. Trees have tree rights, insects have insect rights, rivers have river rights, mountains have mountain rights" and we do not have the right to interfere with their well-being.[9] We are firm believers in and passionate defenders of rights, but by making this conceptual split between humans and nature, by viewing nature as separate and different from us, we can deny the nonhuman world its rights with impunity.

Physicist Fritjof Capra argued that the conceptual split of nature and humans emerged along with the Enlightenment view of the universe (discussed further in Chapter 3) as an object for scientific and analytic observation.[10] This worldview has persisted through the centuries to create a philosophical foundation in which the mind (human) and matter (nature) are separated, creating a dualistic relationship of the knower and the known. From this philosophical standpoint, the human mind is capable of dissecting, analyzing, and thus harnessing and exploiting the forces of nature.

In addition to conceptual problems, practical problems stem from viewing nature as separate from humans. One problem is that this view tends to focus our attention on those places of sublime grandeur—the "big out there," as environmental writer William Cronon calls it, where one can get away from civilization—at the expense of the "wildness in our own back yards, of the nature that is all around us if only we had eyes to see it."[11] This view of nature tends to place us on a rather narrow path of environmental concern, diverting attention from the many forms and definitions of nature.

Barbara Deutsch Lynch, professor of city and regional planning, tells a story about Daniel Perez, an immigrant from the Dominican Republic, who planted a vegetable garden in the median strip of a busy New York city street.[12] Environmentalism that is concerned only with the "big out there" fails to give consideration to Mr. Perez and his small plot of nature, yet for him, this represents the very essence and relevance of nature in his lifeworld. The pollutants in the air, soil, and water that feed his small patch of nature are products of the same human practices that pollute forests, lakes, and rivers the world over. Protecting the global ecological balance starts with protecting Mr. Perez's garden and our own backyards.

One of the main critiques of the mainstream environmental movement is that it treats nature more like a wilderness where humans are intruders than as a garden where humans are an active and involved part of nature.[13] The problem with this view, as Cronon suggests, is that "we leave ourselves little hope of discovering what an ethical, sustainable, *honorable,* human place in nature might actually look like."[14]

In their controversial essay "The Death of Environmentalism," well-known environmental writers and activists Michael Shellenberger and Ted Nordhaus expand Cronon's critique, suggesting that if one considers humans to be a part of the environment, an assumption that is essential to a sustainable future, then mainstream environmental organizations' designations of certain things as environmental and others as not environmental is arbitrary and self-defeating.[15]

Why, for example, is global warming considered an environmental problem and war is not, when either may kill millions of people and have a devastating impact on the environment over the next century? Why is global warming primarily viewed as an environmental issue when its economic, social, and political impacts are staggering? Why are issues such as health care and tax credits the intellectual domain of politicians and economists when they have such far-reaching impacts on the environment? The weight of health care costs for businesses and individuals leaves fewer financial resources for investing in green homes and businesses, and tax incentives for greening businesses and homes would have a direct and significant impact on environmental concerns.

The critique of mainstream environmentalism for its failure to consider the social problems that are inextricably tied to environmental problems is arguably justified. Yet, the expanded view of environmental concern that Shellenberger and Nordhaus call for creates its own practical dilemmas. If, as they recommend, the scope of environmental concern is expanded to encompass issues such as health care and tax credits, many environmental issues may get lost in the immensity of the scope and swallowed up in the black hole of politics and marketplace economics. Perhaps global warming, with its broad economic and social implications, can be framed to incorporate human-centered values such as prosperity, freedom, and opportunity, as Shellenberger and Nordhaus propose. But where does that leave the endangered silvery minnow, the Florida panther, or the northern spotted owl?

This "new wave of environmentalism" is not likely to embrace the notion that minnows, panthers, and owls have intrinsic value, despite the fact that they may not do much to foster, and may even inhibit, the pursuit of prosperity, freedom, and opportunity for humans.

The line separating concerns about nature from concerns about humans is fluid and arbitrary. Attempting to determine where to draw this line or to determine the "appropriate scope" of environmental concern is beyond the reach and aim of this book. The primary focus of the study of environmental communication is not on defining the scope of environmental concern, but on understanding the multiple ways it is defined and how we come to our understanding of humans' relationship to the natural world. In order to do this, environmental communication scholars look at the highly complex and uniquely human ability to use symbols.

Symbols: Forms and Characteristics

Symbols, the bulk and backbone of human communication, are the primary focus of communication scholars. Consequently, a clear understanding of the nature of symbols, their forms, and their characteristics is essential to understanding human communication.

Symbols can be either discursive or non-discursive (or presentational). **Discursive** symbols are ordered combinations of smaller bits of meaning. Language, the ordered combination of one word at a time to create meaning, fits into this category. **Non-discursive** (or **presentational**) symbols occur all at once and are experienced as a whole rather than in ordered bits. Examples of presentational symbols include such things as paintings, statues, and even buildings. Objects can also be symbolic. The flag with stars and stripes is a presentational symbol that represents the United States. A wedding ring represents a marriage. Many rhetorical messages that we see are made up of both discursive and presentational symbols. A billboard usually has a discursive message in the form of words printed on the billboard, as well as a presentational message, the picture on the billboard.

Symbolic representations come in multiple forms (such as words, objects, paintings, music, or dance) and give meaning to the world around us. In fact, anything can take on symbolic meaning. Thunder, for example, occurs when lightning creates a sudden disturbance of the air with an electrical discharge. However, we often attach symbolic meaning to thunder, such as "the wrath of God" or "the voice of nature."

Symbols have three primary characteristics: they are representative, arbitrary, and ambiguous.

Symbols are representative: they stand for something other than themselves. Symbols take many forms, but the most pervasive human symbol system is language. A word is a symbol used to represent something else, such as an object, event, idea, or relationship. For example, the word "DOG" is a three-letter symbol that we use to represent the four-legged animal that barks and licks your face.

Something is arbitrary if it is not governed by natural law, but based on preference or whim. *Symbols are arbitrary* because they are conventionally agreed-upon representations that have no real association to the things they represent. The symbol "BOOK," for example, represents the thing you are now reading only because we have agreed that it does, not because there is any natural connection between the word and the thing it represents.

Mark Twain humorously illustrates the arbitrary nature of symbols in his short story "Excerpts from Adam's Diary." In this story, Adam records how Eve (whom he calls "the new creature") goes about the task of arbitrarily assigning names to things in the Garden of Eden (which she has named Niagara Falls Park). Adam is perplexed as to the rationale for word selections that seem illogical and capricious to him. Adam writes, "TUESDAY—Been examining the great waterfall. It is the finest thing on the estate, I think. The new creature calls it Niagara Falls—why, I am sure I do not know. Says it LOOKS like Niagara Falls. That is not a reason, it is mere waywardness and imbecility."[16] When etymologists (those who study word origins) trace a word back to its origin (in Latin, Greek or whatever its origin), the connection between the word and the thing is no less perplexing or more obviously logical than Eve's arbitrary "waywardness and imbecility." As you will see later, the name we assign to a thing greatly influences how we perceive and value the thing, no matter how arbitrary, whimsical, or wayward the name may be.

Symbols are ambiguous. In other words, their meanings are not fixed, but variable, so that a single symbol can have multiple interpretations. In fact, the five hundred most frequently used words in the English language have more than fourteen thousand meanings assigned to them.[17] Some words even have contradictory meanings. The word "cleave," for example, can mean either "cut in half" or "stick together." One starts a watch, but finishes a meeting, by "winding it up."[18]

Adding to a word's ambiguity is the abstract nature of words that allow for multiple interpretations. Words such as "prosperity," "progress," and "sustainability" are highly abstract, with multiple layers of attached meanings that vary from person to person. Because of its ambiguity, any given symbol may evoke different meanings in different people, creating the potential, indeed the likelihood, of confusion and misunderstanding.

The extraordinary capability to use symbols is the defining characteristic of the human animal. In the words of philosopher Suzanne Langer, this ability is, "without a doubt, the most momentous and at the same time, the most mysterious product of the human mind."[19] Symbols do far more that just allow us to communicate with one another. Symbols are vehicles of thought. They open to us a life of the mind and a world of knowledge, dreams, and artistic expression.

Symbols give meaning to the world around us as well as to a world we have never experienced. Because of our ability to use symbols, we can conceptualize and talk about a grizzly bear or an atom, even though we may have never experienced these realities. We can conceptualize and communicate about things that have no real-world referents (to the best of my knowledge), such as ghosts and space aliens. We can envision things to come, such as hotels on the moon and solar-powered flying cars, Symbols, in other words, are not just devices for reporting pre-existing reality, but also a way of influencing and even creating reality.

As a reminder, our description of the study of environmental communication states that "the study of environmental communication examines the use of symbols to influence, construct, and maintain humans' relationship to the natural world." The terms "influence" and "construct" are examined in the following discussion.

Symbolic Representation, Influence, and Construction

Three philosophical positions attempt to explain the relationship between symbols and reality: (1) *symbols represent reality;* (2) *symbols influence the way we view reality;* and (3) *symbols construct reality.* Because language is the fundamental and most pervasive component of our symbol system, these three positions deal mainly with the relationship between language and reality.

Symbols Represent Reality

The first philosophical statement of the relationship between symbols and reality is that *symbols represent reality*—that the natural world exists, is knowable, and can be represented (either well or poorly) by language or some other symbol system. From this perspective, language reflects an objective reality, although the representation is necessarily a partial view and often inadequately or inaccurately captures the reality. The way in which language represents reality is the basis for an area of study known as General Semantics.

General Semantics teaches that all linguistic representations leave out most of reality—that no sentence can fully describe a given situation. Alfred Korzybski, commonly thought of as the founder of General Semantics, examined how the structure of language fails to adequately or accurately represent reality.[20] One of the many shortcomings of language representation is what Korzybski characterizes as a two-valued, either/or system. This creates false dichotomies that separate in language that which is not separated in nature. Examples include nature/culture, reason/emotion, rationality/spirituality, and right/wrong. Yet, as Korzybski explains, reality is multifaceted, with numerous realities that lie between such polar distinctions.

Another inadequacy of language is what Samuel I. Hayakawa, another leading General Semantics theorist, refers to as "confused levels of abstraction," which results in treating all things that have the same name as if they were the same.[21] Language, by its very nature, involves a high level of abstraction. For example, the word "environmentalist" is a highly abstract term used to represent all people who are actively involved with raising awareness about or solving environmental problems. The term encompasses a broad spectrum of people, who are involved in a wide range of activities. Yet, all environmentalists are often equated with "radical alarmists" or "ecoterrorists" when, in fact, only a small percentage of environmentalists would fall into these categories. The "confused level of abstraction" treats all environmentalists as if they were the same, ignoring the many shades of concerns and activities.

The view that language is an instrument that merely represents what is already present in nature—a simple mapping of an objective something-out-there—is a useful way of showing the uses and abuses of language, its intricacies and inadequacies. However, this perspective does little to explain how language influences perceptions of reality. For this reason, environmental communication scholars focus mostly on research grounded in one or the other of the next two philosophies regarding the relationship between symbols and reality.

Symbols Influence Reality

A second philosophical position regarding the relationship of language to reality is that *language influences how we view reality*. This position differs from the first in that it not only considers the object and the symbol used to represent it, but also takes into account the interpreter, as is demonstrated by the C. K. Ogden and I. A. Richards's triangle model of meaning (pictured in Figure 1.2).[22] The three points on the triangle are the **referent** (the actual thing being discussed), the **symbol** (the word used to refer to the thing), and the **reference** (our thoughts about the thing). Notice that the line between the symbol and the referent is broken. There is no direct, natural relationship between the word and the thing it represents. The meaning or perceived reality an individual holds for any given symbol grows out of that individual's thought references, which encompass memories of past experiences and feelings about the thing the word stands for, as well as the many socially and culturally created associations attached to it. In other words, symbols carry a lot of meaning baggage—some of it highly consistent with an objective reality and some of it far removed from that reality.

Take the word "fox," for example. If I were to ask you to write down all the thought associations (references) you have attached to the word "fox" (symbol), your list might include some of these commonly shared associations:

a four-legged, canine-like creature

a crafty, cunning, untrustworthy character

a sexy, beautiful woman

Now let's look at the objective reality (the referent) of a fox. The first association— a four-legged, canine-like creature—is comfortably consistent with its referent. This is, in fact, what a fox is. The second reference—crafty, cunning, untrustworthy—is somewhat less obviously connected to the referent. If you were to observe fox behavior in the wild, you would probably see nothing in its behavior that is more crafty or cunning than any other animal with instinctive self-preservation skills. A fox is no more cunning and crafty than a rabbit or a chameleon and every bit as trustworthy as either of them. It is difficult to know how this personality trait came to be associated with foxes. It may have originated in cultural folklore, fables, or fairy tales, but it has little or nothing to do with its real-world referent. (Notice the broken line between the symbol and the referent in Ogden and Richards's meaning triangle in Figure 1.2.) This thought association came about because of the way foxes were talked about—through the symbols we use to communicate about foxes and the references attached to those symbols.

I'll let you try to figure out what it is about the objective reality of a fox that has led to the sexy-beautiful-woman-meaning baggage. This arbitrary version of fox "reality" is purely a function of symbols and seems to leave reality out of the meaning loop altogether. Nevertheless, symbols mediate our version of reality

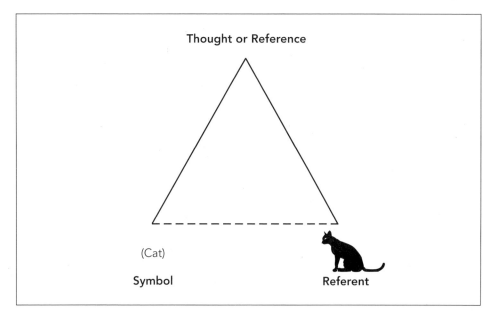

Figure 1.2   Meaning Triangle

Adapted from C. K. Ogden and I. A. Richards, *The Meaning of Meaning*, 8th ed. (New York: Harcourt, Brace, & World, 1946).

through the associations they carry for us—no matter how arbitrary, wayward, or imbecilic they may be. Thus, words, by way of their attached thought references, have the power to define reality and compel particular views of reality. As communication theorist Richard Weaver puts it, "It's not that things give meaning to words, it is that meaning makes things things."[23]

One of the main functions of human communication is to define "reality" through the meanings we believe should be attached to that reality. Names are particularly influential in defining the reality of the things they represent. A great deal of meaning baggage is attached to names. These meanings are superimposed onto the thing and serve to mediate the reality of the thing.

A good example of the reality-mediating influence of names is the word "treehugger," a label frequently given to environmentalists. Communication scholars Mark DeLoach, Michael S. Bruner, and John D. Gossett examined the multiple uses of the epithet in a dispute among loggers, rancher, miners, and environmentalists over rebuilding a road in a national forest in Nevada.[24] In the public discourse surrounding this dispute, "treehugger" was used by environmentalists as a *self-identifier* to proudly acknowledge their solidarity with like-minded people: "I don't mind being called a treehugger. The environmental movement, by any standard, has been a success." In this example, the speaker is attempting to redefine "treehugger" as one who is a part of a unified group of successful activists and to convince others that this meaning baggage is the "right" or "correct" baggage.

DeLoach, Brunner, and Gossett suggest, however, that even when the term is used as a positive self-identifier, it has liabilities for environmental advocacy because of the graphic nature of its objective referent. The image of actually hugging a tree is comically absurd, and the absurdity is superimposed onto the environmental message or advocacy behavior, making it seem likewise absurd. What they are suggesting is that reality actually does have a place in all that meaning baggage and that the reality of hugging a tree is rather absurd. Yet, we must also keep in mind that what is considered "absurd" is likewise mediated through the meanings attached to the act, not the act itself. The physical act of hugging a tree is no more inherently absurd than, say, fan antics at a football game or asking a groundhog to tell us when spring will arrive—to name just two of our cultural absurdities whose meanings are symbolically ascribed.

Another use of the term "treehugger" that emerged from the national forest road dispute is as a form of *attack discourse*. For example, loggers, ranchers, and miners carried signs saying "treehuggers—the other red meat." Here, the associations attached to "red" (communism, anti-American) and "meat" (animals, slaughter) become attached to "treehugger" as part of its meaning baggage. You don't have to analyze this message too deeply to recognize the aggressive attack message it sends when the negative meanings attached to "red" and "meat" are superimposed onto "treehugger."

The third use of the term "treehugger" is as a *moderating device* or a means to differentiate between more "moderate" or "reasonable" environmentalists and "radical" treehuggers, as demonstrated in the following statement: "I'm not some treehugger. I just love trees." This statement implies that one who loves trees is reasonable, whereas a treehugger is not. Hence, another layer of meaning baggage is attached to the word "treehugger"—treehuggers are unreasonable.

And so it goes—layer after layer of meaning is attached to any given word. Proponents of one meaning will compete with proponents of another to define reality and convince others that their meaning is the "right" or "real" reality. The way in which one particular view of reality comes to hold and maintain a privileged place reinforced by laws, institutions, and practices is discussed a little further on in this chapter.

Symbols Construct Reality

Thus far, we have examined two perspectives on the relationship of symbols to reality. We have looked at how symbols are used to represent reality (although poorly), as well as how our perceptions of reality are colored or influenced by language and by the multiple thought references attached to any given word. A third philosophical position takes the relationship of language to reality a step farther, suggesting that language goes beyond merely representing reality or influencing perceptions of reality. This perspective suggests language causes reality to take shape and form—to come into being. As rhetorical scholar Ann Gill explains, through language, "We cull objects from the disorder of sensation and, by giving them a name, make something of them."[25] Thus, *language constructs (or creates) reality.* Another way of saying this is to say that language is **constitutive.**

The strong version of this perspective suggests that humans experience reality only through symbols—that we can never gain access to reality, but can only experience symbolic constructions of it. Because these constructions come to us primarily through the society in which we live, the process is also commonly referred to as the **social construction of reality.**

Construction theorists don't deny the existence of an objective reality, but suggest that if there is no language to talk about or think about any given reality, it remains in "the disorder of sensation." Only when symbols become attached to the reality is it formed and shaped to become something all its own. From this perspective, symbols don't just influence our reality as part of the meaning loop, symbols *are* our reality.

This perspective may seem easy to accept on one level, but harder on another. Let's say, for example, that my only association with grizzly bears is through symbols, in the form of stories I have heard or pictures I have seen. It's easy to see how my reality of grizzlies is constructed through symbols. But let's say that one day I finally do encounter a real, live grizzly on a hiking trail. When staring this reality in the face, it seems difficult to accept the notion that the stark reality of the bear itself is not the primary determinant of my perception of the bear. Yet, according to the constructionist perspective, our only means of processing the information—of thinking about and interpreting the experience, and making sense of our senses—is through language, so even this face-to-face encounter with a grizzly is ultimately a symbolic construction.

Many theorists have attempted to explain the reality-constructing nature of symbols,[26] but arguably, the most noted and quoted in environmental communication is Kenneth Burke. According to Burke, language creates a **terministic screen** through which humans see the world. The screen filters the reality, providing only a selective reality that mirrors and colors parts of reality and screens out or deflects others. As Burke puts it, "Even if any given reality is a *reflection* of reality, by its very nature as a terminology it must be a *selection* of reality; and to this extent it must function also as a *deflection* of reality."[27]

The words we choose are neither neutral nor objective. Each terminological description filters the world, creating a particular version of reality. Thus, language does not just reflect reality; it shapes, colors, and creates a world that is selective and filtered through symbols—a world that is sometimes far removed from the extant objective reality.

Critics of the "purest" form of this theoretical perspective point out the absurdity of suggesting that nothing is "real" outside of the reality created by language. There are some obvious limitations to the practical application of a rigid version of this theoretical perspective. As Ann Gill suggests, "defining speeding trucks out of existence is difficult when one is crossing a busy street."[28] The same thing could be said of grizzly bears on the hiking trails. Even if humans are not there to symbolically construct it, nature will play by its own inscrutable rules, and at some point, the physical reality of the environment cannot be ignored.

Mass media scholars James Shanahan and Katherine McComas offer a useful metaphor for conceptualizing the link between the symbolic construction and the objective reality of the natural world:

> One may conceive of the environment as a rocket that cannot escape the gravitational pull of the objective reality of the natural environment. Although we can power ourselves on fanciful flights, reconceptualizing nature as we go, the reality of the physical environment will inevitably tend to pull us back. Any narrative will have to deal with this gravitational pull.[29]

Despite the gravitation pull of a real, objective reality, the constructed reality is filtered and partial. It sometimes disregards or even contradicts the demands of the physical reality. Yet the constructed reality has profound implications for how we respond to the physical reality. Consider the multiple constructions of Hurricane Katrina, for example, and the ways these constructions direct responses to the disaster.

Katrina, the hurricane that devastated New Orleans and a portion of the Gulf coast in 2005, has been symbolically reconstructed in public discourse as many different realities. One reality is that of an unpreventable natural disaster—an unfortunate fluke of nature or act of God. From this perspective, nothing can be done to prevent or mitigate future disasters. Another reality constructed through the discourse is that it was an engineering issue and the inevitable consequence of expecting a few miles of concrete and earth to hold back an ocean. In this view of reality, the solution can be found in better engineering. Katrina has also been constructed as a racial issue, on the grounds that the destroyed areas would have been better protected by updated and fortified levies if they had been mostly populated by wealthy white people instead of poor African-Americans. Here, the solution lies with the legislative and legal justice systems. Still others may perceive Katrina as a portent of things to come. As warming oceans create stronger storms, this is what we can expect. The solution to this version of reality lies in dealing with the causes of global warming.

The notion that how we reconceptualize nature in our symbolic flights of fancy has a profound influence on how we subsequently treat the natural world has been enthusiastically adopted by players in the art of political spin. In a briefing book compiled for lobbyists and politicians, Republican pollster Frank Luntz advised Republican leaders to use the term "climate change" rather than "global warming" because, according to his firm's focus group research, "climate change" seems less threatening than "global warming" and less in need of urgent and drastic measures.[30]

Connections

What's in a Name?
"Global Warming" or "Global Climate Change"?

Republican pollster Frank Luntz recommended to Republican leaders that instead of saying "global warming," they should say "climate change." According to his firm's focus group research, "climate change" connotes something less threatening and more controllable. As one focus group participant observed, "Climate change sounds like you are going from Pittsburgh to Fort Lauderdale."

Professor Tim Flannery, a well-known Australian mammalogist, paleontologist, and outspoken global warming activist, offers a different take on the term "global warming." He suggests that one reason for society's reluctance to tackle the climate crisis has to do with humans' evolutionary response to the threat of cold. "Warming," suggests Flannery, "creates an illusion of a comfortable, warm future that is deeply appealing, for we are an essentially tropical species that has spread into all corners of our globe, and cold has long been our greatest enemy."

Apparently, there is a discrepancy between the meaning associations reported by the focus group and the human evolution perspective Flannery offers. This discrepancy is not surprising, as the discourse of global warming covers wide terrain, spanning multiple academic disciplines, as well as multiple political, social, and cultural sites of meaning production. Coming to a consensus on whether to call it "global warming" or "climate change" would most likely be an extended exercise in futility.

Ultimately, both terms are accurate, but one refers to cause, the other to effect. (A warming globe is causing the climate to change.) The terms are frequently used interchangeably, but "climate change" is perhaps less prone to eliciting anecdotal responses such as, "How can it be warming when it's been such a cold winter?" People often conflate "weather" and "climate." As explained by climate experts Ann Bostrom and Daniel Lashof, **Weather** is "the state of the atmosphere at a definite time and place." **Climate** is "the average course or condition of weather at a particular place over a period of many years."

Anomalous temperature change can often be seen only through tracking the average daily temperatures over an extended time period. Global warming is a change in the frequency of warmer than normal times. So while the frequency of warm times will increase, there can still be colder than normal times as well. Thus, "climate change" rather than "global warming" might be a less confusing term.

Well-known essayist, activist, and global warming prophet Bill McKibben suggests that we should give the issue "a new scarier name" than either "climate change" or "global warming." "*El Piquante Grande* perhaps or *La Chaleur Enorme*? How about Hell on Earth? Maybe then it will start to sink in."

Sources: Frank Luntz, "The Environment: A Cleaner, Safer, Healthier America," The Luntz Research Companies, February 2004, http://www.ewg.org/briefings/luntzmemo/pdf/LuntzResearch_environment.pdf (accessed June 9, 2005). Tim Flannery, *The Weather Makers: How Man Is Changing the Climate and What It Means for Life on Earth* (New York: Atlantic Monthly Press, 2005), 237. Ann Bostrom and Daniel Lashof, "Weather or Climate Change? In *Creating a Climate for Change*, ed. S. C. Moser and L. Dilling (Cambridge, MA: Cambridge University Press, 2007). Bill McKibben, "Maybe We Should Call It Something Scarier," *Boston Globe*, October 26, 1997, E7.

It would be comforting to think that by merely renaming "global warming" as "climate change," we could mitigate its impacts. Unfortunately, if scientific consensus is right, the gravitational pull of a distressed planet will bring us back from this irresponsible flight of fancy to a catastrophic reality.

Symbols and the Maintenance of Reality

One final term in the definition of the study of environmental communication is "maintain." Recall once again that the study of environmental communication examines the use of symbols to influence, construct, and maintain humans' relationship to the natural world. Because symbols are arbitrary and ambiguous, our perceptions of the natural world and humans' relationship to it are likewise arbitrary and ambiguous, with many competing and even conflicting versions. Amidst the cacophony of realities created through multiple symbolic constructions, some versions of reality are given privileged status—a status that is maintained through the dominant ideologies of a culture.

Ideologies and the Maintenance of Reality

An **ideology** is "a pattern or set of ideas, assumptions, beliefs, values, or interpretations of the world by which a culture or group operates."[31] A **dominant ideology** is one that is privileged over others. There is an unquestioned sense that its meanings or ways of thinking are the right or natural ones. Its privileged status is reinforced and maintained by a culture's laws, institutions, and practices. The ideal of private property ownership, for example, is reinforced by laws that protect rights of ownership, by institutions that lend money to purchase property, and by practices to protect private property (such as building fences or killing predator wolves), and so on.

One way a culture's ideologies are revealed is through its ideographs. An **ideograph** is a word that functions as a "one-term sum of an orientation" and carries a great deal of persuasive power.[32] Words such as "justice," "liberty," "democracy," or "sustainability" encapsulate our most valued ideals. The meanings of these words are highly abstract, however, and can be interpreted in many different ways by different groups within a culture. This is, in fact, one reason ideographs are so powerful. Almost everyone can identify with justice, liberty, and sustainability, even though we may hold vastly different ideas about what these abstract terms mean.

Another way a culture's ideologies are revealed is through its practices. The early settlers of the American West, for instance, believed it was their responsibility to bring civilization to the savage wilderness. The resulting assault on the environment was a natural outcome of their ideologies or sets of belief about nature. A different set of beliefs ground many contemporary environmental activities. As you will read in Chapter 4, deep ecologists believe that nature has an intrinsic value that is independent of its benefits to humans, and that it has as much right to live and survive as humans do. Activists, rather than trying to "civilize" the wilderness, try to protect it from the destructive forces of civilization.

Hegemony is the privileging of one set of ideologies over another, creating a kind of social control or form of domination that reinforces and maintains the dominant ideologies. Hegemonic power is maintained through dominant groups' ongoing efforts to forge a consensus that legitimates the status quo as natural and rational. In order to do this, says communication theorist Lawrence Grossberg, "people have to see the world in ways that reproduce their subordination (as well as the domination of those already in power). The majority of people living in subordinate political positions generally accept their oppression because they are living in someone else's ideological universe."[33] So, for example, the practice of borrowing and lending is almost universally accepted. Institutions such as banks, savings and loan associations, and mortgage lenders operate to maintain and encourage borrowing and lending practices. The "ideological universe" of this system is rarely questioned—it is simply the way we do business. Those who struggle under the weight of credit card bills, for example, tend to blame the oppression on their own profligate spending or lack of income and do not question the ideological universe of our borrowing and lending institutions. Yet, our ideologically driven way of doing business has a profound impact on the natural world.

One of the most, perhaps *the* most powerful force in our culture is **capitalism,** an economic system in which the means of production and distribution are privately owned and operated for profit. The hegemonic power of capitalism is reinforced and maintained by our belief in the goodness and rightness of ideographs such as technological progress, material well-being, and free enterprise. Yet, the ideological universe of capitalism has led us to a state of affairs where nature is sacrificed to these ideological deities. Inextricably tied to capitalism is consumerism—the notion that we can purchase progress and material well-being in attractive packages. Each product we purchase has an impact on the natural world, from the smokestacks and resources used in its production to the smokestacks or landfills used in its disposal.

It is important to keep in mind that hegemony is not a "thing" that is manipulated by the rich and powerful or some kind of unified, deliberate conspiracy. It is a combination of institutions and practices in which we all participate, often without question. In the case of capitalism, for example, one cannot identify a single entity (such as Walmart) or a group of entities (such as the World Trade Organization) as the propagator and sustainer of the hegemonic control. We are all implicated in perpetuating the hegemony every time we make a purchase.

It is also important to keep in mind that hegemony is constantly contested. Its power must be won and re-won, negotiated and renegotiated. However, hegemonic institutions have advantages over those who challenge their control because they have greater control of and access to the bases of power.

Communication scholar Andrew A. King identifies three bases from which power is derived.[34] The first base of power is **material resources,** which include access to money as well as information and technical expertise. Although the Internet has leveled the playing field in significant ways, material resources remain more readily available to those who operate within and are sanctioned by the hegemony.

King terms the second base of power the **psycho-social base of power.** This is derived from the sense of identity for group members who are bound together by common interests and values and the symbols that represent them. An important part of the psycho-social unity of a group lies in ideologies that are legitimized and reinforced by invoking ideographs such as God, the founding fathers, or the Constitution, as well as through ritualistic practices such as singing the national anthem at sporting events.

The third base of power is the **organizational base of power,** which is derived from institutional networks or organized collections of knowledge, resources, and procedures. Organizational power includes the sanctioning power of rules and laws, systems of education, and the justice system, as well as the control of and/or access to media organizations.

Anyone wishing to challenge the hegemony must contend with the laws, customs, and insignias of authority and legitimacy granted to institutions. Yet, a hegemony is a relational process of competing discourses with openings for resistance and change. Consider, for example, the competing discourses and the struggle for ideological dominance in the highly contested reality of nuclear weapons.

Competing Discourses in an Ideological Struggle

On August 6, 1945, the headline of *The New York Times* read:

> FIRST ATOMIC BOMB DROPPED ON JAPAN;
> MISSILE IS EQUAL TO 20,000 TONS OF TNT;
> TRUMAN WARNS FOE OF A 'RAIN OF RUIN.'

So began the rhetoric of the atomic age. In stunned disbelief, Americans read of the awesome power of what President Truman called "the greatest achievement of organized science in history" and "a powerful and forceful instrument of world peace." As news of the devastation and horror began to register in the American consciousness, many people began to question Truman's version of the reality. Several weeks after the bombing of Hiroshima and Nagasaki, letters to the editor of *The New York Times* magazine referred to it as a "barbaric, inhuman type of warfare," and "mass murder, sheer terrorism." Another asserted that the bomb set the stage "for the sudden and final destruction of mankind."[35]

Was the atomic bomb a moral weapon of world peace? Some would argue that it was. After all, one week after the bomb was dropped on Hiroshima, World War II was over. Was this an act of barbaric warfare and mass murder? Some would make a claim to this reality. The combined death count of Hiroshima and Nagasaki is estimated to be somewhere between 190,000 and 200,000 people. The lingering radiation effects on human health and the environment are inestimable.[36] The two competing realities were both constructed through the symbols that were used to describe and talk about the bombing.

The symbolic construction of weapons of mass destruction as "war deterrence" or "guardians of democracy" has gained and maintained hegemonic force, and created a staggering and highly contested reality. Since 1942, the United States nuclear weapons production complex has built in excess of seventy thousand nuclear warheads. Because of humans' symbol-using capabilities, we can now destroy ourselves, along with everything else on the planet. In many ways, the extraordinary capability to use symbols is, as communication theorist Frank E. X. Dance suggests, both our highest excellence and our most tragic flaw.[37]

Our history is replete with challenges that have been instrumental in reforming or collapsing oppressive institutions. We are, after all, the products of a revolutionary history. Although challenges may not lead to immediate liberation from the influence of dominant ideologies and hegemonic controls, the process of attempting change is, itself, liberating. As rhetorical scholar Barry Brummett explains, "It is almost always liberating to realize that you have more options in deciding how to experience life, to be able to see and understand experience in more than one way, to be able to find many meanings in a situation."[38]

Concluding and Looking Ahead

As environmental communication scholars, our goal is to understand how multiple views of nature come into being and how they, in turn, influence the way we experience and understand the natural world and humans' relationship to it. In so doing, we challenge and transform the realities that create and maintain our unsustainable human/nature relationship. One underestimates the power of symbols if all this seems like more than mere communication scholars can do. As rhetorical theorists Sonja K. Foss, Karen A. Foss, and Robert Trapp explain, "Humans construct the world in which they live through symbolic choices . . . . Every word choice we make—every perspective we choose to apply—results in seeing the world one way rather than another . . . . Because we create our worlds through symbols, changing our symbols changes our worlds."[39]

This chapter has covered a lot of ground, beginning with the assumptions that anchor the work of environmental communication scholars and following with a detailed discussion of the component parts of the definition of environmental communication as a field of study. I hope it has left you with a sense of the vital role that human communication plays in determining how we view and treat the natural world. Symbols influence, construct, and maintain humans' relationship to the natural world. Since this relationship is fundamentally unsustainable, we should closely scrutinize the symbols that are used to communicate about the natural world and the ideologies that serve to reinforce and maintain this flawed and destructive relationship.

Soon you will be examining the dominant Western ideologies and the mainstream perspectives that ground most of our current environmental policies and practices, as well as environmental perspectives that challenge the dominant ideologies. But before blasting off on these flights of philosophical fancy, it is important to recognize the gravitational pull of our natural environment. Chapter 2, then, takes us back to earth with a sobering look at some of the environmental problems we currently face.

Discussion Questions and Exercises

1. What are some of the problems of viewing nature as "the big out there"— a place separate and distant from humans and their culture?

2. Briefly describe and explain each of the three philosophical positions regarding the relationship of symbols and reality.

3. When you hear the term "treehugger," what meanings does it connote or what images does it conjure in your mind? In your opinion, is it a negative or a positive label? Think of other terms you have heard to refer to environmentalists. What do these terms connote?

4. Let's say that you are a small grass-roots organization of local citizens that has formed to preserve as open space an undeveloped parcel of land owned by the city. You have gotten wind of the city's plan to sell this property to a developer who plans to turn it into a housing development. Discuss the obstacles your group might face with regard to Andrew King's bases of power.

Suggested Readings

James G. Cantrill and Christine L. Oravec. *The Symbolic Earth: Discourse and the Creation of the Environment.* Lexington: University Press of Kentucky, 1996.

Andrew Simms. *Ecological Debt: The Health of the Planet and the Wealth of Nations.* London: Pluto, 2005.

Notes

1. Carl Sagan, *The Pale Blue Dot: A Vision of the Human Future in Space* (New York: Random House, 1994), 5.

2. In late December 1968, the popular earth image known as "Earthrise" was taken by *Apollo 8* astronauts. The "Blue Marble," taken by the crew of *Apollo 17* on December 7, 1972, replaced Earthrise as the iconic image of our day and is believed to be the most widely reproduced and distributed photographic image in history. *Apollo 17* was the last manned lunar spaceflight and the last opportunity for taking such a photo. (NASA History Series Publications On-Line, http://history.nasa.gov)

3. Jimmy Carter, "Remarks at the Congressional Space Medal Honor Awards Ceremony," *Weekly Compilation of Presidential Documents* 14, October 1, 1978, 1685.

4. Union of Concerned Scientists, "Warning to Humanity," 1992, http://www.ucsusa.org/ucs/about/1992-world-scientists-warning-to-humanity.html (accessed July 10, 2005).

5. Alan S. Miller, *Gaia Connections: An Introduction to Ecology, Ecoethics, and Economics,* 2nd ed. (New York: Rowman & Littlefield, 2003), 4.

6. Susan L. Senecah, "The Sacredness of Natural Places: How a Big Canyon Became a Grand Icon," in *Proceedings from the Conference on the Discourse of Environmental Advocacy,* ed. C. L. Oravec and J. G. Cantrill (Salt Lake City: University of Utah Humanities Center, 1992), 209.

7. M. Henberg, "Wilderness, Myth, and American Character," *The Key Reporter* 59, (Spring 1994): 7–11.

8. Anne Whiston Spirn, "Constructing Nature: The Legacy of Frederick Law Olmsted," in *Uncommon Ground: Toward Reinventing Nature,* ed. W. Cronon (New York: Norton, 1995), 98.

9. Thomas Berry, *The Great Work: Our Way into the Future* (New York: Bell Tower, 1999), 4–5.

10. Fritjof Capra, *The Web of Life: A New Scientific Understanding of Living Systems* (New York: Anchor, 1996).

11. William Cronon, ed., *Uncommon Ground: Toward Reinventing Nature* (New York: Norton, 1995), 86.

12. Barbara Deutsch Lynch, "The Garden and the Sea: U.S. Latino Environmental Discourses and Mainstream Environmentalism," *Social Problems* 40 (1993): 108–124.

13. J. D. Proctor, "Whose Nature? The Contested Moral Terrain of Ancient Forests," in *Uncommon Ground: Toward Reinventing Nature,* ed. W. Cronon (New York: Norton, 1995), 269–297.

14. Cronon, *Uncommon Ground,* 81.

15. Michael Shellenberger and Ted Nordhaus, "The Death of Environmentalism: Global Warming Politics in a Post-Environmental World," *Grist Magazine* (January 13, 2005), http://www.grist.org/news/maindish/2005/01/13/doe-reprint (accessed February 17, 2005).

16. Mark Twain, *Extracts from Adam's Diary: A Short Story by Mark Twain* (New York: Harper, 1904).

17. Bill Bryson, *The Mother Tongue: English and How It Got That Way* (New York: Avon, 1990).

18. J. D. Rothwell, *In the Company of Others: An Introduction to Communication* (Mountainview, CA: Mayfield, 2000), 89.

19. Suzanne Langer, *Philosophy in a New Key* (New York: New American Library, 1951), 94.

20. Alfred Korzybski, *Science and Sanity: An Introduction to Non-Aristotelian Systems and General Semantics* (Lakeville, CT: International Non-Aristotelian Library, 1958).

21. Samuel I. Hayakawa, *Language in Thought and Action,* 4th ed. (New York: Harcourt Brace Jovanovich, 1978).

22. C. K. Ogden and I. A. Richards, *The Meaning of Meaning,* 8th ed. (New York: Harcourt, Brace, & World, 1946).

23. Richard Weaver, *Language is Sermonic: Richard M. Weaver on the Nature of Rhetoric* (Baton Rouge: Louisiana State University Press, 1970), 23.

24. Mark DeLoach, Michael S. Bruner, and John D. Gossett, "An Analysis of the 'Tree-Hugger' Label," in *Enviropop: Studies in Environmental Rhetoric and Popular Culture,* ed. M. Meister and P. M. Japp (Westport, CT: Praeger, 2002), 95–110.

25. Ann Gill, *Rhetoric and Human Understanding* (Prospect Heights, IL: Waveland, 1994), 246.

26. See for example Jacques Derrida, *Of Grammatology* (Baltimore, MD: Johns Hopkins University Press, 1976); Michael Foucault, *The Archeology of Knowledge and the Discourse on Language,* trans. A. M. Sheridan Smith (New York: Pantheon, 1972); Jean-François Lyotard, *The Postmodern Condition: A Report on Knowledge* (Manchester, UK: University of Manchester Press, 1984); Ferdinand de Saussure, *Course in General Linguistics,* ed. C. Bally and A. Sechehaye (London: Peter Owen, 1960); John Shotter, *Cultural Politics of Everyday Life: Social Constructionism, Rhetoric, and Knowing of the Third Kind* (Toronto: University of Toronto Press, 1993).

27. Kenneth Burke, *Language as Symbolic Action: Essays on Life, Literature, and Method* (Berkeley: University of California Press, 1966), 45.

28. Gill, *Rhetoric and Human Understanding,* 243.

29. James Shanahan and Katherine McComas, *Nature Stories: Depictions of the Environment and Their Effects* (Cresskill, NJ: Hampton, 1999), 5.

30. Frank Luntz, "The Environment: A Cleaner, Safer, Healthier America," Luntz Research Companies, February 2004, http://www.ewg.org/briefings/luntzmemo/pdf/LuntzResearch_environment.pdf (accessed June 9, 2005).

31. Sonja K. Foss, *Rhetorical Criticism: Exploration and Practice,* 2nd ed. (Prospect Heights, IL: Waveland, 1996), 291.

32. Michael C. McGee, "The 'Ideograph': A Link between Rhetoric and Ideology," *Quarterly Journal of Speech* 66 (1980): 1–16.

33. Lawrence Grossberg, *We Gotta Get Out of This Place: Popular Conservatism and Postmodern Culture* (New York: Routledge, 1992), 90–91.

34. Andrew A. King, *Power and Communication* (Prospect Heights, IL: Waveland, 1987).

35. "Letters to the Editor," *New York Times,* August 20, 1945.

36. The Atomic Bomb Museum, "Health Effects: Counting the Dead." http://www.AtomicBombMuseum.org/3_health.shtml (accessed November 30, 2008).

37. Frank E. X. Dance, "Swift, Slow, Sweet, Sour, Adazzle, Dim: What Makes Human Communication Human," *Western Journal of Speech Communication* 44 (1980): 60–63.

38. Barry Brummett, *Rhetoric in Popular Culture* (New York: St. Martin's, 1994), 77.

39. Sonja K. Foss, Karen A. Foss, and Robert Trapp, *Contemporary Perspectives on Rhetoric,* 3rd ed. (Prospect Heights, IL: Waveland, 2002), 2.

Chapter 2
Our Changing Environment

Even the event organizers didn't fully anticipate the overwhelming and unprecedented grassroots response to the first Earth Day on April 21, 1970. Senator Gaylord Nelson, who headed up the efforts to organize the nationwide mobilization of demonstrations and events, states, "Earth Day worked because of the spontaneous response at the grassroots level. . . . That was the remarkable thing about Earth Day. It organized itself."[1] Over twenty million people—10 percent of the nation's population—took to the streets in what was and remains the largest single-day demonstration in United States history.

The goal of the organizers of the first Earth Day was, as Nelson describes it, "to shake the political establishment out of its lethargy and force the environmental issue onto the national political agenda."[2] And that's exactly what happened. Over the next ten years, Congress would pass twenty-eight major laws protecting such things as our water, air, wetlands, and endangered species. Substantial gains have been made in environmental protection since the first Earth Day, yet many of the old problems remain. We are now faced with the complicated and seemingly overwhelming challenges brought on by a rapidly warming planet.

As environmental communication scholars, we do not need an in-depth understanding of ecological systems or scientific explanations for all of the environmental concerns that are before us. Indeed, a complete understanding of the relationships in the intricately interconnected web of our natural systems is beyond the capability of even the most knowledgeable scientists and experts. Nevertheless, the first step toward addressing the problems stemming from humans' relationship to the natural world is an awareness of the human impact on nature.

This chapter offers a rudimentary overview of some of the environmental challenges on the local, national, and global scale. It is not possible to cover all of the environmental concerns that we face, but the following discussion covers some of the more significant and exigent problems.

A caution to the reader is in order. The following litany of environmental problems can seem discouraging and insurmountable. As you read through the long list of problems we face, I would encourage you to keep in mind the words of novelist and historian Wallace Stegner:

> We are the most dangerous species of life on the planet, and every other
> species, even the earth itself, has cause to fear our power to exterminate.
> But we are also the only species which, when it chooses to do so, will go
> to great effort to save what it might destroy.[3]

Global Climate Change

"Today, we are hearing and seeing dire warnings of the worst potential catastrophe in the history of human civilization: a global climate crisis that is deepening and rapidly becoming more dangerous than anything we have ever faced."[4] These are the words of Al Gore, probably the most recognized of all global warming prognosticators. He is only one of many voices sounding urgent alarms. It seems the verdict is in and the warnings are grim and unequivocal: the earth is warming as a result of human activities; it is happening at a rate alarmingly faster than earlier climate models predicted; if unchecked, it will threaten the survival of most of the earth's inhabitants.

Amid the groundswell of urgent warnings, there is still a handful of skeptics and naysayers, and there is still uncertainty with regard to how much and how fast warming will occur, as well as how it will affect the climate system. But as information is amassed, as climate models become increasingly reliable, and as the impact becomes more and more apparent in our everyday lives, the consensus among the world's scientists and experts is overwhelming. A study published in *Science* magazine by Naomi Oreskes reveals just how overwhelming consensus is within the scientific community. She reviewed over nine hundred juried articles published in science journals over an eleven-year period (1993–2003) and found that not a single author disagreed with the consensus opinion that global climate change is happening and that it is **anthropogenic** (or human-caused).[5]

The foremost cause for global warming is the increased concentration of "greenhouse gases" in the atmosphere. Greenhouse gases are present naturally in the earth's atmosphere and are, in fact, essential to our survival. Without them, the average global temperature would be colder by about 60° F (33.3° C).[6]

The primary greenhouse gases that occur naturally are water vapor, carbon dioxide (CO_2), methane (CH_4), and nitrous oxide (N_2O). Greenhouse gases affect global warming by allowing short-wave radiation (visible light) to pass largely undeterred through the atmosphere. Light striking the surface of the earth heats it up. The surface heat then radiates back up as infrared radiation. Greenhouse gases trap most of the heat, preventing it from escaping into the upper atmosphere. The trapped heat keeps the earth warmer, in an effect called **radiative forcing.**

Human activities have led to a significant increase in the concentration of greenhouse gases and the resulting radiative forcing. Levels of CO_2, which account for 80 percent of total greenhouse gas emissions, have risen mainly because of fossil fuel burning, deforestation (resulting in reduced oxygen-producing photosynthesis), and cement production. The main anthropogenic sources of methane are intensive rice cultivation and livestock farming. Anthropogenic sources of nitrous oxide include fertilizers, fossil fuels, and forests fires.

A study of air bubbles trapped in a 3.2-kilometer (2-mile) ice core drilled in Antarctica revealed that concentrations of greenhouse gases in the atmosphere are higher than at any time in the past 650,000 years.[7] The increased concentration of greenhouse gases will lead to a global temperature rise; however, there is uncertainty as to how much and how fast it will rise. The uncertainty is due, in large part, to unknown human factors, especially with regard to future emissions. The projections indicate an average temperature rise of 2° F to 11.5° F (1.1° C to 6.4° C) by the end of the twenty-first century, with a best estimate of 3.2° F to 7.2° F (1.8° C to 4.0° C).[8]

The effects of global warming are likewise uncertain, but scientists warn of some probable consequences. The predicted effects include more frequent and more violent storms, drier weather in mid-continent areas, increased precipitation in coastal areas, and the northward migration of species. Plague and disease-causing microbes that thrive in warmer climates are predicted to increase. Soil productivity would decrease because of soil microbes' sensitivity to temperature and moisture variation. Another ominous threat of global warming is that as the polar ice caps melt, the ocean levels would rise, inundating coastal areas. The predicted rise in sea levels is estimated to be from 9 to 88 centimeters or 3.54 to 34.65 inches.[9]

The earth's atmosphere, like its terrestrial ecosystems, is a complex and highly interactive system. Because the projected human-related changes are beyond the

Connections

The Prestigious Nobel Peace Prize
Places the Spotlight on Climate Change

On October 12, 2007, the Nobel committee announced that the prestigious Nobel Peace Prize was awarded to former United States vice president Al Gore and the Intergovernmental Panel on Climate Change (IPCC). The award recognizes the recipients as the leaders in their respective fields and brings attention to the essential relationship between these two widely divergent fields.

Al Gore's film, *An Inconvenient Truth*, won the 2007 Academy Award for best documentary. His untiring efforts to bring the science of climate change to an often ambivalent public is largely credited with shifting the tide of awareness and changing the debate about global climate change. The Nobel committee stated that Mr. Gore has probably done more than any other individual "to create greater worldwide understanding of the measures that need to be adopted."

Since it was formed in 1988, the IPCC has made an enormous effort to synthesize and report climate science findings about the earth's climate system and its relationship to human activities. The collaborative effort and meticulous work of the world's leading scientists have resulted in comprehensive assessments of climate change, which were published in 1990, 1996, 2001, and 2007. In its formal citation, the Nobel committee praised the IPCC for creating an "informed consensus about the connection between human activities and global warming."

This prestigious prize communicates a powerful message to the world. In honoring both the IPCC and Mr. Gore, the Nobel Committee draws global attention to the broadening scientific knowledge and consensus while also recognizing the critical importance of communicating this knowledge to global audiences. The marriage of science and rhetoric represented in this award recognizes the essential roles of both in stemming the problem that *An Inconvenient Truth* calls "the worst potential catastrophe in the history of human civilization."

Sources: W. Gibbs and S. Lyall, "Gore Shares Peace Prize for Climate Change Work," *The New York Times*, October 13, 2007, http://www.nytimes.com/2007/10/13/world/13nobel.html (accessed October 14, 2007). Al Gore, *An Inconvenient Truth: The Planetary Emergence of Global Warming and What We Can Do about It* (New York: Rodale, 2006), 3.

range of observed experience of global climate change, there is still some uncertainty about the predictive accuracy of scientific models. Some uncertainty has to do with the unpredictability of the positive feedbacks that are set in motion once the earth's temperature begins to rise and amplify warming. One such feedback is the planet's **albedo** or reflectivity. The higher the albedo, the more energy is reflected off the surface, causing less energy to be absorbed in the form of heat. As the polar ice caps melt, exposing more dry land and open water, additional warming will occur because land and water absorb more solar radiation than ice.

A second area of uncertainty in climate change models is the water vapor feedback. Because warm air holds more moisture than cool air, higher temperatures will produce an atmosphere with more water vapor, which, in the form of high thin clouds, warms the planet.

Yet a third positive feedback is in the form of melting Arctic permafrost. As temperatures rise, organic materials that have been frozen for millennia in the permafrost will begin to break down, giving off carbon dioxide and methane, and further contributing greenhouse gases to the atmosphere.

There are also some negative feedbacks, which slow the warming trend, that are difficult to figure into the climate models. For example, an increase in low clouds, a result of increased evaporation due to warming temperatures, will cool the climate by blocking sunlight from reaching the earth's surface. The fact that water vapor in the higher atmosphere serves as a blanket to create more warming, while water vapor as low cloud cover reflects the light and cools the earth, gives insight into just how complicated climate models must be in order to account for all the factors that impact the earth's climate. Many other feedbacks, both positive and negative, will likely influence the rate of warming. However, the net effect of known feedbacks, according to projections, is almost certainly an accelerated warming, although the exact magnitude of feedback impacts remains uncertain.[10]

Despite the uncertainties, mounting scientific evidence points convincingly toward the conclusion that global warming poses a real and significant threat for the twenty-first century. In response to growing concern, the **Intergovernmental Panel on Climate Change (IPCC)** was created in 1988 by the World Meteorological Association and the United Nations Environment Programme. The role of the IPCC is to review worldwide research and issue assessment reports of the scientific community's findings with regard to global warming. IPCC's first assessment report, issued in 1990, reflected the global scientific consensus of four hundred scientists and brought international attention to the threats posed by global warming.

The panel's findings spurred governments to create an international treaty on global warming called the **United Nations Framework Convention on Climate Change (UNFCCC).** The **Kyoto Protocol** (formally called the Kyoto Protocol to the United Nations Framework Convention on Climate Change) was an amendment to the UNFCCC that was negotiated in Kyoto, Japan, in December 1997. This agreement committed the participating industrialized countries to reduce their emissions of greenhouse gases by a combined total of 5.2 percent below 1990 levels between 2008 and 2012. If participating countries were unable to meet their reduction targets, they could engage in emissions trading, whereby they could purchase emission credits from countries who were below their agreed-upon targets. As of February 16, 2005, when the Kyoto Protocol entered into force, 141 countries had ratified the agreement, with the United States and Australia as conspicuous exceptions. Even if met, however, the Kyoto targets would merely have scratched the surface of the climate change problem.

With a growing recognition of the urgency to reduce greenhouse gas emissions, world leaders met in Copenhagen, Denmark, in December of 2009 to craft an agreement to replace the Kyoto Protocol. Despite years of negotiations leading up to the highly anticipated **Copenhagen Climate Change Conference (COP15),** delegates failed to produce a treaty with binding caps on emissions. The Copenhagen Accord, while not binding, does pledge both rich and poor countries to curb emissions. The meeting also garnered a commitment from the industrialized countries to help developing countries adapt to the impacts of climate change and to implement renewable energy technologies. But perhaps the most significant outcome of COP15 is the substantial shift in thinking that was evident in the talks. As a BBC news editorial put it, "There is no longer any

Connections

The Climate Change Solution in Wedges

The effort required to cut greenhouse emissions in half by 2055 is staggering: it can overwhelm even the most optimistic prognosticator. Researchers Stephen Pacala and Robert Socolow suggest that, as with any seemingly overwhelming problem, breaking the task down into more manageable blocks makes it more understandable and easier to address. That is precisely what they have done—they have broken emission-reduction options into more manageable components, which they term "stabilization wedges."

Each wedge represents a step that would be sufficient to prevent one billion metric tons of carbon per year from being emitted. Since emissions need to be cut by a minimum of seven billion tons, at least seven wedges would theoretically be needed. Altogether, Pacala and Socolow came up with fifteen wedges, any seven of which we could choose to implement to meet the required reduction levels. The following seven examples of wedges demonstrate the good news (the technologies we already have to do it) and the bad news (the magnitude of effort it will take).

- Wedge #1: Fuel economy: Increase fuel economy for 2 billion cars from 30 to 60 miles per gallon.

- Wedge #2: Reduced vehicle use: Reduce travel for 2 billion cars from 10,000 to 5,000 miles per year.

- Wedge #3: Efficient buildings and appliances: Cut carbon emissions by one-fourth in buildings and appliances.

- Wedge #9: Nuclear power: Add 700 gigawatts of nuclear power (twice the current global nuclear power capacity) to displace coal power.

- Wedge #10: Wind power: Add 2 million 1-megawatt-peak windmills (50 times the current capacity).

- Wedge #11: Solar power: Add 2000 1-gigawatt-peak photovoltaic cells (700 times the current capacity).

- Wedge #13: Biomass fuel: Add 100 times the current Brazil or U.S. ethanol production.

Let's put the effort required to implement these wedges into perspective. One million wind turbans, as called for by wedge #10, would take up an area roughly the size of New York state. The solar power wedge (#11) would require enough photo-voltaic cells to cover the surface of Connecticut. It would require one-sixth of all the world's cropland to produce enough biofuels to meet the goals set in wedge #13.

Nobody said it would be easy, but it can be done—and we still have eight wedges left to consider.

The model upon which Pacala and Socolow based their predictions has been criticized for not being rigorous enough. Physicist Martin Hoffert believes it will take as many as twelve wedges to simply keep emissions on the same upward trajectory.

Source: Stephen Pacala and Robert Socolow, "Stabilization Wedges: Solving the Climate Problem for the Next 50 Years with Current Technologies," *Science* 305 (August 13, 2004): 968–972. Martin Hoffert, cited in Elizabeth Kolbert, *Field Notes from a Catastrophe: Man, Nature, and Climate Change* (New York: Bloomsbury, 2006).

question that climate change is central to the political thinking of every country on the planet."[11] There is hope that the universally recognized need to act will create the political will to combat global warming aggressively as negotiations move forward.

Human Population Growth

From the global perspective, human population growth is approaching the earth's limited capacity to sustain us. Climate change, air and water pollution, resource depletion, species extinction, and a myriad of other environmental problems are all related to the fact that too many people are competing for a finite number of resources.

In his 1968 book, *The Population Bomb,* Stanford conservation biologist Paul R. Ehrlich raised the specter of environmental collapse as a result of exponential population growth and dwindling resources.[12] Through the mathematical calculation of doubling rates (the time it takes the Earth's population to double), Ehrlich predicted that if the rate of growth continued on the same path it was on in the late 1960s for 900 years, there would be some 60 million billion people, or about 100 people per square yard of the Earth's surface.

Global growth is difficult to calculate because of insufficient world census data as well as the complex weave of variables that must be factored into the equation. In addition to birth and death rates, factors such as the age structure of the population (percentage of prereproductive, reproductive, and postreproductive populations), fertility rates (number of births per woman), and emigration numbers must all be taken into consideration. It is not surprising, therefore, that Ehrlich's predictions are somewhat off the mark. For example, he predicted that the city of Calcutta would have 66 million inhabitants in the year 2000. According to 2001 census data, the population of Calcutta metropolitan area was approximately 13.2 million—far short of Ehrlich's projection.[13] Although there were some flaws in the models used in his calculations, Ehrlich nevertheless gained the world's attention and brought the problem of population growth to a broad public audience.

In his highly acclaimed book, *How Many People Can the Earth Support?,* mathematician Joel E. Cohen assesses several population-projection models by comparing the models to actual population data.[14] He points out that Ehrlich's model is fundamentally flawed—that human population growth is not a simple exponential process. Cohen emphasizes the effects of social, cultural, economic, and political variables and how they have affected population patterns in the past. Although Cohen's calculations, like Ehrlich's, produce dire predictions, a glimmer of hope can be found in his emphasis on one highly variable component in the equation—how humans *choose* to interact with the environment and with each other. The earth's **carrying capacity** (or how many people the earth can support) is uncertain and dynamic. Cohen's mathematics demonstrates the significance of the choices we make and offers at least some cause for optimism if the right choices are made.

The 2007 U.S. Census Bureau International Data Base estimates that the overall world population growth rate is 1.14 percent, which translates into a doubling rate of approximately 61 years.[15] There is, however, a significant discrepancy between developed and developing nations. For example, the growth rate in the United Kingdom is 0.2 percent; in France it is 0.4 percent; in Germany it is 0.0 percent.

Many Asian and African countries have much higher growth rates. Afghanistan, for example, has a growth rate of 4.8 percent or a doubling time of 14.5 years.

Although these numbers are more encouraging than the grim predictions that Ehrlich made in 1968, optimism must be tempered with an understanding that even a small percentage rate increase quickly translates into millions of people. The world population projection for the year 2050 is 9.3 billion people.

But the most troubling implication of population growth at any level is the escalating rate of resource consumption as underdeveloped nations raise their standards of living and the increasing resource demands begin to approach those of the developed nations. Consider, for example, that the United States, whose population comprises only 4.64 percent of the world's population, consumes 25.32 percent of the world's energy resources.[16] It is clear that the world's natural resources cannot sustain a future that is dependent upon increasing production and harvesting resources to meet the needs of the expanding world populations and consumer markets.

Species Extinction and Loss of Biodiversity

The extinction of species is not a new phenomenon. Organisms have been disappearing from the face of the earth for billions of years. There is extensive evidence of five mass extinctions, the largest of which occurred 225 million years ago, when 95 percent of all marine species living at that time became extinct. Undoubtedly, the most captivating mass extinction occurred 65 million years ago, when the dinosaurs disappeared. The fate of the dinosaurs has fascinated children, movie producers, and scientists alike, and many theories have attempted to explain the demise of these extraordinary creatures. The most accepted theory advances the notion that a large asteroid struck the earth, causing an enormous dust cloud that obscured the sun for several years and greatly reduced the earth's vegetation, which led to the starvation of the giant herbivores and their predators.

A more recent mass extinction occurred in North America a little more than eleven thousand years ago, at the end of the last Ice Age. This extinction, called the **Pleistocene extinction,** involved many large animals, including mammoths, mastodons, giant beavers, and saber-toothed tigers. It is estimated that only about 30 percent of the big game animals that were in existence at the time survived. Those that somehow managed to avoid annihilation include moose, caribou, horses, and camels.

There is no generally supported theory that explains what caused this mass extinction. One theory advanced the idea that the large animals were hunted to extinction.[17] A more recent theory suggests that the Pleistocene extinction was caused by diseases carried by the newly arrived humans and their pet dogs.[18] Whether the cause was climate change, human intervention, disease, or a combination of factors is a matter of conjecture. Today, however, it is evident that humans are the primary agent in the alarmingly accelerating rate of species extinction. The **International Union for Conservation of Nature and Natural Resources (IUCN)** estimates that current rates of human-caused extinctions are one hundred to one thousand times the **background rate** (or naturally occurring rate).

The IUCN keeps a "Red List of Threatened Species," a comprehensive assessment of the conservation status of species classified according to their risk of global extinction.[19] The IUCN uses a nine-category classification system:

Extinct: The last known individual has died.

Extinct in the Wild: The last known individual has died in the wild, but there are still some in captivity.

Critically Endangered: Extreme high risk of extinction.

Endangered: Very high risk of extinction.

Vulnerable: High risk of extinction.

Near Threatened: May soon move into above categories.

Least Concern: Species is abundant and widespread.

Data Deficient: Not enough data currently exists about the status of the species to classify it.

Not Evaluated: The species has never had a conservation status assessment. Most of the world's species are in this category.

Two of the more spectacular **charismatic megafauna** (animals that have popular appeal and are often used to spotlight conservation campaigns) to appear on the Red List in recent years are polar bears and the common hippopotamus. In 2006, polar bears were listed with a grim prediction. The IUCN forecasts that their population will decline by 50 percent to 100 percent over the next fifty to one hundred years because of melting Arctic ice floes, which are essential for their hunting. The 2006 Red List also added the common hippopotamus to the list of "vulnerable" species. Obviously, it has become not so common. There has been a sharp decline in common hippopotamus populations in the Democratic Republic of Congo (about 95 percent in ten years), where unregulated hunting for meat and ivory teeth has proliferated as a result of the country's unstable political situation. Regional conflicts and political turbulence in some African countries have created extreme hardship and devastation for many of their human inhabitants, causing a devastating impact on the nonhuman populations.

Why should we concern ourselves with disappearing species? What has a common hippopotamus or a northern hairy-nosed wombat ever done for me? Many environmentalists and conservationists would respond to these questions by pointing out the intrinsic value of nature—that nature has value regardless of its usefulness to humans. This nature-centered view is sometimes referred to as **ecocentric** or **biocentric.** However, the mainstream view of nature is an **anthropocentric,** or human-centered, perspective, which focuses on the merits of nature in its service to humankind.

Nature's services to humankind are innumerable. Along with goods such as seafood and timber, the natural world provides many services to humans. We need plants, animals, microbes, and fungi to fertilize and regenerate soils, pollinate crops, disperse seeds, decompose wastes, purify water, and carry out many other vital functions that are often overlooked until a disruption in the natural system impedes the delivery of these services. According to Stanford ecologist Gretchen C. Daily, to replace these "natural utilities" would cost more than the gross national product of all the nations of the world combined—and these are just the known services.[20]

Harvard biologist Edward O. Wilson asks us to consider the unknown factors and what might potentially be lost along with biodiversity:

Why should we care? What difference does it make if some species are extinguished, if even half of all the species on earth disappear? Let me count

Figure 2.1   Greenpeace Advertisement

Greenpeace makes good use of these spectacularly photogenic charismatic megafauna in Project Thin Ice, a campaign to save the polar bears. The U.S. Fish and Wildlife Service officially listed polar bears as a "threatened species" in 2006. Global warming has led to diminishing of the Arctic ice floes, upon which the bears depend for hunting and breeding.

© Greenpeace / Daniel Beltrá

the ways. New sources of information will be lost. Vast potential biological wealth will be destroyed. Still undeveloped medicines, crops, pharmaceuticals, timber, fibers, pulp, soil-restoring vegetation, petroleum substitutes, and other products and amenities will never come to light.[21]

Wilson goes on to point out that the cure for Hodgkin's disease and childhood lymphocytic leukemia comes from the rosy periwinkle, a chemical extract from the saliva of leeches dissolves blood clots during surgery, and the bark of the Pacific yew offers a promising new treatment for ovarian and breast cancer. A long list of pharmaceutical services is rendered to the human community, compliments of the natural community.

Perhaps the most compelling argument for the preservation of biodiversity focuses not on the contribution of individual species to human well-being, but on the role of diversity in the ecosystem as a whole. In an intricately woven web of interdependence, diversity is what keeps ecosystems functioning. We depend on healthy, productive ecosystems to replenish our soil, cleanse our water, and filter the air we breathe. Biodiversity is both the consequence of a healthy planet and the instrument of its self-repair. (To find out what is being done to preserve biological diversity and how you can help, visit the Center for Biological Diversity at www.biologicaldiversity.org or the National Wildlife Federation at www.nwf.org.)

Humans have contributed to species extinction and loss of biodiversity in several ways. The following section looks at humans' role in extinction through fishing and hunting for food and commercial products, the introduction of alien or exotic species, and, most significantly, the destruction or alteration of natural habitats.

Fishing

Nearly one in four people worldwide depend on the oceans' bounty for food and livelihood. Industrial fishing practices have taken a heavy toll on marine species and ecosystems. A comprehensive analysis published in 2003 revealed that over 90 percent of the world's large predatory fishes (tuna, blue marlins, swordfish, and others) have been lost, with some populations alarmingly close to extinction.[22] A subsequent report, published in 2006, drew further attention to the increasingly dire status of global fisheries. The authors report that trends in loss of marine biodiversity, if continued at the current rate, would mean "the global collapse of all taxa [categories of organisms] currently fished by the mid-21st century."[23]

The collapses in marine species have several causes. As fish populations dwindle, fisheries extend into ever-deeper ocean zones, which are largely unregulated, allowing for industry corruption and exploitation. Poverty likewise plays a role, especially in developing countries where growing populations demand the food and income provided by the oceans.

The decimation of species not only impacts the ability of marine ecosystems to feed a growing human population, it also impacts the ecosystem's stability and potential for recovery. The loss of a single species can have cascading effects up and down the food chain. For example, the decline in perch and herring off the coast of Alaska caused a decline in seals and sea lions, which prey on the fish. The killer whales, which prey on seals and sea lions, then had to feed on otters, causing a collapse in otter populations. This, in turn, led to an explosion in the otters' favorite prey, sea urchins. The explosion of sea urchins diminished the kelp on which they feed, placing many other species of fish, invertebrates, and birds in jeopardy—and on it goes.[24]

Concern for the global fisheries prompted delegates to the 2002 U.N. World Summit on Sustainable Development in Johannesburg to pass a resolution to restore global fish stocks to maximum sustainable yield by 2015. This will require nations to reduce and enforce catch limits, reduce by-catch (species unintentionally caught in trawls and nets), and establish marine reserves. Once restored, well-managed fisheries can produce both sustainable yields of seafood and good economic returns for those who depend on fishing for food and livelihood. (To find out more about what is being done to preserve marine biodiversity, go to http://environmentaldefense.org.)

Hunting

Many examples could be cited of hunting as the cause of the annihilation of a given species. Here are just a few:

- The dodo bird that once lived on the island of Mauritius in the Indian Ocean was hunted to extinction in the late 1600s by Dutchmen living in a penal colony on that island. The flightless dodo was easy prey for hunters because the bird had previously had no predators and, therefore, had no fear of humans.

- In 1914, the last passenger pigeon, named Martha, died in the Cincinnati Zoo. The population had once been so abundant that flocks numbered in the billions. Yet in less than half a century, hunters extinguished the species.

- Three of the eight subspecies of modern tigers have disappeared in the last sixty years: the Bali tiger, the Caspian/Iranian tiger, and the Javan tiger. The population of the remaining five subspecies is estimated to be between forty-six hundred and seventy-seven hundred. Tigers have been poached for their skins and for body parts that are used for traditional Chinese medicines.

These are just a few on the long list of species that have been hunted out of existence. Hunting does also play a role in species conservation, through the managed control of species populations as well as through the actions of organizations of hunting enthusiasts dedicated to protecting wildlife populations and hunting traditions. Among such organizations are Ducks Unlimited, The Izaak Walton League of America, The National Wild Turkey Federation, Pheasants Forever, and Quail Forever.

The list of animals that have been hunted to extinction or near extinction through unregulated or unlawful hunting is extensive. I will leave you with one final example.

- In 1894, the last eleven Steven Island wrens that once lived on an island of the same name in New Zealand were killed by a lighthouse keeper's pet cat. Although the hunter in this case was not human, the guilty feline was introduced to the island by humans.

Nonnative species that have been intentionally or unintentionally introduced into an ecosystem can cause serious problems for the native species, as discussed in the following section.

Nonnative Species Introduction

For as long as humans have traveled around the world, they have carried with them many species of plants and animals that they have introduced to new geographic areas and their endemic species. A species is **endemic** to a certain location if it originated there and is confined to that place. The international spread of non-native species, also called **alien** or **exotic** species, is referred to as **bioinvasion.** In many cases, the introduced alien is a superior competitor and threatens the endemic populations. In fact, bioinvasion now ranks as the second greatest threat to biodiversity, just after habitat loss or alteration.[25]

The introduction of nonnative species can be intentional or accidental. An example of endemic species devastation caused by accidental introduction is the case of the zebra mussel, a freshwater species of mollusks. It is believed that the zebra mussel larva was carried from Europe in the ballast tanks of ships and introduced into the ecosystem of the Great Lakes, where it reproduces abundantly, has no natural predators, and has forced out the native mollusk species. It has migrated all the way down the Mississippi River to New Orleans.[26]

An example of a devastating species that was intentionally introduced is the cane toad, which was brought from Hawaii to the northeast coast of Australia in 1935 to eat cane beetles. Today the toad population has spread across the country, killing native predators with the deadly poison on its skin. A sadly ironic twist to this tale is that the cane toads found such an abundance of nourishment in their new habitat that they didn't eat the cane beetles.[27] (For a comprehensive list of invasive species, go to www.issg.org or to www.invasive.org.)

Destruction and Alteration of Natural Habitats

The law doth punish man or woman
That steals the goose from off the common,
But lets the greater felon loose,
That steals the common from the goose.

(18th Century—Anonymous)

Inextricably linked to species extinction and loss of biodiversity is the destruction or alteration of natural habitats. Humans have altered or destroyed natural eco-systems through the extensive burning of fossil fuels, urban encroachment, farming, grazing, logging, mining, and road construction (and the list goes on). No country is immune to the disappearance of life-supporting habitats, but certain places and types of habitat are especially vulnerable. High on the critical list are forests, wetlands, and coral reefs.

Forests

Particularly species-rich "hot spots" are the tropical rain forests, which comprise only 7 percent of the earth's surface but are home to an estimated 50 to 90 percent of the earth's species. Entomologist Terry L. Erwin found that a single tree could host up to as many as fifteen hundred different species of beetle. Erwin believes that inhabiting the tropical forests may be thirty million species of anthropods (a phylum that includes insects and crustaceans) alone.[28]

The rain forests are disappearing at an alarming rate. According to Chris Bright of the World Watch Institute, clearing and burning destroys at least fourteen million hectares (34.6 million acres) each year.[29] Despite recent public awareness of the global impacts of tropical deforestation, the pace of destruction has not appreciably slowed. Nor is the destruction limited to tropical forests. Almost half the world's original forest cover is gone, most of it destroyed within the last three decades. Only one-fifth remains as "frontier forest," tracts of relatively undisturbed forest.[30]

Many factors contribute to the alarming rate of deforestation. The demand for forest resources has risen dramatically with growing economies and consumption rates. For example, between 1961 and 1994, the per capita consumption of paper increased by 80 percent globally and by 350 percent in developing countries.[31] Much of the forest land in developing countries is cleared for grazing and farming, often by burning large tracts of forests. The "colonization" of rainforest land offers immediate economic resources for countries such as Brazil, where much of the population lives in extreme poverty.

Continued forest loss will have serious local, regional, and global implications. The losses to biodiversity are incalculable. Forests provide essential ecological services, including nutrient recycling and watershed management. Forests also play a vital role in climate regulation. Tropical deforestation is responsible for an estimated 20 percent of the total human-caused atmospheric build-up of CO_2.[32]

Coral Reefs

Coral reefs, some of the most ancient and biologically diverse ecosystems on the earth, comprise less than 1 percent of the earth's marine environment but are home to more than a quarter of all known marine species. Coastal development, fishing,

Connections

Chocolate Can Help Save the Rainforests—Sweet!!

Among the many efforts underway to save the rainforests is one particularly savory option. Organically grown cacao (or cocoa, as it is called in the United States) is a forest-friendly product, especially when one considers the alternatives. Cacao is the fruit from which the nectar of the gods—chocolate—is produced. It is a shade-grown, forest understory crop that depends on rainforest canopy for cover.

The biggest threats to rainforests are logging and deforestation for cattle ranching and agriculture. The ecological benefits of growing cacao in rainforests are twofold: it preserves forests and boosts rural employment. Because the cacao trees require shade cover from the forest, farmers plant the small cacao trees amid the plants in the jungle with very little clearing. The large variety of trees and plants makes cacao's cropland a diverse habitat for birds and animals.

When the cacao crop in Costa Rica failed in the 1970s, due, in large part, to a fungal disease that spread across Central and South America, farmers turned to growing bananas, which requires clearing the rainforest land for planting. By the 1990s, the fungal epidemic had spread to South America, leaving some ninety thousand farm laborers out of work in Brazil alone and forcing cacao farmers to convert their plantations to other uses.

A number of organizations have been promoting the regeneration of the cacao industry in the rainforests of Central and South America. (Fungus-resistant cacao varieties are now available.) "Forest cacao" could be used to preserve biological diversity in rainforests as well as to boost rural economies. But in order to make this a reality, markets for organically grown "eco-chocolate" must be established. One such entrepreneurial enterprise has been established by the Milwaukee Public Museum, which has introduced and marketed "Cacao de Vida," a dark chocolate bar made from cacao grown in Costa Rican rainforests. Another such endeavor was launched by Yachana Gourmet, a green company that promotes "Yachana Jungle Chocolate" from chocolate grown in Ecuador. For a small fee, you can adopt a chocolate tree in Ecuador's Amazon Rainforest (www.yachanagourmet.com/adopt_tree.htm). Worldwatch Institute is likewise promoting a program for forest venture capitalists in Brazil.

Eat chocolate—save a rainforest!

Sources: S. Quick, "Chocolate May Help Preserve Rainforests," 2003, http://www.jsonline.com/story/index.aspx?id=169506 (accessed October 9, 2007). Worldwatch Institute, "Chocolate Offers New Hope for Saving Endangered Rain Forests," 2003, http://www.worldwatch.org/press/news/2003/12/04 (accessed October 2, 2007). C. Bright and R. Sarin, "Worldwatch Report #168: Venture Capitalism for a Tropical Forest: Cocoa in the Mata Atlantica," 2003, http://www.worldwatch.org/pubs/paper/168 (accessed October 2, 2007).

marine pollution, and warming waters have put an estimated 58 percent of these "rainforests of the sea" at risk and turned many into bleached graveyards devoid of fish and other marine life.[33]

Global warming plays a significant role in the accelerated degradation of the world's reefs. Coral is extremely vulnerable to heat stress: the increasing sea surface temperatures over the past three decades have resulted in "bleaching," a process in

Figure 2.2   Coral Reefs

Coral reefs are the largest living structures and the most biologically diverse ecosystems on earth, supporting nearly one-quarter of all marine species. Warming oceans, coastal development, pollution, and fishing are among the threats that have put these colorful underwater gardens at risk.

Claire Fackler, NOAA National Marine Sanctuaries

which the coral expels the algae living in it, turning the coral white. The algae are necessary to help feed the coral. Many coral reefs have not been able to rebound from the massive bleaching. A 1998 global assessment of coral reefs published by the World Watch Institute reported that nearly 60 percent of the earth's coral reefs are threatened.[34]

Some of the most degraded reefs are those off popular Caribbean vacation spots, including the islands of Jamaica, Barbados, and Dominica. Most United States reefs are also in jeopardy, including almost all those off the Florida coast and nearly half of Hawaii's. The most threatened of all are the reefs of Southeast Asia, which are also the most species-rich on earth.[35]

Coral reefs are among the least protected and monitored natural habitats in the world, leaving much of the world's marine biodiversity at risk. In addition to hosting a rich diversity of species, reefs provide food, coastal protection, new medications, and tourist revenue for millions of people. (For more information on coral reefs and what you can do, go to the National Oceanic and Atmospheric Administration's web page at www.publicaffairs.noaa.gov/coral-reef.html or visit the Nature Conservancy at www.nature.org/joinanddonate/rescuereef/explore/help.html.)

Wetlands

The disappearance of wetlands, which include fresh and saltwater marshes, swamps, mangroves, and estuaries, is another significant environmental concern.

Wetlands support a wide variety of species, including many fish, mollusks, and migratory birds. They also serve as nature's sponge—absorbing ocean tidal surges and excess stream flow in times of river flooding, then releasing the excess water at low tide and times of low river flow. But perhaps the most vital role of the wetlands is that of an efficient and effective water purification system. Wetland water retains and recirculates organic matter and pollutants. In this recycling process, it purifies the water before it again reaches the ocean, lake, or river.

Wetlands are among the most threatened ecosystems in the United States and other populated areas in the world where they are drained to make room for urban development or agriculture. The U.S. Environmental Protection Agency reports that over half of the 220 million acres of wetlands that existed in the lower 48 states in the seventeenth century have been drained and converted to other uses. An estimated 58,500 acres of wetlands were lost each year between 1986 and 1997. Since then, there has been an encouraging decline in the loss rate, due to the enforcement of wetland protection measures, wetland restoration and creation programs, and monitoring and protection programs, as well as public education and outreach about the importance of wetlands.[36]

Another threat to wetlands is climate change. Increasing temperatures and the increasing frequency of storms, droughts, and floods, as well as rising sea levels, are likely to significantly impact wetlands and the essential services they provide.[37] (To learn more about the plight of wetlands and what you can do to help, go to the EPA web site at www.epa.gov/owow/wetlands/awm.)

Forests, coral reefs, and wetlands represent only a few of the species-rich ecosystems that have been negatively impacted by human intervention. Lakes, rivers, topsoil, desert landscapes, old growth forests, as well as countless local and regional sites have also been subjected to environmental degradation that jeopardizes the diversity of life these ecosystems support.

If you are feeling overwhelmed by all the problems that we face, this would be a good time to recall the battle that was launched with the first Earth Day and the challenges that can be met by energized and imaginative environmental action. As former vice president Al Gore tells us, "It's our time to rise again to secure our future."[38] As you will read later in this book, a great deal of evidence suggests that a new restlessness is emerging to challenge our leaders and create the political will necessary to mobilize the next great push for a more sustainable future. So take a deep breath and read on—environmentalism is not for the faint of heart.

Waste Disposal

We live in a throw-away society. The problem with this, as pointed out by Barry Commoner, a well-known environmental writer and thinker, is that "Everything must go somewhere."[39] The following sections examine the problems of the disposal of solid wastes, hazardous wastes, and radioactive wastes, as well as where the "somewhere" is when they are thrown away.

Solid Wastes

The volume of waste generated in many developed countries has grown substantially in recent decades. In the United States it has more than doubled since 1960. U.S. households generate over two hundred million tons of waste each year. That figure increases to eleven billion tons when industrial wastes are added to the equation.[40]

Paper accounts for the largest share of municipal solid waste. In the United States, paper makes up 39 percent of all household waste. Even though almost half the paper we use is now recycled, we still throw away more paper each year than China consumes in a year.[41]

Throughout much of our nation's history, garbage was tossed into the city streets, where hogs were allowed to wander freely and eat the organic wastes. In the late 1800s, garbage accumulated in such large amounts along some New York city streets that it impeded pedestrian and horse traffic. Public health concerns eventually forced some reforms, but strict federal regulation on waste disposal was not enacted until 1976, with the passage of the **Resource Conservation and Recovery Act (RCRA).**

Prior to the passage of RCRA, most municipal waste was hauled to unregulated open dump sites outside municipalities. These sites served as breeding grounds for rodents and created air pollution problems because of gases produced in decomposition and the smoke from fires that frequently burned in the dumps. Ground water pollution was also a big problem because leachate (contaminated liquid from waste dumps) seeped through the ground into groundwater reservoirs.

Because the open dump sites were unregulated, hazardous materials were dumped along with household trash, resulting in health hazards that, in many cases, are still present and cost taxpayers billions of dollars for cleanup. Public attention was drawn to the problem of improper waste disposal in the late 1970s, when a leaking abandoned dump site at **Love Canal** in New York was found to have seriously contaminated the surrounding areas. From 1942 to 1952 the dump site had been used by what was then Hooker Chemicals, for the disposal of over 21,000 tons of various chemical wastes, including many highly toxic substances such as pesticides and dioxins. In 1953 the area was covered over with soil. Homes and an elementary school were constructed on land near the dump site.

Problems with odors were first reported in the late 1960s, but extensive studies were not done the early 1970s. These studies revealed that the toxic leachate had migrated to the surrounding residential areas and into streams that fed the Niagara River upstream from the Niagara Falls water treatment plant, which served 77,000 people. In 1978 and again in 1980, President Jimmy Carter issued an environmental emergency at Love Canal. Eventually, 950 families were evacuated from the area.

The serious contamination problem at Love Canal focused national attention on the problem of abandoned waste sites and their adverse effects on human health, and ultimately led to legislation governing abandoned sites. Hazardous waste was dumped on many more such sites in the United States prior to the establishment of our current laws and regulations. After years of remediation and hundreds of millions of dollars spent, The Environmental Protection Agency (EPA) deemed Love Canal to be once again safe for residents. Because the name "Love Canal" will remain imprinted with its toxic legacy, the area has been renamed Bear Creek Village.

The Resource Conservation and Recovery Act of 1976 required states to close all open dumps by 1983 and replace them with sanitary landfills, in which wastes are compacted and sealed between layers of clean dirt each day. Most residential and industrial waste ends up in landfills. However, because of rapidly diminishing landfill capacity and the problems of finding sites for new landfills, municipalities are increasingly turning to incineration as a means of waste disposal. Although incinerators are more expensive to build and operate than landfills, in many municipalities they are the only viable means of dealing with the enormous amount of wastes generated each day.

In addition to providing waste disposal, incinerators are used in cities across the country to generate electricity or steam. The first commercial waste-to-energy plant began operating in 1975 in Saugus, Massachusetts, and is still operating today. State-of-the-art emission control systems and advanced incineration technologies, along with aggressive composting and recycling programs, offer feasible and promising solutions to the ever-increasing landfill capacity problems.

Hazardous Wastes

The problem of hazardous wastes is recognized by the EPA as one of the most serious and costly environmental dilemmas in the United States today. The **Comprehensive Environmental Response, Compensation, and Liability Act of 1980 (CERCLA),** also known as the **Superfund Act,** created a multibillion dollar "superfund" for the remediation of hazardous waste sites that pose public health or environmental threats.

Hazardous wastes (also called **PTBs:** persistent, toxic, and bioaccumulative chemicals) include such things as acids, explosives, combustible solvents, and toxic chemicals. The EPA considers three characteristics when determining a given chemical's potential adverse effects. A chemical is *persistent* if it doesn't readily break down in the environment. It is *bioaccumulative* if it concentrates in animal or plant tissues, and it is *toxic* if it is hazardous to human health and environment. PTBs may have many adverse effects such as cancer, birth defects, and declines in species populations.

RCRA sets national standards for the generation, transport, storage, and disposal of hazardous wastes, which are highly regulated by the EPA and state agencies. Most hazardous wastes are disposed of in **secure landfills** that are carefully located, constructed, and monitored to minimize the chances of migrating leachate or toxic fumes. High temperature incinerators (1200° C) are also used to dispose of combustible liquids and hazardous solids.

The stringent laws and regulations that govern the disposal of hazardous wastes have gone a long way toward preventing disasters like Love Canal. (To locate the Superfund sites in your area, go to www.scorecard.org.) However, the costs of treating and disposing of hazardous waste are often staggering. Unfortunately, these high costs have provided an incentive for "midnight dumpers" to illegally dispose of hazardous wastes. Perhaps the most famous case of this kind occurred in Times Beach, Missouri.

In the late 1970s, a waste hauler was subcontracted by a chemical manufacturing company to dispose of its hazardous waste—and dispose of it, he did. He mixed the waste with oil and sprayed it on the gravel streets of Times Beach, as well as on more than two dozen other sites in eastern Missouri. That oil contained, among other things, dioxin, a cancer-causing agent that is known to be one of the most toxic chemical by-products in existence. When investigations in the early 1980s revealed the extent of the contamination, the federal government purchased most of the city of Times Beach for $32 million so that the residents could afford to move elsewhere, making a toxic ghost town of this once vibrant community of some two thousand people. The cleanup of Times Beach was completed in 1997. The site has since been turned over to the Missouri State Parks division.

The problem of illegal dumping of toxic wastes is not limited to "midnight dumpers." Another problem is that of household toxic wastes (paint thinners, insecticides, solvents, and so on) that, through carelessness or lack of awareness, are thrown into household trash collection containers and delivered to municipal landfills or incinerators. What may seem like harmless household products underneath your kitchen sink may have serious environmental consequences once they leave your home.

Barry Commoner, in his highly influential book, *The Closing Circle,* gives an example of what may happen to a typical household dry-cell battery, which contains mercury. When the battery is incinerated, the mercury in the battery is heated, producing mercury vapor, which is then emitted from the incinerator's smokestack. This toxic vapor is then carried by wind and brought to earth in rain or snow, which in turn enters a mountain lake, where the mercury condenses and sinks to the bottom. Here bacteria convert it into methyl mercury, which is taken in by fish and accumulates in their organs and flesh. If a tainted fish is then caught and eaten by a fisherman, the mercury becomes deposited into his organs—and so on. Commoner urges us to remember a basic law of physics—"everything must go somewhere."[42] Matter is indestructible; all trash goes somewhere when you throw it away.

Household batteries containing mercury are now banned in many countries, including the United States, but a new concern for mercury has arisen with the increasing use of **compact fluorescent light bulbs (CFLs).** Many environmental organizations, including the U.S. Environmental Protection Agency, have encouraged use of CFLs, because they use up to 75 percent less energy than incandescent bulbs and can last up to ten times longer.[43] Each CFL has an average of five milligrams of mercury sealed in its glass tubing. Although this is a small amount of mercury (about the amount that would cover the tip of a ballpoint pen), CFLs in landfills and incinerators could have the same effect that Commoner described in his household battery example. Spent bulbs should be brought to recycling centers that have services for CFL disposal. Many major retailers who sell CFLs also have recycling repositories.

Unfortunately, the kind of waste discussed in the next section has greatly limited disposal options. The amount of radioactive waste grows worldwide. The following discussion is limited, for the sake of space, to the problems and ways of dealing with radioactive waste in the United States.

Radioactive Waste

Increasingly, world-wide attention is being focused on the ecological legacy of over fifty years of nuclear weapons and nuclear energy production. There are more than one hundred nuclear power plants operating in the United States alone, producing 20 percent of the nation's power. The International Atomic Energy Agency reported that worldwide, as of 2007, a total of 439 nuclear power reactors were operating in thirty-one different countries.[44]

Nuclear power plants produce high-level radioactive wastes in the form of spent fuel rod assemblies, which are stored in water-filled basins at the nuclear power plant sites. Each year, a typical nuclear power station (which produces a thousand megawatts of electricity) adds approximately thirty metric tons of spent fuel rods to its storage facility.[45]

In addition to the waste generated from nuclear power production is the waste associated with producing nuclear weapons. In the past fifty-five years, the United States government has built more than seventy thousand nuclear weapons, resulting in millions of cubic meters of radioactive waste.[46] In addition, a tremendous amount of radioactive waste is generated from the post–Cold War decommissioning of nuclear weapons.

A radioactive substance emits radiation until it gradually becomes stable and no longer radioactive. This transformation towards stability is called **radioactive decay.** The rate of decay is measured by the element's **half-life,** the time required for 50 percent of the radioactive element to decay. It generally takes ten half-lives before a highly radioactive substance no longer constitutes a serious radiation threat. The half-life of any given kind of radioactive material varies widely—from fractions of a second to billion of years. The half-life of plutonium-239, an essential ingredient in nuclear weaponry, is 24,000 years; its radiation lasts for 240,000 years.[47]

Until quite recently, the radioactive wastes generated from producing nuclear weapons have been stored in drums and tanks on production sites in numerous Department of Defense and Department of Energy installations across the United States. These on-site storage facilities were never designed to serve as permanent storage facilities, but as temporary means of disposal until a "better solution" presents itself. In the past, there have been a number of problems with leaking drums and storage tanks at on-site facilities. The worst spill at a federal installation occurred at the Hanford site in Washington state, where estimates as high as eight hundred thousand to one million gallons are reported to have leaked from tanks containing the waste from forty-five years of plutonium production.[48]

The first permanent nuclear waste burial facility opened its doors for business on March 26, 1999, near Carlsbad, New Mexico. The **Waste Isolation Pilot Plant (WIPP)** was authorized by Congress in 1979 as a research and development facility for demonstrating safe disposal of radioactive waste from government nuclear defense activities. It took more than twenty years for the plant to make it through the permitting process and begin receiving the shipments of low-level radioactive waste for interment deep into the salt beds of southeastern New Mexico.

Currently, there is no facility for the permanent disposal of high-level radioactive waste, most of which is in the form of spent nuclear fuel from power plants. Nevada's **Yucca Mountain,** located about one hundred miles northwest of Las Vegas, was targeted as the location for the first such facility. Although to date over 13.5 billion dollars have been spent on studies, permits, and construction, the federal budget recently slashed spending on the project, which was tentatively scheduled to open in 2017. The nearly sixty thousand tons of reactor fuel will remain in storage at nuclear power plants around the country.[49]

The push to lower global carbon emissions has sparked renewed interest and debate about nuclear power generation as a clean, reliable, alternative energy source. Nuclear energy does offer a way to lower our dependence on fossil fuels. (Coal plants provide more than half the electricity consumed in the United States and 40 percent worldwide.) Alternative energy sources are essential components of any serious effort to cut back on carbon emissions. However, the social and ecological implications of continuing or accelerating the production of radioactive waste must be factored into alternative energy decisions. It is unreasonable to expect that radioactive wastes can remain in temporary storage or that we can find and secure permanent storage sites for the tens of thousands of years that it will take for the radiation to decay to safe levels.

Concluding and Looking Ahead

The preceding discussion of environmental concerns is but a sampling of the complex issues of which we, as environmental communicators, should be aware. It would be much more comfortable to leave the environmental problems of the world to scientists and hope for a "technofix" that can halt or reverse the damage we have inflicted upon our natural environment. Unfortunately, it seems highly unlikely that scientists alone can stem the tide of environmental degradation. Technological solutions tend to focus on a single problem or set of problems. This "band-aid" response often fails to address the systemic problems that exist in a natural system of unfathomable complexity and inextricable interdependency with the social system.

It is essential that our experts keep working toward solutions to specific environmental problems, but an essential part of any real solution to the problems of our natural systems lies in our social systems. Murray Bookchin, noted author and environmental philosopher, suggested that "We do not simply live in a world of problems but in a highly problematical world, an inherently anti-ecological society."[50] What is called for in this "highly problematical" world is a whole new ethic that reconceptualizes humans' relationship to the natural world—an ethic that, in the words of Aldo Leopold, perhaps the most noted (and quoted) philosopher of the modern environmental movement, "changes the role of *homo sapiens* from conqueror of the land to plain member and citizen of it."[51]

The study of environmental communication employs multiple approaches and perspectives in the search to understand the role of communication in defining the natural world and our relationship to it. You will find as you continue in your study that environmental communication scholars, like environmentalists, often disagree on how to define that relationship and the most effective way to bring about the necessary changes. I do not presume to know the form and fashion that this "new ethic" should take. Nor do I believe that there is only one "right" or appropriate way to view the natural world and our relationship to it. A social system, like a natural system, is a collection of diverse, interrelated components. Only by incorporating multiple and varied controls into the system can we deal with the multiple and varied challenges posed by the environment.

As individuals, the challenges we face are indeed daunting. Yet collectively, we can address the many environmental problems that threaten the well-being of the planet and its human and nonhuman inhabitants. How we communicate about the environment influences our view of the natural world, which, in turn, determines how we treat it. As journalists, rhetoricians, conflict managers, team builders, and activists, environmental communicators are poised in a central position to influence attitudes, behaviors, policies, and practices.

I urge you to pick your "environmental cause" and get involved. As the twenty-first century unfolds, our individual actions will create the collective collateral for shaping a sustainable future.

The following chapter takes us from this rather grim look at our environmental problems to an examination of the influences and ideologies that have led us to this state of affairs. Chapter 3 examines the historical influences and the mainstream environmental perspectives that ground Western environmental policies and practices.

Discussion Questions and Exercises:

1. Calculate the demand your lifestyle places on the natural world (your "ecological footprint") by going to www.footprintnetwork.org. Report your score.

2. Find out about hazardous sites in your own area by going to www.scorecard.org and report what you find.

3. Tim Flannery, in his influential book *The Weather Makers* (2005), makes the statement that "One of the biggest obstacles to making a start on climate change is that it has become cliché before it has even been understood." What do you think he means by this? Do you agree or disagree with this statement?

4. With the looming threat of global warming, there has been a great deal of renewed interest in nuclear power as an alternative to fossil fuels. State and support your opinion on this issue.

Suggested Readings

Tim Flannery. *The Weather Makers: How Man Is Changing the Climate and What It Means for Life on Earth*. New York: Atlantic Monthly Press, 2005.

Ross Gelbspan. *Boiling Point*. New York: Basic Books, 2004.

Al Gore. *An Inconvenient Truth*. New York: Rodale, 2006.

Elizabeth Kolbert. *Field Notes from a Catastrophe: Man, Nature, and Climate Change*. New York: Bloomsbury, 2006.

Gaylord Nelson. *Beyond Earth Day: Fulfilling the Promise*. Madison: University of Wisconsin Press, 2002.

Naomi Oreskes. "The Scientific Consensus on Climate Change." *Science* 306.5702 (December 3, 2004): 1686.

Spencer R. Weart. *The Discovery of Global Warming*. Cambridge, MA: Harvard University Press, 2003.

Edward O. Wilson. *The Creation: An Appeal to Save Life on Earth*. New York: Norton, 2006.

Notes

1. Gaylord Nelson, *Beyond Earth Day: Fulfilling the Promise* (Madison: University of Wisconsin Press, 2002), 9.
2. Nelson, *Beyond Earth Day,* 3.
3. Wallace Stegner, ed., *This is Dinosaur: Echo Park Country and Its Magic Rivers* (New York: Knopf, 1995), 17.
4. Al Gore, *An Inconvenient Truth: The Planetary Emergence of Global Warming and What We Can Do about It* (New York: Rodale, 2006), 3.
5. Naomi Oreskes, "The Scientific Consensus on Climate Change," *Science* 306 (December 3, 2004): 1686.
6. U.S. Environmental Protection Agency, "Climate Change Science," 2007. http://www.epa.gov/climatechange/science/index.html (accessed October 4, 2007).
7. E. J. Brook, "Atmospheric Science: Tiny Bubbles Tell All," *Science* 310 (November 25, 2005): 1285–1287.
8. Intergovernmental Panel on Climate Change, "The Physical Science Basis: Contribution of Working Group I to the Fourth Assessment Report of the Intergovernmental Panel on Climate Change," ed. S. Solomon, D. Qin, and M. Manning (2007).
9. United Nations Framework Convention on Climate Change, "Future Effects: A Question of Degree," 2005. http://unfccc.int/essential_background/feeling_the_heat/items/2005.php (accessed June 5, 2005).
10. National Research Council, "Abrupt Climate Change: Inevitable Surprise" (Washington, DC: National Academy Press, 2002).

11. Tom Brookes and Tim Nuthall, "What Did Copenhagen Achieve?" December 21, 2009. http://news.bbc.co.uk/go/pr/fr/-/2/hi/science/nature/8424522.stm (accessed December 21, 2009).

12. Paul R. Ehrlich, *The Population Bomb* (New York: Ballantine, 1968).

13. "Kolkata," Microsoft® Encarta® Online Encyclopedia (2007). http://encarta.msn.com.

14. Joel E. Cohen, *How Many People Can the Earth Support?* (New York: Norton, 1995).

15. U. S. Census Bureau International Data Base, "World Population Information," 2007. http://www.census.gov/ipc/www/idb/worldpopinfo.html (accessed September 29, 2007).

16. American Association for the Advancement of Science, "AAAS Atlas of Population and Environment: Population and Natural Resources," 2007. http://atlas.aaas.org/index/php?parts=2 (accessed October 1, 2007).

17. P. S. Martin and H. E. Wright, eds., *Pleistocene Extinctions: The Search for a Cause* (New Haven, CT: Yale University Press, 1967).

18. R. D. E. MacFee and P. A. Marx, "The 40,000-Year Plague: Humans, Hyperdisease, and First Contact Extinctions," in *Natural Change and Human Impact in Madagascar,* eds. S. Goodman and B. Patterson (Washington, DC: Smithsonian Institution Press, 1997), 169–217.

19. To view the Red List of Threatened Species go to http://iucn.org.

20. Gretchen C. Daily, ed., *Nature's Services: Societal Dependence on Natural Ecosystems* (Washington, DC: Island Press, 1997).

21. Edward O. Wilson, *The Diversity of Life* (New York: Norton, 1993).

22. R. A. Myer and B. Worm, "Rapid Worldwide Depletion of Predatory Fish Communities," *Nature* 423 (May 15, 2003): 280–283.

23. Boris Worm, Edward B. Barbier, Nicola Beaumont, J. Emmett Duffy, Carl Folke, Benjamin S. Halpern, Jeremy B. C. Jackson, Heike K. Lotze, Fiorenza Micheli, Stephen R. Palumbi, Enric Sala, Kimberley A. Selkoe, John J. Stachowicz, and Reg Watson, "Impacts of Biodiversity Loss on Ocean Ecosystem Services," *Science* 314 (November 3, 2006): 790.

24. J. A. Estes, M. T. Tinker, T. M. Williams, and D. F. Doak, "Killer Whale Predation on Sea Otters Linking Oceanic and Near Shore Ecosystems," *Science* 282 (October 16, 1998): 473–476.

25. Chris Bright, "Anticipating Environmental 'Surprise,'" in *State of the World 2000: Worldwatch Institute Report on Progress toward a Sustainable Society,* eds. L. R. Brown, C. Flavin, and H. French (New York: Norton, 2000), 22–38.

26. A. Becher, *Biodiversity: A Reference Handbook* (Santa Barbara, CA: ABC-CLIO, 1998).

27. M. Parfit, "A Harsh Awakening: Australia," *National Geographic* 198 (July 2002), 2–31.

28. Terry L. Erwin, "The Tropical Forest Canopy: The Heart of Biotic Diversity," in *Biodiversity,* ed. E. O. Wilson (Washington, DC: National Academy Press, 1988), 123–129.

29. Bright, "Anticipating Environmental 'Surprise,'" 22–38.

30. D. Bryant, D. Nielson, and L. Tangley, *The Last Frontier Forests: Ecosystems and Economies on the Edge* (Washington, DC: World Resources Institute, 1997).

31. Bryant, Nielson, and Tangley, *The Last Frontier Forests.*

32. D. Bryant, L. Burke, J. W. McManus, and M. Spalding, *Reefs at Risk: A Map-Based Indicator of Threats to the World's Coral Reefs* (Washington, DC: World Resources Institute, 1998).

33. Bryant, et al., *Reefs at Risk.*

34. Bryant, et al., *Reefs at Risk.*

35. Bryant, et al., *Reefs at Risk.*

36. U.S. Environmental Protection Agency, "Wetlands: Status and Trends," 2006. http://www.epa.gov/owow/wetlands/vital/status/html (accessed October 3, 2007).

37. U.S. Environmental Protection Agency, "Wetlands: Status and Trends."

38. Gore, *An Inconvenient Truth,* 300

39. Barry Commoner, *The Closing Circle: Man, Nature, and Technology* (New York: Knopf, 1971).

40. Franklin and Associates, *Characterizations of Municipal Solid Wastes in the United States: 1997 Update* (Washington, DC: U.S. Environmental Protection Agency, 1997).

41. J. N. Abramovitz and A. T. Mattoon, "Recovering the Paper," in *State of the World 2000: A Worldwatch Institute Report on Progress toward a Sustainable Society,* eds. L. R. Brown, C. Flavin, and H. French (New York: Norton, 2000), 101–120.

42. Commoner, *The Closing Circle.*

43. Energy Star, "Frequently Asked Questions: Information on Compact Florescent Light Bulbs (CFLs) and Mercury," May 2007. http://www.energystar.gov (accessed October 3, 2007).

44. International Atomic Energy Agency, "Latest News Related to PRIS and the Status of Nuclear Power Plants," 2007. http://www.iaea.org (accessed October 15, 2007).

45. International Atomic Energy Agency, "Latest News."

46. D. Hancock, "What's Happening with WIPP?" *Green Forest Report* (Santa Fe: New Mexico Environmental Law Center, 1998–99).

47. National Research Council, *The Waste Isolation Pilot Plant: A Potential Solution for the Disposal of Transuranic Waste* (Washington, DC: National Academy Press, 1996).

48. L. Lange, "Hanford Leak Bigger Than Originally Thought," *Seattle Post-Intelligencer,* October 12, 1990, B2.

49. John Fleck, "Sandia Labs May Shift Yucca Employees," *Albuquerque Journal,* March 16, 2009, A1, A5.

50. Murray Bookchin, "Death of a Small Planet," *Progressive,* August 1989, 19–23.

51. Aldo Leopold, *A Sand County Almanac: And Sketches Here and There.* (Oxford, UK: Oxford University Press, 1949/1977). By permission of Oxford University Press, Inc.

Part II

Environmental Worldviews

Chapter 3

Mainstream Environmental Perspectives

In little more than two centuries, the United States has emerged as the wealthiest nation in the world. It is the home of great institutions of learning and science, of medical miracles and mind-boggling technological advancements. Yet, we are becoming increasingly aware of the consequences of our heavily mortgaged American dream: stress, obesity, substance abuse, broken families, rising greenhouse gas emissions, and unchecked species loss, to name only a few.

The founders of this great experiment in democracy left a legacy of ideals to which we tenaciously cling—ideals that, in Charles Dickens' famous words, have given rise to "the best of times" and "the worst of times." In the face of a growing environmental crisis, a number of environmental philosophers and communication theorists have begun to scrutinize the ideological legacy that grounds the contemporary Western worldview, as well as its influence on our perceptions and practices with regard to the natural world.

Influences on the Western View of Nature

As discussed in Chapter 1, an ideology is "a pattern or set of ideas, assumptions, beliefs, values, or interpretations of the world by which a group operates."[1] The ideologies that ground the way we view the world are so fundamental that they exist on an almost subconscious or subliminal level and are so taken for granted that we may not even be aware that they exist.

Ideological assumptions vary in significant ways from culture to culture. For example, the Western worldview holds that there is an objective reality in which the natural or nonhuman world is physical and material and does not have a soul or spirit. Native Americans, on the other hand, hold a strong belief in a spirit world in which the natural world, be it animate or inanimate, is comprised of conscious beings with spirit and power that must be treated with respect and care.

Multiple ideologies exist in any given culture; however, some ideologies are accepted as dominant. As we discussed in Chapter 1, hegemony, the privileging of one group's way of thinking over another's, directs us to understand the world in certain ways and to view those who hold alternative views as "abnormal," "radical," or "strange." As such, the hegemonic ideology serves as a kind of social control by muting or marginalizing alternative ways of viewing the world.

The dominant ideologies that ground the Western view of the natural world and our relationship to it are products of many historical, cultural, economic, and political factors. The following sections will discuss four of the major influences: Enlightenment thought, Judeo-Christian beliefs, the Industrial Revolution, and consumerism and capitalism.

The Enlightenment

The Enlightenment era, roughly covering the sixteenth and seventeenth centuries, was a time of scientific revolution that marked the beginning of modern, rationalist thinking. Inspired by the scientists and philosophers of the age, such as Francis Bacon (1561–1626), Galileo (1564–1642), René Descartes (1596–1650), John Locke (1632–1704), and Isaac Newton (1642–1727), reason, progress, and scientific advancements were the dominating themes.

During this age of reason, nature came to be viewed as something that could be observed and understood through scientific methods of inquiry. The universe was no longer thought to be controlled by mythical or spiritual forces, but worked according to natural laws that could be explained by theories of physics and through the precision of mathematics and astronomy.

One of the most celebrated of the Enlightenment philosophers was Francis Bacon, whose major contribution to philosophy was his application of the induction method of scientific inquiry. Bacon was among the first to articulate the idea that the hidden laws of nature could be discovered through scientific methods of observation. Nature, according to Bacon, could be "forced out of her natural state and squeezed and molded." In so doing, humanity could recover that which was lost in the fall from the Garden of Eden, "the right over nature that belongs to it by divine behest."[2]

The new controlling imagery, heralded by Bacon and other natural philosophers of the time, challenged the earlier Renaissance view of nature as a living organism, a nurturing and sometimes capricious mother. This imagery of *nature as a holistic organism* was replaced with a *mechanistic view of nature,* wherein nature was seen as something that could be dissected into its component parts like a machine and "bound into service" through scientific inquiry.

The scientific and technological advancements spurred by Enlightenment philosophers brought with them new ideological assumptions about humans' relationship to the natural world. Manipulating nature was now within the realm of human intellectual capacities, redefining humans' role from nature's servant to nature's master. As the power to manipulate nature advanced, so too, did our power to destroy nature.

The assumptions of Enlightenment thought still dominate contemporary Western ideologies and our perception of the natural world. As a culture, we place great faith in scientific method as a means of solving our environmental problems. Scientific and technological advancements have indeed led to many innovative solutions. Yet, in many ways, science and the natural world are linked in a paradoxical relationship, wherein our ability to control and master nature is called on to solve the problems created by the control and mastery of nature. As our environmental problems multiply and intensify, many people have come to realize that our environmental crisis cannot be viewed as solely a crisis of nature that can be solved by more advanced science and technology. Rather, it is a cultural, social, and political crisis that must be addressed by a fundamental change in our way of thinking about the natural world. In the famous words of Albert Einstein, "The significant problems we face cannot be solved at the same level of thinking we were at when we created them."

Judeo-Christian Beliefs

A number of scholars have examined the human/nature relationship set forth in Judeo-Christian beliefs and the Biblical grounding of those beliefs. The book of Genesis, for example, spells out humans' position in the world that God created: "be fruitful and multiply, and replenish the earth and *subdue* it; And have *dominion* over the fish of the sea, and over the fowl of the air, and over every living thing that moveth upon the earth."[3] This Biblical passage, among others, articulates the theological justification for the Western view of humans' relationship to the natural world. God's mandate to Adam and Eve to subdue and have dominion over all

Figure 3.1   "American Progress"

This lithograph, made from an 1872 painting by John Gast titled "American Progress," richly symbolizes the concept of "manifest destiny"—the idea that the United States was destined and divinely ordained to reach across the North American Continent "from sea to shining sea." American progress is depicted as a fair-skinned woman who holds a book in one hand and strings the transcontinental telegraph cable with the other. Native Americans and wild animals flee as she guides miners, farmers, covered wagons, railroads, and a stagecoach on their way west.

Library of Congress

living things that inhabit the earth sanctifies human control and domination of the natural world. It establishes a hierarchy in which nature is a sharply separated inferior realm, thereby creating a conceptual framework for exploiting the inferior realm.

Lynn White, Jr., in his controversial essay "The Historical Roots of Our Ecological Crisis," advanced the argument that Christianity, in promoting a world view that portrays humans as separate from and superior to nature, is largely responsible for our ecological crisis. Included in White's indictment are science and technology which, having developed within a Christian matrix, "are permeated with Christian arrogance toward nature."[4]

The divine mandate to subdue nature fueled the fervor and courage of the settlers during the westward expansion of the United States as they struggled to endure the unimaginable hardships of a seemingly endless and often hostile wilderness. "Manifest destiny," a term made popular by John O'Sullivan, an influential editor and political writer of the time, became the rallying cry and the symbolic torch for the westward expansion movement.

"In its magnificent domain of space and time," wrote O'Sullivan, "the nation of many nations is destined to manifest to mankind the excellence of divine principles; to establish on earth the noblest temple ever dedicated to the most high."

Settlers pushed across the continent, ordained by God to subdue the wilderness and to "carry the glad tidings of peace and goodwill where myriads endure an existence scarcely more enviable than that of the beasts of the field."[5]

Our cherished legends of the "Wild West" celebrate the heroic spirit and courage of the settlers, but tend to overlook the injustices and cruelties levied against indigenous peoples and the environmental destruction that resulted from their fervent drive to "civilize" the wilderness. As environmental historian Roderick Nash explains:

> A massive assault was directed at the new world environment in the name of civilization and Christianity. Progress became synonymous with exploitation. Men slashed the earth in pursuit of raw materials . . . . A scarcity of natural resources? Absurd! Over the next ridge was a cornucopia of wood, water, soil, and game![6]

A number of scholars have reexamined the Western experience, offering a more balanced view or, as historian Elliot West describes it, "a longer, grimmer, but more interesting story."[7] The "new Western history" takes into account the social complexity of the western expansion in which women, as well as ethnic and racial groups, played a vital role. It challenges the moral complacency of traditional historical accounts of the treatment of indigenous peoples and denounces the violence with which the wilderness was vanquished. The new story celebrates the valor, while acknowledging the "grimmer," less flattering side of the western movement.

Likewise, communities of faith have begun to reexamine what theologian Thomas Berry refers to as "the old story, the account of how the world came to be and how we fit into it . . . ."[8] The U.S. Catholics Bishops' statement "Renewing the Earth," the Presbyterian statement "Hope for a Global Future," and the Evangelical Environmental Network's "Declaration of the Care for Creation" are evidence of a growing concern for environmental problems among communities of faith. In fact, religious organizations in the United States and abroad have become one of the fastest growing venues of environmental awareness and activism.

The Industrial Revolution

The transcontinental railroad was the crowning achievement of the manifest destiny–driven westward expansion. Workers for the Union Pacific Railroad laid track westward from Omaha, Nebraska, while the Central Pacific Railroad laborers built eastward from Sacramento, California. The two met at Promontory Point, Utah, on May 10, 1869, to drive the Golden Spike, signaling the "end" of the frontier and initiating a new era of travel and development.

As railroads opened the frontier, the vast empty spaces on the map quickly filled, giving rise to urban centers of trade. A growing demand and market for goods, along with a bounty of natural resources from which to supply the goods, set the stage for the Industrial Revolution. As the population increased, markets and economies likewise expanded, fueling the drive for new technologies needed to meet the demand.

The second half of the nineteenth century saw the emergence of factories with large-scale production and machine tools. The rapid development of innovations, such as steam power, the internal combustion engine, electrical power generation, new smelting and metal working technologies, and the assembly line, dramatically increased production capabilities and gave credence to the Enlightenment philosophers' conviction that nature could be bound into service through human ingenuity.

As production capabilities increased, so too did the number of factories, causing urban centers to boom as workers migrated to the cities to find employment. In 1830, there were only 23 towns with populations over 10,000. New York, with a population of 200,000, was the largest followed by Philadelphia with 160,000 people. However, as farmers and immigrants flocked to industrial centers, the size of cities doubled every decade. By 1910, some 50 cities had populations greater than 100,000.[9]

As the nation moved from a predominantly agrarian society to an urban society, the relationship between consumers and the sources of the products they consumed became more distant and obscured. Nature's bounty was packaged as consumer products. Those who purchased the products had little connection with or concern for the field or forest in which the product originated. Growth, progress, and profit were seen as the sign of a healthy society, whereas the ecological consequences of growth, progress, and profit were largely ignored.

Consumerism and Capitalism

As evidenced by our mass consumption of manufactured products, Western cultures tend to place a great value on consumer goods and the material comforts that modern technology provides. Our voracious consumption is frequently brought to our attention—a critique that is not new to contemporary society. The eighteenth century philosopher Charles Fourier bemoaned the self-indulgence of a consumer-driven civilization, but how much more critical he would be if he were to observe the consumer habits of contemporary society. Political scientist Joan Roelofs extends Fourier's critique to today's society by pointing out that "each family must have not merely a cider press and a goose roaster, but cars, VCRs, crockpots, stockpots, candlepins, recycling bins, wine racks, Nordic Tracks, mowers, rowers, and blowers."[10] Vast shopping malls and warehouse-sized supermarkets can be found in almost any city in the United States. A typical supermarket stocks over twenty-five thousand items. We have a choice from over one thousand varieties of shampoo and over two thousand skin care products.[11] We do, indeed, live in a land of extraordinary, attractively packaged abundance.

Inextricably linked to our consumer habits is capitalism. Based on what environmental philosopher Murray Bookchin describes as "mindless 'laws' of supply and demand, grow or die, eat or be eaten,"[12] capitalism feeds consumerism and technological innovation through its fierce competition to create new products and market them to consumers. Food companies in the United States alone spend an estimated $30 billion annually to market their products to consumers.[13] And as consumers, we respond in force. For example, with less than 5 percent of the world's population, the United States consumes 30 percent of the world's paper goods and 25 percent of the world's petroleum products.[14]

Our mass consumption takes a heavy toll on the natural resources necessary to produce the products we consume. The environmental impacts are magnified globally with the emergence of transnational corporations. It is sadly ironic that developing countries around the world are now facing environmental problems that are, in many cases, the result of the growing consumer demands of the industrialized nations. For example, the world's eight largest industrial countries account for 74 percent of the world's timber imports.[15] Despite the environmental consequences of resource extraction and the toxic by-products of manufacturing processes, developing nations often have no choice but to maintain and even accelerate the exploitation of their natural resources. One out of every three children under the age of five in developing countries is malnourished.[16] The struggle for basic survival leaves little room for concerns about such things as long-term exposure to toxins, deforestation, and global warming.

Enlightenment thought, Judeo-Christian beliefs, the Industrial Revolution, consumerism, and capitalism are only a few of the multiple influences that ground dominant Western ideologies and that have led to contemporary mainstream views about nature and humans' relationship to the natural world. The following section examines the mainstream environmental philosophies. These philosophies are premised on the anthropocentric views engendered by dominant Western ideologies. **Anthropocentrism** refers to the view that regards human values as the measure of all values. From an anthropocentric perspective, the natural world has value only as an instrument for human ends. **Ecocentrism** or **biocentrism,** on the other hand, recognizes an intrinsic value of the natural world regardless of its benefits to humans.

Anthropocentric Reformism

Most of our current environmental policies and practices are grounded within the mainstream philosophy of **anthropocentric reformism.** According to this perspective, the primary value of nature is based on its value as an instrument for human ends. These ends range from the resources necessary for human survival, such as food and fuel, to the aesthetic or recreational pleasure provided by the natural landscape.

Anthropocentric reformists argue that our current environmental problems stem from the over-exploitation of natural resources because of shortsightedness, greed, or a lack of understanding of the consequences. As such, environmental problems can be addressed through laws, policies, and practices that encourage the prudent use and conservation of natural resources without radically challenging the status quo. The following sections discuss several key terms that are associated with anthropocentric reformist perspectives: *stewardship, conservation, preservation,* and *sustainable development.*

Stewardship

The term **stewardship** refers to holding something in trust for another. Historically, a steward was one who was appointed to protect lands and resources while the owners were away or, in some cases, to govern for an underage king. The notion of environmental stewardship is expressed by poet, essayist, and farmer Wendell Berry: "We must take care of the land, which is never a possession, but an inheritance to the living, borrowed from the unborn."[17]

The stewardship perspective operates within an anthropocentric, or human-centered, ethic. This perspective does not question humans' separation from and dominance of the natural world, but it emphasizes humans' responsibility to wisely oversee and manage natural resources for future generations. It does not call for radical changes in how we view our relationship to the natural world, but calls on us as individuals to use prudence and restraint as stewards of the inheritance.

The stewardship perspective is clearly exemplified in the 1989 best-selling book *50 Simple Things You Can Do to Save the Earth,*[18] which many people praised for empowering "everyday people" to become a part of the solution and offering specific recommendations on how to do so. These recommendations include "Stop Junk Mail," "Plant a Tree," "Recharge Your Batteries," and "Snip Six-Pack Rings." Other publications in this genre include *Hints for a Healthy Planet*[19] and *The Green Lifestyle Handbook: 1001 Ways You Can Heal the Earth,*[20] as well as green shopping guides and specialized magazines designed to empower the individual through prudence and restraint.

Critics of this approach to environmental activism argue that while such actions are important, these books may lull people into a false sense of security if they believe that doing some or all of these things is enough to stem the tide of environmental destruction. Environmental writer J. Robert Hunter, in his book *Simple Things Won't Save the Earth,* levels a provocative critique against the individual-as-steward approach to environmental advocacy, suggesting that promoting this approach to environmental activism is misleading and even dangerous.[21]

John Javna (author of the 1989 book *50 Simple Things You Can Do to Save the Earth*) agreed with Hunter and pulled his book from publication in 1995. As Javna explains, "They're useful tips and they have an impact, and I believe we should continue making them a part of our lives. But after nearly two decades, I also think it's time to acknowledge that they won't save the earth—or more to the point, they won't preserve our planet's life support system."[22]

Javna has since published a new version of the book, now titled *50 Simple Things You Can Do to Save the Earth: Completely New and Updated for the 21st Century.*[23] This version still offers useful ecotips, but focuses primarily on informing readers about environmental advocacy groups, what they do, and how to get involved. Javna encourages readers to find a single cause that will inspire a sustained, committed effort rather than focusing efforts on "random acts" of individual stewardship activities. He points out that it doesn't really matter what cause you choose to adopt, because they are all connected.

Although stewardship advocacy defined as individual acts of stewardship may not save the earth, it has nevertheless resulted in some significant positive trends in things such as recycling rates and home energy and water conservation. But perhaps more important, it has raised awareness about our individual complicity in the plundering of the planet and offers an accessible means of doing at least something about it.

Before moving on to the next mainstream environmental perspective, I should note that the word "stewardship" has become, to some extent, a catch-all term for almost any kind of environment-related activity. One example of the permutation of the word is the "Stockpile Stewardship Program" initiated by the Department of Energy in 1994. This was a massively complex system of programs, involving multiple facilities across the country, designed to maintain the safety and reliability of the U.S. stockpile of nuclear weapons. The use of "stewardship" in this context is conspicuously inconsistent with its traditional use, in that the term, generally used to signify an individual stewarding resources for the benefit of future generations, was being used to refer to stewarding resources through one of the largest and most expensive bureaucratic systems of nuclear research programs ever funded, for the potential mass destruction of future generations.[24] I bring this usage to your attention merely to point out that the term has many uses that stretch or even contradict its traditional meaning.

Conservation

The **conservationist** approach to environmental protection and management, like the stewardship approach, operates within the anthropocentric reformist perspective. It views the primary value of nature in terms of its usefulness to humans and, therefore, advocates managing natural resources wisely to insure that they will be available for future generations. Whereas stewardship calls on the individual to use prudence and restraint in everyday consumption habits and behaviors, conservation relies on the science of ecology and trained resource managers to protect and sustain natural resources.

The conservation movement emerged in the early 1900s in response to a growing national population, the excesses and wastes of the industrial age, and a realization that wilderness areas were rapidly disappearing. Conservationists argued for the creation of government policies for planned use of resources through scientific principles of resource management. Conservation leaders emerged from such fields as geology, hydrology, biology, and forestry.

The most influential proponent of the conservation movement was Theodore Roosevelt, who believed that the health and prosperity of the nation depended on the careful and "intelligent" use of our natural resources. He also believed that government, with the help of science and technology, could best and most fairly manage, protect, and allocate the nation's natural resources. During his presidency (1901–1909), Congress expanded the national forests from 42 million acres to 172 million acres, created 51 national wildlife refuges, established 18 national monuments including the Grand Canyon and the Petrified Forest, and established Glacier National Park and Yosemite.

The Roosevelt administration also created the United States Forest Service in 1905 and appointed Gifford Pinchot to head the new agency. Pinchot was instrumental in defining conservation through his forest management policies. Under Pinchot's direction, conservation came to mean a belief in using government and science to "intelligently" manage natural resources and protect them from the rampages of profit-oriented commercial enterprises.

The notion of forest management through scientific principles was new at this time. When Pinchot entered Yale University in 1885, there were no degrees or even courses offered in forestry in U.S. colleges. After graduating from Yale, Pinchot spent a year in France, where he learned the principles of scientific forest management that were to guide his management policies in the years to come as our nation's first chief forester.

The government's role in natural resource management has expanded significantly since Roosevelt's time. Today, the **U.S. Forest Service** is responsible for managing 155 national forests, comprising 191 million acres. Other agencies that manage federal lands include the **U.S. Bureau of Land Management,** which oversees 262 million acres of public lands, and the **U.S. Park Service,** which manages our 391 national parks, monuments, memorials, and historical sites, covering more than 83 million acres.

The conservation movement of the early twentieth century did much to heighten public awareness of the fact that our nation's natural resources were, in fact, finite and needed to be protected and conserved. Not everyone, however, was in agreement with the new policies established by the conservationists. Land use policies, especially in the western states, were often challenged by competing interests. Farmers, ranchers, and timber and mining companies resented limitations to free enterprise

Figure 3.2   Teddy Roosevelt and John Muir

In 1903 President Theodore Roosevelt went on a three-day wilderness trip in Yosemite, guided by naturalist John Muir. Muir took the opportunity to make a plea to the president for placing Yosemite Valley and Mariposa Grove under federal protection. In 1906, Roosevelt signed the bill that added the forty-square-mile valley and the ancient grove of giant sequoias to Yosemite National Park.

Library of Congress

that the new policies imposed and questioned the government's right to control resources. Environmental historian Roderick Nash describes the attitudes of many: "For most Westerners, conservation (they sometimes called it 'Pinchotism') was the arbitrary and un-American policy of snobbish Eastern bureaucrats unsympathetic to the needs of and desires of the West."[25] This view of the federal management of lands is still held by many farmers, ranchers, miners, and loggers from western states, as well as by others who would like to see national wilderness areas opened for expanded recreational use for off-road vehicles and snowmobiles.

Preservation

Another challenger of the conservation movement was the preservation movement, which emerged at the same time as the conservation movement. The goal of the **preservationists** was to set aside large areas of wilderness from commercial use and to preserve nature in its pristine state. Preservationists had mixed feelings about Pinchot's forest policies. On the one hand, they supported government initiatives to protect natural areas through policies that emphasized the wise use and management of resources. On the other hand, they felt that conservationist policies failed to consider that nature had a value beyond its economic or practical usefulness to humans, and that some wilderness areas should be preserved in their natural state.

The philosophical clash between conservationists and preservationists gained a great deal of public attention in the 1912 debate over the proposal to dam the Tuolumne River in Yosemite National Park. The proposed dam would provide the city of San Francisco with a much-needed water supply, but in so doing would flood the spectacular Hetch Hetchy Valley within the borders of Yosemite. The debate between proponents of the valley's aesthetic values and proponents of its practical values clearly defined the opposing positions and influenced environmental debate for years to come.

A leading opponent of the dam was John Muir, one of the founders and the first president of the Sierra Club. Muir argued that "Everybody needs beauty as well as bread, places to play in and pray in, where nature may heal and cheer and give strength to body and soul."[26] The Sierra Club published numerous books, articles, and pamphlets strongly denouncing the plan for the proposed dam. In one such publication, Muir writes, "Dam the Hetch Hetchy! As well dam for water tanks the people's cathedrals and churches, for no holier temple has ever been consecrated by the heart of man."[27]

Conservationists criticized such thinking as idealist, elitist, and absurdly sentimental in the face of the public interest that would be served by the dam. They called for the "highest use" of the resources defined, in this case, as the domestic use of the water by the people of San Francisco. Conservationists argued that "public interest" was best served by invoking "the utilitarian principle of 'the greatest good for the greatest number'"[28]

Congress passed the Hetch Hetchy bill in 1913, allowing the dam to be built. The first water from the reservoir reached San Francisco twenty-one years later. The reservoir today remains a significant source of water and hydroelectric power for the Bay area.

Although preservationists lost the battle to preserve the valley, the controversy served to focus a great deal of attention on wilderness preservation. It also served to introduce an alternative view of humans' relationship to the natural world that was not solely or predominantly grounded within the anthropocentric perspective. While much of the early preservationists' rhetoric called for preservation for human purposes (such as recreational or aesthetic pleasure), some of their rhetoric leaned toward an ecocentric or biocentric view, in which nature is seen as having intrinsic value regardless of its value to humans. This perspective represented a departure from previous views of humans' relationship to the natural world. The next chapter looks at some of the contemporary environmental philosophies that are based on this radical perspective.

Sustainable Development

Perhaps today's most commonplace environmental catchphrase is **sustainable development.** The term was proposed by the 1987 report of the U.N. World Commission on Environment and Development, *Our Common Future,* commonly referred to as the **Brundtland Report** after the former Prime Minister of Norway who chaired the commission, Gro Harlem Brundtland. The report signified a historical awakening to the environmental consequences of rampant global development and economic growth, directed world attention to the contrast between the dehumanizing poverty of many and the wasteful consumption of the world's affluent, and addressed what M. Jimmie Killingsworth and Jacqueline S. Palmer refer to as "a crisis of Western liberalism." They explain, "Briefly put, the dilemma is this: How can the standard of living attained through technological progress in the developed nations be maintained (and extended to developing and undeveloped nations) if the ecological consequences are prohibitive?"[29] In an attempt to address this dilemma, the Commission called for "sustainable development," defined by the report as "development that meets the needs of the present without compromising the ability of future generations to meet their own needs."

The concept of sustainable development was further engrained in public consciousness when it was endorsed at the **1992 Earth Summit in Rio de Janeiro** as the dominant environmental paradigm. This historic summit was attended by 177 representatives from almost every nation in the world, many of whom were heads of states. The summit drew worldwide attention with hundreds of thousands of participants and on-lookers, as well as seven thousand members of the media covering the event. Two significant outcomes of this summit were a document entitled *Agenda 21,* which outlined sustainable development practices, and the United Nations's subsequent creation of a Commission on Sustainable Development to oversee the implementation of these practices.

As you have probably realized by now, when the subject is associated with environmentalism, there will inevitably be multiple and conflicting viewpoints. Sustainable development is no exception. Proponents of sustainable development recognize the inevitability of and need for continued technological and economic development, but call for boundaries determined by the ecological limits of the global environment. Critics argue that the concept of sustainable development is ambiguous and that the ecological limits to development are not clearly defined, leaving much room for multiple interpretations, misapplications, and misuse. Some environmentalists have gone so far as to label sustainable development as "a thundering oxymoron" and a "giant exercise in self-deception."[30] As Leslie Paul Thiele explains, "The problem is that the developmental focus of sustainable development often serves as a guise for business as usual . . . . What certain sustainable developers chiefly want to sustain, it appears, is unlimited economic growth."[31]

This critique is perhaps warranted. Five years after the 1992 Earth Summit, the Rio Plus Five conference convened in New York in June of 1997 to assess the progress of sustainable development practices. The chairperson of the U.N. General Assembly, Razali Ismail, referred to the results of the review as "sobering" and stated that "Our words have not been matched by deeds."[32]

The 2002 United Nations World Summit of Sustainable Development (Rio Plus Ten) in Johannesburg, South Africa, yielded some encouraging developments, among them the promise to cut by half the number of people living with inadequate water and sanitation and to do so within the next decade and a half. Also encouraging to many was the prominent representation of private corporations at the summit. Some seven hundred companies and fifty chief executives attended the Johannesburg talks, whereas ten years earlier, at the Rio Summit, business was barely present. One significant outcome of the summit was the agreement among various corporations to help developing countries with improvements such as extending the electrical grid to reach broader populations and developing more clean water and sanitation technologies.

Others, however, criticized the "corporate takeover" of the meeting, calling it "a victory for greed and a tragedy for the poor and for the environment."[33] They argued that the summit, "hijacked by free-market ideology," would prove to be merely a public relations ploy, resulting in business-as-usual with few substantive changes for protecting the natural resources of the developing world.[34]

In recognition and response to a growing global threat, the Rio Plus 15 summit, held in Jakarta, Indonesia, in 2007, resulted in the approval of some monumental and ambitious measures. The summit called on developed nations of the world to slow their rates of production and consumption, stating that in the coming decades, world consumption of energy and other natural resources must be cut in half. Summit delegates also called for, among other things, the creation of an International Court on Foreign Debt as well as the development of social and environmental debt indicators that would adjust foreign debt to take into account these previously unaccounted debts. The creation of this court has the potential to redefine and redistribute wealth as the developed nations repay their ecological debts to the global community.

Despite the conflicting and often sobering reviews of current sustainable development practices, despite the skepticism of many with regard to the likelihood of achieving the bold new measures that summit delegates called for, many environmentalists believe that development and environmental practices can and must go hand in hand. The relief of poverty and an improved standard of living enhance everyone's capacity to protect the environment. Likewise, environmental protection is essential to development. As environmental communication scholar Tarla Rai Peterson explains, "Sustainable development is a banner under which transformed environmentalism has marched in the public consciousness. . . . It says that care for the environment is essential to economic progress; that the natural resources of our planet are the base of all agriculture and industry; and that only by sustaining that base can we sustain human development."[35] The two concepts of environmental protection and development are inseparably linked.

Sustainable development falls within the anthropocentric reformist perspective in that its primary focus is on humans' right to an improved quality of life through sustainable technologies and economic development. Its principles, in one way or another, encompass all the perspectives that have been discussed in this chapter. Sustainable development calls for individual stewardship of our natural inheritance, for conserving nature by advancing technologies and expert management, and for preserving such things as rain forests and biodiversity. As such, sustainable development, as it is most commonly interpreted, is consistent with mainstream environmental perspectives, although some measures called for in the last round of Earth Summit talks have stretched the boundaries of mainstream thinking, crossing the invisible and fluid line between mainstream and radical thinking.

However one cares to interpret the environmental philosophy that grounds sustainable development, the notion of sustainable development represents an increasing global concern for the environment and a global dialog about how to address these concerns. In joining both ecology and human development, sustainable development provides a dialog for promoting both social justice and environmental protections.

Concluding and Looking Ahead

This chapter has examined some of the major influences on the Western worldview and the environmental perspectives that fall under the general rubric of anthropocentric reformist philosophy. The ideologies grounding Enlightenment thought, Judeo-Christian beliefs, the Industrial Revolution, and consumerism/capitalism served to define the Western worldview and continue to ground contemporary views of humans' relationship to the natural world. Operating under these assumptions, the anthropocentric reformist perspectives of stewardship, conservation, preservation, and sustainable development have led to important reforms and environmental protection measures. Yet, with growing environmental concerns, many have begun to question whether reform policies can bring about the changes necessary to address the global sustainability crisis.

The following chapter looks at environmental philosophies that challenge the mainstream perspectives and the human/nature relationship they construct and sustain. These philosophies have been placed under the general heading of "radical" environmental philosophies. Such categorizing and labeling serves as a useful means of comparison and contrast among the various perspectives. You should keep in mind, however, that the creation of neat categorical divisions in the complicated, messy, and contested domain of environmental philosophies is largely an academic exercise that is laden with inconsistencies and contradictions. There is a fluid and sometimes indistinguishable line between what is considered "radical" and what is considered "mainstream." Although in practice the distinctions are sometimes blurred, the assumptions grounding radical perspectives represent significant departures from those that ground the mainstream perspectives and challenge the human/nature relationship implied in the mainstream perspectives.

Discussion Questions and Exercises

1. On what grounds have critics questioned the overall environmental benefits of books such as *50 Simple Things You Can Do to Save the Earth?* Do you agree or disagree with these critics?

2. The term "stewardship" has become a catch-all to refer to many different kinds of environment-related activities. Do an online search using the phrase "stewardship organizations" and report what you find. What are some organizations whose activities would fall under the traditional definition of the term? What are some that stretch or contradict the traditional usage?

3. What do critics argue are some of the problems of sustainable development as it is sometimes translated into practice? Do you think sustainable development is possible or do you think it is oxymoronic?

4. The environmental protection measures ushered in by reform policies grounded in conservation, preservation, stewardship, and sustainable development have improved our quality of life. Conduct a day-in-your-life inventory that catalogs the daily benefits you enjoy from these reforms. For example, start with brushing your teeth—how have the reforms made this simple part of your daily routine more healthy, risk-free, or enjoyable? Then move on to breakfast or to your means of transportation to school, and so forth.

Suggested Readings

Roderick Nash. *Wilderness and the American Mind*. New Haven, CT: Yale University Press, 1967.

Christine Oravec. "Conservationism vs. Preservationism: The 'Public Interest' in the Hetch Hetchy Controversy," *Quarterly Journal of Speech,* 70 (1984): 444–458.

Tarla Rai Peterson. *Sharing the Earth. The Rhetoric of Sustainable Development.* Columbia: University of South Carolina Press, 1997.

Notes

1. Sonja K. Foss, *Rhetorical Criticism: Exploration and Practice,* 2nd ed. (Prospect Heights, IL: Waveland, 1996), 291.

2. Cited in P. Rossi, *Francis Bacon: From Magic to Science* (London: Routledge & Kegan Paul, 1968).

3. Genesis 1:28.

4. Lynn White, Jr., "The Historical Roots of Our Ecological Crisis," in *Western Man and Environmental Ethics,* ed. I. G. Barbour (Reading, MA: Addison-Wesley, 1973), 19.

5. J. O'Sullivan, "The Great Nation of Futurity," *The United States Democratic Review* 6 (1839): 426–430.

6. Roderick Nash, *Wilderness and the American Mind* (New Haven, CT: Yale University Press, 1967), 3.

7. Elliot West, "A Longer, Grimmer, but More Interesting Story," in *Trails: Toward a New Western History,* eds. P. Nelson Limerick, C. A. Milner II, and C. E. Rankin (Lawrence: University Press of Kansas, 1991), 103.

8. Thomas Berry, *The Great Work: Our Way into the Future* (New York: Bell Tower, 1999), 20.

9. Benjamin Kline, *First along the River: A Brief History of the U.S. Environmental Movement,* 2nd ed. (San Francisco: Acada, 2000).

10. Joan Roelofs, "Charles Fourier: Proto Red-Green," in *Minding Nature: The Philosophers of Ecology,* ed. D. Macauley (New York: Guilford, 1996), 51.

11. P. C. Whybrow, *American Mania: When More is Not Enough* (New York: Norton, 2005).

12. Murray Bookchin, "What is Social Ecology?" in *Environmental Philosophy: From Animal Rights to Radical Ecology,* ed. M. E. Zimmerman, J. B. Callicott, G. Sessions, K. J. Warren, and J. Clark (Englewood Cliffs, NJ: Prentice Hall, 1993), 368.

13. Worldwatch Institute, *State of the World: 2000* (New York: Norton, 2000).

14. Worldwatch Institute, *State of the World: 2000.*

15. Worldwatch Institute, *State of the World: 2000.*

16. L. C. Smith and L. Haddad, "Research Report III: Explaining Child Malnutrition in Developing Countries: A Cross-Country Analysis" (2000). http://www.ifpri.org (accessed January 24, 2007).

17. Wendell Berry, *The Unsettling of America* (San Francisco: Sierra Club, 1977), 22.

18. John Javna, *50 Simple Things You Can Do to Save the Earth* (Berkeley, CA: Earth Works, 1989).

19. Heloise, *Hints for a Healthy Planet* (New York: Perigee, 1990).

20. J. Rifkin, ed., *The Green Lifestyle Handbook: 1001 Ways You Can Heal the Earth* (New York: Henry Holt, 1990).

21. J. Robert Hunter, *Simple Things Won't Save the Earth* (Austin, TX: University of Texas Press, 1997).

22. J. Javna, S. Javna, and J. Javna, "The New Environmentalism: Issues, Not Eco-Tips," *The Huffington Post* (April 2008). http://www.huffingtonpost.com/john-javna-sophie-javna -and/the-new-environmentalism_b_97825.html (accessed July 7, 2008).

23. J. Javna, S. Javna, and J. Javna, *50 Simple Things You Can Do to Save the Earth: Completely New and Updated for the 21st Century* (New York: Hyperion, 2008).

24. Judith Hendry, "Mystery, Paradox, and Occupational Psychosis in the Stewardship Discourse of Nuclear Weapons" (paper presented at the National Communication Association Convention, Boston, November 2005).

25. Roderick Nash, *The American Environment: Readings in the History of Conservation* (London: Addison-Wesley, 1968), 64.

26. John Muir, *The Yosemite* (New York: Century, 1912), 256.

27. Muir, *The Yosemite,* 196–197.

28. Christine L. Oravec, "Conservationism vs. Preservationism: The 'Public Interest' in the Hetch Hetchy Controversy," *Quarterly Journal of Speech* 70 (1984): 444.

29. M. Jimmie Killingsworth and Jacqueline S. Palmer, *Ecospeak: Rhetoric and Environmental Politics in America* (Carbondale: Southern Illinois University Press, 1992), 3.

30. Garrett Hardin, *Living within Limits: Ecology, Economics, and Population Taboo* (New York: Oxford University Press, 1993), 206.

31. Leslie Paul Thiele, *Environmentalism for a New Millennium: A Challenge of Coevolution* (New York: Oxford University Press, 1999), 52.

32. Quoted in "Five Years after Rio and Still Questions Left Unanswered," *Reuters,* June 28, 1997, B14.

33. "The Bubble-and-Squeak Summit," *The Economist,* September 7, 2002, 70.

34. "Small Is Alright," *The Economist,* September 7, 2002, 14.

35. Tarla Rai Peterson, *Sharing the Earth: The Rhetoric of Sustainable Development* (Columbia: University of South Carolina Press, 1997), 6.

Chapter 4
Radical Environmental Perspectives

"These are the times that try men's souls." These are the opening words of *Common Sense,* Thomas Paine's famous 1776 treatise that inspired a nascent country to revolution. The comparatively short but turbulent history of the United States is rife with the voices of malcontents—those orators, essayists, song writers, and poets whose radical and incendiary ideas challenged the mainstream ideologies of their times. See if you can identify the originators of these famous words:

Name That Rabble-Rouser: (The answers are at the end of the chapter.)

"It was we, the people, not we the white male citizens, nor yet we, the male citizens; but we, the whole people, who formed the union."

"I have a dream that my four little children will one day live in a nation where they will not be judged by the color of their skin, but by the content of their character."

"They paved paradise and put up a parking lot."

"I believe that without recognizing it, we have already stepped over the threshold . . . that we are at the end of nature."

It is hard to believe that only a little more than fifty years ago, Rosa Parks, an African-American seamstress from Montgomery, Alabama, was arrested and fined for refusing to give up her seat on a city bus to a white man. Ideas that were once seen as "radical" are now part of mainstream thinking, as new rabble-rousers, rebels, and dissidents take to the stage, the airwaves, and the book shelves. As communication scholar John D. Ramage puts it, "It is a never-ending dialectical process. Every thesis provokes an antithesis from whence a synthesis arises, only to itself become a thesis sure to provoke another antithesis."[1]

Figuring predominantly among the thesis-provokers have been environmentalists—you know, those granola-munching, tree-hugging, Birkenstock-wearing lunatics who have challenged the view towards nature that the dominant ideologies cultivate. These alternative views are considered radical in that they represent a paradigmatic departure from mainstream views of humans' relationship to the natural world.

The term **radical** stems from the Latin word *radix* which means "root" or "foundation." Something is radical when it challenges or threatens the roots or foundations of a belief system. Radical environmental philosophers maintain that the current attempts to address environmental problems may help alleviate the symptoms, but fail to address the roots of the ecological crisis. Radical philosophies call for drastic changes in our fundamental ways of thinking about and behaving toward the natural world.

Radical environmental philosophies can be divided into roughly three major fields: deep ecology, ecofeminism, and social ecology. Their philosophical perspectives are similar in that they all call for major reforms to our current ways of thinking and behaving towards the environment. However, they differ with regard to their ideas about the fundamental roots of the environmental crisis.

Deep ecologists believe that the root of the environmental crisis lies in anthropocentrism, the view that regards humans as the center or measure of all value. Deep ecologists take an ecocentric or biocentric view of nature, which places humans and nature on equal par. This view calls for an ethical consideration of nature, just as we give ethical consideration to humans. **Ecofeminists** reject the idea that anthropocentrism is the root cause of the environmental crisis and focus instead on the patriarchal or male-dominated system that creates and perpetuates the exploitation of both women and nature. For **social ecologists,** the root cause is neither anthropocentrism nor patriarchal dominance. It is an issue of human social power relations, specifically the problem of social class domination that is created and perpetuated by a capitalist, free-market system.

The following sections will briefly discuss each of these areas of radical environmentalist thought and introduce some of the influential philosophers and writers in each field, who represent what social movement theorists David A. Snow and Robert D. Benford describe as "The progenitors of the master frames that provide the ideational and interpretive anchoring for subsequent movements."[2] Although many of these ideas have not gained a prominent foothold in our current ideological terrain, radical philosophies play an important role as the impetus for critical conversations about our ways of viewing the natural world and humans' relationship to it.

Deep Ecology

The term "deep ecology" came into common use in the 1970s through the writings of Norwegian philosopher Arne Naess, who is credited with developing a "sophisticated philosophic basis" of deep ecology.[3] A central tenet of deep ecology is the idea that anthropocentrism is at the root of our environmental problems, and that in order to create lasting solutions we must first address this ideological basis for the problems. Essentially, deep ecologists believe that nonhuman life has intrinsic value that is independent of its usefulness to humans. As Naess explains, those who adhere to the tenets of deep ecology believe in "a core democracy in the biosphere. The shallow ecology movement tends to talk only about resources for humans, whereas in deep ecology we talk about resources for each species."[4]

Drawing on the work of Naess and others, deep ecologists have articulated the following basic principles of deep ecology, as outlined by Bill Devall and George Sessions:

(1) there is intrinsic value in both human and nonhuman life on earth, independent of utilitarian purpose,

(2) richness and diversity of life forms are values in themselves,

(3) humans do not have the right to cause a decrease in this richness and diversity except to meet survival needs,

(4) human population must be reduced,

(5) present human interference with the nonhuman world is excessive and worsening rapidly,

(6) policies affecting economic, technological, and ideological structures must change,

(7) life quality should replace standard of living as a goal, and

(8) those who subscribe to these beliefs have an obligation to make the necessary changes.[5]

The essence of deep ecology, according to Naess, is to ask deeper questions that challenge our most fundamental beliefs and move us toward an ecocentric

Figure 4.1
Henry David Thoreau

Writing about the essential human need for leisure, contemplation, and a harmonious coexistence with nature in an era of rapid urban and industrial expansion, Henry David Thoreau (1817–1862) was not widely popular in his lifetime. His work inspired many who came after him, however, including John Muir and Aldo Leopold. Today Thoreau is celebrated as one of the leading figures in the U.S. literary canon.

Library of Congress

view of the natural world. In so doing, we transform ourselves from an ego state in which we identify with other humans, to what he terms the **ecological self.** This new ego state encompasses a wider identification of self with other species and the ecosystem. According to Naess, the spiritual/psychological growth process of becoming the ecological self will lead to a fundamentally and radically different way of viewing the natural world and humans' relationship to it.

Although Naess did not coin the term "deep ecology" until 1973, his philosophy was inspired by the writings of deep ecologists who came before him. One such highly influential writer was Henry David Thoreau.

A naturalist, essayist, and poet, Thoreau died in 1862 at the age of forty-five, unaware that his inspirational writings would have a major influence on the environmental movement a century later. Amid the birth of the Industrial Revolution, Thoreau cautioned his contemporaries about prizing only the material value of nature and laid the foundation for an environmental ethic that embodied both spiritual and moral considerations. Consider, for example, nature's spiritual and moral standing, implied in the question Thoreau poses in his essay "Huckleberries." In speaking of the founders of New England villages, he asks, "At the same time they built meeting houses, why did they not preserve from desecration and destruction far greater temples not made with hands?"[6]

Another early challenger of the anthropocentric view was John Muir, an avid naturalist, who became the late nineteenth century's most influential voice for wilderness protection. The establishment of Yosemite National Park and the creation of the Sierra Club are attributed, in large part, to his vigorous campaigns and eloquence in the cause of protecting the wilderness areas he so loved. Like Thoreau, Muir criticized society's obsession with material wealth. He cynically referred to modern Western humans as "Lord Man." Muir (1916) wrote:

> The world, we are told, was made especially for man—a presumption not supported by all the facts. . . . From the dust of the earth, from the common elementary fund, the Creator has made Homo sapiens. From the same material he has made every other creature, however noxious and insignificant to us. They are earth-born companions and our fellow mortals.[7]

One of the most inspiring voices of the early challengers of anthropocentrism was that of Aldo Leopold, "to whom" as contemporary environmental writer Charles Little states, "every self-respecting environmentalist repairs when in need of understanding or a good quote."[8] Leopold's posthumously published book, *A Sand County Almanac* (1949), played such a major role in shaping the environmental movement of the 1970s that it has been termed the "environmentalists' bible."

In his classic essay "The Land Ethic," Leopold sets forth the idea that the land, plants, animals, and human inhabitants should be thought of as one community. "In short," states Leopold, "a land ethic changes the role of Homo Sapiens from conqueror of the land community to plain member and citizen of it."[9]

The writer who arguably had the most influence on the re-articulation and reinvigoration of deep ecological perspectives was Rachel Carson. Many have asserted that the modern environmental movement was set in motion by the 1962 publication of her book *Silent Spring*. Carson, a marine biologist and former researcher for the Fish and Wildlife Service, alarmed the nation with her powerful and eloquent warning about the dangers created by the widespread use of the insecticide DDT and other synthetic chemicals. "We have put poisonous and biologically potent chemicals indiscriminately into the hands of persons largely or wholly ignorant of their potentials for harm," she warned, "with little or no advance investigation of their effect on soil, water, wildlife, and man himself."[10] The realization of the potentially disastrous consequences of the chemicals that were being used in industry and agriculture quickly captured public attention and led to the federal ban on the use of DDT in 1972.

Carson not only exposed the dangers of the use of chemicals, but brought into question the anthropocentrism of the Western worldview. In the final paragraph of *Silent Spring* she asserts that "the 'control of nature' is a phrase conceived in arrogance, born of the Neanderthal age of biology and philosophy, when it was supposed that nature exists for the convenience of man."[11]

Naess, Thoreau, Muir, Leopold, and Carson are but a few of the many environmental writers, theorists, and advocates who have contributed to the development of the modern perspective of deep ecology. The following section discusses another radical perspective that grew out of the writings of modern environmental philosophers, but in a very different direction.

Social Ecology

Whereas deep ecologists view our environmental crisis as rooted in anthropocentrism and call for us, as individuals, to change our psychological orientations, social ecologists view the problem as stemming from our social structures and class domination and call for us to make changes in our social systems. Social ecologists believe that the human urge to dominate nature stems from humans' domination of other humans. They challenge the social institutions that perpetuate such practices of domination. These practices include market capitalism, industrial expansion, and corporate competition.

Environmental philosopher George Bradford explains the fundamental rift between deep ecology and social ecology by arguing that the environmental crisis is not a product of our anthropocentrism, as deep ecologists suggest, but a product of our social institutions—most predominantly our capitalist market system: "No development scheme, no poisoning of water, no squandering of the soil, no leveling of forests and no mass exodus or slaughter of human populations occurs as a response to 'human need' or 'human-centeredness.'" These atrocities, suggests Bradford, are products of our capitalist system and are carried out "to continue the accumulation of capital and the smooth functioning of a global, imperial work pyramid."[12]

Political theorist Murray Bookchin, whose writings of over forty years developed and refined the principles of social ecology, explains the basic tenet of this philosophical perspective by pointing out that all of our current ecological problems stem from our deep-seated social problems,[13] including conflicts stemming from economic, ethnic, cultural, and gender inequalities. Bookchin affirms one of the basic premises of the study of environmental communication when he states that "the real battleground on which the ecological future of the planet will be decided is clearly a social one. . . . The way human beings deal with each other as social beings is crucial to addressing the ecological crisis."[14]

The problems of nature are, according to Bookchin, products of social evolution gone awry. He believed that the world and its life forms, both human and nonhuman, are part of a natural evolution toward increasing complexity. Living organisms, through the process of adaptation, have evolved from single cell organisms to intelligent creatures with complex neural systems. Through mutual cooperation and a kind of mutually supportive symbiosis of life forms, nature has evolved into a self-organizing and self-maintaining unity in which the emergence of human societies is not a separation from or aberration of the natural world, but a part of its ongoing evolution. Just as nonhuman inhabitants of the ecocommunity engage in survival activities, Bookchin suggests humans engage in activities for survival that, in principle, are no different from those of nonhumans. Humans build homes for the same reason gophers dig holes.[15]

On another level, however, human evolution has taken a markedly different turn from that of the nonhuman world. Largely freed from instinctive behaviors, humans engage in social development. Communities bonded together through ideologies and institutions have created an environment that often conflicts with or is detrimental to the well-being of both humans and nonhumans.[16]

Bookchin explains how early human civilizations created societies in which humans' relations with each other and with the natural world were organized in such a way as to support the mutual cooperation of natural evolution. From this perspective, human and nonhuman inhabitants of an ecosystem are inseparable parts of a community in which all inhabitants benefit in a kind of symbiotic cooperation. However, as human societies evolved and as institutions and ideologies emerged, they began to go against the natural process of a mutually supporting evolution, as they developed "the hierarchical mentality and class relationships" that define humans' relationships to each other as well as to the natural world.[17]

The "hierarchical mentality" of which Bookchin speaks is derived primarily from a "hierarchical chain of being" that stems from, among other things, the biblical injunction that gave Adam "dominion over the fish of the sea, and over the fowl of the air, and over every living thing that moveth upon the earth."[18] Thus, society evolved to create structures and institutions that reinforce the God-sanctioned hierarchy of God over humans and humans over nature. The hierarchical mentality is further extended by institutions, rules, and laws that sanction and encourage the domination of humans over humans, as well as of humans over nature.

Human societies have evolved into hierarchical structures of power and domination—the most powerful of which are those institutions that support, govern, and control free enterprise and our capitalistic market system. This system, according to Bookchin, supports and even demands "dehumanizing competition" and the need to continually grow or be swallowed by rival companies or forced out of existence.[19] The competitive imperative to "grow or die" goes against the continued evolution of mutually supportive ecocommunities. When our institutions and structures promote, reward, and demand consumerism, industrial expansion, and corporate self-interest, the inevitable result is the exploitation of labor and resources to meet the growth imperative.

Though human social evolution has gone awry, human societies, according to Bookchin, can be an integral part of the mutual cooperation of all life forms and "can be placed at the service of natural evolution to consciously increase biotic diversity, diminish suffering, and foster the further development of new and ecologically valuable life forms."[20] For Bookchin, the way to re-establish mutually supportive human and nonhuman evolution is through the decentralization of the social and economic powers that have led to the destructive capitalistic imperative of "grow or die." In practice, this would require building sustainable communities that are ecologically sensitive to their locations, use alternative energy sources such as solar and wind power, and rely on locally grown, organic agriculture. It would require creating industries that produce high quality, durable goods to meet local and regional needs. The mutually supportive community also calls for adapting lifestyles to promote leisure, the arts, and community involvement.[21]

While many view Bookchin's ideas as radically subversive anarchism with unrealistic utopian goals, his critique of the modern capitalistic system has greatly influenced contemporary environmental thought. Many agree with him that the first step toward halting the destructive domination of humans over nature is to confront the destructive domination of humans over humans, as well as the institutions and practices of a brutal market system that perpetuate this relationship.

Ecofeminism

Ecofeminism has evolved in many directions in the past three decades. It grew out of the feminist movement of the 1970s and, like feminism, encompasses a wide range of perspectives. While ecofeminist thought is far from homogenous, the unifying theme is that our environmental crisis is a feminist issue, as pointed out by Rosemary Radford Ruether in her book *New Woman/New World:* "Women must see that there can be no liberation for them and no solution to the ecological crisis within a society whose fundamental model of relationships continues to be one of domination."[22]

Ecofeminists believe that the root of our environmental crisis lies not in anthropocentrism (as suggested by deep ecologists), nor in the social institutions of hierarchy (as suggested by social ecologists). For ecofeminists, the root of the environmental crisis lies in **patriarchal** (male dominated) or **androcentric** (male-centered) ideologies, which have historically devalued and exploited both women and nature. Ecofeminists assume that the oppression of women, races, classes, and nature are all interconnected in what ecofeminist Karen J. Warren describes as a "conceptual framework of oppression."[23] Such frameworks justify and explain relationships of domination and exploitation. Ecofeminism examines the connections between women and nature and how domination has led to the exploitation of both.

What are the connections between women and nature? A number of woman-nature connections can be found in ecofeminist literature. Space will not allow for a complete discussion of this rich and diversified body of research; however, we will examine a few of the major directions of inquiry.[24]

Several *historical connections* have been examined in ecofeminist literature. Historical accounts of the domination of women closely parallel historical accounts of the domination of nature. Ecofeminist writer Carolyn Merchant examines how, prior to the Enlightenment of the sixteenth and seventeenth centuries, nature was viewed as "organic," as a living, nurturing, "mother," a "kindly beneficent female who provided for the needs of mankind in an ordered, planned universe." This nurturing mother image acted as a cultural restraint on how the natural world was treated. "One does not readily slay a mother, or dig her entrails or mutilate her body," writes Merchant.[25] The nature-as-nurturing-mother perspective changed with the Scientific Revolution and its technological advances. The constraints that restricted the destruction of a living, nurturing organism were no longer in place when nature came to be viewed from the "mechanistic" perspective. Nature was then something that could be "bound into service" and "molded" (Merchant quotes these words of Francis Bacon) by mechanical innovations.

A second area of ecofeminist inquiry looks at *conceptual connections* that construct women and nature in ways that promote a negative bias towards both. One such conceptual bias is found in **value dualisms** that give higher value or status to one element in a dichotomous pair over the other item. Examples of value dualisms include human/nature, reason/emotion, rationality/spirituality, and controlling/nurturing.

Dualisms tend to separate and devalue characteristics that are historically associated with women (nature, emotion, spirituality, nurturing). Ecofeminist writer Val Plumwood suggests that the features that are identified with men (reason, rationality, control) are viewed as special characteristics of humans that are not shared with women and nature. According to Plumwood, this conceptual separation constructs a view of nature, and the feminine with which nature is identified, as "sharply divided off from the human, alien and usually hostile and inferior."[26] This view offers a cultural justification for the domination and exploitation of both women and nature. As Plumwood explains:

> Because western culture has conceived the central features of humanity in terms of the dominator identity of the master, and has empowered qualities and areas of life classed as masculine over those classed as feminine, it has evolved as hierarchical, aggressive, and destructive of nature and of life, including human life.[27]

A third area of ecofeminist inquiry is that of *experiential connections* between women and nature. Researchers working within this philosophical perspective look

Connections

Gaia

Mathematician James Lovelock presented a radical new way of viewing the Earth's ecosystem with his 1979 book, *Gaia: A New Look at Life on Earth*. Lovelock argued that all parts of the Earth—the living and the nonliving—make up a single, giant, self-regulating organism that maintains and stabilizes the conditions suitable for life on Earth (in particular the temperature and chemistry of the atmosphere). He named this complex system "Gaia" after the Greek earth goddess. Lovelock defined Gaia as "a complex entity involving the Earth's biosphere, atmosphere, oceans, and soil; the totality constituting a feedback or cybernetic system which seeks an optimal physical and chemical environment for life on this planet."

Lovelock's hypothesis was vociferously criticized and even ridiculed by many for, among other things, its lack of scientific rigor and its nontestability. Lovelock's use of language created a sense of spiritual mysticism that also fueled criticism of its neo-paganistic tone. For example, he states that "she [Gaia] is now through us awake and aware of herself. She has seen the reflection of her face through the eyes of astronauts. . . . our sensations of wonder and pleasure, our capacity for conscious thought and speculation, our restless curiosity and drive are hers to share." In Lovelock's later iterations of the theory, he was careful to clarify that the name "Gaia" was used metaphorically, that he did not intend to imply that Gaia acts "consciously" or "intentionally" to maintain the Earth's balance.

Mysticism aside, the notion that the Earth is a single, huge ecosystem and that the biota, oceans, and atmosphere are capable of cooperating globally seemed to be a far-fetched, improbable idea to many people, who held that chance alone created the multiple conditions for a stable, liveable planet. Lovelock asserted that the likelihood of this happening by chance alone was about the same as the chances of someone driving blindfolded through peak rush hour traffic. Yet, as biologist W. Ford Doolittle points out, "surely if a large enough number of blindfolded drivers launched themselves into rush hour traffic, one would survive."

Evan Eisenberg, author of the book *The Ecology of Eden,* sides with Lovelock when he points out that if it were chance occurrence, a lucky roll of the dice, it would have to

at the real, lived, "experiential" connections between the domination of nature and the domination of women. For example, Australian ecofeminist writer and activist Ariel Salleh examines how the exploitation of nature often results in "institutionalized theft" for women. She points out that women "put in 65 percent of the world's work, and get back only 10 percent of all income paid."[28] She goes on to suggest that:

> Traditionally, women, children, animals, and plants have been accorded no rights and have existed solely for the enhancement of God and Man. New modes of production simply extend the underlying logic, as both "nature" and those who labour with nature are treated as "resources" without intrinsic value.[29]

be a long run of luck—"a throwing of sevens and elevens day in and day out for three billion years . . . . Every day that goes by in which the proportion of oxygen in the air remains at 19 percent is a fresh miracle, a thing to gape at—unless, of course, some explanation is proposed." (Note: Eisenberg is in error here—according to NASA, the actual percentage of oxygen in the air is 20.9 percent.)

Since its original iteration, Gaia theory has developed considerably. Lovelock gives a great deal of credit for its advancement to Lynn Margulis, a noted micro-biologist and one of his strongest supporters and collaborators. Although the extraordinary complexity of interactions among the multiple parts of the global system are far from understood, our rapidly advancing earth sciences, especially climate science, have verified a closely linked, highly complex relationship. Lovelock's notion of Gaia is today largely supported by the scientific community (although there is still debate) and has become a major field of study most commonly referred to as "earth systems science."

Unlike other radical environmental perspectives (deep ecology, social ecology, and ecofeminism), Gaia is not an environmental philosophy but a scientific theory. Nevertheless, it offers a clear theoretic grounding for an ecocentric philosophy of humans' relationship to the natural world. The basic tenet of Gaia—that human and nonhuman, living and nonliving are all components of a larger, co-evolving, insepa-rable whole—contradicts the anthropocentric view of humans' privileged place in the ecosystem. Gaia, as a self-regulating system, may be able to correct for the abuses that humans have imposed and maintain conditions for life on earth, but the condi-tions may be inhospitable for humans as well as for many other life forms. In fact, Lovelock believes that runaway global warming will make much of the earth uninhabit-able for humans.

Sources: James Lovelock, *Gaia: A New Look at Life on Earth* (Oxford, UK: Oxford University Press, 1979). W. Ford Doolittle, cited in E. Strong, "*Gaia* and the Selfish Genes: Differing Perspectives on Life," *The New York Times on the Web*, January 1, 2001, http://endeavor.med.nyu.edu/~strone01/gaia.html (accessed May 9, 2007). Evan Eisenberg, *The Ecology of Eden* (New York: Knopf, 1998). James Lovelock, *The Vanishing Face of Gaia: A Final Warning* (London: Allen Lane, 2009).

Other ecofeminist writers have explored a fourth woman-nature connec-tion—*symbolic connection*. They examine ways in which nature and women are portrayed in the language of film, religion, art, literature, and so forth, as well as how these symbolic representations perpetuate the domination and inferiorization of both women and nature. Karen J. Warren gives examples of how language is used to construct this connection. Women, she says,

are often described in animal terms (e.g., as cows, foxes, chicks, serpents, bitches, beavers, old bats, pussycats, cats, bird-brains, hare-brains). Nature is often described in sexual terms: nature is raped, mastered, conquered, controlled, mined. Her "secrets" are "penetrated" and her "womb" is put into the services of the "man of science." "Virgin timber" is felled. . . . "Fertile soil" is tilled and the land that lies "fallow" is "barren," useless.[30]

Ecofeminism is a growing field of study; these are but a few of the directions the inquiry has taken. Many ecofeminism proponents view it as the only true libratory perspective with the potential to radically re-articulate humans' relationship to the natural world.[31] Ecofeminists believe that, unlike deep ecology or social ecology, ecofeminism has the potential to challenge contemporary Western views in ways that other radical environmental philosophies ignore. Although other radical perspectives also call for paradigmatic change in the way we view the natural world, ecofeminists point out that both the deep ecology emphasis on the psychological self and the social ecology focus on our unsustainable social systems ignore the fundamental and unsustainable logic of domination that is responsible for creating and perpetuating our environmental problems. According to ecofeminists, the logic of domination allows for and encourages humans' domination of other humans and of the natural world. Many ecofeminists believe that in failing to critique the discourse of dominance, deep ecology and social ecology actually reproduce rather than transform the dominant paradigm.

The Messy Domain of Environmental Perspectives

The previous two chapters have examined numerous environmental perspectives and philosophies, and categorized them as either mainstream or radical perspectives. These various perspectives are not necessarily exclusive or incompatible, however. We should exercise caution when attempting to apply a blanket classification to any given individual, group, or organization. Aldo Leopold, for example, is cited in this chapter as an influential voice in advancing the ideas of deep ecology. Yet, he spent his life as a forester trained in conservation methods; much of his writing reflects his love and admiration for fellow foresters and conservationists. John Muir is mentioned in this chapter as an important voice of the deep ecology perspective, but in the last chapter he is cited as a leading voice of the preservationist movement. Categorizing environmental perspectives is a useful academic exercise, but the boundaries often become obscured when applied to the "real world" of environmental advocacy.

To illustrate this point, I will attempt to classify my own environmental stance based on the categories previously discussed. My father was a farmer who took advantage of many government-sponsored agricultural programs to incorporate the latest techniques in soil and water conservation. I was very proud of the awards he received for his innovative farming techniques. Coming from this background of environmental management based on scientific and technological land management expertise, I would have to classify myself as a *conservationist*. As an adult, I have worked extensively as an open-space preservation activist in my community. So I guess that makes me a *preservationist*. I recycle, use water and energy carefully, try to buy environmentally friendly products, and engage in other *stewardship* activities. But somewhere in the depths of my belief system, I feel that if we are to stem the tide of environmental destruction, we must drastically alter the way we view the natural world and our relationship to it. We must give moral consideration to the natural world; expose and alter a way of thinking that allows for the domination of women, the underprivileged, and nature; and restructure the institutions and economic policies that have compromised our ecological well-being. This way of thinking then makes me a *deep ecologist,* an *ecofeminist,* and a *social ecologist.*

Categorizing and labeling can help us understand these perspectives and the differences among them, but they may do an injustice to any given individual or group. In fact, labeling is often used as a rhetorical tactic for establishing false divisions—us versus them, mainstream versus radical, green versus brown, developer versus environmentalist. Influential environmental writers M. Jimmie Killingsworth and Jacqueline S. Palmer refer to such dichotomous categorizations as "**ecospeak,**" which, like Orwell's newspeak, "becomes a form of language and a way of framing arguments that stops thinking and inhibits social cooperation rather than extending thinking and promoting cooperation through communication."[32]

Regardless of the philosophical differences among the varying camps of radical critique or the differences between mainstream and radical perspectives, all these perspectives share a deep and meaningful concern for the natural world and its health and sustainability. Rather than trying to decide which perspective is the right or most right, it is best to take, from each perspective, that which offers the best explanation for or response to any given situation or circumstance. The mainstream perspectives of stewardship, conservation, preservation, and sustainable development, as well as the radical critiques offered by deep ecology, social ecology, and ecofeminism, all bring significant insights to the complex relationship between humans and the natural world. Just as there is no single solution to our environmental problems, no one philosophy offers the only reasonable or right way to re-envision or re-construct this relationship.

Concluding and Looking Ahead

This chapter has introduced you to environmental philosophies that call for fundamental or radical changes in our ways of thinking about the natural world and humans' relationship to it, as well as to some of the philosophers and writers who have developed and refined these status quo–challenging perspectives. The fundamental assumptions that ground deep ecology, social ecology, and ecofeminism, while not holding a privileged or dominant ideological position in the Western worldview, have nevertheless added significantly to the critical conversations about our ways of viewing and treating the natural world. Many forces resist change, but hegemonic restraints are weakened as new ways of seeing and understanding the world are brought to light. These critical conversations are essential to constructing a new, more sustainable human/nature relationship.

We now move from examining the perspectives that explain and define the human/nature relationship to looking at environmental rhetoric, the various ways in which this relationship is symbolically represented, and how these representations impact our perceptions, policies, and practices.

Environmental communication scholars view the environment not so much as a thing of nature, but as a concept with an associated set of meanings and values that have been created through the way we communicate about the environment. This is not to say that environmental communication scholars deny the existence of an objective natural world. One can go out into the forest and touch, feel, see, and smell the objective version of the reality of a tree. Yet, the meaning of that tree does not reside primarily in the bark and leaves that one can touch and see. Meaning is not a forest product, it is a social product. The management of our natural resources is largely a function of the management of our symbolic resources. As you will soon learn, rhetoric is defined as precisely that—the management of symbolic resources. Rhetoric then, plays a central role in shaping how we view and treat the natural world.

> Answers to Name That Rabble-Rouser: (1) Susan B. Anthony, Women's Right to Suffrage Address, 1873; (2) Martin Luther King, Civil Rights March on Washington, D.C., August 23, 1963; (3) Joni Mitchell, "Big Yellow Taxi," from the album *Ladies of the Canyon,* released in 1970; (4) Bill McKibben, *The End of Nature* (New York: Random House, 1989), p. 7.

Discussion Questions and Exercises

1. The author of this book discusses the influences in her life that have led to her own environmental perspectives. Do this for yourself—outline your own historically grounded environmental position.

2. Literary critic Harold Fromm (2005) states, "I don't believe that anything human can ever be anything other than anthropocentric—and that biocentrism is just anthropocentrism in drag, like Jerry Falwell telling us what God wants, a god who always turns out to have the atavistic brain of Jerry Falwell."[33] Interpret this in your own words. Do you agree or disagree?

3. Read Aldo Leopold's classic essay, "Thinking Like a Mountain," included in the appendix of this book. What do you think it means to "think like a mountain?"

4. Let's debate: Set up three teams—one to represent each of the following perspectives: deep ecology, social ecology, and ecofeminism. Now refer back to Chapter 2 and pick an environmental problem (such as loss of diversity, global warming, or waste disposal). Debate the causes and possible solutions to that problem from the perspective your team has been assigned.

5. Of the three environmental perspectives presented in this chapter, which, if any, do you find the most compelling? Explain your answer.

6. The seventh basic principle of deep ecology states that our goal should be "life quality" rather than "standard of living." Explain and expand this idea. What does "life quality" mean to you?

Suggested Readings

Rachel Carson. *Silent Spring.* New York: Fawcett, 1962.

M. Jimmie Killingsworth and Jacqueline S. Palmer. *Ecospeak: Rhetoric and Environmental Politics in America.* Carbondale: Southern Illinois University Press, 1992.

Aldo Leopold. *A Sand County Almanac: And Sketches Here and There.* Oxford, UK: Oxford University Press, 1949, 1977.

Michael E. Zimmerman, J. Baird Callicott, George Sessions, Karen J. Warren, and John Clark (Eds.). *Environmental Philosophies: From Animal Rights to Radical Ecology.* Englewood Cliffs, NJ: Prentice Hall, (1993).

Notes

1. John D. Ramage, *Rhetoric: A User's Guide* (New York: Pearson Education, 2006), 210.
2. David A. Snow and Robert D. Benford, "Master Frames and Cycles of Protest," in *Frontiers in Social Movement Theory,* eds. A. D. Morris and C. McClurg Mueller (New Haven, CT: Yale University Press, 1992), 144.

3. George Sessions, "Deep Ecology: Introduction," in *Environmental Philosophy: From Animal Rights to Radical Ecology*, eds. M. E. Zimmerman, J. B. Callicott, G. Sessions, K. J. Warren, and J. Clark (Englewood Cliffs, NJ: Prentice Hall, 1993).

4. Arne Naess, "Simple in Means, Rich in Ends: An Interview with Arne Naess by Stephen Bodian," in *Environmental Philosophy: From Animal Rights to Radical Ecology,* eds. M. E. Zimmerman, J. B. Callicott, G. Sessions, K. J. Warren, and J. Clark (Englewood Cliffs, NJ: Prentice Hall, 1993), 185. This interview was originally published in 1982 by *The Ten Directions,* Los Angeles Zen Center.

5. Bill Devall and George Sessions, *Deep Ecology* (Salt Lake City: Peregrine, 1985), 70.

6. Henry David Thoreau, *Huckleberries* (Iowa City: Windhover Press, University of Iowa, 1971).

7. John Muir, "Man's Place in the Universe," in *A Thousand-Mile Walk to the Gulf,* ed. W. F. Badè (New York: Houghton Mifflin, 1916), 1.

8. Charles E. Little, *The Dying of the Trees: The Pandemic in American Forests* (New York: Viking, 1995), 223.

9. Aldo Leopold, *A Sand County Almanac: And Sketches Here and There* (Oxford, UK: Oxford University Press, 1949/1977), 209. By permission of Oxford University Press, Inc.

10. Rachel Carson, *Silent Spring* (New York: Fawcett, 1962), 12.

11. Carson, *Silent Spring,* 11.

12. George Bradford, "Toward a Deep Social Ecology," in *Environmental Philosophy: From Animal Rights to Radical Ecology,* eds. M. E. Zimmerman, J. B. Callicott, G. Sessions, K. J. Warren, and J. Clark (Englewood Cliffs, NJ: Prentice Hall, 1993), 433.

13. Murray Bookchin, "What is Social Ecology?" in *Environmental Philosophy: From Animal Rights to Radical Ecology,* eds. M. E. Zimmerman, J. B. Callicott, G. Sessions, K. J. Warren, and J. Clark (Englewood Cliffs, NJ: Prentice Hall, 1993), 354.

14. Bookchin, "What is Social Ecology?" 354.

15. Bookchin, "What is Social Ecology?" 360.

16. Bookchin, "What is Social Ecology?" 361.

17. Bookchin, "What is Social Ecology?" 354–355.

18. Genesis 1:28.

19. Bookchin, "What is Social Ecology?" 367.

20. Murray Bookchin, "Social Ecology versus Deep Ecology," *Socialist Review,* 18 (1988): 8.

21. Bookchin, "What is Social Ecology?" 370.

22. Rosemary Radford Ruether, *New Women/New Earth: Sexist Ideologies and Human Liberation* (New York: Seabury, 1975), 204.

23. Karen J. Warren, "The Power and Promise of Ecological Feminism," *Environmental Ethics* 12 (1990): 125–144.

24. For a more detailed summary see Karen J. Warren, "Ecofeminism," in *Environmental Philosophy: From Animal Rights to Radical Ecology,* eds. M. E. Zimmerman, J. B. Callicott, G. Sessions, K. J. Warren, and J. Clark (Englewood Cliffs, NJ: Prentice Hall, 1993).

25. Carolyn Merchant, *The Death of Nature* (New York: Harper & Row, 1980), 270.

26. Val Plumwood, "Nature, Self, and Gender: Feminism, Environmental Philosophy, and the Critique of Rationalism," in *Hypathia* VI, No 1 (Spring 1991): 3–27.

27. Val Plumwood, *Feminism and the Mastery of Nature* (New York: Routledge, 1993), 30.

28. Ariel Salleh, "Living with Nature: Reciprocity or Control?" in *Ethics of Environmental Development,* eds. J. Ronald Engle and Joan Gibb Engle (Tucson: University of Arizona Press, 1990). 245–253.

29. Salleh, "Living with Nature," 250.

30. Karen J. Warren, "Ecofeminism," in *Environmental Philosophy: From Animal Rights to Radical Ecology,* eds. M. E. Zimmerman, J. B. Callicott, G. Sessions, K. J. Warren, and J. Clark (Englewood Cliffs, NJ: Prentice Hall, 1993), 259.

31. See, for example, Connie Bullis, "Retalking Environmental Discourse from Feminist Perspectives: The Radical Potential of Ecofeminism," in *The Symbolic Earth: Discourse and the Creation of the Environment,* ed. J. G. Cantrill and C. Oravec (Lexington: University Press of Kentucky, 1996); Val Plumwood, *Feminism and the Mastery of Nature* (New York: Routledge, 1993); Karen J. Warren, "The Power and Promise of Ecological Feminism," *Environmental Ethics* 12 (1990): 125–144.

32. M. Jimmie Killingsworth and Jacqueline S. Palmer, *Ecospeak: Rhetoric and Environmental Politics in America* (Carbondale: Southern Illinois University Press, 1992), 9.

33. Harold Fromm, "Full-Stomach Wilderness and the Suburban Esthetic," in *Holding Common Ground,* eds. P. Lindholt and D. Knowles, 36–40. Spokane, WA: Eastern Washington University Press, 2005.

Part III

Rhetoric and the Environment

Chapter 5

An Introduction to Environmental Rhetoric

Rhetorical scholar John D. Ramage created a fictitious "anti-rhetoric" persona to articulate some of the commonly held ideas about how rhetoric is used and by whom. According to this anti-rhetoric persona (whom Ramage calls a "supercilious twit"):

> Those quacks and mountebanks on late-night TV who flog fat-burning elastic belts practice rhetoric; those "Sabbath gasbags" who pontificate endlessly on Sunday news shows practice rhetoric; those shameless mopes who phone during dinner and plead with us to buy a time-share in Orlando practice rhetoric; that ingratiating little weasel who sat next to you in French and got a C on the midterm but managed to wheedle a B- out of the teacher practiced rhetoric.[1]

Although fictitious, this character's sentiments reflect a perception that many people hold about rhetoric—twits and non-twits alike. You have probably heard someone say something like "that's just a lot of rhetoric" to refer to bombastic or empty speech by persons of dubious character and questionable motives, but this is not how rhetoric is characterized in the communication discipline. While rhetoric may be bombastic or empty, it may also be principled and honorable.

Environmental communication scholars have focused a great deal of attention on the rhetorical practices that are employed in communicating about the natural world. These scholars operate under the assumption that symbols have a force in the world that shapes and even creates our environmental realities. Essential to understanding human interaction with nature is understanding the fundamentally "rhetorical nature of nature." By that I mean that the environment is not so much a "thing of nature" or something one can go out and find in the woods, as it is a concept with associated meanings and values that are constructed through the symbols we use to communicate about it.

Over the course of history, many voices have articulated multiple perspectives about the natural world and humans' place in it. The influential rhetoric of prophets and pundits, academics and activists, politicians and the press, and yes, quacks and mountebanks, as well as countless others, have all helped create, nurture, and sustain the still-unfolding drama of the environmental movement.

The chapters in Part 3 introduce you to the study of environmental rhetoric and some areas of inquiry within this domain, in the hope of heightening your understanding of how symbols influence the meanings and values we ascribe to the natural world. I hope they will also move you toward an enlightened, critical awareness of how rhetoric works in our everyday lives.

A comprehensive examination of the many rhetorical theories and the multiple sites of inquiry is beyond the scope of this book. Indeed, the literature on the subject of rhetoric spans centuries and academic disciplines, and encompasses multiple ways of knowing and seeing the world. The topics in this chapter introduce some of the major perspectives and ways of knowing that inform this rich and timely area of study.

Because the way we communicate about the natural world influences and sometimes even determines the values we ascribe to it, it is important to be critically cognizant of the rhetoric we encounter and its profound influence on the way we view and subsequently treat the natural world. An understanding of the functions and forms of rhetoric in everyday life is an important step toward this critical awareness.

This chapter discusses the functions of rhetoric (instrumental and constitutive) and some broadly categorized forms of rhetoric (reasoned argumentation, narrative, myth, image events, and aesthetic rhetoric). The following chapters will go on to explore some of the particular themes commonly used in environmental discourse. But before we go too much farther, a definition of rhetoric is in order.

Defining Rhetoric

Since its beginning in ancient Greece, the study of rhetoric has taken many directions; there is no single, agreed-upon definition. Many scholars draw on Aristotle's definition of rhetoric as "the art of persuasion." They describe an artist of rhetoric as a person who has the capacity and knowledge to understand and appropriately employ "the available means of persuasion" in a given situation. Aristotle's view of rhetoric focuses on the instrumental function of language, which is to persuade others. Aristotle's writings focus solely on spoken and written language. Contemporary rhetorical scholars expand their view of rhetoric to encompass multiple forms, beyond spoken or written language. They define rhetoric as *the management of symbolic resources;* the purposeful selection and arrangement of symbols. As rhetorical scholar Gerard A. Hauser describes it, "rhetoric is discourse by design."[2]

The expanded scope of this definition allows for consideration of nondiscursive or presentational symbols, such as music, art, and dance, that have a strong persuasive force that is not primarily dependent upon language. Scholars of environmental rhetoric have examined many forms of messages, from paintings and sculptures to landscape architecture and city parks. For example, the spectacular photographic images of Yosemite Valley that Carleton Watkins created in the 1860s were instrumental in persuading Congress to create the world's first wilderness park.[3] Depictions of nature in greeting cards, weather maps, and theme parks send messages about what nature is, what it is for, and what it should look like. Similarly, acts such as sit-ins, marches, and direct acts of property destruction send rhetorical messages (as discussed in the next chapter).

This view of rhetoric also encompasses its use for purposes other than the instrumental function of persuading others, with which Aristotle was concerned. It allows for the consideration of the constitutive function of rhetoric, as discussed in the following section.

Instrumental and Constitutive
Functions of Rhetoric

Something is **instrumental** if it serves as a purposeful means or an agency for accomplishing something—to persuade, alert, mobilize, and so forth. A politician's speech, for example, may be instrumental in persuading Congress to pass a certain piece of legislation. A television advertisement may be instrumental in influencing you to purchase a certain brand of toothpaste. A focus on the instrumental function of rhetoric implies that the **rhetor** (the person who sends the rhetorical message)

Figure 5.1   Carleton Watkins's Yosemite

Carleton Watkins (1829–1916) began photographing the sublime wonders of Yosemite Valley in 1861. The spectacular and daring shots he took in his explorations of precipitous and forbidding terrain (while transporting heavy and cumbersome equipment, including a portable darkroom), along with the superb technical quality of his work, established his reputation as one of the finest landscape photographers of the nineteenth century. His photographs influenced President Abraham Lincoln to sign the Yosemite Grant, which set aside a large tract of the Yosemite Valley for preservation and public use, and paved the way for a national park system.

Library of Congress

consciously selects a particular rhetorical means or variety of means from several communication options, with a certain goal in mind. The creator of the toothpaste advertisement made very purposeful communication choices about what language and visual cues to use in the thirty-second spot to create the most impact on potential toothpaste purchasers.

The second function of rhetoric is its **constitutive** function, by which realities come into being or are *created* (constituted or constructed) through symbols. A focus on the constitutive function suggests that the way we view and subsequently treat the natural world is not so much based on an extant, objective reality, but on how we symbolically construct our reality. In other words, symbols don't just represent an existing reality, such as a tree in the forest, they serve to create the reality—the tree has no meaningful existence independent of the meaning given to it through symbols. As Russian psychologist L. S. Vygotsky put it, we "see the tree just as much through our words as through our eyes."[4] Thus, our reality of the tree is a product of our "mental representations" of the tree, which is a product of the symbols we use to represent it.

The constitutive function of rhetoric operates on three levels—constructing reality for the audience, for the rhetor, and for society. For the audience, a rhetor's words can constitute reality by evoking a world—a symbolic world—and causing it to come into being. Rhetorical scholar Ann Gill explains it like this: "By naming, we create objects. We cull objects from the disorder of sensation and by giving them a name, make something of them."[5] The Arctic National Wildlife Refuge, for example, constructed as "a magnificent expanse of pristine wilderness," creates a very different meaning of the reality than a construction of it as "an endless wasteland of barren nothingness."

Rhetoric also functions as a means of identity construction and self-affirmation for the rhetor. This is referred to as the **ego function** of rhetoric, a form of self-persuasion wherein the act of verbalizing or participating in rhetorical acts serves as a means of realizing and affirming one's selfhood.[6] Rhetoric that extols the strengths and virtues of the self and that vilifies the oppressor creates for the individual a sense of moral superiority. Protestors, for example, experience the communal ego-building identification and affirmation associated with membership in the superior group and with participation in the excitement, dangers, and camaraderie of the crusade. The self-persuasion that occurs in the process of engaging in a rhetorical act not only reaffirms and strengthens one's beliefs in the cause, but constitutes selfhood—who I perceive myself to be emerges from my verbalization of the rhetoric or from my participation in the rhetorical acts. If one were to translate this internal process, it might sound something like this: "through my participation in the cause, I know where I stand and I have become a good, dedicated, moral person."

In contrast to instrumental rhetoric that is used to persuade others, the rhetoric associated with the ego function often purposely ignores the kind of communication that would create identification with and move an audience toward a cause. The goal is not to find a common cause in order to persuade, but to create distance from an adversary and to construct for the self and like-minded others an alternative reality. For example, in accusing others of being greedy destroyers of the planet, you are not attempting to persuade them to change their evil ways. This would, in fact, be an ineffective way to persuade them to change their planet-destroying behaviors and join your cause. Rather, such rhetoric distances you from others by constructing yourself and your cohorts-in-the-cause as righteously different from them.

A third level of constitutive rhetoric works to transform the identity of a society—a kind of society-ego function. As environmental communication scholar Kevin M. DeLuca points out, rhetoric serves to "reconstitute the identity of the dominant culture by challenging and transforming mainstream society's key discourses and ideographs."[7] Consider, for example, the profoundly transformed cultural identity called for in Aldo Leopold's famous axiom from *A Sand County Almanac:* "A thing is right when it tends to preserve the integrity, stability, and beauty of the biotic community. It is wrong when it tends otherwise."[8] This construction of what is "right" profoundly transforms such ideographs as progress, freedom, and independence, and gives them new meaning. Whereas we tend to view these ideographs as good if they don't harm the human community, Leopold suggests they are good only if they don't harm the biotic community. The articulation of alternative versions of reality that challenge the prevailing ideologies and redefine ideographic meanings offers a new way for a society to view itself—always a good place to start when change is needed.

Rhetorical Forms

We can choose from several rhetorical forms to articulate a message. Each form invites us to reason in a particular way and to come to judgment based on its own criteria. The following section discusses five broad forms of rhetoric: reasoned argumentation, narrative, myth, image events, and "aesthetic rhetoric" in the form of performance, art, and literature.

Reasoned Argumentation

Reasoned argumentation is the kind of persuasion and decision-making that calls on logic, proofs, scientific methods of testing, and so on. This form of rhetoric holds great sway in Western legal, legislative, scientific, and educational institutions. Many theorists have added to our understanding of reasoned argumentation and the elements of an effective persuasive appeal. One thing that almost all of these rhetorical theorists have in common is a grounding in the classical Greek tradition, most notably, the teachings and philosophies of Aristotle. In fact, **Aristotle's Rhetoric,** a well-known and much studied treatise that categorizes the "available means of persuasion," is often referred to as the beginning of the communication discipline.

Aristotle, in the Greek tradition, believed that the art of persuasion was the means of weighing and testing all sides of an issue through the reasoned arguments of those who were skilled in employing the rules of advocacy. Because decisions about human affairs rarely involve absolute certainties, Aristotle believed the process of constructing arguments and engaging in critical deliberation would yield the best decisions or "probable truth" rather than absolute truth. Aristotle devoted a large portion of the *Rhetoric* to the modes of proof by which a rhetor can establish or an audience can evaluate probable truth: *ethos, pathos,* and *logos.*

Ethos refers to the credibility or character of the speaker, which Aristotle believed was the most potent of all components of persuasion. A rhetor's *ethos* is a function of attributes such as moral character, trustworthiness, and intelligence. We tend to trust the views of those whom we believe possess these attributes. Rhetors will often call on the expertise or character of other highly respected personages to reinforce their own credibility.

Pathos refers to the appeals a rhetor uses to move the audience to become emotionally engaged and to move the audience to action. Aristotle believed that, because all rational people experience emotions, they were part of any rational response to persuasion and should be considered as a component of any carefully reasoned argument. To that end, he provided a list of fourteen basic human emotions to which a rhetor could appeal. Two that he believed were especially powerful in moving an audience to act were pity and fear. Three fears, he believed, were common to everyone: fear of death or physical harm, fear of loss (loss of health, wealth, security, et cetera), and fear of being deprived of rights or freedoms (freedom of choice and actions, the right to be heard).

Logos refers to the logical soundness of the case itself and the proof provided to support the case. *Logos* calls on the logical reasoning of the audience and uses such things as scientific facts, expert testimony, and historical analogy to persuade the audience of the reasonableness or soundness of the rhetor's claim, but it involves more than logic alone. Aristotle was also concerned with the way people reason and the patterns or conventions of reasoning that audiences find persuasive. Thus, in constructing a persuasive appeal to move an audience, Aristotle believed that a rhetor should answer the question, what commonly shared beliefs, feelings, and ideas does the audience have?

Aristotle and the Greek philosophers articulated the foundation of reasoned argumentation as a rhetorical form that today remains a template for both how to "do" rhetoric and how to evaluate the rhetoric of others. This form, and the adaptations and variations advanced by contemporary scholars, holds great sway with Western audiences, who tend to view themselves as "reasoning beings" who make decisions based on sound rational arguments. However, contemporary rhetorical theorist Walter R. Fisher pointed out that "humans as rhetorical beings are as much valuing as they are reasoning animals."[9] He argued that the **rational paradigm,** a term he used to refer to the Aristotelian legacy, doesn't always adequately explain why we are or are not persuaded, and that reason is not necessarily expressed only in sound, logical arguments.

Fisher believed that Western tradition gives too much attention to conventional rationality, in which evidence, facts, logic, and formal argumentation are emphasized as the primary and "rational" means of persuasion or deliberative decision-making. Fisher argued that we should consider the importance of a different kind of logic in our everyday lives, "narrative rationality." The following section will look at narrative as a form of rhetoric and explore Fisher's ideas in more detail.

Narrative

The recognition of the persuasive power of stories has led many scholars to study narratives or storytelling as a form of rhetoric.[10] Narrative inquiry is grounded in diverse disciplines and encompasses multiple theoretical perspectives. A good place to start as an introduction to the study of narrative as rhetoric is with Fisher's **narrative paradigm,** which challenged the classical view of rhetoric and has had considerable influence in provoking new ways of thinking about persuasion.

According to Fisher, storytelling is not an occasional activity that we practice only to put a child to sleep or to introduce a speech. It is an ongoing human activity by which we weave discrete and disconnected facts and experiences together into a coherent pattern: "They are the stories we tell ourselves and each other to establish a meaningful life world."[11] Fisher goes so far as to suggest that most of our communication takes the form of a story with plot, characters, a beginning, and an end, and that the dominant mode of human decision-making involves sharing these stories. People choose from a set of stories that provide insight into the proper or best course of action.

Fisher believed that a compelling story is often more persuasive than evidence or experts. Award winning journalist Elizabeth Kolbert demonstrates the veracity of this assertion in her book *Field Notes from a Catastrophe,* where she tells of her travels to the Arctic and recounts the stories of those who live there. Through interviews with researchers and environmentalists, she explains the science and the studies behind global warming. But the stories of people whose lives have been impacted by a rapidly changing Arctic environment present the most compelling and persuasive "evidence" of the stark reality—people who must move from their island home because ice no longer protects its shores from being washed away, Fairbanks residents whose homes have collapsed because of the melting permafrost upon which they sit, the Inuit bartender who tells of seeing robins for the first time and having no word in the Inuit language for this previously nonexistent bird.[12] Research data and climate models warn us that global warming will radically alter human existence, but the stories of people who experience the effects in their day-to-day lives bring rhetorical force to the seemingly distant and incomprehensible warnings.

Fisher suggested that stories have their own kind of rationality (he called it **narrative rationality**) that offers alternative forms of "good reasons" to believe or not believe any particular story. According to Fisher, we judge stories on the basis of two standards for assessing narrative rationality: narrative coherence and narrative fidelity. **Narrative coherence** concerns whether all the parts of a story fit together in a believable manner. Evaluating the coherence of a story involves asking questions such as whether the story includes all the details necessary to make it believable or whether there are holes in the story. Are the characters' actions, as described by the storyteller, consistent with their motivations and personalities? Is it probable that events could have happened in this way?

The second standard for assessing narrative rationality is what Fisher termed **narrative fidelity,** which is concerned with the extent to which a story rings true or resonates with the listener's own experiences, values, and beliefs or with previously accepted stories. Whereas coherence deals with the internal structure of the story, fidelity looks at things external to the story that impact its believability.

The stories people hear and tell offer "good reasons" to act or believe in a particular way. While the reasons may not always meet the normative standards of the rational paradigm or reasoned argumentation, the stories are accepted because of their narrative rationality—they are consistent with what people know to be true in their lives.

The successes of some of the most influential environmental writers have been due, in large part, to their individual genius as storytellers. Consider, for example, the powerful prose of Henry David Thoreau, John Muir, Rachel Carson, or Ralph Waldo Emerson. One of my all-time favorite stories is Aldo Leopold's moving account of his life-changing experience of shooting a wolf. The following excerpt from his essay "Thinking Like a Mountain," from his classic work, *A Sand County Almanac,* demonstrates the persuasive power of a gifted storyteller. (The complete essay is included in the appendix.)

> In those days, we had never heard of passing up a chance to kill a wolf. In a second, we were pumping lead into the pack, but with more excitement than accuracy . . . . When our rifles were empty, the old wolf was down, and a pup was dragging a leg into impassible slide-rocks. We reached the old wolf in time to watch a fierce green fire dying in her eyes. I realized then, and have known ever since, that there was something new to me in those eyes—something known only to her and the mountain. I was young then, and full of trigger itch; I thought that because fewer wolves meant more deer, that no wolves would mean hunters' paradise. But after seeing the green fire die, I sensed that neither the wolf nor the mountain agreed with such a view.[13]

Leopold's famous essay makes a powerfully persuasive case for wolf preservation. Its rhetorical force lies not in well-structured arguments supported with evidence and facts (although Leopold also effectively used these in his writings). The power of this essay lies in Leopold's ability to create for the reader a visualization of "fierce green fire" dying from the wolf's eyes and the cries of the frightened pups.

A Sand County Almanac was published posthumously in 1949 to little fanfare. Aldo Leopold's writings were rediscovered and became widely acclaimed in the 1960s with the mobilization of the modern environmental movement. Many believe that the work of another storyteller, Rachel Carson, whose book *Silent Spring* swept the nation in 1962, served as one of the principal catalysts for this widespread mobilization.[14] Perhaps the most well-known of all environmental narratives is "A Fable for Tomorrow," the prologue to *Silent Spring* (included in the appendix of this book).

Much of our understanding of the natural environment comes to us through the stories we hear from many sources—television, newspapers, books, magazines, movies, advertisements, and so on. The narrative voices compete in a struggle to frame their stories in ways that privilege their own particular views of nature over others. The narratives of the Arctic National Wildlife Refuge are stories about the life of caribou, as well as stories about a growing need for oil. Narratives of bioengineering are Frankenstein-like stories of altering life forms, as well as narratives of human ingenuity brought into play to feed the world's hungry or cure diseases.

Not all stories, however, receive equal billing through the mainstream commercial media. While environmentalists attempt to frame a more sustainable human/nature narrative, the social and cultural conceptions of nature perpetuated by mainstream Western narratives tend to dominate public discourse. One form of narrative that is particularly influential in the maintenance of hegemonic views of nature is myth.

Myth

Myths are cultural narratives—the stories told by a people. Our way of behaving, of seeing the world, of knowing what is right and good, are embedded in our cultural myths. The stories are told over and over again in multiple versions through multiple forms of media. Mythic themes appear in movies, books, political speeches, and even television situation comedies. They are familiar to all of us. Take for example the classic narrative of the American cowboys of the West—you know, those whisky swillin', gun-slingin', honest, hard-working, courageous, yet humble, white guys. We can envision them sitting around the campfire, far from civilization, with a magnificent canopy of stars overhead and the other-worldly sounds of coyotes accompanying the lone harmonica player. All seems right with the world, but you can hear the Indian war drums in the distance and you know that the cattle-rustlin' Mexican banditos are hanging out somewhere in the canyon waiting to strike. Despite the perils, we know that in the end, the good guy gets the stagecoach robber and, of course, the girl (Aw shucks, ma'am!).

Although any given version of the narrative will vary in details, the basic mythic themes tend to be universal and celebrate the values and beliefs a culture holds dear. By embracing myth, a rhetor establishes *ethos* and *pathos* by creating identification with the listener, as a person who shares the same deeply held values and beliefs. Conversely, people who dare to question this venerated font of culture are often characterized as irrational or lacking common sense.

Scholars engaged in mythic criticism are admonished to avoid the colloquial view of myth as a popularly perpetuated fictitious story or falsehood. Indeed, the cultural ideals and deeply held values expressed in myth are products of both historical realities and popular beliefs. Yet, critics must also keep in mind that the "truths" contained in myth, as composites of cultural beliefs and values, operate at the deepest level of cultural understanding. As such, they tend to be taken for granted and are rarely subjected to critical reflection. The evaluative criteria of narrative coherence and narrative fidelity tend to be overlooked when myth is invoked to support an argument. In this way, these deeply held "truths" can serve as a means of blinding the myth-sharing community to the possible contradictions in the logic of the myth. The following section looks at some of our most persistent and influential myths grounding Western perceptions of the human/nature relationship, as well as some of the contradictions inherent in the mythic constructions.

Many myths inform Western perceptions of humans' relationship to the natural world. Among the most persistent, recognized, and influential are the *agrarian myth,* the *frontier myth,* and the *Arcadian myth.*

The **agrarian myth** is credited largely to the ideas and writings of Thomas Jefferson, who envisioned a nation with 90 percent of its people engaged in farming. Donald Worster, a historian of the American West, described the principal narrative of the agrarian myth as the story about a simple ordinary people moving into an extraordinary frontier land, "turning it into the garden of the world,"[15] and there creating a peaceful productive life free of the depravity and contaminating influence of urban civilization.

The yeoman farmer, according to Jefferson, held all the traits of the ideal citizen—traits that our cultural narratives persist in attributing to farmers even today. A farmer is often portrayed as an honest, hard-working, independent, moral person who, along with the nuclear farm family, lives a life of wholesome simplicity. The mythical farmer is perpetuated through multiple sites of popular culture, such as films, novels, commercials, country songs, and cartoons, all of which color and shape our "common sense" view of farmers and farming practices.

Emerging from the agrarian myth and reinforcing its cultural ideals was the **frontier myth,** also referred to as the **Turner thesis** because it was advanced and popularized by Frederick Jackson Turner, an early twentieth century U.S. historian.[16] This self-flattering vision of the United States' past extolled the virtues of the courageous settlers who endured the hardships of the wilderness to create a unique form of democracy where equal hardship and opportunity leveled the playing field for all. According to Turner, the settling of the western frontier was not merely a colorful phase of our history, it actually shaped and defined our national character. Environmental historian Roderick Nash, in his classic book *Wilderness and the American Mind,* said, "Turner believed, in short, that democracy was a forest product."[17] The frontier brought forth and molded the "rugged individualists" who conquered adversity on the strength of their own self-reliance. Unassisted by government intervention and unencumbered by the external restraints of Eastern power elites, the frontier fostered individualism, independence, and a belief in the common person's ability to self-govern.

Many critics have explored the contradictions in logic in the agrarian myth and the frontier myth. For example, historian Stephanie Coontz points out one of the inconsistencies in the mythic frontier theme of the "rugged individualists" who braved it on their own, unassisted by government handouts or intervention. "It would be hard to find a western family today or at any time in the past," says Coontz, "whose land rights, transportation options, economic existence, and even access to water were not dependent on federal funds."[18]

In the same vein, historian Donald Worster discusses the "unresolved contradictions of innocence" of the agrarian myth of the garden as a place to escape the depravity and contamination of industrialization and urbanization. Paradoxically, as Worster points out, the pioneering era quickly evolved into "a new open-ended period of expanding technology and enterprise that had no limits in sight. . . . We might call it the myth of the world of the Chamber of Commerce, for whom the West will be unfinished frontier until it is one with Hoboken, New Jersey."[19]

A third influential myth has persisted even longer than the agrarian myth or the frontier myth. The **Arcadian myth** has influenced cultural views of nature for over two thousand years. Arcadia was a mountainous region of ancient Greece known for its picturesque streams, forests, meadows, and lush grazing for sheep. Our notions of Arcadia, which stem largely from the pastoral writings of the third century B.C. poet, Theocrites, were re-invigorated two centuries later in the *Eclogues* of Virgil. The bucolic charm of the Arcadian landscape and the contented innocence of its inhabitants have been the subject of some of Western civilization's greatest poetry, dramas, operas, and paintings. Familiar Arcadian themes, as described by Evan Eisenberg in his book *The Ecology of Eden,* include "the babbling brooks, the dallying nymphs, the shepherds piping and pining . . . They are joined by cowherds and goatherds, shepherdesses . . . cyclops and giants, the god, Pan, and his satyrs, and the occasional visitor from the big city."[20]

Although the pastoral as a literary form has gone out of vogue, it resurfaces in multiple disguises. One manifestation of this persistent myth can be found in U.S. suburbia, sometimes referred to as "the middle landscape" where one can find "the perfect midpoint between wilderness and civilization."[21] The dream of Arcadia has led to the expansion of city boundaries through "greenfield development." **Greenfields** are farmlands or areas with little or no previous development. Among the negative environmental impacts of ever-expanding greenfield developments are the destruction and fragmentation of wildlife habitat, the draining of wetlands and felling of trees, and increased CO_2 emissions from commuter vehicles.

Many city planners, architects, developers, and environmental groups have begun to take a serious look at the environmental and social consequences of decades of almost unchecked suburban development. Arcadia has turned into urban sprawl where nary a pan is piping, sheep grazing is mostly prohibited by community codes and covenants, and the closest thing to a babbling brook is the water feature at the miniature golf park.

New trends in green urban development emphasize the redevelopment of already existing urban areas rather than expanding the city's reach into greenfield areas. **Infill development** is done on sites of abandoned housing projects or buildings in the inner city. **Greyfield development** occurs on sites that formerly housed strip malls or other large commercial establishments. **Brownfield development** utilizes previously industrial land and commercial sites where redevelopment is complicated by environmental contaminants.

Arcadia, as with all myths, is riddled with contradictions, the most glaring of which is that one certain way to destroy Arcadia is to move there. You can't have your wilderness cake and eat it too. As the open spaces of Arcadia fill in with shopping malls and fast food restaurants, one must continue the search for a more authentic Arcadia further from the city center, thus extending the sprawl into the next comparatively pristine, unpopulated landscape until that, too, loses its pastoral innocence—and on it goes. As Eisenberg says, "Nostalgia sets in before the paint is dry."[22] Yet it is nostalgia for something that never really existed in the first place and couldn't be sustained even if it did exist. Even Theocrites's Arcadia was "largely deforested and well on its way toward its present magnificent bleakness" when Virgil began writing his pastoral poetry two hundred years later. Today, Virgil's Arcadia is nearly as bleak.[23]

Connections

New Arcadia or Suburban Sprawl?

Environmental communication scholar Barb Willard observed the use of the Arcadian myth as a rhetorical device in the promotional literature of "green" suburban development. Part of an urban planning movement, **new urbanism** has arisen and gained momentum in response to the many problems of urban sprawl and to the environmental and human stress of our fast-paced consumer culture. She believes that part of the popularity of these suburban developments is due to their success in rhetorically tapping into the Arcadian myth.

Her analysis of promotional literature produced and distributed by new urbanist development companies revealed how the commonly held beliefs and understandings that ground the Arcadian myth were used to influence suburban dwellers' view of nature in their surroundings. The promotional literature appeals to the human desire for a place of refuge and tranquility, for living in harmony with nature, and for a shared sense of community.

New urban development designs aim to facilitate community interaction through public open spaces and parks, houses with front porches, walking paths, and so forth. In short, the design allows for a return to the fantasy of small town life and the shared community values of a simpler, more harmonious environment. Willard describes this fantasy as "a desire for the past that never existed but rather was ascribed to the suburbs by vintage TV programs." In fact, several promotional brochures made specific references to the old classic television shows, *Leave it to Beaver* and *Mayberry*.

Although new urbanism and green development philosophies might translate into kinder, gentler, less environmentally destructive suburban developments, they are ultimately unsustainable. Consider, for example, that in order to create that Arcadia, one must first carve out a neighborhood in a previously undeveloped place. Thus, the starting point for new urban development is the destruction of pristine or minimally developed greenfields, from which one must then commute to the city.

Arcadians live in a symbolic fantasy world, walled off from the industrial and commercial ravages of the city. Yet, as Willard points out, Arcadia is always a temporary state and can only operate in a given landscape for a period of time. As civilization encroaches and Arcadia's innocence is lost, "like a bored, middle-aged spouse," the original property owners will leave to find a more authentic and less defiled Arcadia.

Source: Barb Willard "Mythic Arcadia: Reading the Landscapes of Conservation Communities," in *Proceedings of the 7th Biennial Conference on Communication and Environment*, eds. G. B. Walker and W. J. Kinsella (Silver Falls State Park, OR, July 2003), 205.

Image Events

The next form of rhetoric takes us from the "middle ground" of mainstream culture to the periphery and challenges the mainstream ideologies that ground much of the culture's environmental discourse. **Image events** are events specifically staged for the television cameras to create or manipulate an image. Politicians, business leaders, and corporate public relations specialists have made strategic use of media to control their public images. With their easy access to the media, those in positions of institutionalized power have a distinct advantage in the creation of mass-mediated reality. For grassroots environmental groups or those not in positions of institutionalized power, image events provide a way of gaining access to media and getting the most "bang for the buck"—so to speak.

For grassroots organizations operating outside of the traditional centers of power (such as courtrooms, legislative bodies, or executive boardrooms), image events are *tactical* rather than *strategic*. The difference between strategic and tactical rhetoric is important when we are looking at image events. **Strategic rhetoric** is used by those who hold an advantageous position of power, whereas **tactical rhetoric** is used by those who are operating within the enemy's territory to oppose the institutional powers of control. Image events of radical environmental groups fall primarily into the category of tactical operations that are carried out by those who lack strategic advantages of power.

Rhetorical scholar Kevin M. DeLuca, in his book *Image Politics,* looks at the tactical use of image events by **subaltern counterpublics,** groups that have been excluded, for political reasons, from the traditional forums of influence and so must find alternative forums for challenging the power elite. He begins by describing an image event staged by Greenpeace, the largest environmental organization in the world, whose primary form of rhetorical activity is image events. DeLuca writes:

> On June 27, 1975, 50 miles off the coast of California, the Soviet whaling ship, the *Vlastny,* armed with 90-millimeter canon loaded with a 160-pound exploding grenade harpoon, departs from the factory ship *Dalniy Vostok* in pursuit of sperm whales. Unlike any previous hunt, though, the *Vlastny* finds itself pursued by six Greenpeace activists in three Zodiacs (inflatable rubber dinghies) "armed" with one film camera and intent on confronting the whaler and intervening on behalf of the whales. One Zodiac, bobbing in and out of sight on the rough swells, manages to position itself between the harpoon ship and the nearest whale. The two activists in the Zodiac are betting that the whalers will not risk killing humans in order to kill whales. They lose. Without warning, the whalers fire over the heads of the activists, striking the whale. The steel harpoon cable slashes into the water less than five feet from the zodiac.[24]

Although Greenpeace failed in its immediate goal of saving the whale, the image event was nevertheless highly effective. Video footage of the event was shown on news reports around the world. Robert Hunter, who was the director of Greenpeace at the time and one of the activists precariously positioned in the path of the harpoon, explained that "with a single act of filming ourselves in front of the harpoon, we had entered the mass consciousness of modern America."[25] The dramatic footage seen around the world created a moving, visual narrative of the defenseless environmentalists in their precarious dinghies in a courageous stand to save the whales, against the giant whaling ship and its deadly harpoons. Even the most dynamic speaker or gifted writer could not have challenged the whaling industry as eloquently.

According to DeLuca, image events are more that just a means of creating media attention and generating publicity, "they are crystallized philosophical fragments, mind bombs"[26] that radically challenge mainstream values and authority. Image events, then, are more than "gimmicks or antics of the unruly" that are used to create media attention for "the real rhetoric." They serve "as a social medium through which to hold corporations and states accountable, help form public opinion, and constitute their own identities as subaltern counterpublics. Critique through spectacle, not critique versus spectacle."[27]

Aesthetic Rhetoric

One final form of rhetoric that profoundly influences cultural attitudes toward nature is what is very broadly categorized as "aesthetic rhetoric," or rhetoric that appeals to a sense of the artistic or beautiful. This broad categorization includes the literary arts (nature writing in the form of prose, poetry, fairy tales, and so forth), visual arts (painting, photography), performance art (music and drama), and architecture (building and landscape). The obviously expansive scope of this subject will not allow for a comprehensive discussion of any particular form or even a particular genre within a form, so the following discussion is necessarily highly selective, partial, and painted in very broad strokes. Its intent is simply to bring to light some of the significant sites of meaning-making within this unwieldy categorization and introduce you to a few of the major players in a few of these aesthetic genres.

The Romantic Era

Nature writing has existed since ancient times, but it was at its height of popularity during the late nineteenth and early twentieth centuries, when nearly every issue of popular magazines featured at least one nature story or essay. Many believe that the surge in popularity of nature writing during this time was a response, in part, to Charles Darwin's theory of evolution that was sweeping the world, leaving in its wake a stunned and disillusioned public. Writers and visual artists tended to focus on themes such as nature's sublime grandeur and sacred qualities, its ability to heal the human soul, and the nobility of its nonhuman inhabitants. As one critic explained, because "we are only a little higher than the dog, we may as well make the dog out to be as fine a fellow as possible."[28]

Representations of animals tended to overlook their "wildness" and instead imbued them with traits that resembled those of admirable humans, such as dignity, individuality, and intelligence. Ernest Thompson Seton, a well-known naturalist and animal storyteller of the time, tells of a vixen feeding her cub poisoned meat to save him from the indignity of being chained.[29] Another popular writer, William J. Long, tells his readers about watching a woodcock placing a plaster cast of mud and grass on its broken leg.[30]

The flagrant **anthropomorphism** (attributing human characteristics to nonhuman things) employed by many of these nature writers was vociferously criticized, bringing even President Theodore Roosevelt into the fray. Referring to Long's woodcock story, Roosevelt wrote that "It seems a pity not to have added that it made itself a crutch to use while the splint was on."[31] Roosevelt stressed the importance of accuracy when writing about nature and harshly criticized as "nature fakers" those who romanticized animal characteristics. His strong stance on the accurate representation of animals leads one to wonder what he thought about his namesake, the teddy bear, which bears little resemblance to nature's not-so-cuddly version of bears.

Other prominent nature writers of the time included such well-known names as Henry David Thoreau (1817–1862), Ralph Waldo Emerson (1803–1882), Walt Whitman (1819–1892), John Burroughs (1837–1921), and John Muir (1838–1914). Muir, like many of these writers, spent many years of his life in wilderness excursions. He wrote about everything from his harrowing trek across an Alaskan

Figure 5.2

Anthropomorphizing Bears

This cartoon's anthropomorphic representation of bears may lead to more than just a chuckle. While we might be inclined to accommodate the comestible cravings of these adorable delinquents, it is against the law to feed the bears and one can be fined and even jailed for doing so. The law protects both bears and humans, since bears that become habituated are extremely dangerous and often must be destroyed.

Cartoon by Tony Mangnall

glacier to his beloved Sierra Nevada mountains of California. (An excerpt from Muir's book, *Our National Parks,* is included in the appendix.)

The nature writers and artists of the day played a large role in generating public support for wilderness preservation, support which became highly visible in the course of the national debate surrounding the controversial damming of the Hetch Hetchy Valley in Yosemite (discussed in Chapter 3). In fact, the enactment of the 1916 National Park System Organic Act can be traced to the public outcry that accompanied this controversy.[32] The beauty and grandeur of nature, so eloquently depicted in the aesthetic re-creations of writers and artists, inspired a national movement for wilderness preservation.

Despite the irresistible lure of this celebratory rhetoric and its powerful rhetorical force, the rhetorical critic would do well to take a deeper look at the impact of romantic representations on our perceptions of nature. Environmental communication scholar Christine L. Oravec explains how these "sublime" representations of nature "functioned actively to screen or project human expectations and desires upon the landscape."[33] This vision is what we have come to expect and desire of nature—the "authentic" natural that we care to preserve and protect. Yet, these depictions are carefully framed, cropped, and airbrushed. They make liberal use of poetic license and hyperbole in their symbolic representations of nature. When the real world experience of nature fails to live up to sublime expectations, as it inevitably will, "then nature itself is subject to the deflation of expectations, trivialization, and denigration."[34]

Imagine the public outrage if a housing development or factory were to be built overlooking the South Rim of the Grand Canyon. Many would think that a better place to put it would be farther up the canyon so as not to add unsightly clutter to the sublime photo op. Our homage to the sublime can deflect attention from and concern for the less-than-sublime, yet critical, habitats further down the metaphorical canyon.

Unfortunately, this is more than just a hypothetical example. Several miles downstream from Grand Canyon National Park, on the Hualapai reservation, a cantilevered, horseshoe-shaped, glass walkway juts seventy feet beyond the canyon's edge, nearly a mile above the canyon floor. The tourist attraction has generated a great deal of controversy over what critics view as the defacement of a national treasure.[35]

Like the potentially negative implications of sublime representations of nature, when we project desirable human characteristics on to animals, we also construct perceptions of reality that can have negative repercussions for both humans and animals. For example, when you actually encounter the reality of a bear in its natural habitat doing its natural bear thing, it doesn't seem exactly cuddly. It probably smells and makes ill-mannered demands for your energy bars—a craving the bear developed through previous interpersonal interactions with humans. While it is unwise to attempt to correct his boorish behavior, it is usually the bear that loses the turf war in the end. When a bear actually does **habituate,** or become accustomed to human presence, it becomes an extremely dangerous "nuisance" and may have to be killed by game managers to protect the area's hikers, campers, or residents.

Contemporary Nature Writers

Contemporary writers of nature, many of whom emerged from the spirit of protest in the 1960s and '70s, have moved beyond the narratives of human encounters of sublime wildness to explore alternative views of the human/nature relationship. The rhapsodies of the romantic writers have given way to a markedly different and less airbrushed version of nature that starkly confronts the wounded human/nature relationship. Consider, for example, the following excerpt from Pulitzer Prize–winning ecopoet and essayist Gary Snyder:

> Much life will be lost in the wake of human agency on earth, that of the twentieth and twenty-first centuries. Much is already lost—the soils and water unravel:
>
> > "What's that dark thing in the water?
> > Is it not an oil-soaked otter?"
>
> Where do we start to resolve the dichotomy of the civilized and the wild?[36]

The difference between nineteenth-century environmental writing and twentieth-century ecopoetry, suggests literary critic Roger Thompson, is "the shift from conceptions of nature as divine metaphor to nature as location of social responsibility and action."[37] Note the indictment of human conceit and the call for change implied in the following excerpt from W. S. Merwin's poem "For a Coming Extinction." Through the poet's skillful use of irony, one is struck with the remorseless arrogance of the request made to a dying whale:

> Gray whale
> Now that we are sending you to The End
> That great god
> Tell him
> That we who follow you invented forgiveness
> And forgive nothing[38]

Connections

Performance as Rhetoric: "Bear"

Performance can be a powerful rhetorical instrument to raise awareness and influence attitudes and beliefs. Conference attendees at the 2005 Conference on Communication and Environment were treated to a "nature" performance by environmental communication scholar and performance artist Jonathan Gray. His artistry and insight combined to move the audience to simultaneous laughter and tears in an extraordinarily thought-provoking performance.

Among the original selections Gray performed was one entitled "Bear," in which he takes on the character of an angry, cynical, foul-mouthed bear-with-an-attitude—not exactly the anthropomorphized cute, cuddly bear persona we have come to know and love. "Oh what?" says Bear. "Did I cross yet another line? Do you think I am an inappropriate representation of a bear? What kind of bullshit is that? What, don't I do the stepnfetchit of Smokey for you?"

Bear opens his monologue with the following introduction: "I am a charismatic megafauna! A celebrity. A star. Yeah, right. I am an endangered species, threatened with extinction by your value system, your weapons of enforcement, and your willingness to use both."

Bear then commences to level a resounding rebuke to his human listeners for their arrogance and hypocrisy and for their encroachment on his ever-diminishing terrain. "Cross that imaginary line," says Bear, "between the place set aside for me and your space, so much larger, and suddenly there are rednecks with guns."

The poem challenges the assumption of humans' privileged place and calls on the reader to question the essential anthropocentric construction that humans are more significant creatures than whales or other citizens of the nonhuman lifeworld. Thompson explains it this way: "So in the final lines of the poem, the condemnation [of humanity] culminates in an ironic request that the whale, at its death, tell the god 'That it is we who are important.'"[39]

The poet-as-activist emerges in Merwin's elegant use of irony as a rhetorical appeal to humanity to reflect on its anthropocentric arrogance. Thus, as Thompson explains, the poem becomes the location of argument for social change—"an argument self-consciously rhetorical and openly persuasive."[40]

As with the romantic representations, contemporary aesthetic nature representations challenge the ecologically and socially destructive forces that divide contemporary society—humans versus nature, intellect versus emotions, rationality versus spirituality. Contemporary representations go a step farther to examine alternative ways of viewing humans' relationship to the natural world that were largely ignored by earlier nature aestheticism. Yet, even contemporary writers and artists pause to ponder and celebrate nature's magnificence—as does contemporary poet, theologian, and essayist Thomas Berry:

But even as we glance over the grimy world before us, the sun shines radiantly over the earth, the aspen leaves shimmer in the evening breeze, the coo of the mourning dove and the swelling chorus of the insects fill the land, while down

Even though, as Bear explains, "no self-respecting bear WANTS to be in suburbia" he has learned to adapt. He has figured out that all he has to do is "work up some schtick for the cameras, maybe give some pointers on style, provide a little interior decorating, accentuate my cuddliness and you guys will give me all the garbage I want." You see, Bear has habituated:

> I've been around you people so much that I've grown used to your presence, I've grown accustomed to your face. I'm comfortable with you. In truth, I've become a little like you. I am used to you and your sense of contradiction, your own tendencies toward violence, your own hypocrisy. Can't have that. Eeek. He knows the secret we won't tell ourselves. Gotta put an end to that public nuisance.

> Bear is luckier than some. "Mostly," says Bear, "I just nod my head and wait for the sedatives to wear off. So far, I've been too cute, too charismatic for anyone to want to do serious harm. So far." The sad reality is that once bears lose their fear of people, they often must be destroyed. We love bears because they are celebrities, they are charismatic megafauna. Yet, because of our culturally constructed versions of bears, we tend to forget that they are not Smokeys, Teddies, or Poohs. They are, in fact, powerfully dangerous wild animals. So far, Bear has managed to stay alive, but for many of his kind, to habituate is a death sentence.

> PLEASE DON'T FEED THE BEARS!

Source: Jonathan Gray, "Trail Mix: A Sojourn on the Muddy Divide between Nature and Culture," *Text and Performance Quarterly* 30 (2010) (in press)

in the hollows the mist deepens the fragrance of the honeysuckle. Soon the last summer moon will give a light sheen to the landscape. Something of a dream experience. Perhaps on occasion, we participate in the original dream of the earth.[41]

Sometimes, it seems, celebration is the only appropriate and "natural" response to nature's sublime offerings.

Concluding and Looking Ahead

This chapter has introduced the highly diverse field of environmental rhetoric, beginning with a discussion of the instrumental and constitutive functions of rhetoric. Next, we looked at various broad forms of rhetoric, including reasoned argumentation, narrative, myth, image events, and aesthetic rhetoric. By now, you have probably come to the conclusion that almost any environmental message is rhetorical—that if you look deep enough, you will find the underlying persuasive or perspective-inducing component in almost any message. This is precisely the conclusion I was hoping and expecting you to draw. In coming to this realization, you have made a big step towards the ability to think rhetorically, an ability that, in the words of rhetorical theorist Kenneth Burke, is "equipment for living."[42] This ability will serve as a valuable tool for understanding and thinking critically about the instrumental and constitutive messages with which we are confronted daily, and about the frequently taken for granted, yet highly influential force of rhetoric in our everyday lives.

The next chapter looks at particular rhetorical themes articulated within these broad forms of rhetoric. Chapter 6 looks at the rhetoric of polarization via the rhetoric of two groups who are poles apart in their philosophies about the natural world and humans' place in it.

One can easily become overwhelmed by the competing voices, incompatible realities, and vitriolic rhetoric that often accompany environmental discourse. Narcotized by the rhetorical onslaught and numbed into apathy, we may feel as if the best solution to our environmental problems is indifference and a cold beer. An effective antidote to this self-defeating, status-quo-maintaining, nature-destroying means of coping is to become informed and engaged critics and practitioners of rhetoric. In the words of Gerard A. Hauser:

> Amid our many differences, rhetoric provides the means to forge an expression of the future that all concerned can abide. Rhetoric is our last best alternative to a world run by power or privilege; it offers a world run by the people. In the final analysis, it may also be our last best hope for avoiding mutual obliteration, for a world of political, social, and personal amity.[43]

Listen! Learn! Speak up and speak out!

Discussion Questions and Exercises

1. This chapter discusses the woodcock story told by William J. Long. Examine the narrative rationality of this story in terms of Fisher's notion of narrative fidelity and narrative coherence.

2. Think of a movie, book, or short story that employs the mythic themes of the agrarian myth, the frontier myth, or the Arcadian myth (or a combination of them). Explain how the mythic themes are portrayed in the story. Does the message reinforce or challenge the myth?

3. Create two versions of a message about global warming or some other environmental problem or threat. In the first version, create the message to meet an instrumental function of rhetoric. In the second version, create the message to meet a constitutive function.

4. Find a nature poem from a contemporary poet and analyze its rhetorical message. Some things you might want to discuss are the following:
   - Does the poem address the value dichotomies that divide contemporary culture (for example, humans/nature, intellect/senses, reason/emotion)? Give examples.
   - Does the poem use the celebratory rhetoric of the Romantic writers? Give examples.
   - Does the poem challenge the anthropocentric view of the primary value of nature? Give examples.
   - Does the poem draw on or challenge mythic themes from the agrarian myth, the frontier myth, or the Arcadian myth? Give examples.

5. Divide into teams. Each team is responsible for choosing a cause to bring to peoples' attention and planning an image event that you could carry out on campus (without disrupting classes or defacing campus property). Give a detailed description of the event and how you could carry this out.

Suggested Readings

Kevin M. DeLuca. *Image Politics: The New Rhetoric of Environmental Activism.*
New York: Guilford, 1999.

Evan Eisenberg. *The Ecology of Eden.* New York: Knopf, 1998.

Christine L. Oravec. "To Stand Outside Oneself: The Sublime in the Discourse of
Natural Scenery." In J. G. Cantrill & C. L. Oravec (Eds.), *The Symbolic Earth:
Discourse and the Creation of the Environment.* Lexington: University Press of
Kentucky, 1996, pp. 58–75.

Craig Waddell (Ed.). *Landmark Essays on Rhetoric and the Environment.* Mahwah,
NJ: Erlbaum, 1998.

A Few of My Favorite Contemporary Nature Writers

Thomas Berry. *The Great Work: Our Way into the Future.* New York: Bell Tower,
1999.

Wendell Berry. *The Unsettling of America.* San Francisco: Sierra, 1977.

Mary Oliver. *White Pine.* New York: Harcourt Brace, 1994.

Gary Snyder. *Turtle Island.* New York: New Directions, 1974.

Wallace Stegner. *Marking the Sparrow's Fall: Wallace Stegner's American West.*
New York: Henry Holt, 1998.

Notes

1. John D. Ramage, *Rhetoric: A User's Guide* (New York: Pearson Education, 2006), 2–3.
2. Gerard A. Hauser, *Introduction to Rhetorical Theory* (Prospect Heights, IL: Waveland,
    1986), 23.
3. Kevin M. DeLuca and Anne T. Demo, "Imaging Nature: Watkins, Yosemite, and the
    Birth of Environmentalism," *Critical Studies in Media Communication* 17 (2000):
    241–261.
4. L. S. Vygotsky, *Mind in Society: The Development of Higher Psychological Processes,*
    eds. M. Cole, V. John-Steiner, S. Scribner, and E. Souberman (Cambridge, MA: Harvard
    University Press, 1978), 32.
5. Ann Gill, *Rhetoric and Human Understanding* (Prospect Heights, IL: Waveland, 1994),
    46.
6. Richard B. Gregg, "The Ego Function of the Rhetoric of Protest," reprinted in *Readings
    on the Rhetoric of Social Protest,* eds. C. E. Morris III and S. H. Browne (State College,
    PA: Strata, 2001).
7. Kevin M. DeLuca, *Image Politics: The New Rhetoric of Environmental Activism* (New
    York: Guilford, 1999), 16.
8. Aldo Leopold, *A Sand County Almanac: And Sketches Here and There* (Oxford, UK:
    Oxford University Press, 1949/1977), 211. By permission of Oxford University Press, Inc.
9. Walter R. Fisher, "Narration as a Human Communication Paradigm: The Case of Public
    Moral Argument," *Communication Monographs* 51 (1984): 1.
10. Some of the more influential theories in this area include Walter R. Fisher's narrative
    paradigm (1984), Ernest Bormann's theory of symbolic convergence and fantasy theme
    analysis (1985), Kenneth Burke's dramatism and pentad (1945), and Irving Goffman's
    dramaturgical model of social interaction (1959).
11. Fisher, "Narration," 6.
12. Elizabeth Kolbert, *Field Notes from a Catastrophe: Man, Nature, and Climate Change*
    (New York: Bloomsbury, 2006).
13. Leopold, *A Sand County Almanac,* 211. By permission of Oxford University Press, Inc.
14. Rachel Carson, *Silent Spring* (New York: Fawcett, 1962).
15. Donald Worster, "Beyond the Agrarian Myth," in *Trails: Toward a New Western History,*
    eds. P. N. Limerick, C. A. Milner II, and C. E. Rankin (Lawrence: University of Kansas
    Press, 1991), 8.

16. Frederick Jackson Turner, *The Frontier in American History* (New York: Henry Holt, 1947).
17. Roderick Nash, *Wilderness and the American Mind* (New Haven, CT: Yale University Press, 1967), 146.
18. Stephanie Coontz, *The Way We Never Were: American Families and the Nostalgia Trap* (New York: Basic Books, 1992), 73.
19. Worster, "Beyond the Agrarian Myth," 12–13.
20. Evan Eisenberg, *The Ecology of Eden* (New York: Knopf, 1998), 145.
21. Eisenberg, *Ecology of Eden,* 146.
22. Eisenberg, *Ecology of Eden,* 157.
23. Eisenberg, *Ecology of Eden,* 165.
24. Kevin M. DeLuca, *Image Politics: The New Rhetoric of Environmental Activism* (New York: Guilford, 1999), 1.
25. R. Hunter, *Warriors of the Rainbow: A Chronicle of the Greenpeace Movement* (New York: Holt, Rinehart and Winston, 1979), 231.
26. DeLuca, *Image Politics,* 6.
27. DeLuca, *Image Politics,* 21–22.
28. H. W. Boynton, "Books New and Old: Nature and Human Nature," *Atlantic Monthly,* January 1902, 135.
29. Ernest Thompson Seton, *Wild Animals I Have Known* (New York: Scribners, 1898).
30. William J. Long, "Animal Surgery," *Outlook,* September 12, 1903, 126.
31. Theodore Roosevelt, "Nature Fakers," *Everybody's Magazine,* September 1907, 430.
32. Nash, *Wilderness and the American Mind.*
33. Christine L. Oravec, "To Stand Outside Oneself: The Sublime in the Discourse of Natural Scenery," in *The Symbolic Earth: Discourse and the Creation of the Environment,* eds. J. G. Cantrill and C. L. Oravec (Lexington: University Press of Kentucky, 1996).
34. Oravec, "To Stand Outside," 70.
35. J. Cart, "Tribe's Canyon Skywalk Opens One Deep Divide." *Los Angeles Times,* February 11, 2007, http://www.latimes.com/news/nationworld/la-na-skywalk (accessed August 12, 2007).
36. Gary Snyder, from *The Practice of the Wild: Essays.* Reprinted by permission of Counterpoint. (San Francisco: North Point, 1990), 15.
37. Roger Thompson, "Emerson, Divinity, and Rhetoric in Transcendentalist Nature Writing and Twentieth-Century Ecopoetry," in *Ecopoetry: A Critical Introduction,* ed. S. Bryson (Salt Lake City: University of Utah Press, 2002), 35.
38. W. S. Merwin, *The Lice* (New York: Atheneum, 1967), 69.
39. Thompson, "Emerson, Divinity, and Rhetoric," 35.
40. Thompson, "Emerson, Divinity, and Rhetoric," 40.
41. Thomas Berry, *Creative Energy: Bearing Witness for the Earth* (San Francisco: Sierra Club, 1988), 90.
42. Kenneth Burke, *The Philosophy of Literary Form: Studies in Symbolic Action* (New York: Vintage, 1957/1973).
43. Hauser, *Introduction to Rhetorical Theory,* 203.

Chapter 6
Rhetoric of Polarization

"Save a Logger, Eat an Owl"

"Save an Owl, Educate a Logger"

"This Family Supported by Timber Dollars"

"This Family Supported by Intact Ecosystems"

"I ♥ Spotted Owls"

"I ♥ Spotted Owls . . . Fried"

The above are bumpers sticker slogans that were created to represent each side in the dispute between environmentalists, who are attempting to protect the threatened Northern Spotted Owl and the old growth forest upon which the owl depends for survival, and loggers, who want to log the valuable old-growth timber—a bitter dispute that has been raging for over three decades. It's difficult to judge which side wins the creative polarizing slogan contest.

Environmental conflict often takes place in the public arena. All parties in the conflict strive to bring their viewpoints to the public's attention in a persuasive and compelling manner while undermining the opposition. **Polarizing rhetoric** creates an "us-versus-them" dichotomy, with clear distinctions between the "evil other" and the "virtuous self." This rhetoric serves to magnify the differences between groups and minimize differences within the group, creating a high degree of internal solidarity.

A number of environmental communication scholars have examined the rhetoric of polarization by looking at the tactics used to construct each side's version of "reality." The following discussion looks at the rhetorical tactics employed by two different activist groups. The first section examines the highly controversial rhetoric of **Earth First!**, a radical environmental group best known for its use of **ecotage,** sabotage done in the name of protecting nature. The second section examines the use of dichotomies in the rhetoric of the **Wise Use Movement,** a well-organized and powerful anti-environmental group. These two groups represent vastly divergent philosophical positions about humans' relationship to the natural world. Earth First! subscribes to the ecocentric philosophy of deep ecology. The Wise Use movement could best be described as adhering to a highly anthropocentric form of stewardship that advocates doing away with many government-mandated environmental controls and regulations and turning more of the management of public lands over to those whose livelihood depends on the extraction or use of the natural resources.

Recognizing and understanding the tactics used in public campaigns to construct any given environmental "reality" helps us to become more critical consumers of the rhetoric. These taxonomies of polarizing themes can also serve as tools of analysis in performing your own examination of other public campaigns.

Earth First! and the Rhetoric of Polarization

"No Compromise in Defense of Mother Earth!" This is the motto and prevailing rhetorical stance of Earth First!, a controversial environmental group best known for the dramatic image events and unconventional tactics it uses to publicize environmental issues. Founded in 1980 by five environmental activists who were disillusioned with what they saw as co-optation and compromise by the mainstream environmental groups, Earth First! has taken actions that have raised the stakes in the environmental struggle.

Dave Foreman, cofounder and charismatic leader of Earth First!, had previously served as chief lobbyist for the Wilderness Society, one of the country's largest and most respected environmental lobbying groups. After one particularly disappointing political setback, Foreman left his position with the Wilderness Society in 1979 and called some friends together for a camping trip in the Pinacate Desert in Mexico. As one popular magazine described the now-legendary camping trip:

> They hit the Mexican border running on beer and tequila and an agenda: preserve natural diversity by any means, legal or not, and reclaim lost ground—close logging roads, tear down dams, reintroduce grizzlies and wolves and elk. They united as a 'disorganization' with no official members and no directors, and called themselves "Earth First!"[1]

Foreman and his colleagues were inspired by a book by Edward Abbey (a friend of Foreman's), *The Monkey Wrench Gang*, about a group known as the Eco-Raiders who used unconventional and unlawful tactics in their struggle to slow the growth of the Tucson suburbs.[2] Today, the "disorganization," with no paid staff, no centralized hierarchical structure, and no bylaws, includes a diverse group of "nonmembers." The Round River Rendezvous, a meeting held once a year in a wilderness area, draws an assorted mix of participants described by rhetorical scholar Jonathan I. Lange as "'rednecks' and 'hippies,' vegetarians and hunters, agnostics and Taoists, drop-outs and tenured professors. There are anarchists, Marxists, those who 'don't give a damn about economic issues since saving the earth is the real issue,' teenagers dubbed 'Little Wolves,' and a Pulitzer Prize winning poet."[3]

Although Foreman resigned from Earth First! in 1990 due to increasing philosophical differences among its leaders, throughout his years with the "disorganization" he provided inspiration to a generation of disillusioned environmentalists and enough rhetoric to inflame opponents for years to come.

Earth First!'s founding doctrine reflects the radical, ecocentric philosophy of deep ecology that motivates the actions of its followers. Earth First! principles hold that all life forms have an inherent and equal right to exist and that no form of life has a legitimate claim to dominate and destroy the natural world.

Its web site (www.EarthFirst.org) describes the movement as a "diverse, passionate, committed, and uncompromising group of environmental activists," and goes on to say that "Our direct actions in defense of the last wild places only seem radical compared to an entire paradigm of denial and control, where the individual is convinced they are powerless, and the organizations set up to protect the wilderness continue to bargain it away." With its motto of "No compromise in defense of Mother Earth," Earth First! understandably uses rhetoric, both discursive and nondiscursive, that is likewise uncompromising and polarizing.

The Nondiscursive Rhetoric of Earth First!

The radical rhetoric of Earth First! employs both nondiscursive and discursive tactics. Its nondiscursive rhetorical tactics include nonviolent civil disobedience and confrontation. In the past, the tactics also included private property destruction that called attention to activities that were destroying nature. (The Supreme Court has ruled that some acts of civil disobedience, such as marches, sit-ins, and parading in costumes, are "symbolic speech" entitled to First Amendment protection. However, direct acts of violence, such as vandalism, arson, and property destruction, are not protected.)

The direct acts of property destruction have been given various labels, including **monkeywrenching, ecotage,** and **ecodefense.** The FBI has given yet another label to these acts—**ecoterrorism.** Whether they are labeled "ecodefense" or "ecoterrorism," they are rhetorical acts in which the message is not sent primarily though discursive means. They are image events that draw attention to the particular environmental issue in question and offer "critique through spectacle"[4] of environmentally destructive practices. Not surprisingly, many people denounce ecotage tactics as morally reprehensible, but Earth First! activists saw protecting the earth as a moral imperative, no matter what the cost.

In his book *Ecodefense: A Field Guide to Monkeywrenching,* Foreman outlined the principles and tactics of ecotage and called on activists "to act heroically and admittedly illegally in defense of the wild, to put a monkeywrench into the gears of the machine destroying natural diversity."[5] Ecotage activists were encouraged to work alone or in small groups, and Earth First! claimed no "official" support for ecotage activities. Foreman explained that "while Earth First! doesn't officially engage in monkeywrenching, or even officially advocate it, we also don't *not* advocate it."[6]

Early Earth First! activists maintained that monkeywrenching was nonviolent because "it is not directed toward human beings or other forms of life. It is aimed at inanimate machines and tools."[7] For groups with limited resources and limited access to bases of political power, this kind of direct action is a cost-effective and resource-efficient means of drawing public attention to a particular environmental issue and, at the same time, increasing the costs for the target of the campaign. (Earth First! no longer condones, officially or unofficially, acts that result in private property destruction. Those who disagreed with this anti-destruction stance broke from Earth First! and became a part of a group calling itself the Earth Liberation Front, discussed later in this chapter.)

An example of the nondiscursive rhetorical tactics that Earth First! activists employed was tree spiking, which involved driving metal spikes into trees to prevent them from being cut. Tree spiking received a great deal of criticism because it risked injuring loggers if their saw blades struck the almost invisible spikes in the process of felling the tree or milling the log. Because the goal of Earth First! activists was not to harm loggers but to prevent logging, Earth First! activists let it be widely known that trees had been spiked.

Other acts of ecotage for which Earth First! was credited include road spiking, where spikes were placed in logging roads to destroy truck tires; pulling up survey stakes to confuse developers; disabling heavy equipment and power lines; using paint bags to splatter billboards and buildings; cementing themselves into roadblocks; chaining themselves to trees and logging equipment; and parading down Wall Street dressed as spotted owls.

One of the most publicized and well-known acts of nonviolent nondiscursive rhetoric occurred in March 1981, at the opening ceremonies of the Glen Canyon Dam in Arizona. While demonstrators distracted police, Earth First! activists unfurled a three hundred–foot black plastic "crack" from the dam's parapet, creating an illusion of the dam's destruction. Another famous act of confrontation occurred at

Mount Rushmore, where Earth First! activists draped a 160 by 80 foot banner across the face of George Washington with a message that read, "We the People Say No to Acid Rain."

Earth First!ers have also gained public attention for tree-sitting as a means of protesting the logging of old-growth trees and giant redwoods. The most famous of all tree-sitters is Julia Hill, also known as Butterfly. On December 10, 1997, she took up residence on a six by eight–foot platform high up in a 180-foot redwood that activists had named Luna. For over two years she slept, cooked, and weathered the violent storms of the Pacific Northwest in her treetop protest perch. Finally, on December 18, 1999, an agreement was reached with the various logging companies. In exchange for $50,000, the logging companies agreed to allow Luna to remain standing, along with a 2.9 acre buffer zone surrounding the tree. The next day, Butterfly descended from the tree, fell to the ground, and wept amidst the roots of her ancient friend.

In 1992 the **Earth Liberation Front (E.L.F.),** an extreme offshoot of Earth First!, was established in Brighton, England, by radical members of Earth First! who felt that the organization was becoming too mainstream. The first time a United States E.L.F. group claimed responsibility for an ecotage action was in 1996, when the locks at two McDonalds's in Eugene, Oregon, were glued and spray painted to protest corporate environmental destruction. Since then, the E.L.F. has claimed responsibility for dozens of destructive actions.

The costliest act of ecotage to date occurred on August 1, 2003, when a five-story 206-unit apartment complex under construction was set fire and destroyed in a San Diego neighborhood. The cost of this act of arson was estimated to be $50 million.[8] A twelve-foot banner left at the scene of the fire read "If you build it, we will burn it." It was signed "The E.L.F.s are mad."

Another highly destructive act for which E.L.F. claimed responsibility was setting fire to Vail Mountain, Colorado, in 1998, damaging several ski lifts and destroying a restaurant, a patrol building, and a picnic shelter. The total cost of the arson was estimated to be over $12 million. This was done to draw attention to the plight of the lynx, whose habitat was being devastated by resort construction and development.

E.L.F. activists have likewise targeted sports utility vehicles (SUVs), which are criticized by E.L.F. activists as air polluting, gas-guzzling despoilers of the earth. Slogans with words like "avarice" and "gluttony" were painted on Land Rovers at a Santa Fe dealership and on SUVs in four dealerships in California.

Although the E.L.F. activities tend to be more destructive than were those of Earth First!, E.L.F. also publicly disavows the harming of any human being. Nevertheless, the FBI has classified E.L.F. as the number one domestic terrorist group in the United States today. The actions of E.L.F. represent the extreme end of the ecotage continuum and are the exception rather than the rule. For the most part, Earth First! activities have remained largely symbolic and nonviolent.

Discursive Rhetorical Themes of Earth First!

Consistent with Earth First!'s use of unconventional nondiscursive tactics, the discursive rhetoric of Earth First! is likewise radical and extreme in defense of Mother Earth. The following discussion examines three rhetorical themes that predominate in Earth First! rhetoric: *war, moral action,* and *vilification.*

Figure 6.1   Julia Hill

Julia "Butterfly" Hill looks out from her 180-foot perch in a 1,000-year-old redwood that activists named Luna, where she made history for her world record tree-sit. When her supporters finally made a deal with the lumber company to spare the tree, she came down after having spent 738 days in the tree through some of the worst storms in California history—a dedicated activist, indeed.

AP/WIDE WORLD PHOTOS

The *war* or warrior metaphor is repeatedly stressed in Earth First! rhetoric. Dave Foreman, as its primary spokesperson for nearly ten years, was largely instrumental in establishing Earth First! as a "warrior society."[9] "Earth First! is warriors!" screams Foreman at the 1987 annual rendezvous, "and if you aren't a warrior, then I suggest you find another group." Earth First! activists "are not a debating society," says Foreman. They are "men and women who are planting their spears in the ground and who are taking a stand."[10]

Earth First! activists attempt to legitimize acts of confrontation discursively, by drawing a parallel between their war and others. As one Earth First! activist states, "Now . . . the 50th anniversary of D-Day will also be remembered as D-Day for the forests, the day the final assault on our tattered remnant of an ancient forest system was sanctioned by the very groups who should have stood shoulder to shoulder in uncompromising defense."[11] Drawing on the words of John Muir, Foreman urged his audience to pick a side in the war: "John Muir said that if it ever came to a war between the races, he would side with the bears. That day has arrived."[12]

Moral action is another rhetorical theme that is stressed by Earth First! activists. Establishing the moral righteousness of the cause to justify their actions is of critical importance to the movement. Foreman counseled Earth First! activists to remember that monkeywrenching was "not a casual or flippant affair," to "keep a pure heart and mind about it," and to "remember that they are engaged in the most moral of all actions: protecting the earth."[13]

A great deal of Earth First! rhetoric is used to identify and *vilify the enemy,* another prevalent theme. Foreman clearly identifies the enemy in the following example:

> With bulldozer, earth mover, chainsaw and dynamite, the international timber, mining and beef industries are invading our public lands . . . bashing their way into our forests, mountains and range-lands and looting them for everything they can get away with. This for the sake of short-term profits in the corporate sector and multi-million dollar annual salaries for the three-piece-suited gangsters . . . who control and manage these bandit enterprises.[14]

Ridicule is a common strategy used to vilify the enemy. In formal argumentation, ridicule is eschewed for establishing a claim without proof. In other words, name-calling is not proof of the "wrongness" of another's ideas. Nevertheless, ridicule does serve a purpose, even though it doesn't meet the criteria of sound reasoning in formal argumentation. Ridicule serves two functions: it reduces the worth of the enemy and, at the same time, creates a confirmatory sense of superiority and unity for Earth First! activists.[15]

Earth First! rhetoric employs a great deal of inflammatory name-calling as a form of ridicule. Rhetorical scholar Lisa Heller offers examples of Earth First! rhetoric used to mock and inflame the opposition. Forest Service employees are "fascist Freddies." Corporate CEOs are "the slugs and thugs of industry." A law officer is "Deputy Dipshit" and a politician is a "puke." They are all "corrupt," "sleazy" "bastards with greed glands."[16]

The Legacy of Earth First!

Not surprisingly, the extreme discursive and nondiscursive rhetoric of Earth First! has garnered strong retaliatory rhetoric from the opposition. Environmental communication scholar Brant Short summarizes a few of these opposition voices from the media: The *Missoulian* called tree-spikers "no more than rural versions of the valueless human vermin." The *Idaho State Journal* called Earth First! the "skunk at the picnic." The *Idaho Statesman* called tree-spikers the "eco-equivalent of neo-Nazi skinheads."[17]

Earth First! activists have likewise received criticism from mainstream environmental groups. Their past monkeywrenching tactics were denounced by mainstream environmental groups, who have given them such labels as "terrorists" and "irresponsible, beer-drinking adolescents."[18] Earth First! activists have been criticized for alienating the public by their acts of ecotage. Many people believe that all environmental groups suffer in the public's eye because of the "dirty deeds" committed by activists involved with a group that, in reality, represents only a small percentage of environmentalists in the United States.

While these criticisms may be warranted, communication scholar Jonathan I. Lange suggests that the radical texts of Earth First! and other radical groups, when viewed in the larger context of the environmental movement, may actually aid the cause of environmental protection in at least three ways.[19] First, the media attention that activists receive through their outrageous discursive and nondiscursive rhetoric draws public attention and increases awareness of environmental issues. So, for example, while many may have felt that the E.L.F. activists' arson at the Vail ski resort (discussed earlier in this chapter) was a reprehensible act of willful and irresponsible destruction, media consumers were nonetheless made aware of the problem of the disappearing lynx habitat.

A second function that radical groups such as Earth First! serve in the larger environmental picture is that they make mainstream groups working within the system seem "reasonable" and "responsible" by comparison. T. O. Hellenbach, a contributing author in Foreman's *Ecodefense: A Field Guide to Monkeywrenching*, explains, "Industry considers mainstream environmentalists to be radical until they get a taste of real radical activism. Suddenly the soft-sell of the Sierra Club and other white-shirt-and-tie ecobureaucrats becomes much more attractive and worthy of serious negotiation."[20]

A third way in which Earth First! serves the goals of the larger environmental movement is by broadening and transforming the environmental debate. Lange suggests that the radical rhetoric of Earth First! activists offers dreams of "the ideal environmental vision" through the stated belief in possibilities such as the re-introduction of nearly vanished species and the reclamation of wilderness areas. This vision serves to express the possibilities and expand the boundaries of the environmental debate for both radical and mainstream environmentalists.[21]

Dave Foreman resigned from Earth First! in 1990 due to increasing discontent with the philosophical turn that was beginning to create rifts in many environmental organizations at that time. He believed that the deep ecological tenets of wilderness preservation, upon which the group was founded, were being diluted or obscured by the organization's shift, from what many criticized as its misanthropic emphasis on biocentrism and wilderness protection, to a more anthropocentric emphasis on social justice and issues of urban pollution.

Foreman has remained true to his unyielding commitment to wilderness protection. In 1991 he started the Wildlands Project, with Michael Soulé (www.wildlandsproject.org). Its slogan is "Reconnect, Restore, Rewild." In his 2004 book, *Rewilding North America: A Vision for Conservation in the 21st Century,*[22] Foreman lays out a carefully constructed and meticulously researched plan for a continental wildlands network based on the science of conservation biology. In place of the current island-like protected wildlands, his plan for a network would provide a way to link existing wildlands, allowing for the movement of wide-ranging species through protected corridors—movement that is critical for the viability of many species as well as the ecosystems that support them. Although his rhetoric is considerably less polarizing than it was in his early years with Earth First!, Foreman's eloquence and insight continue to inspire news ways of thinking and a new generation of "earth warriors."

Whether or not the radical rhetoric and tactics of Earth First! are ultimately contributing to the protection of the natural world remains an open question. Yet, most would agree that these activists have redefined the parameters of the environmental debate by articulating alternative views of reality that challenge the largely unsustainable mainstream views. As author and columnist Susan Zakin explains:

> Beneath their beer-drinking, gonzo forays into guerilla theatre—and occasional lapses into guerilla war—Earth First!'s founders shared the goals of the great innovative environmentalists who preceded them, people like Aldo Leopold, Bob Marshall, and David Brower. With these historic figures very much in mind, the hardscrabble Earth First! cowboys expanded the reach of the hundred-year-old environmental movement to include a truly ecological worldview.[23]

We move now from an examination of the extreme rhetoric of Earth First! to the extreme rhetoric of the Wise Use movement that gained momentum in the 1990s. Although Earth First! and Wise Use are poles apart philosophically and politically, you will see a great deal of similarity in their use of polarizing rhetoric.

Wise Use and the Rhetoric of Polarization

Sporting a bright red tie depicting a baby triceratops, former Speaker of the House Newt Gingrich stepped to the speaker's podium in front of several hundred environmentalists and policy makers and quipped, "these things happen, life is like that." This cavalier attitude toward species extinction reflected the anti-environmental sentiments that swept the country in the 1990s. A well-organized, anti-environmental coalition calling itself the "Wise Use" movement emerged to challenge the environmental protections that had gained a foothold in U.S. policies since the first Earth Day in 1970. While environmentalists first dismissed the Wise Use movement as anti-environmental extremists, they soon began to realize that they were facing perhaps the most aggressive adversary in the history of the environmental movement.

"Wise Use" takes its name from a 1907 quotation by Gifford Pinchot, the first chief of the U.S. Forest Service, who said, "Conservation is the *wise use* of resources." However, the use of Pinchot's phrase to name the movement is disingenuous in that Wise Use literature explicitly points out that the modern wise use movement views Pinchot as a federal bureaucrat who believed that it was the government's role to protect and conserve natural resources.[24] Wise Use organizations reject government interference in resource use, including the policies and regulations that Pinchot was instrumental in establishing.

Much of Wise Use literature is disseminated via the web site of the Center for the Defense of Free Enterprise (www.cdfe.org/center-projects/wise-use). This organization, founded by Alan Gottlieb in 1980 with Ron Arnold as executive vice president, was instrumental in organizing the movement, articulating its manifesto and operating principles, and creating links among the scattered and diverse groups of supporters.

Wise Use leaders claim an "exotic miscellany" of more than fifteen hundred affiliated organizations scattered across the county. Those gathered at the 1988 Wise Use Leadership Conference held in Reno, Nevada, give a sense of the "hodgepodge" that makes up the roster of Wise Use supporters—including western ranchers concerned about their grazing subsidies on public lands; fishermen, loggers, and miners whose jobs have been negatively impacted by environmental regulations; and snowmobile and other off-road vehicle clubs seeking greater access to public lands.[25]

Wise Use organizations portray themselves as the "grassroots" insurgence of "the oppressed little guy" who has been hurt by restrictive environmental regulations. Yet, in some ways, this "grassroots" portrayal is misleading, in that the movement is heavily funded by the large corporations of the extractive industries and the manufacturers of off-road vehicles. J. D. Hair, president of the National Wildlife Federation from 1981 to 1995, described these organizations as "the wallet heavy industries—big timber, big logging, big mining, and big development, that stand to profit handsomely by linking their goals with what they hope to define as a grassroots populists movement."[26]

Perhaps the wisest tactic of the Wise Use movement is in giving its affiliated organizations names that imply environmental advocacy but in such an abstract way that the organizations cannot actually be accused of blatant misrepresentation of their underlying agendas. (J. D. Hair has labeled it a "wise disguise.") For example, *The National Wetlands Coalition,* sponsored by oil and gas companies and developers, is one of the leading opponents of wetlands regulations. *The Environmental*

Conservation Association is a coalition of farm associations, builders, and developers that lobbies against wetland protection legislation. *The Marine Preservation Association* is an organization of oil companies whose purpose is to promote the interests of the petroleum and energy industries.[27]

One must be careful, however, not to minimize the movement as just the grumbling of those with self-serving interests spurred on by big business. Doing so, says environmental writer Phil Brick, "underestimates the rage on the range and the potential power of committed Wise Use activists to torpedo environmental progress in the West."[28] It also underestimates the sacrifices demanded of those who are impacted most by across-the-board environmental policies. As Jon Roush, former president of The Wilderness Society, explains:

> Policies [such as] protecting endangered species . . . demand that people change deep habits of environmental behavior. They restrict access to resources and limit their use. They demand that people not use available technologies and materials. They claim benefits that are obscure and hard to prove. They ask us to forego concrete benefits today for theoretical ones in an indeterminate future.[29]

Environmentalists would do well to remember that the sacrifices demanded by environmental protection policies are often not shared equally by all.

Key Political Issues of Wise Use

The Wise Use movement grew out of the **Sagebrush Rebellion** of the 1970s, a movement of western ranchers, loggers, and miners to return control of federal lands to individual states or private owners. The eleven states involved in the rebellion felt that the land was rightfully theirs and that the extraction of resources through mining, grazing, and logging was the best use of the land.

The 1980s marked a reversal in the move toward environmental protections. Ronald Reagan was the first U.S. president to make a determined push to drastically roll back environmental regulations. His administration, with widespread support from industry and landowners, dismantled or repealed many existing environmental regulations and drastically cut the budgets of environmental regulatory agencies. His appointments to key environmental positions reflected Reagan's hostility toward environmental regulations. For example, Donald Hodel, whom he appointed as Energy Secretary, became notorious for suggesting that the way to deal with ozone depletion is to apply stronger suntan lotion. Reagan's Secretary of the Interior, James Watt, and his head of the Environmental Protection Agency, Ann Gorsuch Burford, have gone down in history for their fanatical zeal in dismantling environmental protection programs.

The conservative backlash was driven by three key political issues that anti-environmental groups have rigorously promoted. The first is anti-regulation—the drive to limit government regulatory intrusion into the livelihoods of private citizens. The Wise Use movement portrays environmentalists as supporters of big bureaucratic government and intrusive regulations. The main goal of the Center for the Defense of Free Enterprise, the organization that coordinates Wise Use activities and serves as its campaign headquarters, is "to defend the right of individual Americans and American businesses to participate in the free market without hindrance by government."[30]

Figure 6.2   Loggers vs. Greenpeace

The bitter dispute between the timber industry and environmentalists over logging old-growth forests has been raging for decades and remains a fiercely polarizing issue today. In a 1997 protest against Greenpeace's ongoing efforts to stop logging in old-growth forests, angry members of the International Woodworkers Association (IWA) blockaded Greenpeace's ship, the *Arctic Sunrise*, with a log boom that prevented it from leaving harbor in Vancouver, British Columbia. In this photo, Greenpeace Canada executive director Jeanne Moffat confronts Ken Bayers, an IWA member.
REUTERS

A second key political issue for the Wise Use movement is private property rights, for which government regulations are seen as a threat. Property rights advocates have been emboldened by several Supreme Court rulings that have supported the notion of **regulatory takings,** in which property is "taken" or its value is greatly diminished because of environmental regulations.

Environmental writer Phil Brick summarizes the Wise Use stance on regulatory takings: "The Fifth Amendment to the U.S. Constitution guarantees compensation for property taken by eminent domain. Property rights advocates want compensation extended to property 'taken' by government regulations, even if the 'taking' is only partial."[31] They argue, for example, that because endangered species regulations restrict land use options in order to protect the habitat of an endangered species, the land's value is decreased and the government should be required to compensate the landowner. Environmentalists are concerned that the interpretation of the takings clause might be routinely expanded to include regulatory takings, which would have broadly sweeping implications for many environmental protection measures and make them extremely expensive to enforce.

The third key political issue for the Wise Use movement is job loss and economic problems. Its supporters argue, for example, that regulations protecting endangered species or wetlands result in logging or development restrictions, thereby leading to loss of employment. This theme taps into citizens' understandably deep anxiety about the economy and job security.

Although Wise Use has many more political positions, these represent its supporters' major concerns. Many of its rhetorical strategies are grounded in these concerns, as you will see in the following section.

Wise Use and Polar Dichotomies

Wise Use supporters employ rhetorical strategies to construct polar dichotomies in which they characterize themselves as upholding the highest values in a moral struggle against environmentalists, who are characterized as threatening or opposing those values. The following section discusses three polar dichotomies that repeatedly emerge in Wise Use rhetoric: *home folks versus the institutionalized elite; radical alarmists versus reasonable realists;* and *true believers versus pagan tree worshippers.*

Home Folks vs. the Institutionalized Elite

Wise Use rhetoric characterizes the environmental movement as firmly positioned within the establishment, part of the institutional elite. Ron Arnold, executive vice president of the Center for the Defense of Free Enterprise, expresses this view of environmentalism when he states, "Today the Wolf is firmly entrenched in Washington, D.C. . . . They have, in brief, become the establishment."[32]

Names serve as powerful reality-mediating influences (as discussed in Chapter 1). Note the use of "Wolf" to name environmentalists in the above quotation. In attaching this name with all of its common associations, Ron Arnold has rhetorically constructed a vicious, voracious, powerful enemy "entrenched" within the bases of power.

For those who depend on the extractive industries for their livelihood, environmentalists who would advocate such things as tightening the 1872 Mining Act, restricting old growth logging, limiting grazing on federal lands, or mandating the use of turtle excluder devices in shrimp trawl nets are seen as "interfering, power elitists" who impose their will without regard for those whose livelihoods are impacted by such restrictions.

In contrast, Wise Use rhetoric portrays its own constituency as "home folks" who as loggers, ranchers, miners, or farmers are more qualified to understand and protect their natural resources than are the "elitist environmentalists," whom Arnold describes as "urban environmentalists defending their vision of the pastoral ideal against those who actually live the pastoral ideal."[33]

The scenario likewise lends itself to the rhetorical construction of the "oppressed little guy." Arnold draws on this appeal when he claims that "Environmentalism's ideology was promulgated for the ruling elite, not for the farmer or rancher or family forest owner or mineral prospector." [34]

Radical Alarmists vs. Reasonable Realists

Polarizing rhetoric ignores the highly nuanced space between poles, and Wise Use rhetoric is no exception. Although environmentalism spans a broad continuum of perspectives and philosophies (as discussed in Chapters 3 and 4), Wise Use rhetoric ignores the broad distinctions between radical and mainstream environmentalism. Radical environmental rhetoric is quoted by the Wise Use movement as representing the perspectives of all environmentalists. Wise Use advocates have made a virtual cottage industry of reprinting selected excerpts from radical environmental rhetoric, with Dave Foreman's (Earth First!) uncompromising rhetoric supplying a great deal of the inflammatory text.

Much of Wise Use rhetoric is spent attempting to subvert the apocalyptic threats upon which environmentalists have based a large share of their rhetoric. One way Wise Use advocates do this is by simply denying that the planet Earth has any real problems, claiming that anyone who believes otherwise has bought into the scare tactics of the apocalypse abusers. Books with titles such as *Environmental Overkill*,[35] *Eco-Scam*,[36] *Apocalypse Not*,[37] *Eco-Sanity*,[38] and *Environmental Deceptions*,[39] to name only a few, were popular in the 1990s, advancing an "alternative science" that attempts to debunk the environmental "doomsday myths." Dixie Lee Ray, the first woman to head the Atomic Energy Commission and former Governor of Washington, succinctly articulated this perspective at the 1992 Wise Use Leadership Conference: "I don't support that damage to the earth is being done and that man is responsible."[40]

In addition to simply denying that the planet Earth has any real problems, anti-environmental rhetoric devotes a great deal of attention to the notion that nature does more to destroy itself than does any human activity. Speaking on a radio talk show in 1993, Dixie Lee Ray took this position to new heights, claiming that trees create a great deal of smog and that about one-half of acid rain comes from natural sources. According to Ray, however, this is not a problem, as smog is largely harmless and acid rain is beneficial to forests because it releases plant nutrients.[41]

One of the loudest and most powerful voices speaking out against the doomsayers is that of radio and television personality Rush Limbaugh. In his 1992 book, *The Way Things Ought to Be*, Limbaugh argues:

> Mount Pinatuba in the Philippines spewed forth more than a thousand times the amount of ozone-depleting chemicals in one eruption than all the fluorocarbons in history . . . . In other words, Mother Nature has been attacking her own stratospheric ozone for millions of years and yet the ozone is still there, and in sufficient quantities to protect Democrats and environmental wackos alike from skin cancer.[42]

Another way in which anti-environmental rhetoric attempts to subvert apocalyptic fears is through stressing the notion that environmental damage is the unavoidable price of human survival, but "the earth and its life are tough and resilient, not fragile and delicate."[43] A great deal of faith is placed in human ingenuity to overcome any environmental catastrophes that may necessarily occur in the struggle for survival. This attitude of optimism is summarized by Ronald Bailey in his book *Eco-Scam*, when he states, "Human history shows that our energy and creativity will surmount whatever difficulties we encounter . . . as the last fifty years of solid achievement show, there is nothing out there that we cannot handle."[44]

Another way anti-environmentalists have attempted to debunk environmentalists' doomsday warnings is by attributing self-serving agendas to environmentalists. What are those hidden agendas? Limbaugh suggests they are scams perpetuated by environmental scientists to increase research funding. Other hidden agendas attributed to environmentalists include the propagation of pantheistic religious beliefs and advancing socialism through the elimination of individual rights and property ownership—two themes used repeatedly in the polarizing rhetoric of Wise Use.

True Believers vs. Pagan Tree Worshippers

The philosophical differences between anthropocentric and ecocentric views of the human/nature relationship have been used extensively in the Wise Use movement to create polarization. The Biblical anthropocentric view, which holds that God gave humans "dominion over the fish of the sea, and over the fowls of the air, and over every living thing that moveth upon the earth,"[45] is the basis upon which the Wise Use view of the human/nature relationship is sanctioned.

Wise Use rhetoric portrays environmentalists as "toad stool worshipers and land embalmers"[46] who are attempting to create a world in which humans are sacrificed to the god of nature. Examples of environmentalists' radical rhetoric are used to drive an emotionally charged wedge between "pagan environmentalists" and "true believers." Helen Chenoweth, Representative from Idaho, forwarded this view when she said in a speech on the floor of the House in 1996, "This religion, a cloudy mixture of New Age mysticism, Native American folklore and primitive earth worship—pantheism—is being promoted and enforced . . . in violation of our rights and jobs."[47] Chenoweth's statement employs ideographs in a rhetorical appeal to some of our most valued ideals. Wise Use advocates are called on to unite in a moral struggle against those who threaten "religion," "rights," and "jobs."

The Wise Use Legacy

The political influence of Wise Use peaked with the 1994 Republican "Contract with America," which supported many tenets of the Wise Use agenda. By the end of the 1990s, the movement had begun to fade from the headlines. Environmental communication scholar Jennifer A. Peeples suggested that "Wise Use members may have chosen to relax their vigilance, having been emboldened by the Republican sweep [in the 2000 elections], and further reassured by the election of George W. Bush . . . that their work was in the hands of the federal government."[48] These assumptions were perhaps not unfounded.

The legacy of the Wise Use movement will be felt for generations to come. Many environmental protections succumbed to the policy retrenchments of the conservative administration of George W. Bush (2001–2008). Among other things, the Bush administration rolled back wetlands protections, undermined safeguards in the Clean Air Act, weakened mining regulations, dismissed habitat protections for endangered species, and froze the roadless policy of the Clinton administration. So drastic are these cutbacks in environmental protections that the League of Conservation Voters gave George W. Bush an "F" on its Presidential Report Card—the first failing grade ever given to a president since the League was founded in 1969 for the purpose of informing the voting public on the environmental voting records of political candidates.[49] With the change of administration under the leadership of Barack Obama there is hope for an improved presidential report card, but only the future will reveal whether and how the challenges will be met.

Some Implications of Polarizing Rhetoric

Polarizing rhetoric can be used effectively to unify and mobilize group members against a common foe. However, polarization as a means to divide in order to unite has potential consequences that may ultimately do more to hinder than advance the cause for which it is used. It symbolically creates a falsely dichotomous black-versus-white division that allows for no shades of gray. Yet spanning the distance between the poles are highly complex issues, multiple voices, and alternative perspectives. Failure to recognize and consider the "gray areas" can have consequences that are harmful to both sides.

One consequence of polarizing rhetoric is that *issues tend to be oversimplified and dramatized*. Rhetoric that is intended to unite through division must amplify the "evilness" of the opposition and extol its own righteousness. Issues that are capsized into polar dichotomies—right versus wrong, good versus evil, us versus them—must necessarily be simplified and dramatized. Complex issues are often capsized into a single phrase or sentence, as artfully demonstrated by the T-shirt and bumper sticker slogans mentioned at the start of this chapter. It is easy to discern from this insipid (albeit amusing) rhetoric that very little public education is advanced through such simplification and dramatization of the issues.

Another consequence of polarizing rhetoric is that *it inhibits the possibility of collaborative solutions*. Creating falsely dichotomous choices, in which one side is viewed as morally right and the opposing side as morally defunct, reifies or fixes the issues as moral certainties. This result does not allow for thoughtful consideration of alternative viewpoints. After all, one does not attempt to negotiate with the devil incarnate. The result is often costly and time-consuming lawsuits and appeals that can drag on for years.

A third potential consequence of polarizing rhetoric is that *it tends to create a self-reinforcing, self-perpetuating conflict* as both sides become locked into the spiral of interaction that polarization creates. Negative charges and public vilification of the opposition almost demand a reciprocal response. Those who are targeted by the negative rhetoric are compelled to level charges that are equally or more negative against their opponents, who must then respond with more negative charges, causing more reciprocal charges, and on it goes in a never-ending spiral. As communication scholar Jonathan I. Lange puts it, "The system is the best explanation for itself; a specific communicative act by one interlocutor practically 'forces' a predetermined response by the other. Parties become locked in to a systemic, self-reinforcing, patterned, and repetitive practice."[50]

This pattern of reciprocal responses and the bitter divisiveness it creates can be observed in many political conflicts that we witness through mass-mediated campaigns. The public is often left wondering why parties can't seem to rise above the trivialized and dramatized nature of the conflict. Yet, once the negative spiral is set in motion, the failure of one side to respond to the negative charges of the other could spell disaster for its cause. The system is co-created and self-reinforcing, symbolically constructed and maintained through polarizing rhetoric.

Because of its tendency to simplify and its potential for creating irreconcilable divisiveness, rhetorical scholars have traditionally criticized the use of polarizing rhetoric. Yet, this criticism is based on the assumption that the primary function of rhetoric should be social unification. Environmental communication scholar Steven Schwarze questions this assumption and suggests that rhetorical scholars should perhaps take another, more flexible and tolerant look at polarizing rhetoric—that it has its place and time.[51]

Another View of Polarizing Rhetoric

Steven Schwarze looked at the highly polarizing rhetorical form of the melodrama used by activists in Libby, Montana. As a result of almost a century of mining and milling asbestos-contaminated vermiculite near the town by the mining company,

W. R. Grace, over two hundred people have died from asbestos-related diseases. Many others show evidence of asbestos-related lung abnormalities. Schwarze examined the public discourse that emerged in public meetings, journalistic accounts, and film documentaries, and found that across these multiple genres, the highly polarizing melodramatic form was used consistently.

Although the previous discussion of the rhetoric of Earth First! and Wise Use is organized around common rhetorical themes used to polarize, melodramatic characteristics are also easily recognizable in their rhetoric. The **melodramatic form** has four characteristics: (1) melodrama is social and political conflict (rather than inner or personal conflict); (2) melodrama clarifies through polarization by bringing the characters into sharp bipolar contrast and clearly distinguishing the "good guys" from the "bad guys;" (3) melodrama is moralistic and frames the drama as a moral clash; and (4) melodrama is monopathic (the actors are emotionally unified against a common foe).

The investigation of the Libby public discourse revealed that the use of melodrama went far beyond simplifying the issues and dividing the opposing sides in the controversy. Schwarze suggests that there are times when melodrama can, in fact, perform productive transformative actions. He points out five such actions.

First, *melodrama can frame the conflict as a social and political issue rather than as a private issue.* Sometimes polarization is a necessary first step in recognizing the social and political implications of a given situation. To illustrate this point, Schwarze explains that the W. R. Grace company had downplayed the hazards of asbestos by attributing the health problems of its workers to the high incidence of smoking. As a result, the health problems were "privatized" rather than being perceived as a social or political issue. Newspaper accounts served to transform this perception by exposing company memos that showed that the company did, in fact, know that workers were getting sick from asbestos, thereby transforming the rhetoric from the privatized plane (workers' individual choices to engage in unhealthy behavior) to the social/political plane (innocent victims harmed by the self-serving deception of a powerful company).

A second transformative action of melodrama is that *it can challenge previously unquestioned social relationships.* W. R. Grace was almost universally viewed as a good community citizen that provided jobs to many local residents. The melodramatic rhetoric of newspaper accounts and activists worked to reconfigure that relationship by calling attention to the long-standing trust that the company had violated. Schwarze points out that in this case, "melodrama effectively redefined the characters in the situation; instead of being viewed as a pillar of the community or a partner in cleanup, the company rightfully came to be seen as an enemy of the people and their health."[52]

A third transformative action of melodrama is that *it can reframe the conflict as a moral issue rather than as a scientific or technical issue.* Melodrama is an especially effective frame for foregrounding moral issues because, as Schwarze points out, "it frames situations as confrontations between the virtuous and the villainous, and encourages audiences to take sides in such confrontations in order to repair the moral order."[53] Schwarze tells of one journalist's report that company officials had tracked its workers' health status for years through an annual lung x-ray program, and that W. R. Grace was well aware of the workers' health problems. This report put the inaccuracy of the company's reassuring scientific language on display and, at the same time, demonstrated the moral indifference of the "villainous" toward the trusting "virtuous."

Connections

Rhetorics of Unification:
Words of Wombat Wisdom

The silly-looking, fast-talking wombat created by the Global Mindshift tells us:

All this stuff, the animals, the waters, the sky, the ground, the bugs, the fish, the tacos, the people—they're all connected. Everything's connected. . . . So listen up. It's all one—not two worlds, not three—one, just one. (www.global-mindshift.org/memes/wombat.swf).

Environmental discourse can polarize and divide, but it can also unify and connect people to people, people to issues, and people to nature. In light of the magnitude of the challenges we face, a truly sustainable future will require a cooperative and coordinated global effort. Global Mindshift is only one of many groups working for the unification of our fragmented and fractious world. Here are just a few others you might want to check out.

One unification effort is the "We Campaign," a project of the Alliance for Climate Protection founded by Nobel laureate and former vice president Al Gore. This campaign works to organize and bring together individuals, groups, and companies to "build a movement that creates the political will to solve the climate crisis" (http://wecansolveit.org).

Another unification organization is the Global Ecovillage Network, whose goal is to support the development of sustainable "ecovillages" around the world. Ecovillages are communities that have adopted sustainable practices such as ecological design, permaculture, green buildings, and alternative energy. The vast network includes villages in Sri Lanka, Senegal, Tibet, Argentina, and Australia, as well as urban rejuvenation

Maintaining opposition throughout extended, arduous social conflict and public confrontation takes a great deal of energy. Schwarze suggests that creating the necessary energy is the fourth transformative action of melodrama. Specifically, *melodrama can create a unity of feeling* (or monopathy). In Libby, monopathic identification is sustained through journalistic depictions of entire families who suffer from asbestos disease; photojournalists' displays of hearses, coffins, and white crosses with victims names on them; and stories of local heroes in their struggles against corporate deception and government bureaucracy. Families, friends, and neighbors shared monopathic identification in their mutual loss and anger that the company experts' dispassionate technical rhetoric could not dissipate.

These four actions of melodrama all work together to create the fifth and final transformative action: *"melodrama has the capacity to complicate and transform, not merely simplify and reify public controversies."*[54] Schwarze suggests that the critical view of polarizing rhetoric as oversimplifying and reifying conflict is based on viewing it solely as instrumental rhetoric, rather than considering its constitutive function. He suggests that instead of simplifying and reifying the issues, the Libby discourse actually served to complicate the issues by constructing new ways to view the situation. In this case, melodrama served to rearticulate the community's projects such as the Los Angeles EcoVillage. For further information about these sustainable practices and places go to http://gen.ecovillage.org/index.html.

One final example of a global unification effort is ecotourism, typically defined as low-impact, environmentally responsible travel to unique environments where biological diversity and cultural heritage are the main attractions. The International Ecotourism Society (www.ecotourism.org) is one of a number of organizations that promote ecotourism.

Vacation packages are often linked to established conservation groups. For example, one can experience a Hawaiian "shark encounter" vacation sponsored by Shark Allies, a nonprofit shark conservation organization, or visit the Galapagos Islands on a tour sponsored by the World Wildlife Fund. Tourism dollars create an economic incentive for communities to conserve their local heritage and biological diversity and, at the same time, give travelers the opportunity to become involved in conservation efforts around the world. When done right, ecotourism advances education, encourages activism, funds conservation efforts, benefits economic development in local communities, and fosters understanding and respect for diverse cultures.

With all of this mobilized wombat wisdom, achieving a more unified and sustainable world seems within the realm of possibility and lends credence to Al Gore's prophesy: "By seizing the opportunity that is bound up in this crisis, we can unleash the creativity, innovation, and inspiration that are just as much a part of our human birthright as our vulnerability to greed and pettiness. The choice is ours. The responsibility is ours. The future is ours."*

*Al Gore, *An Inconvenient Truth: The Planetary Emergence of Global Warming and What We Can Do about It* (New York: Rodale, 2006), 297.

relationship with W. R. Grace from "benevolent employer" to "callous victimizer." The previously "unremarkable, taken-for-granted illnesses" were transformed into "an unparalleled environmental health disaster" that resulted in "one of the largest public health screenings in the United States to determine the scope of the disease in the Libby area."[55] Nor did the transformative impacts of the Libby discourse stop at the city limits. A large-scale investigation of vermiculite processing facilities across the nation was set in motion, along with new scientific studies that "placed asbestos back on the environmental and public health agenda in the United States."[56]

As demonstrated in the Libby case, the transformative action of melodrama can be far-reaching and significant. Yet, critics of melodrama are also justified in their warnings of the potential negative impacts of polarizing rhetoric, as previously discussed. Although, in the case of Libby, melodrama worked to clarify and transform, Schwarze acknowledges that the results might be different in other cases. "Melodrama appears less likely to be a productive choice," he explains, "when controversies are well-defined, issues have been thoroughly articulated, and a full range of stakeholders has identified possible means of resolution."[57] Thus, in the case of conflicts that have spanned many years and multiple fronts, the melodramatic form is probably far less transformative than it is in emerging controversies such as Libby, where the issues have not been thoroughly articulated or voices have been left out of the discourse.

Concluding and Looking Ahead

You may begin to get a sense of the multiple realities constructed through the way we symbolically represent the environment. One person's Eden is another's barren wasteland. What some view as moral action is seen as ecoterrorism by others. The polarizing rhetoric of Earth First! and the Wise Use Movement, as well as the melodramatic representation of the Libby asbestos controversy, are prime case studies of how contradictory and seemingly irreconcilable realities are rhetorically constructed.

What can we gain through the study of these multiple realities? In their book *The Symbolic Earth: Discourse and the Creation of the Environment,* James G. Cantrill and Christine L. Oravec answer the question in this way:

> For all intents and purposes, the planet is a captive of our language community; the environment, beyond its physical presence, is a social creation and this fact is often lost in the hoopla of crisis and deliberation. Furthermore, the only hope we ever have of preserving our environment is collectively to understand and alter the fundamental ways we discuss what we continually re-create.[58]

Environmentalists have long attempted to alter ways of talking about the environment. A number of rhetorical forms are commonly used (with varying degrees of success) to achieve this end. One classification of rhetoric that emerges prominently in environmental rhetoric is prophetic rhetoric—rhetoric that foretells or predicts the future. The following chapter examines different kinds of prophetic rhetoric as well as some of the potential outcomes of these commonly used forms of environmental rhetoric.

Discussion Questions and Exercises

1. In your opinion, do the ecotage tactics of E.L.F. activists ultimately help or hurt the environmental cause? Explain your answer.

2. The chapter mentions a number of examples of nondiscursive rhetoric and image events that Earth First! has used in past campaigns. Do some research to find other examples and report what you find.

3. Find an article or one of the books mentioned in the chapter that debunks or is skeptical about the claims of environmentalists. How does the author go about debunking the "doomsday myths" of "environmental apocalypse abusers?" Do the rhetorical themes of polarization emerge in the article's or the book's rhetoric? Give examples. Do the characteristics of melodrama emerge? Give examples. (You may want to do the same exercise, but look instead at the writing of an environmental writer.)

4. Divide the class into two groups, with each group representing one side of a highly polarized environmental dispute (for example, loggers vs. owl protection advocates, wolf re-introduction advocates vs. federal land grazers, proponents of wilderness protection vs. off-road vehicle enthusiasts). Brainstorm bumper stickers and T-shirt slogans to simplify, dramatize, and polarize the issues.

Suggested Readings

Edward Abbey. *The Monkey Wrench Gang*. New York: Avon, 1973.

Dave Foreman. *Ecodefense: A Field Guide to Monkeywrenching*. Tucson, AZ: Ned Ludd, 1985/1987.

Dave Foreman. *Rewilding North America: A Vision for Conservation in the 21st Century*. Washington, DC: Island, 2004.

Jonathan I. Lange. "The Logic of Competing Information Campaigns: Conflict over Old Growth and the Spotted Owl." *Communication Monographs* 60 (1993): 239–257.

Jonathan I. Lange. "Refusal to Compromise: The Case of Earth First!" *Western Journal of Speech Communication* 54 (1990): 473–494.

Brant Short. "Earth First! and the Rhetoric of Moral Confrontation." *Communication Studies* 42 (1991): 172–188.

Notes

1. J. Kane, "Mother Nature's Army: Guerilla Warfare Comes to the American Forest," *Esquire,* February 1987, 100–101.
2. Edward Abbey, *The Monkey Wrench Gang* (New York: Avon, 1973).
3. Jonathan I. Lange, "Refusal to Compromise: The Case of Earth First!" *Western Journal of Speech Communication* 54 (1990): 481.
4. Kevin M. DeLuca, *Image Politics: The New Rhetoric of Environmental Activism* (New York: Guilford, 1999), 22.
5. Dave Foreman, *Ecodefense: A Field Guide to Monkeywrenching* (Tucson, AZ: Ned Ludd, 1985), 14.
6. Foreman, *Ecodefense,* 21.
7. Foreman, *Ecodefense,* 14.
8. S. Hettena and L. Wides, "Sabotage Campaign Spreads in U.S.: Radical Group Suspected in Attack on SUVs in Santa Fe," *Albuquerque Journal,* October 2, 2003, A1, A8.
9. Lisa K. Heller, "The Rhetoric of Ecotage: Earth First! and the Language of Violence," *Speaker and Gavel* 31 (1994): 50–65.
10. Dave Foreman, "We Aren't a Debating Society." [Transcript] Speech Given at the Grand Canyon River Rendezvous, quoted in *Earth First! Journal,* December 21, 1992, 8.
11. J. Time, "D-Day for Northwest Forests." *Earth First! The Radical Environmental Journal* (June 21, 1994): 31.
12. Foreman, "We Aren't a Debating Society," 17.
13. Foreman, *Ecodefense,* 11–12.
14. Foreman, *Ecodefense,* 7.
15. C. J. Stewart, A. S. Smith, and R. E. Denton, Jr., *Persuasion and Social Movements,* 2nd ed. (Prospect Heights, IL: Waveland, 2001).
16. Heller, "Rhetoric of Ecotage," 59.
17. Brant Short, "Earth First! and the Rhetoric of Moral Confrontation," *Communication Studies* 42 (1991): 181.
18. Elizabeth Kaufman, "Earth-Saving: Here Is a Gang of Real Environmental Extremists," *Audubon,* July 1982, 116–120.
19. Lange, "Refusal to Compromise."
20. T. O. Hellenbach, "The Future of Monkeywrenching," in *Ecodefense: A Field Guide to Monkeywrenching,* ed. D. Foreman and B. Haywood (Tucson, AZ: Ned Ludd, 1987), 22.
21. Lange, "Refusal to Compromise."
22. Dave Foreman, *Rewilding North America: A Vision for Conservation in the 21st Century* (Washington, DC: Island, 2004).
23. Susan Zakin, *Coyotes and Town Dogs: Earth First! and the Environmental Movement* (Tucson: University of Arizona Press, 2002), 10.

24. Ron Arnold, "Overcoming Ideology," in *A Wolf in the Garden: The Land Rights Movement and the New Environmental Debate,* eds. Phillip D. Brick and R. McGregor Cawley (Lanham, MD: Rowman & Littlefield, 1996), 15–26.
25. Arnold, "Overcoming Ideology."
26. Cited in W. Poole, "Neither Wise Nor Well," *Sierra,* November/December 1992, 61.
27. T. A. Lewis, "Cloaked in a Wise Disguise," *National Wildlife,* October/November 1992, 4–9.
28. Phil Brick, "Taking Back the Rural West," in *Let the People Judge,* eds. J. D. Echeverria and R. B. Eby (Washington, DC: Island, 1995), 61.
29. Jon Roush, "Freedom and Responsibility: What We Can Learn from the Wise Use Movement" in *Let the People Judge,* eds. J. D. Echeverria and R. B. Eby (Washington, DC: Island, 1995), 8.
30. http://www.cdfe.org/about-us/mission-statement.
31. Phil Brick, "Determined Opposition: The Wise Use Movement Challenges Environmentalism," in *Landmark Essays on Rhetoric and the Environment,* ed. C. Waddell (Mahwah, NJ: Erlbaum, 1998), 201.
32. Arnold, "Overcoming Ideology," 18
33. Arnold, "Overcoming Ideology," 19.
34. Arnold, "Overcoming Ideology," 19.
35. Dixie Lee Ray and L. R. Guzzo, *Environmental Overkill: Whatever Happened to Common Sense?* (Washington, DC: Regnery Gateway, 1993).
36. Ron Bailey, *Eco-Scam: The False Prophets of Ecological Apocalypse* (New York: St. Martin's, 1993).
37. B. Bolch and H. Lyons, *Apocalypse Not: Science, Economics, and Environmentalism* (Washington, DC: Cato Institute, 1993).
38. J. L. Bast, P. J. Hill, and R. Rue, *Eco-Sanity: A Common Sense Guide to Environmentalism* (Lanham, MD: Madison, 1994).
39. M. A. Cahn, *Environmental Deceptions* (Albany: State University of New York Press, 1995).
40. Dixie Lee Ray, cited in Poole, "Neither Wise Nor Well," 59.
41. Cited in T. Callahan, "Trees and Volcanoes Cause Smog! More Myths from the 'Wise Use' Movement," *The Humanist,* January/February 1996, 29–34.
42. Rush Limbaugh, *The Way Things Ought to Be* (New York: Simon & Schuster, 1992), 155–156.
43. Arnold, "Overcoming Ideology," 23.
44. Bailey, *Eco-Scam,* xiii.
45. Genesis 1:26.
46. M. Dowie, *Losing Ground: American Environmentalism at the Close of the Twentieth Century* (Cambridge, MA: MIT Press, 1995), 91.
47. Helen Chenoweth, cited in Timothy Egan, "Look Who's Hugging Trees Now." http://www.nytimes.com/1996/07/07/magazine/look-who-s-hugging-trees-now.html (accessed July 23, 2009).
48. Jennifer A. Peeples, "Aggressive Mimicry: The Rhetoric of Wise Use and the Environmental Movement," in *The Environmental Communication Yearbook, Vol. 2,* ed. S. L. Senecah (Mahwah, NJ: Erlbaum, 2005), 14.
49. League of Conservation Voters, "2004 Presidential Candidates Profile," http://www.lcv.org/images/client/pdfs/bush_profile.pdf (accessed July 4, 2007).
50. Jonathan I. Lange, "The Logic of Competing Information Campaigns: Conflict over Old Growth and the Spotted Owl," *Communication Monographs* 60 (1993): 254.
51. Steven Schwarze, "Environmental Melodrama," *Quarterly Journal of Speech* 92 (2006): 239–261.
52. Schwarze, "Environmental Melodrama," 249.
53. Schwarze, "Environmental Melodrama," 251.
54. Schwarze, "Environmental Melodrama," 253.

55. Schwarze, "Environmental Melodrama," 253–254.
56. Schwarze, "Environmental Melodrama," 253.
57. Schwarze, "Environmental Melodrama," 255.
58. James G. Cantrill and Christine L. Oravec, eds., *The Symbolic Earth: Discourse and the Creation of the Environment* (Lexington: University Press of Kentucky, 1996), 2.

Chapter 7

Prophetic Rhetoric: Apocalyptic, Irreparable, Utopian, and Jeremiadic

One of the most outspoken and influential of modern day environmental prophets is Bill McKibben. His book *The End of Nature,* published in 1989, was one of the first books about global warming written for a general audience. His apocalyptic prophecy begins with these words:

> Changes in our world can happen in our lifetime—not just changes like wars, but bigger and more total events. I believe that, without recognizing it, we have already stepped over the threshold of such a change: that we are at the end of nature.[1]

When McKibben makes the claim that "we are at the end of nature," he does not mean the end of the world. He goes on to say that "though they may change dramatically, the rain will still fall and the sun shine."[2] What he means by the "end of nature" is that because humans have changed the climate, nature is no longer natural. McKibben explains it like this:

> We have changed the atmosphere, and thus we are changing the weather. By changing the weather, we make every spot on earth man-made and artificial. We have deprived nature of its independence, and that is fatal to its meaning. Nature's independence *is* its meaning; without it, there is nothing but us.[3]

At the time the book was published, McKibben was part of a small minority whose concerns about global warming and its effects had been largely ignored. Now his views are widely accepted and nations of the world have begun to make steps (albeit slow and halting) toward lessening the amount of greenhouse gases released into the air. The response to McKibben and other global warming prophets has been, at best, lukewarm. McKibben expresses his frustration with the marginal response to the growing threat when he states,

> For fifteen years now, some small percentage of the world's scientists and diplomats and activists has inhabited one of those strange dreams where the dreamer desperately needs to warn someone about something bad and imminent; but somehow, no matter how hard he shouts, the other person in the dream—standing, smiling perhaps, with his back to an oncoming train— can't hear him.[4]

Unfortunately, the threat of global warming is not a strange dream, and if scientific predictions are accurate, the oncoming train portends an ominous future.

Environmental communication scholars and environmental rhetors play a vital role by attempting to understand more clearly the discourse from which perceptions of the natural world emerge and the ways in which people create and transform the constructed realities. With the train approaching, now would be a good time to understand what works when it comes to changing ideas about nature and inciting action. In an attempt to do just that, the following looks at the themes and structures of prophetic rhetoric.

Figure 7.1   Rachel Carson

Rachel Carson (1907–1964) initially earned her reputation as a noted marine biologist and oceanographer with her books *Under the Sea Wind* (1941), *The Sea Around Us* (1951), and *The Edge of the Sea* (1955). By far her best-known work, *Silent Spring* (1962) shocked the world with its indictment of the devastating effects of agricultural chemicals. Many people believe this book was the catalyst for the modern environmental movement.

U.S. Fish and Wildlife Service

Apocalyptic Rhetoric

Apocalyptic narratives have long been a major theme in modern literature and film. The term "apocalypse" simply means "revelation." It comes from the last book of the Christian Bible, the Book of Revelation, also known as the Apocalypse of Saint John. This book foresees the events that will attend the second coming of Christ, beginning with a period of destruction and the Battle of Armageddon, in which the forces of good and evil will fight the last decisive battle.

Apocalyptic rhetoric has emerged as a central theme in environmental rhetoric. In common usage, the term **apocalyptic** has come to refer to the threat to human survival through large-scale destruction. While other forms of rhetoric emphasize protection of nature for nature's sake, apocalyptic rhetoric focuses on protecting nature for the sake of the survival of humanity. Like the prophets of old, environmental prophets predict or foreshadow a grim scenario of what could happen if we don't make drastic changes in the way we view and treat nature.

Apocalyptic rhetoric has been used effectively by environmentalists to bring the urgency and severity of environmental problems to the public's attention. Many would agree that the most successful of all environmental prophets of apocalypse was Rachel Carson. As rhetorical scholars M. Jimmie Killingsworth and Jacqueline S. Palmer observe, "[Carson's] *Silent Spring* possessed a rhetorical power unmatched in its day. The book's accessibility and the popularity of its author made it much more visible and influential than any to have preceded it in the environmental movement."[5]

The Apocalyptic Rhetoric of *Silent Spring*

The prophetic prologue to *Silent Spring*, "A Fable for Tomorrow," is barely two pages long, but it was one of the most controversial and response-provoking narratives in environmental history.[6] "There once was a town in the heart of America," begins Carson, "where all life seemed to live in harmony with its surroundings." The fictitious town is located in an ideal pastoral setting of a farming community. The peace and tranquility of the community was shattered as "a strange blight crept over the area and everything began to change. Some evil spell had settled over the community." The cattle, sheep, and chickens sickened and died. The doctors were puzzled by the new kinds of sickness appearing in the town and the sudden and unexplained deaths. There was a strange stillness because the birds had vanished. "It was a spring without voices." The bees in the orchard and the fish in the streams had likewise disappeared. Who was responsible for silencing the voices of spring? "No witchcraft, no enemy action had silenced the rebirth of new life in this stricken world. The people had done it themselves." Carson ends the prologue with a disclaimer that explains that this town does not actually exist, but that communities all over America have experienced the adverse symptoms described in the fabled town. She warns that "A grim specter has crept upon us almost unnoticed, and this imagined tragedy may easily become a stark reality we all shall know." ("A Fable for Tomorrow" is included in the Appendix.)

The book then sets out to explain the apocalyptic prophesy of the allegorical prologue. Carson describes the negative impacts of insecticides, such as DDT and other industrial and agricultural chemicals, and levels an angry critique at the agricultural-chemical industry and the scientists who support it.

Implications of Apocalyptic Rhetoric

Killingsworth and Palmer examined the apocalyptic forms used in environmental writing and drew several conclusions about the significance of this rhetorical form. They claim that apocalyptic rhetoric has three implications: (1) it implies a need for radical change; (2) it marks the apocalyptic prophet as an outsider who then risks alienation; and (3) it urges others into political rebellion.[7]

Apocalyptic rhetoric implies a need for radical change in that it attacks the master narrative of "progress"—a word that carries an almost unquestioned connotation of "righteousness" and "good." To challenge progress is to challenge a dominant ideology of our culture. Apocalyptic rhetoric calls for a revolutionary change in the way we view and deal with technology and its consequences. The challenge to that ideology is related to the intensity of the apocalyptic prediction. If the predicted devastation is extreme, the recommended changes in the social, political, and economic system are correspondingly radical. Carson predicted the devastating consequences of unchecked use of agricultural chemicals and called for radical changes in the way we view and use these chemicals.

Apocalyptic prophets are often viewed as outsiders and risk alienation. Herself a scientist, Carson "jumped ship" when she challenged the dominant ideology of science and technology by calling for a revolution in science that, rather than aiming to control nature, would "work-with-nature" through a holistic model of ecology. Not surprisingly, Carson's critique of science and her angry attack against the chemical industry marked her as a "radical outsider" and a voice of dissent within the scientific community.

The reviews of *Silent Spring* from the scientific community were mixed. While a few distinguished authors praised her work, agribusiness and the chemical industry quickly acted to flood the media with "expert" refutation of her claims. As Killingsworth and Palmer state, "Unwilling to give up their share in the mythic status of modern science, industry scientists launched a frenetic counterattack on Carson's position."[8] For example, in an imitation of Carson's "Fable for Tomorrow," Monsanto Chemical Company published its own version of an apocalyptic narrative that warned of the famine that would result if farmers were deprived of agricultural chemicals.

The public attacks on Carson were not limited to criticism of her science-based predictions. Some took the form of highly personalized ***ad hominem*** attacks, which are attacks on the person rather than the issue. A Federal Pest Control Review Board member went so far as to say that "He thought she was a spinster, so what's she so worried about genetics for?"[9]

Apocalyptic rhetoric urges others out into the open air of political rebellion. Carson's popularity and the overwhelming public response to her message made *Silent Spring* the most recognized and influential book of its day. The wave of environmental awareness that followed the publication of the book spawned renewed interest in and appreciation for past environmental writers, such as John Muir and Aldo Leopold. Not only was Carson almost single-handedly responsible for banning DDT, she demonstrated the power of the pen, inspiring others of her time to challenge the political powers and dominant ideologies of the day.

The rhetorical impact of Carson's book was immense. Yet not all apocalyptic rhetoric is as successful. Killingsworth and Palmer urge environmental rhetors to recognize the importance of situation and context in any given environmental discourse. Carson's apocalyptic narrative succeeded where others have failed not only because of her talent as a writer or because of the truly alarming nature of her warning, but also because of the historical period in which the book was written.[10]

The 1960s was a decade of social turbulence, in which many activist groups challenged traditional American views. This decade saw the emergence of the civil rights movement, the feminist movement, and the anti–Vietnam War movement. Carson tapped into "the temper of the times," in which the historical, social, and political factors, as well as the strength of the message all combined to create a colossal public response. Media historian Priscilla Coit Murphy describes that response as a "cultural 'perfect storm' that enjoyed a confluence of circumstances that made the episode a landmark not only in environmental history but in book history as well."[11]

Yet, as Murphy suggests, the reason for the book's tremendous impact was more than just the confluence of circumstances. The fact that *Silent Spring* is still in print implies that some exceptional quality made it more than a passing sensation. "It is important to acknowledge," says Murphy, "that in the esteem of many, her book is a classic of environmentalist writing—at once accessible and intellectually defensible."[12]

Another reason for the book's phenomenal success, suggests Murphy, was the dynamic between the book and other media forms. The controversy over *Silent Spring* and the organized counter-campaign against it kept the book in the media spotlight and on the public agenda. As Murphy states, "From garden club meetings to the floor of Congress, *Silent Spring* drew its advocates and its detractors into sometimes acrimonious debate, one not only covered by the media but engaging the media as participants as well."[13] It was evident that the press, the public, and the policy makers viewed Carson's prophetic revelation as a matter of significant concern, making *Silent Spring* what many believe to be the most influential environmental text in the history of the environmental movement.

Potential Backlash Responses to Apocalyptic Rhetoric

Environmental rhetors would be well advised to exercise caution in their use of apocalyptic rhetoric. Environmental communication scholar Star A. Muir points out several potential backlash responses to apocalyptic rhetoric. The first is the **cumulative numbing effect,** also referred to as the **Chicken Little effect,** that results from the repeated presentation of gloom and doom predictions.[14] A common criticism is that environmentalists use exaggerated scare tactics in order to gain public support for environmental protections. As Muir points out, many of these doomsday predictions have not come true or have been only partially realized. As a result, they have provided powerful ammunition for skeptics of environmental claims.

Another potential response to apocalyptic rhetoric is that it encourages a centrist approach to decisions concerning environmental protections, which Muir refers to as the **hegemony of the center.** Anti-environmental rhetoric denies the doomsday appeals of environmentalists by painting an optimistic picture of the state of the planet and humans' ability to fix whatever problems may exist. When confronted with contradictory interpretations of highly complex scientific "facts," we tend to believe that the truth probably lies somewhere in the middle. Muir uses the example of the greenhouse debate to demonstrate how attitudes about environmental issues get caught in the "hegemony of the center." He points out that media reporting about climate change has given as much attention to a few skeptical scientists as it has given to the large body of scientists who share the consensus agreement that warming is happening and will have serious consequences. "Much of the American public," explains Muir, "confronted by the two 'equal' sides of this controversy, believes that the truth probably lies somewhere in the middle, and support for policies that address the problems of fossil fuel consumption are thereby muted to a significant degree."[15]

The following section discusses a form of rhetoric that is similar to apocalyptic rhetoric—**a locus of the irreparable.** Apocalyptic rhetoric tends to predict total or mass destruction that threatens the survival of humankind. A locus of the irreparable, on the other hand, tends to be more situation-bound (a specific place or hazard), where the destruction may or may not have a profound impact on human survival; but where, once the predicted event or situation occurs, there is no recovering what is lost or repairing what is destroyed.

A Locus of the Irreparable

You have probably seen bumper stickers or slogans that say something like "Extinction means forever" or "What about GONE FOREVER don't you understand?" When an action leads to an irreversible outcome, rhetors often appeal to what is termed a locus of the irreparable.[16] "Locus" refers to a general category or line of argument. An action is irreparable if that which is lost by the action can never be recovered or regained.

Environmental communication scholar J. Robert Cox examined the features and strategies of this very common form of environmental rhetoric. According to Cox, appeals to a locus of the irreparable consist of three components: the identification of a place or situation as *unique,* the identification of the *precarious* or fragile nature of the place or situation, and the identification of the *timeliness* or urgency of the action required to save that which is irreparable.[17]

Building on Cox's work, environmental communication scholar Terence Check analyzed an environmental organization's fundraising and promotional letters in an effort to understand how a locus of the irreparable is used and to further explore the components and implications of this kind of appeal.[18] Check's study gives numerous examples of specific rhetorical appeals that demonstrate the components of a locus of the irreparable (uniqueness, precariousness, and timeliness). Check further discusses how these rhetorical tactics may be successful in the short term but may actually frustrate pro-environmental action in the long run. The following discussion uses examples borrowed from Check's examination of letters from the Natural Resources Defense Counsel (NRDC) to its membership, regarding the proposed plan to drill for oil in the Arctic National Wildlife Refuge (ANWR) in northern Alaska.

Appeals to Uniqueness

In their letter campaign to stop the proposed drilling in the Alaska Reserve, the NRDC characterized the place as unique, or if not unique, a very rare place. Often, this characterization takes the form of **Edenic narratives,** or presentations that evoke images of the biblical account of the Garden of Eden—a rare place of ideal, exceptional, pristine beauty. One letter states, for example, "There are very few places left in the world like the Alaska Reserve. As big as the state of Indiana, this is a land of snow clad peaks, glacial valleys, rolling tundra meadows, and extensive ice floes."

The value of what is unique or rare can be rhetorically enhanced by contrasting it to something that is usual, ordinary, or trivial. The letters point out that this unique place will be sacrificed for comparatively ordinary or trivial gains in the form of "about a half-billion barrels of oil—about a month's supply of energy for the United States."

Appeals to Precariousness

In addition to focusing on the unique or rare aspects of the place, a locus of the irreparable appeals to the precariousness of the place or situation. Rhetors can establish something as precarious by portraying it as fragile or easy to destroy; or if not necessarily fragile, threatened by a powerful agent. The following excerpt from a Natural Resources Defense Counsel letter is an appeal to the fragility of the nesting birds of ANWR: "It's no mystery why so many birds choose the Alaska Reserve at this most vulnerable moment in their annual life cycle. There is simply nowhere else for them to go that is so free from human disturbance."

Oftentimes, the precariousness of a place or situation is established by rhetorically creating a powerful "evil" or "devil" that threatens to harm or destroy it. In the case of ANWR, the powerful evil that threatens the refuge is the "greedy industrial giants" who, according to the NRDC, will not be satisfied until they have "plundered the last acre of wilderness—not to meet any pressing need for energy, but to sell the oil overseas for a fast buck."

Appeals to Timeliness

The final component of a locus of the irreparable, according to Cox, is timeliness. Appeals to timeliness call for immediate, urgent action to save something rare or to forestall an action that would cause irreparable harm. A sense of urgency is rhetorically established in the following excerpt from a NRDC letter. "There is no time to lose," the letter warned, because (then) Interior Secretary Bruce Babbitt "has just given the green light to drill in the spectacular Alaskan Reserve. . . . You and I have one last chance to keep the Alaska Reserve wild and free. . . . if we take swift and effective legal action now." The letter concludes by urging readers to immediately send a tax-deductible donation.

Potential Backlash Responses to Rhetoric of the Irreparable

Just as apocalyptic appeals can backfire, so can appeals to the locus of the irreparable. Check cautions that although appeals to uniqueness may lead to short-term success for a specific campaign, they may, in the long run, promote ideals that inhibit or discourage pro-environmental action. There are several reasons why this outcome may occur. The first is that by framing places as Edenic, a rhetor may send the unintended message that places that are not rare or of exceptional beauty are not worthy of protection. The uniqueness criterion makes it rhetorically difficult to justify the preservation of places that fail to meet this exacting standard. Likewise, when a place is framed as Edenic, opponents need only show that the place does not meet these lofty visions of ecological paradise. An editorial in the *Wall Street Journal* for instance, accused environmentalists of trying to "slap a wilderness label" on what is "basically a frozen desert, wind-swept and bleak even in summer."[19]

Although appeals to the precariousness of a place can be an effective way to mobilize public support, Check warns that this rhetorical tactic can likewise frustrate pro-environmental action. Repeated appeals to precariousness can lead to a kind of "psychic numbing" as a coping mechanism for dealing with the overwhelming enormity of the many environmental problems.

Likewise, appeals to timeliness can be very effective if the place or situation is, in fact, in imminent danger. However, Check points out that environmentalists run the risk of being labeled as "unreasonable alarmists" or "doomsayers" if appeals are premature. Environmental advocates should also be mindful of the possibility that urgent actions may serve only as a "first aid" response to immediate needs and may fail to address more fundamental, systemic problems.

An examination of environmental appeals to a locus of the irreparable offers insight in to the way a culture views itself and its ability to affect its future. Ultimately, a locus of the irreparable, says Cox, "is grounded in a fundamental presupposition of a culture: the preservation of future choice."[20] The use of a locus of the irreparable can be effective only in a society that believes it has the authority and capability to change the future. If people lack belief in this ability, a locus of the irreparable has little power to persuade, leaving only a sense of hopelessness and helplessness in the face of a looming crisis.

Utopian Rhetoric

Utopia was the title of a book written by Sir Thomas More in 1516 about an imaginary island with a perfect political and social system. In everyday use, **utopian** has come to represent an ideally perfect social order in a perfect "nowhere land" where people are perfectly content. Utopian philosophers attempt to prophesy what this "perfect social order" would look like, allowing the reader to escape his or her own world and imagine a better one.

The works of utopian philosophers span the centuries, beginning as early as Plato (427–347 B.C.), whose treatise, *The Republic,* is a detailed model of an improved society. They continued through the Enlightenment, with thinkers such as Sir Thomas More (*Utopia,* 1516) and Francis Bacon (*New Atlantis,* 1627). Modern utopian narratives include works by philosophers such as Henry David Thoreau (*Walden,* 1854), Peter Kropotkin (*Fields, Factories, and Workshops,* 1904), Ernest Callenbach (*Ecotopia,* 1975), and Murray Bookchin (*The Ecology of Freedom,* 1982). Fantasy worlds with utopian themes are popular in children's literature as well. Children are enraptured with the make-believe worlds of Oz, Narnia, Hogwarts, and Middle Earth.

Whether the utopia is in the form of the philosophical tome of Plato's *Republic* or the fantastical fiction of J. K. Rowling's Hogwarts School of Witchcraft and Wizardry, the world created by utopian thinkers is a reflection of the social ills of this world. Utopian visions compel the reader to reflect on "the real world" through comparison and contrast to the world presented by the author.

Utopia is a work in progress, in which perfection is never quite achieved but perpetually sought by the inhabitants of the utopian society. There is always some imperfection in the form of uncertainty, danger, or dissent woven into the narrative of the almost-perfect world—an essential element for keeping the struggle for and re-invention of the society alive. In fact, when "perfection" is achieved, the narrative is almost always a "dystopian" narrative in which inhabitants live in a colorless world of total, stifling conformity.

Dystopia is the anti-utopia—the social order gone bad. Like utopian narratives, dystopian writers ask us to reflect on our own world through comparison and contrast to the dystopian world created by the writer. Dystopian narratives warn the reader of a very bleak future if the destructive path of the status quo is not altered. An example of dystopian narratives is George Orwell's novel *Nineteen Eighty-Four* (published in 1949), which portrays a terrifying world of constant surveillance by totalitarian rulers. Another, more recent example of a dystopian narrative is the 2004 movie *The Day After Tomorrow,* which depicts a world in the throes of natural disasters brought about by abrupt climate change.

An extremely disquieting dystopian vision was commissioned by the Department of Defense in 2003. Its purpose is "to imagine the unthinkable—to push the current research on climate change so we may better understand the potential implications on United States national security."[21] The report, authored by Peter Schwartz and Doug Randall, paints a bleak future of floods, famine, drought, and disease, leading to political instability as angry, displaced populations turn to rioting, civil conflicts, increased terrorist activities, and nuclear proliferation.

Ecological Utopian Visions

Ecological utopian visions are often called "ecotopias," a name that comes from a well-known 1975 novel, *Ecotopia,* by Ernest Callenbach.[22] This is a story about a journalist who, at the request of the president of the United States, travels to the country of Ecotopia to learn about this remarkable society and how the inhabitants live their lives. Ecological utopian writers theorize about the kind of social order required to create a mutually reinforcing, sustainable human/nature relationship.

Political theorist Marius de Geus makes a distinction between two kinds of utopian visions: "technological utopias" (or "utopias of abundance,") and "ecological utopias" or ("utopias of sufficiency").[23] **Technological utopias** or **utopias**

of abundance celebrate the benefits of spectacular technological achievements that lead to abundant, carefree lifestyles. In utopias of abundance, happiness and well-being are equated with an increase in goods and services; nature satisfies the demands for material wealth and comfort through innovative technologies. Elements of technological utopian thought are evident in modern fantasy worlds, such as the Starship *Enterprise*, from the classic television series *Star Trek*, which began in 1966 and, through its spin-offs (*The Next Generation, Deep Space Nine, Voyager*, and *Enterprise*), remained in production and on the air until 2005. In this utopian world, technology has evolved to perfectly serve human needs and create comfortable, affluent lifestyles.

Conversely, **ecological utopias** or **utopias of sufficiency** are opposed to abundant production and consumption. Instead, they promote the ideals of satisfaction and sufficiency. In these narratives, happiness is not found through riches and excess, but through simplicity, moderation, and self-restraint.

In his extensive examination of ecological utopias, de Geus observed a number of common characteristics that emerged from the narratives. The following list of these characteristics is extracted from his work as well as from the work of others who have looked at various utopian forms.[24] This list of characteristics is not all-inclusive, since each utopian philosopher will bring in his or her own visions of the perfect order, but one can observe most or all of these characteristics in any given ecological utopian narrative.

- *Ecological utopias present a radically changed vision of the "good life" from one of abundance and excess to one of sufficiency and moderation.* Inhabitants live simpler lives with fewer consumer goods and more time for leisure and rest. There is a strengthened sense of community and of belonging to a place and its people.

- *Ecological utopian communities are redesigned to promote economic self-sufficiency and green living.* In these communities, essential goods and services are locally produced. Local farmers and gardeners supply the food. Energy from renewable resources is likewise locally produced. The community's infrastructure incorporates mass transit networks, abundant green spaces, and homes made from natural green materials.

- *Ecological utopian industries are clean and efficient in their use of energy and resources.* Utopian industries strive for quality rather than quantity of goods. The economic system encourages and rewards green practices and green products rather than unlimited growth and expansion. The products they make are durable, reusable, repairable, and recyclable.

- *Ecological utopias have participatory governance characterized by democracy, transparency, and openness.* They operate under the assumption that in an ecologically sustainable society, the influences of power and wealth must be unmasked and weakened. Many ecological utopian thinkers call for decentralized government with locally autonomous communities.

- *Ecological utopias promote equality, diversity, and justice for all life forms.* The disparity in living standards between the wealthy and the poor no longer exists. All life forms are treated with dignity and respect.

The changes to the social order address what their creators view as the prevailing ills of the current social, economic, and political systems. Although the changes are radical, one finds a number of things left untouched in the writer's refashioning. Utopian narratives, then, not only prescribe how to "fix" society's ills, but also celebrate that which is good in the existing society. The following is an ecological utopian narrative in which the authors describe a utopian world that came about because of the work of present-day activists. Although many things are different in this new world, the role of citizen involvement and activism remain as central and critical characteristics of the social order.

"History of the Future"—An Ecological Utopian Narrative

A striking example of an ecological utopia is provided by the Global Scenario Group through its Great Transition Initiative. The Global Scenario Group is an international panel of experts from diverse fields, convened to envision alternative futures for world development. Its 2002 report, *Great Transition,* identifies the values, strategies, and agents of change that can lead to a globally sustainable future.[25] In the final chapter of the report, "History of the Future," the narrator writes of our current times from the perspective of a historian writing in the year 2068. The history chronicles the "Great Transition" that occurred in the mid-2020s and the events that led up to it.

The history tells a disquieting story of the "Era of Inclusive Growth" (2002–2015), described by the narrator as "an emancipatory tale of wealth generation, modernization, and democracy. But it's also a heartless saga of social disruption, crushing poverty, and economic imperialism."[26] This was a time of industrial capitalism that encouraged and handsomely rewarded powerful corporate giants that were blind to and unaccountable for the negative social and ecological impacts of their voracious assault.

In response to failed attempts at reform and in the face of growing social and ecological problems, a global coalition began to form in the mid 2020s. "In a kind of spontaneous global assembly from below," the coalition "mushroomed into a planetary mass movement for basic change."[27] Joining in the massive chorus for change were people who supported movements such as sustainable diets, organic agriculture, and animal rights, as well as environmentalists, antipoverty activists, and peace advocates.

Playing a critical role in the ultimate success of the global coalition were the world's youth. The "Yin-Yang Movement" unified a global youth culture in a "search for more fulfilling lifestyles and the quest for a sustainable and just world."[28] The proliferation of activist alliances representing all walks of life and all parts of the world created "a simple but fundamental transformation in world history—the willingness of people, individually and in groups, to take responsibility for solving problems themselves."[29] Thus was the "Great Transition" ushered in; this is what the history of the future (2025–2068) tells us about the world it created.

The family is now both smaller in size and expanded through involvement with the human and biotic communities. People take pride not in material possessions, but in living healthier, happier lives rich in time and diversity in a shared community of activities and values. Spurred by the Yin-Yang Movement of the youth, the values promoted by consumerism, competition, and individualism have been replaced by values of simplicity, tranquility, and community. Reduced work hours leave more time for studies, arts, and personal relationships in a "culturally rich and materially sufficient lifestyle."[30]

It is an era of greatly expanded transparency and accountability for private and government institutions, brought about by global networks of VBOs (Value-Based Organizations) that monitor corporate behavior. Information about their working conditions and wages, the quality and durability of their products, and their polluting practices are disseminated through global digital networks with video footage. Retailers and consumers band together to boycott those corporations who fail to meet sustainability requirements. The transparency and accountability enforced by VBO watchdog groups create "a rapid and powerful social feedback mechanism, far more potent than formal regulatory efforts of governments and intergovernmental bodies."[31] Global manufacturing companies have adopted "zero impact" goals of producing no waste or pollution, and implement programs for the post-consumer recovery and recycling of their products.

In like fashion, VBOs are able to pressure those governments that violate human rights or fail to protect their natural resources. The greatly expanded public participation in world governance brings new values and direction to policy decisions. Equality, justice, and sustainability drive the new political force.

Small pockets of poverty still survive, and conflict and intolerance occasionally flare. The planet's wounds are not yet healed, and "the lure of economic greed and political domination" must be vigilantly contained.[32] But the core commitments of this era are firmly implanted in the social, economic, and political institutions and structures: "The right of all to pursue a high quality of life, cultural pluralism within global unity, and humanity as part of a vibrant community of life on planet Earth."[33] Now, back to the present reality of the Great Transition's past.

Utopia as Dialogue

It is clear that the change from our contemporary consumer-driven society to the kind of sustainable global society described by the Global Scenario Group would indeed require a "great transition"—a drastic shift in cultural values and in the social, political, and economic institutions of control. One obvious limitation of utopian thinking is that it tends to ignore the practical implementation of a large-scale overhaul. Creating this imagined alternative future would present almost insurmountable obstacles. And since there is no such thing as a perfect society, the changes would inevitably produce a whole new set of problems, uncertainties, and conflict.

Environmental communication scholar John W. Delicath suggests that, rather than attempting to envision the specific "blueprints" of the ideal society, we should view utopia not as a place, but as "a dialogue, debate, an artistic creation" that "presents the future as one in the making, being crafted by the cooperative interaction of humans with humans and of humanity with the natural environment."[34] In a similar vein, Marius de Geus suggests that the utopian vision should be viewed as a navigational compass to guide society's general direction rather than its specific path.[35]

What is most significant about utopian rhetoric, according to Delicath, is that it provides a sense of hope and possibility as an alternative to the gloom-and-doom rhetoric that often characterizes the messages of environmental prophets. H. G. Wells recognized the importance of the utopian hope factor when he stated in a 1939 speech, "For 24 centuries at least men have been telling utopian stories, and they are all stories arising out of discontent and escaping towards dreamland. They all express a certain appetite for life—'if only'—"[36] A better vision of the future must start with a vision that articulates those "if onlys." It is this vision that renders utopian narratives useful, and even essential, to a new, more sustainable future.

The Jeremiad

A **jeremiad** is a morally weighted political sermon that incorporates some or all of the previously mentioned themes (apocalyptic, a locus of the irreparable, and utopian) in a consistently recognizable form. The jeremiadic form starts with a chastisement or scolding for misbehavior, followed by a call to change these evil ways and return to the right ways of behaving. This call leads to the third part of the jeremiadic form—a visualization of the good life to come.

The name is taken from the Biblical Old Testament book of the prophet Jeremiah, who castigates the Israelites for having failed to live up to the covenants of God. Jeremiah's ritualistic verbal flogging elevates the reprimand to an art form. Take, for example, this passage from chapter four of the Book of Jeremiah: "This is your doom and it is bitter . . . . For my people are foolish, they know me not; they are stupid children, they have no understanding. They are skilled in evil, but how to do good they know not." Jeremiah also warns at great length of things to come in the form of disease, famine, and wars. After painting a bleak picture of the future, he tells the Israelites what they must do in order to again find favor with an angry God, and in so doing, be returned to peace and prosperity. Thus, Jeremiah's message is ultimately one of hope and redemption.

Rhetorical Goals of the Jeremiad

Communication scholars John Opie and Norbert Elliot examined a number of environmental texts that could be classified as jeremiads, including a sermon by the Puritan preacher Samuel Danforth given in 1670; Ralph Waldo Emerson's *Nature* (1836); John Muir's *Yosemite* (1912); Aldo Leopold's "Land Ethic" from *A Sand County Almanac* (1949); Rachel Carson's "Fable for Tomorrow" from *Silent Spring* (1962); Bill McKibben's *The End of Nature* (1989); and Al Gore's 1992 book, *Earth in the Balance*.[37]

Opie and Elliot observed that, despite widely divergent rhetorical strategies among the authors, these writings all shared a highly consistent unity of purpose. First, they all *chastise the audience for its failures*. Just as the prophet Jeremiah scolds the Israelites for their failure to live up to the covenants of God, environmental Jeremiahs chastise their audiences for the destruction done to the natural world. The wrath of John Muir, for example, rains down on "the despoiling gain-seekers and mischief-makers of every degree, from Satan to Senators" who would dam Yosemite's beautiful Hetch Hetchy Valley. "Those temple destroyers and devotees of raging commercialism," admonishes Muir, "seem to have perfect contempt for Nature, and instead of lifting their eyes to the God of the Mountains, lift them to the Almighty Dollar."[38]

The second purpose of the jeremiad is to *persuade—to elicit a particular emotion or action*. It is a rhetoric of advocacy. For Jeremiah, the purpose was to restore the covenant. For John Muir, it was to preserve Yosemite. For Aldo Leopold, it was to make a case for an "ethical relation to the land." Leopold states his case clearly and succinctly in this frequently quoted statement: "A thing is right when it tends to preserve the integrity, stability, and beauty of the biotic community. It is wrong when it tends otherwise."[39]

The third purpose of the jeremiad is to *revitalize or rekindle a renewed faith.* Whereas Jeremiah's purpose was to turn people from their lawlessness and worship of false gods and to return them to the one true God, environmental Jeremiahs attempt to turn humans from the destructive path of civilization and to rekindle the love of nature. Often the call for renewed faith by environmental writers closely resembles the religious renewal called for by Jeremiah. Consider, for example, the religious tone of Ralph Waldo Emerson's call for renewal. "In the woods," says Emerson, "we return to reason and faith. There I feel that nothing can befall me in life—no disgrace, no calamity (leaving me my eyes), which nature cannot repair."[40]

The fourth purpose of the jeremiad is to *obviate (or reconcile) opposing views and, in so doing, provide a message of hope.* For the Israelites, the choice was between unrestricted hedonistic pleasures and the constraints imposed by the commandments of God. In environmental jeremiads, opposing views often translate into the comforts of the "good life" versus the sacrifices necessary to save the environment, especially the economic impacts of protection measures. The jeremiad stresses how these views can be reconciled. If they returned to their faith, the Israelites would be allowed to return to a land of abundance. The Puritan preacher Samuel Danforth assured his audiences that devotion to Puritan religious behaviors would insure secular success. John Muir likewise assured his readers that nature provides "for good men of every nation. Let them be as free to pick gold and gems from the hills, to cut and hew, dig and plant for homes and bread, as the birds are to pick wild berries from the bushes, and moss and leaves for nests." This abundance, however, is only offered to "good men." Muir calls on the government "to cast out and make an end of" the "mere destroyers . . . tree-killers, wool and mutton men, spreading death and confusion in the fairest groves and gardens ever planted . . . ."[41]

Rhetorical Strategies of the Jeremiad

Although the various texts examined by Opie and Elliot revealed a consistent unity of purpose, the authors of these texts used widely divergent rhetorical strategies to achieve their goals. These strategies can be placed into two general categories, evocative strategies and methodological strategies.

Evocative strategies can be likened to Aristotle's notion of *pathos,* or appeals intended to move the audience to fear, pity, or compassion. Opie and Elliot observed three identifiable characteristics of evocative strategies. The first is *the use of rich allusions to other texts, especially biblical and classical texts.* The second characteristic of evocative strategies involves *the extensive use of connotative meanings, poetic language, and metaphor.* Jeremiadic rhetors rely on literary devices such as verbal imagery and metaphor to emotionally arouse listeners. Appeals often take the form of highly personal, moving narratives. A third characteristic of evocative rhetoric is its use of imagery that is *close to the human life-world,* celebrating that which is tangible and concrete, that which we can experience and know in our everyday lives.

Consider, for example, the reference to Roman mythology and the evocative imagery in the following passage from Henry David Thoreau's well-known essay "Walking":

In wildness is the preservation of the world. Every tree sends its fibers forth in search of the Wild. The cities import it at any price. Men plough and sail for it . . . . The story of Romulus and Remus being suckled by a wolf is not

Connections

A Contemporary Jeremiah:
Barbara Kingsolver on the American Eating Disorder

"We don't know beans about beans. Asparagus, potatoes, turkey drumsticks—you name it, we don't have a clue about how the world makes it." In her book *Animal, Vegetable, Miracle,* award-winning author Barbara Kingsolver recounts the story of her family's decision to "step off the nonsustainable food grid" and, for one whole year, eat only food grown by local farmers or in her own garden. She artfully weaves together a humorous and moving memoir, a meticulously researched discussion of industrial agriculture, and the family recipe collection to create a compelling jeremiad, in which she calls on U.S. consumers to change their extravagant, unhealthy, and unsustainable eating habits:

> In our Café Dysfunctional, "eat your vegetables" has become a battle cry for mothers against presumed unwilling subjects. In my observed experience, boys in high school cafeterias treat salad exactly as if it were a feminine hygiene product, and almost nobody touches the green beans.

Humor notwithstanding, Kingsolver's message is serious and thought-provoking. Her goal is to promote human and environmental health by eating locally produced, organically grown, small farm–friendly foods. As we roll the grocery carts down the well-stocked grocery store aisles, we tend to ignore the environmental and human costs of this attractively packaged abundance. Below are just some of the things she asks us to consider when making our food purchasing decisions.

- When we purchase that perfectly red, round, (and usually tasteless) tomato, we subsidize international oil cartels and global climate change. Every food calorie produced uses ten or even a hundred times as many fossil fuel calories in its production (growing, milling, packaging, transporting, and so on). Out-of-season fruits and vegetables transported from all over the country and the world allow for our year-round enjoyment of these foods, but do so at a tremendous cost to the environment.
- Industrial meat production in the form of concentrated animal feeding operations (CAFOs, also known as factory farms) present a number of problems.

a meaningless fable. The founders of every state which have risen to eminence have drawn their nourishment and vigor from a similar wild source.[42]

The second type of rhetorical strategy used in the jeremiad is **methodological** or **implementational strategies,** which, like Aristotle's *logos,* urge the audience to take action through ordered, logical means. Like evocative strategies, implementational rhetoric is rich in the citation of other texts. However, rather than drawing on such texts as the Bible and classical literature as does evocative rhetoric, implementational strategies *draw on scientific and technical writing.*

Whereas evocative strategies draw on connotative meanings, poetic language, and metaphors, implementational strategies capitalize on the denotative aspects of

Among them are animal rights issues that arise from the overcrowding of the animals who may never see grass or sunshine. The physical stressors to the animals resulting from being confined in crowded spaces are treated with antibiotics. The overuse of these antibiotics is encouraging the evolution of resistant strains of bacteria. In addition, the tremendous amount of excrement produced by large numbers of animals in concentrated areas causes problems with waste run-off and the pollution of ground and surface water.

- Agribusiness chemicals used in industrial farming practices sterilize the soil, killing the microscopic soil nutrients, while chemical fertilizers replace only a few of the critical nutrients. In addition to depleting the soils, herbicides and pesticides are creating populations of genetically evolved insects and plant pathogens that are resistant to the chemicals, creating a self-perpetuating need for more and stronger chemicals.

- Through genetic modification, gene engineers can combine, as Kingsolver describes it, "traits of creatures that aren't even on speaking terms in the natural world," to produce such characteristics as uniform appearance and the ability to withstand mechanized harvesting, packing, and shipping. The hybrid plants are also genetically engineered so that the seeds can't reproduce. Farmers must again purchase the patented seed from the company that engineers it, rather than saving seeds to plant the next growing season.

Kingsolver encourages her readers to try gardening (even if it's only a few tomato plants in containers), and to support community garden projects and local farmers' markets. To find a farmers' market near you, go to the USDA Web site at www.ams.usda.gov/farmersmarkets or www.localharvest.org.

The only requirement for developing healthy, eco-friendly eating habits, suggests Kingsolver, is "patience and a pinch of restraint." She urges us to walk past the tempting out-of-season fruits and vegetables and choose instead the seasonal produce of the local growing area. Be willing to let go of "the botanically outrageous condition of having everything, always . . . where whole continents collide discretely on a white tablecloth."

Source: Barbara Kingsolver, *Animal, Vegetable, Miracle: A Year of Food Life* (New York: Harper Perennial, 2007).

language and *focus on precision and accuracy of terminology*. In this form of rhetoric, the language of science and reasoned argumentation is called on in place of poetic language and narratives. Rather than the voice of the author, the depersonalized voice of the expert is used. Thus, implementational rhetoric is *distanced from the life-world* that we can see, touch, and personally experience.

The following example demonstrates the implementational or methodological form of rhetoric. These were the words of Secretary of the Interior James R. Garfield in 1908, as he defended his decision to permit the dam in the Hetch Hetchy Valley. A big part of the debate over the dam centered around two opposing interpretations of the meaning of "public interest." Notice the precision of the language and the depersonalized, reasoned argumentation of Garfield's implementational rhetoric:

On construing the words of a statute [The Yosemite Park Act], the evident and ordinary meaning should be taken . . . . On this broad principle the words "the public interest" should not be confined merely to the public interest in the Yosemite National Park for use as a park only, but rather the broader public interest which requires these reservoir sites to be utilized for the highest good to the greatest number of people.[43]

One of my favorite contemporary jeremiads is the book *Animal, Vegetable, Miracle,* by the well-known author Barbara Kingsolver. She artfully uses both evocative and implementational rhetorical strategies in her narration of her family's year-long mission to eat only locally produced foods or food grown in her own garden. Her use of humor, imagery, and metaphor gives new meaning to the previously unsung tomato: "The first tomato of the season brings me to my knees. Its vital stats are recorded in my journal with the care of a birth announcement: It's an Early Girl! Four ounces! June 16! Blessed event we've awaited so long."[44] Interspersed throughout the humorous and evocative narrative is a methodological treatment (much of it in the form of sidebars written by her biologist husband) of the many problems that result from our culture's extravagant, yet impoverished eating habits and unsustainable farming practices. (See text box for a discussion of these problems.)

In her gentle jeremiad, Kingsolver scolds U.S. consumers for their unhealthy and unsustainable eating habits, and offers tips on how to find redemption by supporting farmers' markets and being more critically aware and selective of the food we buy. Her teenage daughter even supplies the meal plans and recipes to assist the reader in preparing the redemptive, locally grown meals.

Kingsolver reconciles the sacrifices of limiting one's food choices with the rewards that will result from returning to the faith and upholding the locally grown covenant. "Doing the right thing," says Kingsolver, "is not about abstinence-only . . . or dragging around feeling righteous and gloomy. Food is the rare moral arena in which the ethical choice is generally the one more likely to make you groan with pleasure. Why resist that?"[45]

When skillfully employed by a gifted rhetor such as Kingsolver, the jeremiad can be an extraordinarily effective rhetorical form. The evocative rhetoric of those who speak passionately about the natural world can move an audience to care enough to take action, while the implementational rhetoric directs the passion into policy. That is why, according to Opie and Elliot, the jeremiad has endured over the centuries as a ritualistic rhetorical form. "The jeremiad affords our culture the opportunity to rage with displeasure, to evoke the beauty of metaphor, to find safety in method, and to reconcile oppositions."[46]

Concluding and Looking Ahead

The contemporary global climate change prophets are truly "prophets of doom." Their unsettling prophesies portend a future very different from the world we now know. Some of the messages employ apocalyptic themes such as in this excerpt from a speech made by Britain's Prime Minister, Tony Blair, in 2004:

What is now plain is that the emission of greenhouse gases . . . is causing global warming at a rate that began as significant, has become alarming and is simply unsustainable in the long term . . . . By unsustainable, I do not mean a phenomenon causing problems of adjustment. I mean a challenge so far-reaching in its impact that it alters radically human existence.[47]

Other predictions, such as the following from Harvard biologist Edward O. Wilson, in 2006, employ a locus of the irreparable:

> We have, all by our bipedal, wobbly-headed selves, altered Earth's atmosphere . . . . A collateral effect of all this . . . is the continuing extinction of wild ecosystems, along with the species that compose them. This also happens to be the only human impact that is irreversible.[48]

The warnings are indeed dire, yet in true jeremiadic form, after leveling a resounding rebuke, contemporary prophets offer a chance for redemption, as in the following example from scientist and conservationist Tim Flannery in his influential book *The Weather Makers:*

> If everyone who has the means to do so takes concerted action to rid atmospheric carbon emissions from their lives, I believe we can stabilize and then save the cryosphere . . . . But for that to happen, individuals, industry, and governments need to act on climate change now: The delay of even a decade is far too much.[49]

Some prophets, such as Pulitzer Prize winner Ross Gelbspan, even suggest the possibility of a utopian outcome:

> It is just possible that the act of re-wiring the planet could begin to point us toward that optimal calibration of competition and cooperation that would maximize our energy and creativity and productivity, while at the same time, substantially extend the baseline conditions for peace—peace among people, and peace between people and nature.[50]

Rhetoric that attempts to predict or envision the future is inherently risky by virtue of the fact that no one has an infallible crystal ball. Unlike the prophets of old who called on the faith of believers, modern-day environmental oracles must rely on scientific models to persuade their audiences of the validity of their predictions. Yet even the most sound science cannot predict with certainty, especially when dealing with something as complex and enigmatic as our global climate system. It is beyond our capability to understand completely or precisely the innumerable systems and subsystems that make up the complex web of the natural world, much less predict with certainty how these systems will respond in the future. In light of the enormity of the threat posed by global climate change, we would do well to heed the warnings of the prophets. There is compelling evidence to suggest that to do otherwise would be an extremely high-stakes gamble.

We tend to place a great deal of faith in the wisdom of science and technological expertise to inform our environmental decisions, yet, paradoxically, we often fail to heed the warnings of experts. As environmental writer Neil Evernden points out, it has been many years since Rachel Carson first sounded the alert about the dangers of pesticide abuse, yet "a rereading of *Silent Spring* leaves one with the feeling that little has changed but the names of the poisons."[51]

The following chapter looks at the rhetoric of risk, science, and technology and offers some explanations why even the most compelling science sometimes fails to translate into policy and practice. Science offers reliable, replicable information about environmental hazards and how to address them, but relevant wisdom is not limited to the "technical rationality" of scientists and technical experts. As you will see, "cultural rationality" likewise plays an important role in sound environmental decisions.

Discussion Questions and Exercises

1. This chapter offers a number of tools of analysis that can be used as guidelines for analyzing a rhetorical artifact: the three components of a locus of the irreparable, the characteristics of ecological utopias, the four rhetorical goals of the jeremiad, and the two rhetorical strategies of the jeremiad. Find an environmental text (such as a speech, a brochure, a web page, or an editorial) and apply one or more of these tools in a rhetorical analysis of the artifact.

2. One of the most well-known and respected prophets of global climate change is Dr. James Hansen, who heads NASA's Goddard Institute for Space Studies. Do some research to find out about attempts to censor Hansen's public communications about global warming. A good place to begin your research is with a January 29, 2006, article in the *New York Times* by Andrew Revkin (www.nytimes.com/2006/01/29/science/earth/29climate.html). Does Hansen's story support or contradict Killingsworth and Palmer's three implications of apocalyptic rhetoric? Explain your answer.

3. Explain what Delicath means when he says that utopia should not be viewed as a place, but as a dialogue.

4. The "History of the Future" gives the reader an idea of the broad societal changes in this utopian world, but offers few details of what day-to-day life is like. Divide into groups and imagine that you are college students in this utopian era and envision a day in the life of a student. Describe the campus and the classroom, the classes you are taking; what you are wearing, what's for lunch, what you will do for recreation when classes are over, the kind of transportation you use, and so forth. Report your visions to the class.

5. Get to Know Your Tomato: Contemporary Jeremiah and best-selling author Barbara Kingsolver chastises American consumers for their unsustainable eating practices. This exercise requires some creative investigation. Go to your local supermarket and choose a tomato (or an apple, an avocado, an onion, etc.). Ask the produce manager what produce supplier it came from. Then see if you can find out about that supplier and its supply network. Find out how to contact the supplier and see how far you are able to trace the tomato back to its "roots" of origin. Report your findings.

Suggested Readings

J. Robert Cox. "The Die Is Cast: Topical and Ontological Dimensions of a *Locus of the Irreparable*." *Quarterly Journal of Speech* 68 (1982): 227–239.

Marius de Geus. *Ecological Utopias: Envisioning the Sustainable Society*. Utrecht, The Netherlands: International Books, 1999.

M. Jimmie Killingsworth and Jacqueline S. Palmer. "Millennial Ecology: The Apocalyptic Narrative from *Silent Spring* to Global Warming." In C. G. Herndl and S. C. Brown (Eds.). *Green Culture: Environmental Rhetoric in Contemporary America*, 21–45. Madison: University of Wisconsin Press, 1996.

Barbara Kingsolver. *Animal, Vegetable, Miracle: A Year of Food Life*. New York: Harper Perennial, 2007.

John Opie and Norbert Elliot. "Tracking the Elusive Jeremiad: The Rhetorical Character of American Environmental Discourse." In J. G. Cantrill and C. L. Oravec (Eds.), *The Symbolic Earth: Discourse and Our Creation of the Environment*, 9–37. Lexington: University of Kentucky Press, 1996.

Notes

1. Bill McKibben, *The End of Nature* (New York: Random House, 1989), 7.
2. McKibben, *The End of Nature,* 7.
3. McKibben, *The End of Nature,* 54.
4. Bill McKibben, "'Worried? Us?'" *Granta Magazine,* 2005, http://www.granta.com/extracts/2032 (accessed June 11, 2005).
5. M. Jimmie Killingsworth and Jacqueline S. Palmer, "Millennial Ecology: The Apocalyptic Narrative from *Silent Spring* to Global Warming," in *Green Culture: Environmental Rhetoric in Contemporary America,* eds. C. G. Herndl and S. C. Brown (Madison: University of Wisconsin Press, 1996), 27.
6. Rachel Carson, *Silent Spring* (New York: Fawcett, 1962).
7. Killingsworth and Palmer, "Millennial Ecology."
8. Killingsworth and Palmer, "Millennial Ecology," 31.
9. Benjamin Kline, *First Along the River: A Brief History of the U.S. Environmental Movement,* 2nd ed. (San Francisco: Acada, 2000), 75.
10. Killingsworth and Palmer, "Millennial Ecology," 42.
11. Priscilla Coit Murphy, *What a Book Can Do: The Publication and Reception of Silent Spring* (Boston: University of Massachusetts Press, 2005), 190.
12. Murphy, *What a Book Can Do,* 191.
13. Murphy, *What a Book Can Do,* 1.
14. Star A. Muir, "Cultural and Critical Grammars of the Apocalypse: Strategies for a New Millennium," in *Proceedings of the 4th Biennial Conference on Communication and Environment,* ed. S. L. Senecah (Cazenovia, NY: July 1997), 28–36.
15. Muir, "Cultural and Critical Grammars," 34.
16. C. Perelman and L. Olbrechts-Tyteca, *The New Rhetoric: A Treatise on Argumentation,* trans. J. Wilkinson and P. Weaver (Notre Dame: University of Notre Dame Press, 1971).
17. J. Robert Cox, "The Die is Cast: Topical and Ontological Dimensions of a *Locus* of the Irreparable," *Quarterly Journal of Speech* 68 (1982): 227–239.
18. Terence Check, "Re-thinking the Irreparable" (Paper presented at the Annual Convention of the National Communication Association, Chicago, IL, November 1999).
19. Cited in Check, "Re-thinking the Irreparable."
20. Cox, "The Die Is Cast," 234.
21. Peter Schwartz and Doug Randall, "An Abrupt Climate Change Scenario and Its Implications for United States National Security," 2003, http://www.climate.org/PDF/clim_change_scenario.pdf (accessed October 12, 2008).
22. Ernest Callenbach, *Ecotopia* (Berkeley: Banyan Tree, 1975).
23. Marius de Geus, *Ecological Utopias: Envisioning the Sustainable Society* (Utrecht, The Netherlands: International Books, 1999).
24. Marius de Geus, *Ecological Utopias;* K. Kassman, *Envisioning Ecotopia: The U.S. Green Movement and the Politics of Radical Social Change* (Westport, CT: Praeger, 1997); B. L. Ott and E. Aoki, "Popular Imagination and Identity Politics: Reading the Future in 'Star Trek: The Next Generation,'" *Western Journal of Communication* 65 (2001): 92–415; C. Hintz and E. Ostry, eds., *Utopian and Dystopian: Writing for Children and Young Adults* (New York: Routledge, 2003); J. Dickerson, "Utopian and Dystopian Master Narratives in a Posthuman World" (Paper presented at the International Communication Association Annual Meeting, New York, May 26–30, 2005).
25. Global Scenerio Group, *Great Transition,* 2002, http://www.gsg.org (accessed October 1, 2008).
26. Global Scenario Group, *Great Transition,* 26.
27. Global Scenario Group, *Great Transition,* 84.
28. Global Scenario Group, *Great Transition,* 86.
29. Global Scenario Group, *Great Transition,* 87.
30. Global Scenario Group, *Great Transition,* 89.

31. Global Scenario Group, *Great Transition,* 87–88.

32. Global Scenario Group, *Great Transition,* 89.

33. Global Scenario Group, *Great Transition,* 89.

34. John W. Delicath, "In Search of Ecotopia: Radical Environmentalism and the Possibilities of Utopian Rhetorics," In *Earthtalk: Communication Empowerment for Environmental Action,* eds. S. A. Muir and T. L. Veenendall (Westport, CT: Praeger, 1996), 155.

35. Marius de Geus, *The End of Over-Consumption: Towards a Lifestyle of Moderation and Self-restraint* (Utrecht, The Netherlands: International Books, 2003).

36. H. G. Wells, "Utopias" [Transcript of speech given on January 19, 1939, and broadcast over ABC radio], *Science Fiction Studies* 9 (1989): 117.

37. John Opie and Norbert Elliot, "Tracking the Elusive Jeremiad: The Rhetorical Character of American Environmental Discourse," in *The Symbolic Earth: Discourse and Our Creation of the Environment,* eds. J. G. Cantrill and C. L. Oravec (Lexington: University of Kentucky Press, 1996), 9–37.

38. John Muir, *The Yosemite* (New York: Century, 1912), 62.

39. Aldo Leopold, *A Sand County Almanac: And Sketches Here and There* (Oxford, UK: Oxford University Press, 1949/1977), 224–225. By permission of Oxford University Press, Inc.

40. Ralph Waldo Emerson, "Nature", in *The Great New Wilderness Debate,* eds. J. B. Callicott and M. P. Nelson (Athens: University of Georgia Press, 1836/1998), 239.

41. John Muir, "Our National Parks," in *The Great New Wilderness Debate,* eds. J. B. Callicott and M. B. Nelson (Athens: University of Georgia Press, 1901/1998), 61.

42. Henry David Thoreau, "Walking," in *The Great New Wilderness Debate,* eds. J. B. Callicott and M. B. Nelson (Athens: University of Georgia Press, 1862/1998), 37.

43. James R. Garfield, cited in Christine L. Oravec, "Conservationism vs. Preservationism: The 'Public Interest' in the Hetch Hetchy Controversy," *Quarterly Journal of Speech* 70 (1984): 444.

44. Barbara Kingsolver, *Animal, Vegetable, Miracle: A Year of Food Life* (New York: Harper Perennial, 2007), 196.

45. Kingsolver, *Animal, Vegetable, Miracle,* 22.

46. Opie and Elliot, "Tracking the Elusive Jeremiad," 35.

47. Tony Blair, "PM Speech on Climate Change," 2004, http://www.number-10.gov.uk/outpage/page6333.asp (accessed April 18, 2007).

48. Edward O. Wilson, *The Creation: An Appeal to Save Life on Earth* (New York: Norton, 2006), 29.

49. Tim Flannery, *The Weather Makers: How Man is Changing the Climate and What It Means for Life on Earth* (New York: Atlantic Monthly Press, 2005), 296–297.

50. Ross Gelbspan, *Boiling Point: How Politicians, Big Oil and Coal, Journalists, and Activists Have Fueled the Climate Crisis—and What We Can Do to Avert Disaster* (New York: Basic Books, 2004), 205.

51. Neil Evernden, *The Social Creation of Nature* (Baltimore: The Johns Hopkins University Press, 1992), ix.

Chapter 8

Technical Rationality and the Rhetoric of Risk, Science, and Technology

From my years of living in the high desert in rural New Mexico, I have come to know and love coyotes. My relationship with these craggy critters has come about through multiple associations. I have often observed them as they run and hunt on the hillsides outside my window. Stories of the early Spanish settlers in this area tell of how the coyotes warned the villagers of the approaching Comanche raiders, giving them time to hide and arm themselves. The traditional lore of the Pueblo Indians of the Southwest portray the coyote as a lovable trickster who entertains and fascinates but can never be completely trusted. The children are told never to invite a coyote into their homes because his tricks sometimes go too far. The soundness of this advice has been brought home to me as I have commiserated with friends and neighbors who have lost their pets or their free-range chickens to the sometimes not-so-lovable trickster. I will never tire of hearing the strange, dissonant, other-worldly sound of the coyote's cry that has inspired poets and songwriters for centuries. The sound carries for miles in the mountain foothills and leaves me with a profound sense of belonging and love for my home and its human and nonhuman inhabitants. For many years, I have worked to preserve the area's wildlands as a home for these beloved friends.

My way of knowing coyotes—of understanding and valuing their presence in my world—is a product of personal experience, folklore, cultural wisdom, narratives, and poetry. But there is another way of knowing that yields a kind of knowledge very different from my own experiential, culture-based knowledge. Through objective, systematic methods of scientific inquiry, biologists and ecologists have learned about the physiology of coyotes, their distribution in the habitat, their mating habits, their role in the ecosystem, and so forth.

Our ways of knowing and the knowledge they generate serve as the authority for determining our opinions and courses of action. In other words, one's way of knowing carries with it its own kind of thinking and reasoning. Communication scholars Alonzo Plough and Sheldon Krimsky refer to the two spheres of reasoning as "technical rationality" versus "cultural rationality."[1] The following discussion looks at these two vastly different ways of knowing and understanding the world.

Technical Rationality vs. Cultural Rationality

The belief that nature can be observed, understood, and controlled through the precision of scientific method, and the assumptions of rationality that ground this way of knowing, are legacies of the Enlightenment (as discussed in Chapter 3). **Technical rationality** is based on a way of knowing through scientific method or technological expertise. It presents an "objective," "neutral" view of reality based on testable, measurable facts that are independent of human values or opinions. When dealing with environmental issues, technical rationality is often framed in terms of the degree of harm, probability of harm, statistical significance, and so forth. This way of knowing and understanding the world is impersonal and distanced from the experience of everyday life.

In contrast, **cultural rationality** stems from familiar, personal experience and the values that humans place on their surroundings. The values we place on a coyote's cry, a mountain vista, a rural way of life, quiet surroundings, family, and community are examples of nonquantifiable, but deeply cherished values that form the basis of cultural rationality. Cultural rationality is also a product of highly abstract ideals such as democracy, fairness, the right of consent, and control over one's life.

Purveyors of technical rationality sometimes view the nonexpert audience as incapable of understanding the complexities of scientific or technical discourse, and take a "trust us, we're experts" stance when communicating with the public. Similarly, the public audience often views experts as incapable of understanding, or insensitive to the meaning and values that come from personal experiences and values. The outcome is often a clash of these two vastly different spheres of reasoning.

Messages framed in the language of technical rationality tend to hold great sway in legal, legislative, and regulatory forums. Technical rationality has its time and place; virtually every aspect of our lives has been enhanced in some way through experts' ability to communicate the knowledge of the scientific community. Yet, the overreliance on technical rationality as a means of communicating about environmental problems has often proven to be a rhetorically ineffective means of motivating action or achieving desired environmental protection measures. As Walter R. Fisher's narrative paradigm tells us, "Humans as rhetorical beings are as much valuing as they are reasoning animals."[2] A failure to consider the human values that come into play in any given environmental issue is likely to result in an ineffective rhetorical appeal or a clash of rationalities.

This chapter takes a look at technical rationality and the rhetoric of risk, science, and technology, and explores the reasons why the most overwhelming evidence or startling data often fail to translate into individual, social, or legislative action. Environmental communication scholar Pete Bsumek explains this failure as resulting from the inability of rhetors "to move from the 'is' of scientific fact to the 'ought' of social policy."[3] A good way to begin an exploration of the gulf between the "is" and the "ought" is by looking at the forms of technical rationality and their implications. The following sections examine two forms of technical rationality that are used extensively in environmental discourse—risk communication and the highly specialized field of risk inquiry known as epidemiology.

Risk Communication

Every day we are confronted with risk. We hear about the health hazards of smoking, plastics, mercury, and food additives; the dangers of recalled children's toys, defective tires, and aging pipelines; the environmental risks posed by CO_2 emissions, leaking landfills, and industry smokestacks; and so on. The technologies and innovations that have given us the "good life" have also created what German sociologist Ulrich Beck refers to as a "risk society." Beck suggests that we are living in an age in which the ecological hazards created by technologies and innovations increasingly elude controls. Modern society, as a result of "autonomous modernization processes which are blind and deaf to consequences and dangers," is faced with ecological risks that are universal and unaccountable.[4] Many, if not most, of the messages we receive about the environment address the hazards we face living in a risk society.

One form of technical rationality commonly used to address environmental hazards is **risk assessment,** an estimation of potential risks of an action or condition based on quantifiable probabilities of the degree of harm. Ecological risk assessment attempts to predict and quantify the adverse affects that human activity or pollutants will have on a particular ecosystem. Health risk assessment addresses questions such as: What types of health problems are caused by substances in the environment? What is the likelihood and severity of the harm? The following excerpt from an informational brochure about the probabilities of getting cancer from a proposed toxic waste incinerator is an example of risk communication.

> The cumulative potential cancer risk estimated for the Offpost Study Area
> are 1 in 10,000 for Zone 1; 2 in 10,000 for Zone 2; 3 in 10,000 for Zone 3;
> 2 in 10,000 for Zone 4; 3 in 100,000 for Zone 5; and 7 in 100,000 for Zone 6.[5]

Risk communication can take many forms, but as in the example above, the messages always focus on the likelihood or degree of harm, based on the best estimates of scientists and experts. Although it is important to communicate to the public what scientists and experts have to say about the potential hazards of an action or a situation, it is often the nonquantifiable human values, such as quality of life and the well-being of loved ones, that form the basis for public concern.

The risk of cancer from the proposed waste incinerator, in the example above, fails to address community concerns about what an incinerator might to do property values or what its impact might be on blue skies and mountain vistas. It likewise fails to address frustration on the part of the community members who may feel that they have had little say in the decision or have lost control over things that are important in their lives. From a technical reasoning standpoint, such concerns may be dismissed because they cannot be counted or factored into the quantitative risk models. When human values are left out of the equation and the risk is reduced to a single metric, such as the risk of cancer in a particular zone, there is an increased potential for mistrust, misunderstanding, and conflict.

Epidemiology

Communicating issues of health effects are especially challenging for members of the lay, nonexpert public. The narratives of their personal experiences and their claims of adverse health effects are often discredited by the language of science, largely because of the scientific method used to assess the incidents of illness in a highly specialized field of risk assessment known as "epidemiology."

Epidemiology is the science that investigates factors affecting the health of populations. Epidemiologists use a variety of statistical tools in an attempt to find causal relationships between, for example, a toxic waste incinerator and the incidence of cancer in surrounding communities. Because proving causality can be very difficult, epidemiological studies are often unable to verify claims that any given toxic landscape is the cause of illness in the community. One reason is that "confounding variables" pose complications. Such things as smoking cigarettes, alcohol consumption, diet, and genetic predispositions cannot be controlled for when we are looking at human populations in their natural settings. These variables can "confound" the results of a study, making it difficult to know for sure whether, for example, an individual's cancer was caused by smoking cigarettes or by the toxic waste incinerator.

Another reason why epidemiological studies often discredit or fail to verify the health claims of community residents is that the health and toxicity data for particular chemicals may be unavailable or inadequate. Considering that the Environmental Protection Agency (EPA) lists eighty-two thousand chemicals currently in commercial use with seven hundred new chemicals introduced each year, this is not surprising.[6] The unknown effects of exposure to more than one chemical at a time further compounds the uncertainty of the data. Such complexities are especially problematic in communities that host multiple industrial facilities (such as Cancer Alley in Louisiana, which is discussed in further detail in Chapter 13), all of which might emit chemicals into the air, water, and soil.

Additional factors complicate the task of establishing a causal relationship between environmental pollutants and health effects. Many toxic pollutants are invisible. Their effects might not be manifested for years, or it might take long-term exposure to a particular pollutant to cause illness. For these and other reasons, disease rates that appear as obvious public health problems may not turn out to be statistically significant in any given study. Thus, those who would be held accountable for creating the environmental hazard can, and often do, use uncertainty about causality to discredit community claims of health effects or to rationalize inaction.

In her book *When Smoke Ran Like Water,* National Academy of Science scholar Devra Davis examines in depth how industries have repeatedly used the uncertainties of science to deceive policy makers. "When it comes to studying the impact of the environment on health," says Davis, "epidemiology remains an inexact instrument. Most often we fail to find answers . . . . Our track record on environmental effects on health is especially unimpressive. As one of my colleagues remarked, 'an epidemic is something so obvious it can be detected even by epidemiologists.'"[7]

Despite their limitations, risk assessment and epidemiology provide regulators and decision-makers with vital information for protecting ecosystems and human health. Risk assessment and other forms of scientific discovery have figured prominently in policy decisions and have led to the adoption of a great many protection measures. As methods of assessing risk advance, so too does our understanding of the adverse effects of human activities or pollutants.

Yet, the technical rationality that grounds risk assessment and scientific discovery represents only one way of seeing and knowing, and is only a piece of the knowledge and understanding that shapes humans' complex relationship with the natural world. Cultural rationality that stems from personal experience, folk wisdom, tradition, and human values also profoundly informs our understanding, but this way of knowing is often afforded little standing within the constraints imposed by technical rationality.

In recognition of the inherent inadequacies of risk assessment that is detached from its cultural and social context, a number of risk experts have called for ways to broaden risk assessment to draw on the rich source of relevant information that interested and affected "nonexperts" can provide. The National Research Council convened the Committee on Risk Characterization to recommend ways of implementing "analytic-deliberative" processes of risk assessment that incorporate analysis based on scientific methods as well as the deliberation and input of citizen stakeholders. Ultimately, these processes lead to better science. As the Committee's report states, "To be decision-relevant, risk characterization must be accurate, balanced, and informative. This requires getting the science right and getting the right science. Participation helps ask the right questions of the science, check the plausibility of assumptions, and ensure that any synthesis is both balanced and informative."[8]

Case studies that have looked at the actual implementation of analytic-participatory processes have demonstrated differing levels of success. While risk assessment professionals recognize the wisdom of broadening the decision criteria beyond the science to include information and insight from diverse groups and individuals, the process can be highly contentious and difficult to manage (as discussed in further detail in Chapter 12). It is often the case that technical rationality excludes or places restraints on alternative ways of knowing and cultural rationality.

Technical Rationality and Constraints to Alternative Ways of Knowing

Many environmental communication scholars have examined case studies of environmental crisis or threats of crisis in which technical rationality was the primary means of understanding or speaking for the environment. The case studies examine a wide spectrum of concerns, ranging from disappearing Monarch butterflies[9] to a nuclear power plant accident,[10] all of which demonstrate, in some form or another, the chilling effect that technical rationality can have on alternative ways of knowing or seeing the world and, ultimately, on informing and motivating pro-environmental action.

The following is a summary of some of the common themes that have emerged as environmental communication scholars have examined the limitations of technical rationality. Technical rationality can constrain alternative ways of knowing in at least three ways: (1) through exclusion or marginalization of the nonexpert voice through language; (2) through ideological and statutory control, and (3) through the assumption of an incompetent lay public.

Language

The language of science and technology can exclude the public voice because it is often inaccessible to those who lack the necessary specialized expertise. The dialogue is limited to those who have a working knowledge of the arcane language, thus creating an autonomous, self-perpetuating hierarchy of technocratic elite. One means by which the language of science creates and perpetuates that hierarchy is through what rhetorical scholar Edward Schiappa, in his examination of the language of nuclear development, refers to as the **bureaucratization of language,** a rhetorical strategy by which highly technical concepts "are insulated from public inspection by acronyms or sanitized jargon."[11]

Although Schiappa looked at the language of nuclear science and its institutions, his observations can also be applied to other areas of scientific enquiry and technical rationality. The discourse of nuclear technologies serves as an especially potent example of how language is used to create a technocratic elite and constrain the nonexpert voice. As environmental communication scholar William J. Kinsella explains, "the term 'nuclear science' (along with its cognate 'rocket science') is a symbol of intellectual difficulty with wide cultural currency, and a doubly powerful symbol in a culture where the term 'science' alone evokes considerable awe."[12]

Schiappa suggests that acronyms serve as an especially mystifying form of language bureaucratization that can confound and alienate a lay public. **Acronyms** are words formed from the first letter, or first few letters, of several words. Consider, for example, the following excerpt from a U.S. Department of Energy document, which describes the complex internal structure of a single program within a much more complex system designed for maintaining the U.S. nuclear weapons stockpile:

> DSW activities to maintain the nuclear stockpile are accomplished through several DP vehicles, including the 6.X process, the SLEP, and the Production and Planning Directive (P&PD). Under the broad DSW umbrella, each of these vehicles contributes to the formulation and execution of weapons Life Extension Programs (LEPs).[13]

Although acronyms may facilitate communication among institutional members, their use can also restrict or limit dialog with those who are unfamiliar with their meanings.

Another form of language bureaucratization that Schiappa refers to is **sanitized jargon,** language that serves to "sanitize" a concept so that it appears inoffensive or neutral. Environmental communication scholars Bryan C. Taylor and Judith Hendry examined the names used for technologies designed to create and test nuclear weapons. They offer some examples of sanitized jargon.[14] This highly complex testing is carried out through technologies with names borrowed from Greek mythology (Pegasus II, SPHINX, Hermes III) or astronomy (Procyon, Saturn). These names create a sense of something mystical and enigmatic and, at the same time, euphemistically temper the reality of weapons of mass destruction. When we attach mystical characters or celestial bodies to the technologies used to create and test nuclear weapons, the technologies take on an aura of benign inscrutability, thus shielding them from public inspection or questioning. "Hermes III" is far more palatable than "High-Energy Radiation Megavolt Electron Source III," the actual name for which the acronym stands.

Control

Another way in which *technical rationality can exclude or marginalize the lay public is through ideological and statutory control.* In their case study of a community's opposition to the siting of a low-level radioactive waste facility, rhetorical scholars Steven B. Katz and Carolyn R. Miller[15] observed how technical rationality confers these two forms of control. **Ideological control** is the power to determine what kinds of language and arguments are considered legitimate in any given debate or policy deliberation. The power of ideological control carries great weight because, as environmental ethicists Michael Bruner and Max Oelschlaeger observe, "whoever defines the terms of the public debate determines its outcome."[16] Defining the debate in terms of technical rationality serves to invalidate communications that do not fall within the "approved topics" or that are not appropriately framed in the expert or procedural language of technical rationality.

In their case study Katz and Miller observed that the regulatory authority considered only those challenges from the public that accurately used the technical language of the stated regulations and ignored those that were phrased in the interpretive language of a lay person. The exclusion or invalidation of the layman's language placed members of the public in what Katz and Miller refer to as "a classic double bind" by allowing them to be heard only in a language they couldn't speak.[17]

Another form of control is **statutory control,** which is granted to the agency or the entity that is the sanctioned, "official," rule-maker and decision authority. Such authority is most often given to government agencies. Statutory control, as

Katz and Miller explain, puts the decision authority in a position to "set the agenda to which the public has to respond."[18] They observed that the decision authority determined who spoke, when they spoke, and for how long. The citizen stake-holders were given very limited opportunity to give input into the decisions and their input carried little weight in the deliberations. Katz and Miller tell of one citizen's report of having to sit through a three-hour presentation by the company that was proposing to build and operate the radioactive waste facility, after which the Authority voted unanimously to approve all of the company's requests. Citizens were invited to give public comment only after voting was already done.[19]

The two forms of control, ideological and statutory, conferred a great deal of power to the decision authority and disempowered citizens who were not versed in technical language or procedural guidelines, and who were given little opportu-nity to influence the decisions that might greatly impact their lives.

The Assumption of an Incompetent Lay Public

Technical rationality also constrains alternative ways of knowing because *it assumes the lay public is incompetent*. Oftentimes, communicators operating within a framework of technical rationality adopt a patronizing approach that is based on the assumption that citizen fears or concerns are simply the product of a sadly uninformed or misguided public, and that information and education can "correct" public opinion.

Environmental communication scholar Susan Sattell[20] offers an example of how this assumption translates into practice. She examined the risk and policy debates over corn that is genetically engineered to contain the Bt protein (a naturally occur-ring pesticide), and its effect on the monarch butterfly. The controversy ignited with the 1999 publication, in the journal *Nature,* of the results of a laboratory study that examined the negative impact on survival rates when monarch butterflies ate leaves dusted with genetically engineered pollen.[21]

The resulting controversy served as a catalyst for debate about risks that went beyond a single butterfly species to encompass broader concerns about the risks of agricultural biotechnology to human health, the food chain, and the global envi-ronment—risks that antibiotechnology activists assert must be better understood before we permit widespread bioengineering in food production. Having much to lose, the biotechnology industry marshaled its resources and hired three public relations firms to create and carry out an image campaign to counter the antibio-technology "hysteria."[22]

The campaign, carried out mostly through mass-mediated news sources, focused its strategy on characterizing the opposition as "hysterical" and "irrational," claiming that the concerns about the safety of Bt crops were based on "junk science." Sattell points out that such a campaign can obstruct opponents' ability to participate in the public dialogue and policy debates. She goes on to warn, however, that although this strategy may temporarily obstruct opposing voices in any particular campaign, "the very socio-political and environmental concerns that are dismissed are likely to arise at a later date."[23] Dismissing public concerns as merely the irrational response of the misinformed ignores the cultural rationality grounding those concerns and fails to recognize the importance and legitimacy of alternative ways of knowing and understanding the world.

Thus far, this chapter has examined some of the limitations of technical ratio-nality and how it can work to constrain alternative ways of knowing. Ultimately, these limitations can lead to what rhetorical scholars Thomas Farrell and G. Thomas Goodnight refer to as a **rhetorical crisis,** which occurs when "practices of communication and techniques of persuasion break down, proliferating disbelief when informed consensus is demanded and foreclosing options when cooperative action is vital."[24] The following case study demonstrates just such a rhetorical crisis, brought about by a failure of technical rationality and its inability to inform and direct a frightened and angry public.

A Colossal Case of a Failed Rhetoric of Risk:
Three Mile Island

In an extraordinary coincidence, the film "The China Syndrome," was released only days before its plot line was reenacted in real life through an accident at the Three Mile Island nuclear power plant. Little did the producers know that their film would be entirely too close to reality. In the film, Jane Fonda and Michael Douglas play television reporters who, while making a documentary about nuclear technology, capture on film an accident at a power plant that nearly resulted in the **China syndrome,** the overheating of the reactor core causing it to metaphorically blast its way to China. Fonda's and Douglas's characters find themselves trapped between the nuclear industry's desire to cover up the incident and the public's right to know.

The nation was stunned as the real-life events of Three Mile Island began to unfold on March 28, 1979, just twelve days after the release of the movie. Although a total meltdown was avoided both in the movie and in real life, the two events focused the nation's attention on the potentially devastating consequences of a serious accident at a nuclear power plant. They also demonstrated a colossal failure of technical reasoning and of the rhetoric of risk, science, and technology, leaving the public confused, frightened, and with no clear idea of what to do.

Farrell and Goodnight[25] examined the Three Mile Island accident to understand how technical discourse failed to adequately inform public judgment, resulting in widespread uncertainty and alarm. They employ the terms *technical reasoning* and *social reasoning,* which are synonymous with the terms *technical rationality* and *cultural rationality.*

Farrell and Goodnight contend that, in the case of the Three Mile Island incident, technical reason usurped the role of social reason and failed because it was "inadequate to the task of informing public judgment."[26] The failed rhetoric created a rhetorical crisis along with the environmental crisis.

The Three Mile Island Accident

The accident at Three Mile Island was the most serious nuclear power plant accident in U.S. history. Although there were no injuries or lives lost at the time of the incident, the invisible threat of radiation release and the unthinkable consequences of a possible core meltdown created a state of public fear, confusion, and outrage. This public concern was compounded by the rhetorical crisis that accompanied the accident, leaving people unsure of what to think, whom to believe, or what to do. Farrell and Goodnight describe the confusion:

> Reporters were unable to judge the validity of technical statements.
> Technicians often could not sense the relevance of reporters' questions.
> Government sources, frequently at odds with one another, could not decide what information to release or what action to take. Some representatives of

the nuclear power industry made misleading statements. Still others did not speak at all. The people of Middletown and Londonderry did not know whom to believe. Many simply fled.[27]

It all began about 4:00 on the morning of March 28, 1979. A confusing combination of human error, design deficiencies, and technical failures ultimately resulted in the partial melting of fuel rods, the appearance of a hydrogen bubble, and the release of radiation.

Although the status of the reactor core was unclear from the outset and would remain so for the next five days, plant technicians, nuclear industry experts, and representatives from the Nuclear Regulatory Commission quickly attempted to reassure the public that there was nothing to fear from the amount of radiation that had been released and that the problem was under control. Yet, the continuous discharge of radioactive materials on the second day and the appearance of a hydrogen bubble in the reactor core resulted in growing uncertainty on the part of the public, as well as the experts. Industry experts and agency representatives were no longer claiming that a meltdown was impossible since no one really knew what to expect from the hydrogen bubble. As Farrell and Goodnight explain, "the further down the bubble reached, the more it threatened to expose the reactor core ('The China Syndrome'!). The closer it reached to the top of the reactor, the more it appeared likely to detonate."[28]

The press was quick to pick up on the drama and play on the fears of the public, as demonstrated by Walter Cronkite's opening remarks in his evening newscast on the third day of the event: "The danger faced by man for tampering with natural forces, a theme familiar from the myths of Prometheus to the story of Frankenstein, moved closer to fact from fancy . . . ."[29]

Prevailing Conceptions of the Public

Farrell and Goodnight argue that the rhetorical crisis at Three Mile Island can be traced to the prevailing conceptions of the public that were communicated throughout the course of the event, including (1) *the accidental public,* (2) *the public as spectator,* and (3) *the public as "standing reserve of energy."*

The technical discourse of the events produced by the nuclear scientists and regulatory agency officials "seemed to be governed," suggest Farrell and Goodnight, "by a conception of *the public itself as an accident.*"[30] It seemed as if the experts who were called on to explain the situation viewed the public's demands for answers as an accidental and unwelcome intrusion into the information turf of the technical experts.

The technical reasoning offered to the public failed, in part, because the experts failed to recognize that this incident represented not just a technological problem, but a social problem as well. Relevant social questions regarding moral accountability (such as the fundamental morality of dangerous technologies as money-making enterprises) and human values (such as the sense of safety and the feeling of control over the decisions that impact one's life) were considered by the experts to be extraneous to the situation, as was the public itself. It was as if the experts were saying, "we are only talking to you because you are demanding answers and we're only talking about the science stuff."

Further contributing to the rhetorical crisis was the vision of *public as spectator* implicit in much of the discourse. The mass media produced a news-as-spectacle narrative form of the Three Mile Island "story," in which the public was treated as a passive receiver rather than as an active agent. When something new and more dramatic happened (such as the American Airlines Flight 191 crash a few weeks later), stories of Three Mile Island were consigned to the back pages. Thus, as Farrell and Goodnight said, "the public remains a spectator to a parade of endless catastrophes."[31] The news tends to dramatize and report only the surface features of public issues, then move on to the next entertaining drama while "the mass audience remains without impulse, knowledge of alternatives, or direction."[32]

Farrell and Goodnight suggest that while neither the technological institutions nor the mass media treated the public as an active agent, such was not the case with the public relations firms that the nuclear power industry hired to promote nuclear energy. After the initial media furor died down, the nuclear industry launched a massive campaign to cultivate a favorable public opinion about nuclear energy. Here, the public was viewed as a *standing reserve of energy* in which, as Farrell and Goodnight explain, the nuclear power industry treated the public as "a natural resource full of potential power waiting to be harnessed."[33] The power of public "attitude capital" was manipulated to create public support for nuclear power in order to advance the industry itself.

The public relations campaign attempted to downplay the seriousness of the accident and portrayed the opponents of nuclear power as irrational, uninformed alarmists. For example, the nuclear industry hired "advocates" to distribute bumper stickers and placards that read "A Little Nukey Never Hurt Anyone," "More People Have Died in Ted Kennedy's Car Than in Nuclear Accidents," and "Feed Jane Fonda to the Whales." (The actress, Jane Fonda, was an outspoken antinuclear activist.)

The general purpose of the post–Three Mile Island public relations campaign was to convince the public that the system had worked and had not failed—a meltdown had been avoided and the nation's worst fears were not realized. Be that as it may, this accident was a very near miss and the industry grossly downplayed the significance of the potential disaster. The fact is that the problem was not solved because of the technical experts and their ability to control the technology, but because, for some unknown reason, the hydrogen bubble dissolved on its own and the reactor stabilized. As Farrell and Goodnight state,

> If the conclusion of the Atomic Energy Commission is correct, that only luck has prevented more serious accidents from occurring, we wonder whether influencing attitudes only serves to deepen the potentiality for crisis. The Task Force concluded that the perceived need to protect the image of the nuclear industry may have been one of the causes for underestimating the potential significance of the breakdown.[34]

Is it any wonder that the rhetoric of Three Mile Island resulted in a rhetorical crisis that failed to inform and direct an angry, frightened public? When the public is itself viewed as an accident, as passive spectators, and manipulated as a source of "attitude capital," the inevitable response is confusion, mistrust, and fear. But the most significant consequence of the failed rhetoric was fortunately never realized. In a time of crisis, especially one with the destructive potential of a nuclear power plant accident, direction, cooperation, and coordinated action are essential. Should the unthinkable actually have happened, the confusion, mistrust, and fear could have led to a very tragic outcome.

On April 26, 1986, seven years after the Three Mile Island accident, the worst-case scenario was played out as a worldwide audience looked on in dismay. An explosion at the Chernobyl nuclear power plant in Ukraine (formerly the U.S.S.R.)

Figure 8.1
A Crack in a Nuclear Reactor

In 2005, Greenpeace activists disguised as radioactive waste containers infiltrated the nuclear power plant in Borssele, Netherlands. They painted a large crack on the dome of the reactor to symbolize the problems of aging reactors, as well as to demonstrate the plant's security issues. This image event created a major embarrassment for the government and the utility owners.

© Greenpeace / Joël van Houdt

caused the prolonged release of massive quantities of radioactive substance into the atmosphere, resulting in widespread distribution of contaminants throughout the northern hemisphere. The official death count reported by Soviet authorities was thirty-one. Many others suffered radiation sickness. The long-term health effects for those exposed to the radiation are still not fully determined. However, studies have shown that the incidence of thyroid cancer among children under the age of fifteen in the Ukraine has increased significantly.[35] Large tracks of forest and agricultural lands surrounding the plant are still excluded from use. The impacts of radiation contamination and its effects on human health and the natural environment are still being felt, and will be for countless years to come.

As you will read in the next chapter, the way in which the Chernobyl accident was communicated to the U.S. public via news media accounts was largely responsible for creating a rhetorical crisis of its own kind. In the case of Three Mile Island, the technical rhetoric of the experts failed to direct and inform public action. The way in which the news media reported the Chernobyl accident failed the public in much the same way.

The case of Three Mile Island demonstrates several critiques of technical rationality and why it sometimes falls short in its rhetorical task of motivating and directing the actions of a lay public. Conflicting constructions of the risk led to a confused and angry public. Despite attempts by the nuclear power industry to downplay the seriousness of the accident, a great deal of mistrust and fear remained. The Three Mile Island accident ultimately served as a catalyst for the

grassroots mobilization of a highly motivated and vocal antinuclear social movement. The fact that no new nuclear power plants have come online in the U.S.
since 1997 can be attributed, in large part, to the success of the movement in
creating large-scale public opposition to nuclear power. The success of the movement, however, is being challenged today by the growing demand for clean energy
that nuclear energy could potentially supply.

In the case of Three Mile Island, public mistrust, fear, and anger resulted in
the mobilization of the masses to bring about change. Not all perceptions of risk,
however, lead to of collective action. The following section examines three very
different public responses to risk and their implications for environmental action.

Cultural Rationality and Responses to Environmental Risk

The public wants and needs to be informed about environmental hazards and
the likelihood of harm from those hazards. We need to know the risks of a toxic
waste incinerator or a radioactive waste dump in our neighborhood. We need to
be informed about what the experts say about the potential harms to butterflies
and humans from genetically engineered crops. And when the experts don't really
know what the risks are, as in the case of Three Mile Island, we need to know that
as well, in order to make our own judgment calls for our safety and that of our
loved ones.

In many ways, our lives are safer and healthier because experts have effectively
communicated risks. Yet, as the previous examples have demonstrated, overreliance
on the technical rationality of risk and science as a means of communicating to the
public and directing action has often proven to be rhetorically ineffective. When
risk threatens, the public will respond with its own version of rationality that is
driven not by experts and risk probabilities, but by human values, experiential
knowledge, and cherished ideals. It is often cultural rationality that drives responses
to environmental risk. The following examines three such cultural rationality–
driven responses to risk.

NIMBY

One response to risk is public opposition in the form of what is commonly referred
to as the **NIMBY (Not In My Back Yard) syndrome,** which happens when community members unite in opposition to the siting of a **Locally Unwanted Land Use
(LULU)** that they fear will negatively impact the health and/or quality of life of the
surrounding communities. Among the most vociferously protested land uses are
hazardous waste incinerators, landfills, nuclear facilities, and airports.

Public opposition to LULUs is conventionally ascribed to the NIMBY syndrome.
Those who must face a determined and angry public often characterize NIMBY
responses as irrational, self-serving, parochial obstruction of land use projects that
are necessary and will benefit the greater community. Consider, for example, the
following definition of NIMBY offered by human geographer Michael Dear: "NIMBY
is the motivation of people who want to protect their turf" making it "almost impossible to build or locate vital facilities that the city needs to function."[36]

When public opposition is viewed as an obstruction to necessary, "rational"
planning, it should come as no surprise that the response to the opposition
frequently takes the form that Robert Lake, an urban policy researcher, describes as
"overcoming irrationality through attitude adjustment: education to change selfish

attitudes, persuading balky residents of the greater social benefit of a more rational approach, or constructing a legislative or judicial mechanism strong enough to steamroll the parochial impulse."[37]

Characterizing NIMBY opposition as merely an irrational response, by people who are trying to defend their piece of turf at the expense of the greater societal good, fails to take into account several social factors, not the least of which is the significance of the stakes. For many, the "piece of turf" represents their homes, their communities and, often, the biggest share of their material wealth. This characterization of NIMBY also fails to consider that imposing hazards against the will of those who are most impacted is greatly at odds with deeply held values for participatory democracy. Seen from this perspective, NIMBY objections are expressions of the sense of powerlessness that inevitably accompanies exclusion from the democratic process at a time when personal stakes are highest.

Lake offers yet another way to frame the NIMBY phenomenon. The conventional view of NIMBY is based on the assumptions that the LULU in question is necessary and provides an important social benefit—that waste incinerators, for example, are necessary to protect the health and safety of the larger community. Lake calls this assumption into question by suggesting that such facilities are not to benefit society as much as they are to benefit the profit margin of the polluting industry, and that NIMBY opposition does not obstruct societal goals so much as it obstructs the goals of corporate wealth.[38]

The strategy of siting unwanted facilities concentrates costs on local communities. It ignores the alternative strategy of placing the costs on the waste producers to restructure production so as to lessen the problem at its source, by producing less waste. Ultimately, suggests Lake, the short-term fix, whereby the community subsidizes the polluting industry, weakens incentives for producers to reduce waste production, and fails to address the problem at its source.

NIMBY and Implications for Environmental Action

The NIMBY response tends to mobilize and unite a community against a common threat. Community mobilization repeatedly has proven to be successful in stopping LULUs from moving forward, and in compelling industry and government regulators to examine ways to ameliorate problems at their source. New Jersey offers a case in point.

Faced with the dilemma of a growing need for waste treatment and disposal facilities, and after sites in eleven different municipalities were quashed as a result of community opposition or environmental factors, New Jersey lawmakers enacted the Pollution Prevention Act of 1991. This act requires producers to reduce their use of hazardous materials and the production of hazardous wastes. Community activists in New Jersey, through their successful rhetorical campaign to pass the legislation, scored a tactical win for their own communities and, at the same time, created the impetus for strategic pro-environmental planning that ultimately helped protect all communities from being targeted as hosts for LULUs. Thus, the NIMBY response transcended local interests to represent a broader and ultimately more sustainable approach—**NIABY (Not In Anyone's Back Yard).** Most states in the U.S. now have similar forms of pollution prevention legislation in place.

To the extent that local victories lead to proactive strategies for pollution prevention, the outcome is increased environmental protection. Even when communities lose the siting battle, facility plans are often safer and cleaner as a result of community action. Yet, one must be cautious when characterizing NIMBY as pro-environmental action. The NIMBY response represents a wait-until-it-gets-close-and-then-react approach. NIMBY as tactical opposition will not and cannot always be successful. The fact remains that there is an ever-present and increasing demand for the services provided by the unsavory facilities. Successful opposition in one community may only serve to doom someone else's back yard. Local victories may not ultimately translate into greater public good or pro-environmental policies. As sociologist Daniel Faber points out, addressing a particular siting issue solely as a locally unwanted land use without also addressing the source of the hazard "focuses on the symptoms rather than the causes and is therefore only a partial, temporary, and necessarily incomplete and insufficient solution."[39]

Inverted Quarantine

Sociologist Andrew Szasz discusses another response to risk in the form of what he terms **inverted quarantine.**[40] This is a response to risk in which individuals engage in acts of self-protection through the purchase and use of consumer products (such as bottled water, sun screen, or organically grown produce). Unlike traditional quarantine where the purpose is to isolate a diseased individual in order to prevent contamination of the healthy community, inverted quarantine is healthy individuals isolating themselves from a diseased community.

Inverted quarantine is a rapidly growing industry in the United States. Bottled water, for example, is the nation's second best–selling beverage—second only to soft drinks. Inverted quarantine also manifests itself in the organic food market. A few decades ago, organic foods represented only a small share of the food market; but after years of steady growth, they now are mainstream. One can purchase organic foods in local supermarkets and chain stores across the country. Add to that the number of other organic products that consumers purchase—shampoos, soaps, household cleansers, cosmetics, clothing—and one begins to get the sense of the perceived vulnerability to risk that leads the consuming public, at least those members who can afford it, to purchase protection in the form of inverted quarantine goods.

Inverted Quarantine and Implications for Environmental Action

Szasz suggests that one consequence of inverted quarantine is **political anesthesia,** the feeling that one has successfully reduced risks from environmental hazards by insulating oneself from the toxic surroundings. Reducing one's sense of risk, suggests Szasz, also reduces the sense of urgency to do something more about that particular risk. If, for example, you feel easily and adequately protected from the negative effects of pollutants in water by simply purchasing bottled water, you may be less likely to become involved in efforts to protect or clean up the water source. In this way, the inverted quarantine mentality serves as an obstacle to pro-environmental action.

Some collective benefits can and, in fact, do accrue from purchasing many inverted quarantine products. As the market for organic foods increases, for example, the use of chemical fertilizers and pesticides decreases. Unfortunately, not all inverted quarantine products have pro-environmental relationships. Take bottled water, for instance. It takes a tremendous amount of energy and raw materials to produce and transport the billions of plastic bottles, most of which end up in our landfills and lakes.

Connections

Message in a Bottle:
The Environmental Costs of Bottled Water

Charles Fishman, in the July 2007 issue of *Fast Company* magazine, levels a strong critique against Americans' $16 billion-a-year bottled-water "indulgence." "When a whole industry grows up around supplying us with something we don't need," writes Fishman, "when a whole industry is built on the packaging and presentation—it's worth asking how that happened and what the impact is." Here are a few things you may want to consider the next time you purchase a bottle of water:

- Imagine what a convoy of 37,800 eighteen-wheelers would look like. That is the equivalent of the one billion bottles of water transported in the United States each week in ships, trains, and trucks.

- In 2006, we went through 50 billion plastic water bottles—167 for each person.

- Because the recycling rate of PET plastic (polyethylene terephthalate—the kind used in water bottles) is only 23 percent, 38 billion water bottles end up in landfills each year—more than $1 billion worth of plastic.

- 24 percent of the bottled water we buy is tap water repackaged by Coke or Pepsi.

- If we paid the same for the water we use at home as we do for bottled water, our monthly water bill would average $9000.

- *Meanwhile, one out of six people in the world has no safe drinking water.*

Source: Charles Fishman, "Message in a Bottle," *Fast Company Magazine*, July–August 2007, 11. http://www.fastcompany.com/magazine/117/features-message-in-a-bottle.html (accessed February 4, 2008).

Szasz is not suggesting that we should stop eating organic foods or finding other ways to protect ourselves from the very real toxins in our environment. Rather, he is warning us that although inverted quarantine may reduce our exposure somewhat, it does not work well enough to truly protect us from the pervasive hazards. That will require collective environmental activism and rejection of "the comforting illusion" that there are purely individual solutions to our collective problems.

GHOST and the Global Warming Specter

Thus far, we have examined two potential cultural rationality–driven responses to risk and technical rationality—opposition in the form of NIMBY (or NIABY) and self-protection in the form of inverted quarantine. I suggest that there is another potential response to risk in the form of resigned hopelessness and the sense that there is nothing one can do: the **GHOST (Giving up Hope Of Stopping the Threat) response.** This response stems from a conceptual framework that is patently different from either NIMBY or inverted quarantine. The GHOST response is a product of a spectral view of environmental risk.[41] Like the ghosts we see portrayed in popular literature and film, the spectral construction portrays the risk as a mysterious, intangible, unknowable, uncontrollable threat.

Daily we are confronted with the apparitions of our planetary demise—global warming, disappearing rain forests, massive extinctions, and loss of biodiversity—all of which defy the imagination in their immensity and complexity. Other-worldly explanations, commonly used to rationalize natural disasters, are often appropriated to explain human-caused disasters. Indeed, the line between natural and human-caused disasters has become increasingly blurred. Was Hurricane Katrina, which destroyed much of New Orleans and the surrounding Gulf Coast in 2005, the caprice of Mother Nature, the wrath of God, or the product of anthropogenic global warming?

All three responses—NIMBY, inverted quarantine, and GHOST—share a common view of risk as a powerful and foreboding threat. In the case of NIMBY and inverted quarantine, however, the threat is viewed as a tangible, knowable, material reality (the waste incinerator, the chemicals in foods), whereas in the spectral view it is seen as a mysterious, intangible threat. In the case of NIMBY and inverted quarantine, there is a sense that the risk can be controlled (the incinerator can be made to go away by the decision-makers; toxic threats can be eliminated by careful food purchasing choices), whereas with the spectral view, there is a sense that the threat is beyond humans' capacity to control. In the case of NIMBY and inverted quarantine, the risks are imposed by outside forces creating a sense of victimage (the waste management company forced the incinerator on the community; powerful agribusinesses forced toxic chemicals on the consumer), whereas the spectral view recognizes individual and collective responsibility for the creation of the risk. The specter is the product of one's own iniquitous behavior that has come back to haunt the modern world and exact revenge.

The spectral construction emerges prominently in the rhetoric of many environmental prophets and is especially prominent in the global warming discourse. The following section discusses the rhetorical dimensions of the global warming specter and offers a few examples to demonstrate the discursive sorcery that is used to conjure up the awesome apparition.

Rhetorical Dimensions of the Global Warming Specter

The spectral construction of global warming has at least four rhetorical dimensions: (1) the specter is a powerful, foreboding threat; (2) it is mysterious and unknowable; (3) it is a product of our own past iniquities; and (4) it is beyond the capacities of humans to control. Examples of these dimensions are drawn from three influential books that have been published within the last four years: *The Weather Makers,* by Tim Flannery;[42] *Field Notes from a Catastrophe,* by Elizabeth Kolbert;[43] and *Ecological Debt,* by Andrew Simms.[44]

We are repeatedly warned of the *powerful and foreboding threat* that the specter of global warming represents. Global warming literature is rife with examples of this rhetorical dimension. Consider the foreboding future that Flannery implies in the following statement: "Given the scale of change confronting us, I think there is abundant evidence to support Lovelock's idea that climate change may well bring about the end of our civilization."[45]

Despite numerous warnings of the foreboding threat, we also hear a great deal about the uncertainty of this *mysterious, unknowable* specter. The complexity of global warming easily lends itself to this rhetorical construction. Even the most ardent global warming prophets, such as Andrew Simms, recognize our current

Figure 8.2   Damage from Hurricane Katrina

A Federal Emergency Management Agency search and rescue crew looks for survivors in New Orleans after Hurricane Katrina destroyed much of the Louisiana and Mississippi coastal areas in August 2005. Science cannot tell us directly whether Katrina's destructiveness was related to global warming. There is evidence, however, that storms are becoming more intense and that this trend correlates with the increase in sea surface temperatures, which are one degree warmer on average than they were a century ago.

FEMA / Jocelyn Augustino

inability to know for sure exactly what we face: "In fact, nobody knows precisely how the complex interactions in our biosphere will respond to global warming over coming centuries. We could be surprised in a few good ways, and many very bad."[46]

Like many of our most celebrated apparitions, the global warming specter is *a product of our own past iniquities* and cannot rest until vengeance is carried out and justice is served. The public discourse on global warming frequently calls our attention to the fact that we have created the haunting risk by our own thoughtless consumer practices and must now bear the consequences. Flannery reprimands us for our iniquitous behavior and failure to acknowledge our own culpability when he states, "There has been little reason for our blindness except perhaps an unwillingness to look such horror in the face and say, 'you are my creation.'"[47] Elizabeth Kolbert implies intentional, self-destructive behavioral choice when she states, "It may seem impossible to imagine that a technologically advanced society could choose, in essence, to destroy itself, but that is what we are now in the process of doing."[48]

Now that the specter has been let loose on the world as a result of our own iniquitous behaviors, it is *beyond humans' capacity to control*—another discursively constructed characteristic of the global warming specter. Writers, in an effort to motivate action, warn of "tipping points" and "thresholds" towards which we are rapidly advancing and that, if reached, will set in motion irreversible and rapid climate change. Simms warns:

> There is now the real possibility of runaway climate change. The melting of ice shelves, death of vegetation and different factors feeding off each other point in the future to the submergence of the world's major capitals. Even the expected reality of warming based on the continuation of observed patterns creates the specter of a problem beyond the capacity of humans to control.[49]

GHOST and Implications for Environmental Action

Operating on the assumption that any solution requires the recognition of a tangible problem and the identification of the agents who can bring about the necessary changes, constructing the risk as mysterious, intangible, and uncontrollable presents obstacles to pro-environmental action in at least two ways. First, the construction of an environmental problem as a mysterious, unknowable force encourages skepticism regarding the existence or the degree of the problem, and promotes business-as-usual-until-we-know-more responses. The scientific uncertainty of global warming has been rhetorically played out in the public arena as a justification for U.S. policy-makers' failure to act. Republican pollster and political consultant Frank Luntz recommends the strategic use of uncertainty to defer action in his now infamous memo to Republican leaders. "The scientific debate is closing (against us) but not yet closed," writes Luntz. "Voters believe that there is no consensus about global warming in the scientific community. Should the public come to believe that scientific issues are settled, their views about global warming will change accordingly."[50]

Newspapers and other mainstream news outlets have perpetuated the myth of uncertainty. Despite the fact that in scientific circles it is almost impossible to find disagreement about the fundamentals of global warming (that it is real and human-caused), news organizations have created an artificial balance by their tendency to frame it as a conflict between opposing groups of scientists. Adding to this sense of uncertainty are groups such as the Global Climate Coalition, funded by dozens of major corporations in the petroleum, automotive, and energy industries that recognize the economic advantages of promoting perceptions of scientific uncertainty. The Global Climate Coalition was dissolved in 2000 after several major supporters defected in light of the growing scientific consensus and public concern, but not before achieving the wholesale distribution of uncertainty through well-funded campaigns and lobbying efforts.

The second consequence of the spectral view of risk is that it perpetuates the prevailing view that environmental problems must be solved by more advanced science and technology. Since there is little that the individual can do in the face of this invincible foe, we call on the enigmatic sorcery of scientist and engineers to solve our problems. Thus, the specter serves to reinforce the reigning discourse in which science and technology are viewed as the key or only legitimate means of addressing our environmental problems.

Scientists play a crucial role in understanding the interactions of complex natural systems. Climate science and related fields have made rapid advancements in the past decade because of truly heroic efforts on the part of the scientific community. These achievements have been and must continue to be rewarded and funded. A critical component of any solutions will depend on scientific knowledge, creative problem-solving, and technological innovations in alternative fuels and renewable energy. Yet, in the long run, global warming cannot be studied and engineered out of existence.

We are given numerous directives that we, as individuals, can do to mitigate the problem of global warming (using compact florescent bulbs, carpooling, planting a tree, etc.). It is difficult for me to believe, however, that in light of the magnitude of the problem, most people will naïvely accept the illusory notion of individual solutions. Our culpability as consumers is frequently brought to our attention, yet our options for changing our iniquitous behaviors and making restitution are limited. In creating a sense of powerlessness in the face of an invincible foe, the spectral view is unlikely to spark the massive uprising of popular and political will that is needed to combat global warming. Although changes are in the works, they have been hard won, slow in coming, uninspired, and insufficient, in light of the magnitude of the problems we face.

Concluding and Looking Ahead

This chapter has covered a lot of ground, beginning with an introduction to technical rationality and cultural rationality. It followed with a discussion of ways in which technical rationality constrains alternative ways of knowing. After that, it introduced three kinds of cultural rationality–driven responses to risk: NIMBY, inverted quarantine, and GHOST.

Another potential public response to global warming has not yet been discussed. It is the antithesis of the spectral view of global warming and the GHOST response to environmental risk. It involves any and all conceivable pro-environmental responses encompassing individual and collective actions, government and community collaboration, individual and corporate accountability, and active and ongoing efforts at home and on the global stage. This response requires innovation, creativity, the precision of technical rationality and the perspicuity of cultural rationality. I challenge you to come up with an acronym that captures this form of response to environmental risk.

We now move on to another area of inquiry within the rich field of environmental communication, to examine particular sites of the production of rhetoric and the implications of their persuasive messages. The following chapters look at some of the popular culture sites of meaning-making (news, advertising, popular culture), which, with their ubiquitous bombardment of messages and images, operate as powerful means of shaping cultural values and guiding our understanding about a whole range of social issues. Chapters 9 and 10 deal with two of the more conspicuous sites of meaning construction—news and advertising, respectively. Chapter 11 examines less obvious, but profoundly influential sites of meaning construction within the ubiquitous and diverse domain of popular culture.

Discussion Questions and Exercises

1. Communication scholar Edward Schiappa discusses the bureaucratization of language through the use of acronyms and sanitized jargon. Find examples of environmental rhetoric that uses such of language. Examine whether and how the language constrains alternative ways of knowing.

2. Make a list of the inverted quarantine products you use. Do you feel safer from threats of environmental hazards because of these products? Do you agree with Szasz's hypothesis that inverted quarantine leads to "political anesthesia?"

3. Think of the ghost movies you have seen. Are there any other commonly portrayed ghost characteristics that are not included in the discussion of the GHOST response to environmental risk? Can these characteristics be seen as consistent with the global warming specter, or do they call into question the appropriateness of the ghost metaphor?

4. In the "Concluding and Looking Ahead" section of this chapter, you are challenged to come up with an acronym that represents the antithesis of the spectral view of global warming. Divide into groups to do this and report your results.

Suggested Readings

Thomas Farrell and G. Thomas Goodnight. "Accidental Rhetoric: The Root Metaphors of Three Mile Island." *Communication Monographs* 48 (1981): 271–300.

Steven B. Katz and Carolyn R. Miller. "The Low-Level Radioactive Waste Siting Controversy in North Carolina: Toward a Rhetorical Model of Risk Communication." In C. G. Herndl and S. C. Brown (Eds.), *Green Culture: Environmental Rhetoric in Contemporary America,* 111–140. Madison: University of Wisconsin Press, 1996.

Alonzo Plough and Sheldon Krimsky. "The Emergence of Risk Communication Studies: Social and Political Context." *Science, Technology, and Human Values* 12 (1987): 4–10.

Edward Schiappa. "The Rhetoric of Nukespeak." *Communication Monographs* 56 (1989): 253–272.

Andrew Szasz. *Shopping Our Way to Safety: How We Changed from Protecting the Environment to Protecting Ourselves.* Minneapolis: University of Minnesota Press, 2007.

Notes

1. Alonzo Plough and Sheldon Krimsky, "The Emergence of Risk Communication Studies: Social and Political Context," *Science, Technology, and Human Values* 12 (1987): 4–10.

2. Walter R. Fisher, *Human Communication as Narration: Toward a Philosophy of Reason, Value, and Action* (Columbia: University of South Carolina Press, 1987), 1.

3. Pete Bsumek, "The Idea of Rhetoric in the Field of Environmental Communication: Reflecting on 'Ways of Knowing' in Our Own Field and Advancing a Theory of Rhetorical Realism," in *Proceedings of the Seventh Biennial Conference on Communication and Environment,* eds. G. B. Walker and W. J. Kinsella (Sublimity, OR: 2003), 243.

4. Ulrich Beck, "Risk Society and the Provident State," trans. M. Chalmers, in *Risk, Environment, and Modernity: Towards a New Ecology,* eds. S. Lash, B. Szerszynski, and B. Wynne (Thousand Oaks, CA: Sage, 1996), 28.

5. Informational brochure distributed by the Rocky Mountain Arsenal, Denver, CO, 1992.

6. U.S. General Accounting Office, "Chemical Regulations: Options Exist to Improve EPA's Ability to Assess Health Risks and Manage Its Chemical Review Program," GAO-05-458 (Washington, DC: GAO, June, 2005).

7. Devra Davis, *When Smoke Ran Like Fire: Tales of Environmental Deception and the Battle against Pollution* (New York: Basic Books, 2002), 21.

8. National Research Council, *Understanding Risk: Informing Decisions in a Democratic Society* (Washington, DC: National Academy Press, 1996), 7.

9. Susan Sattell, "Framing the Monarchs: A Study of the Monarch Butterfly Controversy and Its Role in the U.S. Debate on Genetically Engineered Crops," in *Proceedings*

of the Sixth Biennial Conference on Communication and Environment, eds. Marie-France Aepli, Stephen P. Depoe, and John W. Delicath (Cincinnati, OH: Center for Environmental Communication Studies, 2001), 121–140.

10. Thomas Farrell and G. Thomas Goodnight, "Accidental Rhetoric: The Root Metaphors of Three Mile Island," *Communication Monographs* 48 (1981): 271–300.

11. Edward Schiappa, "The Rhetoric of Nukespeak," *Communication Monographs* 56 (1989): 253.

12. William J. Kinsella, "One Hundred Years of Nuclear Discourse: Four Master Themes and Their Implications for Environmental Communication," in *Environmental Communication Yearbook* 2, ed. S. Senecah (Mahwah, NJ: Erlbaum, 2005), 53.

13. "U.S. Department of Energy Stockpile Stewardship Program: 30-Day Review," Department of Energy, 1999, http://www.fas.org/nuke/guide/usa/doctrine/doe/index.html (accessed October 11, 2005).

14. Bryan C. Taylor and Judith Hendry, "Insisting on Persisting: The Nuclear Rhetoric of 'Stockpile Stewardship,'" *Rhetoric and Public Affairs* 11, (2008): 303–334.

15. Steven B. Katz and Carolyn R. Miller, "The Low-Level Radioactive Waste Siting Controversy in North Carolina: Toward a Rhetorical Model of Risk Communication," in *Green Culture: Environmental Rhetoric in Contemporary America,* eds. C. G. Herndl and S. C. Brown (Madison: University of Wisconsin Press, 1996).

16. Michael Bruner and Max Oelschlaeger, "Rhetoric, Environmentalism, and Environmental Ethics," in *Landmark Essays on Rhetoric and the Environment,* ed. C. Wadell (Mahwah, NJ: Erlbaum, 1998), 218.

17. Katz and Miller, "Low-Level Radioactive Waste," 125.

18. Katz and Miller, "Low-Level Radioactive Waste," 123.

19. Katz and Miller, "Low-Level Radioactive Waste," 124.

20. Susan Sattell, "Framing the Monarchs."

21. J. E. Losey, L. S. Rayor, and M. E. Carter, "Transgenic Pollen Harms Monarch Larvae," *Nature,* May 29, 1999, 214.

22. Sattell, "Framing the Monarchs," 126.

23. Sattell, "Framing the Monarchs," 135.

24. Farrell and Goodnight, "Accidental Rhetoric," 272.

25. Farrell and Goodnight, "Accidental Rhetoric."

26. Farrell and Goodnight, "Accidental Rhetoric," 273.

27. Farrell and Goodnight, "Accidental Rhetoric," 273.

28. Farrell and Goodnight, "Accidental Rhetoric," 286.

29. Cited in Farrell and Goodnight, "Accidental Rhetoric," 287.

30. Farrell and Goodnight, "Accidental Rhetoric," 296.

31. Farrell and Goodnight, "Accidental Rhetoric," 297.

32. Farrell and Goodnight, "Accidental Rhetoric," 298.

33. Farrell and Goodnight, "Accidental Rhetoric," 298.

34. Farrell and Goodnight, "Accidental Rhetoric," 298–299.

35. Nuclear Energy Institute, "The Chernobyl Accident and Its Consequences," 1998 http://www.nei.org/library/infob20.html.

36. Michael Dear, "Understanding and Overcoming the NIMBY Syndrome," *Journal of the American Planning Association* 58 (1992): 288.

37. Robert W. Lake, "Rethinking NIMBY," *Journal of the American Planning Association* 59 (1993): 88.

38. Lake, "Rethinking NIMBY."

39. Daniel Faber, "A More 'Productive' Environmental Justice Politics: Movement Alliances in Massachusetts for Clean Production and Regional Equity," in *Environmental Justice and Environmentalism: The Social Justice Challenge to the Environmental Movement,* eds. R. Sandler and P. C. Pezzullo (Cambridge, MA: MIT Press, 2007), 145.

40. Andrew Szasz, *Shopping Our Way to Safety: How We Changed from Protecting the Environment to Protecting Ourselves* (Minneapolis: University of Minnesota Press, 2007).

41. Judith Hendry, "Public Discourse and the Rhetorical Construction of the Technospecter," *Environmental Communication: A Journal of Nature and Culture* 2 (2008): 302–319.

42. Tim Flannery, *The Weather Makers: How Man is Changing the Climate and What It Means for Life on Earth* (New York: Atlantic Monthly Press, 2005).

43. Elizabeth Kolbert, *Field Notes from a Catastrophe: Man, Nature, and Climate Change* (New York: Bloomsbury, 2006).

44. Andrew Simms, *Ecological Debt: The Health of the Planet and the Wealth of Nations* (London: Pluto, 2005).

45. Flannery, *The Weather Makers,* 209.

46. Simms, *Ecological Debt,* 5.

47. Flannery, *The Weather Makers,* 210.

48. Kolbert, *Field Notes,* 187.

49. Simms, *Ecological Debt,* 119.

50. Frank Luntz, "The Environment: A Cleaner, Safer, Healthier America," Memo prepared by Frank Luntz, The Luntz Research Companies, February 2004 http://www.ewg.org/briefings/luntzmemo/pdf/LuntzResearch_environment.pdf (accessed June 9, 2005).

Part IV

Media, Popular Culture, and the Environment

Chapter 9
Environmental News Reporting

Most people are not experts on environmental issues. The "average" person does not conduct research or read scientific journals or academic literature dealing with environmental issues. For most people, knowledge and understanding of the environment is derived from popular discourse, through sources such as broadcast news, print media, and advertising, as well as from other less obvious cultural sites of meaning construction such as greeting cards, children's books, animated cartoons, and prime-time entertainment.

It would be difficult to map all the multiple sites of meaning construction that contribute to our understanding of the natural world and our relationship to it. Environmental communication scholars Mark Meister and Phyllis M. Japp explain that "the stream of images and ideas from popular culture is a messy domain, filled with fragments of information, bits of dramatic stories, visual images and examples, literally a kaleidoscope of images of places, spaces, species, geographics, and landscapes."[1] We often fail to question the messages of popular culture, yet its constant stream of symbols is a powerful force in shaping our view of the natural world.

One of the most ubiquitous and conspicuous sites of mass-mediated meaning construction is news reporting. Since the first Earth Day in 1970, the news media's interest in covering environmental issues has been cyclical, with notable peaks and valleys. *Time* magazine's decision in 1989 to name the Earth its "Planet of the Year" marked a high point in media attention to environmental issues. *Time* again spotlighted the environment on March 26, 2006, when its cover read "Be Worried. Be Very Worried" and showed a picture of a polar bear stranded on the shrinking Arctic ice floe.

As would be expected, spectacular environmental events such as the Yellowstone fires in 1988, the *Exxon Valdez* oil spill in 1989, and the massive devastation of Hurricane Katrina in 2005 tend to create short-term peaks in environmental coverage. As would also be expected, spectacular events not related to the environment negatively impact the amount of environmental news coverage. For example, statistics compiled by the *Tyndall Report,* which monitors weekly television news, showed that ABC, CBS, and NBC devoted 617 minutes to environmental issues in 2001 but only 236 minutes in 2002. The terrorist attacks of September 11, 2001, understandably resulted in a significant decline in the number of environmental stories that were reported. When so much attention is taken up by extraordinary news, there are not many broadcast minutes or column inches left for the environmental beat. Yet, even when not upstaged by spectacular news events, environmental stories comprise a small percentage of news coverage when compared to other topics, such as the economy, elections, and crime, although Internet news reporting has significantly increased the number of environmental stories.[2]

Each form of news media has its own advantages and disadvantages when it comes to reporting environmental news. Those who study media reporting generally agree that newspapers are better than television at communicating the details of a complex story. Television tends to be biased toward events that make for good visual coverage and toward brief, succinct reports that more nearly approximate a newspaper's front page than its full contents. Yet both column inches and broadcast minutes are finite. Reporters for both print and broadcast media must deal with these inevitable constraints.

Further compounding the challenges of environmental reporters is the increasing complexity and scope of the subject matter. Sharon Friedman, professor of science and environmental writing, notes that, with the help of the Internet, environmental reporting has become more sophisticated in the past decade; but so, too, has the nature of the subjects that are covered. She points out that stories have changed "from relatively simple, event-driven pollution stories to those of far greater scope and complexity such as land use management, global warming, resource conservation, and biotechnology."[3]

The following discussion applies broadly to the standard coverage of mainstream television and newspaper environmental news reporting. It does not necessarily pertain to those instances when the reporter is given the privilege and space to do an extended, in-depth documentary on an environmental issue. Likewise omitted from this discussion are news magazines, news talk shows, and the multiple forms of online news sources that offer extended coverage or additional information links. An understanding of the challenges and complexities inherent in environmental reporting will serve to make us more responsible media consumers by fostering critical awareness of what we see and read in the news.

Framing the Story

Because there are many different ways to report an event or "tell the story," a journalist must decide how to frame a story. A reporter makes decisions (both consciously and unconsciously) about what facts are important and what are not, what will be included and what will be left out. Each choice the journalist makes plays a crucial role in the "reality" created through that story.

In framing a story, a reporter selects portions of a perceived reality and emphasizes them in such a way as to promote ideas about what happens and what is important to us. Media scholar Anders Hansen refers to these selections as **customized frames,** common interpretational frames that can be identified in environmental reporting.[4] Media scholars William Gamson and Andre Modigliani suggest that these customized frames or "packages" result from three conceptual schemes that influence reporters: cultural resonances, sponsor activities, and media practices.[5] The following takes a more in-depth look at these conceptual schemes. The examples used are drawn from media scholar Conrad Smith's examination of the reporting of two spectacular stories—the Yellowstone fires of 1988 and the *Exxon Valdez* oil spill in Prince William Sound, Alaska, in 1989.[6]

Cultural resonances are those underlying assumptions and cultural myths embedded in a society's values and collective psyche that are often taken for granted. For example, anyone familiar with Smokey Bear and Bambi would likely assume that forest fires are bad. Yet, those who are knowledgeable in forest science know that wild fires are not necessarily harmful; that many forests, especially in the western United States, are biologically adapted to fires; and that fires are important to the maintenance and rejuvenation of forest ecosystems. Nevertheless, this perception of forest fires as beneficial does not resonate with the largely accepted notion that forest fires are bad.

Smith, in his exhaustive examination of the reporting of the 1988 fires in Yellowstone National Park, observed several common themes that served to reinforce prevailing cultural assumptions that fire is bad:

> One is that all large fires are pretty much the same and that fire is bad. The standard fire story is one of the most basic in the journalist's repertoire. The other misconception is that nature is static—that the current state of any

Figure 9.1   The Original Smokey Bear

This black bear cub, rescued from a fire in the Capitan Mountains of New Mexico in 1950, inspired the national symbol for fire prevention. Smokey Bear, in blue jeans and a ranger hat, has become a popular cultural icon, but not without controversy. Environmentalists and fire experts have criticized the Smokey campaign for its failure to acknowledge that some fires are essential to forest health. Smokey's slogan, "Remember, only you can prevent forest fires" has been updated to "Remember, only you can prevent wildfires" to distinguish between uncontrolled, destructive "wildfires" and rejuvenating "prescribed natural fires."

U.S. Forest Service, Southwestern Region

landscape, such as Yellowstone National Park, is pretty much fixed and can be preserved as it is. The notion that green forests in today's Yellowstone were shaped by cataclysmic, stand-replacing fires in past centuries was initially alien to most reporters and media consumers.[7]

Another cultural resonance that Smith observed was the framing of the wildfires from the perspective of urban fires, which destroy property and are usually extinguished in a few hours. When reporters brought these urban firefighting values to Yellowstone, their stories focused on traditional urban fire themes: victims and damage to property.

The victims in Yellowstone were mostly inconvenienced tourists and local residents who were engaged in tourist-dependent business such as hotels and restaurants. Reporters relied heavily on testimony from these victims, many of whom believed the fires were spreading because of the Park's policy of "prescribed natural burn." Under this policy, lightning-caused fires are allowed to burn as long as they meet a certain "prescription" that takes into account such things as the degree of threat to developed areas and other management goals. Once the fire exceeds these prescribed conditions, the fire is reclassified from "natural" to "wild" and firefighters are brought in.

The problem with the cultural resonance of the "urban fire" in this case was that it led to a portrayal of the fires in which the consuming public was poorly served, emphasizing victims and damages, rather than offering information "that would allow an intelligent non-specialists to reach an informed conclusion about whether some fires should be allowed to burn on public lands."[8] Smith further points out that according to the scientists who were consulted for his study, the burn would have been on the same order of magnitude in Yellowstone no matter what the policy was. In this case, the cultural resonance of the urban fire led reporters to frame the story in ways that reinforced the prevailing fires-are-bad assumptions and, in so doing, failed to inform the public about the ecological role of forest fires.

A second conceptual scheme that influences how reporters describe events, according to Gamson and Modigliani, is **sponsor activities,** efforts by stakeholders (individuals or organizations with vested interests) to encourage journalists to frame the news in a way that promotes or is beneficial to their interests. Although the framing of the story is ultimately the decision of the reporter and the news organization, sponsor activities can greatly influence that decision.

One common form of sponsor activity is the appointment of an agency or industry spokesperson—the person charged with "officially" representing the views and interests of the organization. The *Exxon Valdez* oil spill in March 1989 offers a good example of a spokesperson's influence.

When the supertanker ran aground in Alaska's Prince William Sound and released over 240,000 barrels of crude oil, a frenzy of media coverage ensued. Smith reports that by the end of September, the spill was the focus of 179 evening network stories and that America's three elite newspapers (the *New York Times,* the *Washington Post,* and the *Los Angeles Times*) had published 631 stories about it.

The primary stakeholders with vested interests in how the spill was reported included the State of Alaska, which was responsible for overseeing maritime safety and spill preparedness; the Alyeska consortium, which operated the terminal and was in charge of the initial response to the spill; the Exxon Corporation, which owned the tanker; and the local fishermen, whose livelihood was impacted by the spill. The clear winner in the battle among information sponsors was the State of Alaska, represented in large part by Environmental Conservation Commissioner Dennis Kelso as its spokesperson. Kelso quickly recognized "the need to score the media images" and launched a well-articulated and rhetorically effective press campaign.

In his study of the environmental reporting of the *Exxon Valdez* spill, Smith surveyed correspondents who covered the spill. A sample of the comments he received gives a clear indication of the press strategies that Kelso and the Department of Environment and Conservation (DEC) employed:

"DEC was an advocacy group. All of its science was devoted to the prosecution of Exxon." (*National Geographic* correspondent)

"Kelso was easy to reach, but always a political slant." (ABC correspondent)

"Kelso was incredibly accessible and articulate." (*Anchorage Daily News* reporter)

"If you hit Alaska for a few days and ran into Kelso, he defined the story for you." (*Rolling Stone* reporter)

Figure 9.2   *Exxon Valdez* Spill

The supertanker *Exxon Valdez* ran aground on March 24, 1989, in Alaska's Prince William Sound, spilling nearly 11 million gallons of crude oil into the Sound and impacting over 1,100 miles of shoreline. At the height of the response, 1,400 vessels, 85 aircraft, and more than 11,000 workers from local, state, federal, and private agencies were involved in the cleanup efforts. The oil spill cleanup effort was the largest ever mobilized, making it a truly spectacular news event.

Office of Response and Restoration, National Ocean Service, National Oceanic and Atmospheric Administration

As is apparent from these comments, Kelso and the DEC made themselves readily available to the press with a well-defined and well-articulated frame that effectively deflected attention from DEC's responsibility for the oversight of spill preparedness.

Exxon, on the other hand, did not fare as well with reporters in the competition among information sources.

> "Exxon people seemed disorganized and hard to find, but no more evasive than other companies." (ABC environmental reporter)

> "Exxon's 'caution' in dealing with the media made them some of the poorest sources of information." (*Los Angeles Times* reporter).

> "Not very accessible, and when accessible, not very forthcoming." (*Los Angeles Times* reporter)

> "The way Exxon dealt with press constantly made reporters go back to trying to empathize with Alaska." (*Rolling Stone* reporter)

Due, in large part, to the effectiveness of Kelso's sponsor activities, the press portrayed the State of Alaska very positively while presenting Exxon in a negative light. As one *Anchorage Daily News* reporter stated, "The worst coverage saw the disaster as a melodrama—Exxon the villain, DEC a hero, fishermen and anthropomorphic otters as victims."[9] While there were many contributing factors, the sponsor activities of Exxon and the DEC had considerable bearing on how the news media framed the story and portrayed these organizations.

Media scholars Mark Miller and Bonnie Parnell Riechert discuss additional ways that sponsor activities accommodate journalists through **information subsidies,**[10] a wide variety of sponsor activities by which sources assist journalists. The most predominant form of information subsidy is the press release, through which sources tell their own versions of the story or the facts to the press. Other forms of information subsidies include interviews, tours, transportation, and event tickets. Miller and Parnell Riechert explain that "while it is a violation of journalistic ethics to accept direct payment for publishing materials, it is acceptable for journalists to accept assistance (subsidies) for gathering materials."[11] They further point out that, like other sponsor activities, information subsidies do not necessarily determine how the story is framed. The final judgment is left up to the journalist. Information subsidies are nevertheless effective and have an impact on how the story is framed.

The third conceptual scheme that influences the framing of events, Gamson and Modigliani say, is **media practice.**[12] Reporters and news organizations employ standard practices as they gather and report the news. The standard practices of environmental journalists have been examined critically by numerous people— journalists and non-journalists alike. While many criticisms of environmental reporting apply to news gathering practices in general, environmental reporters often face challenges that are unique to environmental reporting—it's a tough beat. Media scholars Holly Stocking and Jennifer Pease Leonard give a brief overview of some of the complexities of environmental reporting:

> The environment story is one of the most pressing and complicated stories
> of our time. It involves abstract and probabilistic science, labyrinthine laws,
> grandstanding politicians, speculative economics, and the complex interplay
> of individuals and societies. Most agree that it concerns the very future of life
> as we know it on the planet. Perhaps more than most stories, it needs careful,
> longer-than-bite-sized reporting and analysis, now.[13]

The following sections look at some of environmental reporters' standard practices and the problems and pitfalls that such reporters face.

Event-Oriented Reporting

Reporters are trained and conditioned to adhere to certain news values that serve as criteria for deciding what is newsworthy. Kathleen Hall Jamieson and Karlyn Kohrs Campbell describe the characteristics of an "ideal" news story: It involves a discrete event with a single act or occurrence that can be coherently related in limited space or time, and that is a matter of community concern or of interest to many people. It is a recent event that is novel or goes beyond the bounds of ordinary, routine daily life. It is a personalized human story that focuses on people rather than processes or ideas. The ideal news story also involves drama or conflict, preferably with a sense of danger or excitement.[14]

Environmental issues often defy some or all of these "ideal" characteristics because they tend to be highly complex, long-term situations (not discrete events) and often lack a clearly defined human element with conflict and drama. Environmental stories often frustrate journalists' need for fast, accurate reporting under deadline pressures. It is not surprising, therefore, that reporters tend to focus on a discrete event or crisis at the expense of the complex, sound bite–defying context of the story.

Environmental stories are often dominated by abbreviated details of what happened in a particular event rather than explanations of the historical, political, or social context in which the event was embedded. One consequence of focusing on the event at the expense of the context is that it contributes to what media scholar Kris M. Wilson terms "the issue-of-the-month syndrome," which ignores the long-term, persistent environmental problems and allows them to "slide out of sight if there is nothing new to report."[15]

The story of climate change, which many scientists view as the most pressing problem facing the world in the next one hundred years, is a good example of how environmental problems fall victim to "the issue-of-the-month syndrome" and then "slide out of sight." Climate change is a highly complex issue that is very difficult to capture as a daily news event because there is often nothing new to report. Consequently, climate change reporting is often linked to particular weather events. Stories of drought with accompanying visuals of scorched land, blazing sun, devastated crops, and dry river beds tend to serve as events from which the climate change story is resurrected. Wilson observed that "Mother Nature cooperated in 1988, providing the visuals of drought as scientists warned about possible future droughts in an enhanced greenhouse world. Whether the two are actually linked is impossible for current science to evaluate, but the images are now part of the televised portrayal of a greenhouse world."[16]

Many of our environmental problems fall into the category of **elusive hazards** that are highly complex, geographically dispersed, and seldom marked by specific events.[17] Climate change reporting is only one example of how focusing on the event can serve to keep long-term, persistent environmental problems from becoming part of the routine news agenda. Many of our most pressing environmental stories, such as the loss of biodiversity, human population growth, and disappearing rainforests, are elusive hazards and lie dormant until some event propels them into the news spotlight.

Often, the complexities of an environmental story do not fit neatly into the conventions of the "event story." Some would even argue that a news report is not the appropriate venue for delivering the historical/contextual background information—that history and news are paradoxical. Nevertheless, when knowledge of the context in which the event is embedded is neglected or treated as unimportant to the story, essential components of the meaning of the crisis, or "the big picture," are obscured. The story lacks the necessary interpretation, explanation, and analysis that would empower news consumers by furnishing the relevant context on which to base their decisions on how to think and act with regard to the crisis.

Focus on Drama

Robert Manoff and Michael Schudson, in their book *Reading the News,* suggest that "Journalism, like any other storytelling activity, is a form of fiction operating out of its own conventions and understandings within its own set of sociological, ideological, and literary constraints."[18] The notion of journalism as "a form of fiction" may seem to contradict the standard journalistic norms of "objectivity," "truth," and "fairness." Yet, news does not exist in a vacuum, and journalistic norms do not inoculate the reporter from the cultural, social, and political influences that shape the multiple realities of any given story.

This is not to suggest that there is no "truth" in news reporting or that journalists deliberately falsify or distort reality. Rather, "reality" is always mediated in and through the telling of the story; in the telling, a journalist must make many decisions about what to report, how to report it, and whose voice will be heard. This coverage by selection implies a nonneutral selection of facts influenced by media values—values that are strongly driven by the essential commercial enterprise of delivering an audience to advertisers. The unfortunate bottom line for most reporters is that the story must be entertaining enough to hold the audience's fleeting attention span.

In order to make the news more entertaining to viewers, reporters often cast the story into the standard model of social drama, which prioritizes the human element through the portrayal of victims, heroes, and villains. While this model may lead to an entertaining narrative, when the story is framed within the constraints of a social drama with its predictable plot patterns and stereotyped villains, heroes, and victims, it ignores many relevant issues.

In humanizing the story, reporters often make what media scholars Lee Wilkins and Phillip Patterson call the **fundamental attribution error,** a term borrowed from the study of interpersonal communication. This is "the tendency to attribute too much responsibility to people for their actions and too little to the social and environmental constraints shaping those behaviors."[19] When the story is humanized, the characters involved in the drama tend to emerge in the stereotypical form of villains, heroes, and victims. The focus is on their actions at the expense of critical observation of the social forces underlying those actions. For example, the news stories about the *Exxon Valdez* accident tended to focus on Exxon as the villain and on fishers and wildlife as the victims, and spent very little time exploring the social, political, and economic forces at work—issues such as our nation's dependence on oil and the almost inevitable consequences of transporting oil to meet those needs.

Villains are especially attractive to news reporters. Wilkins and Patterson examined network news reports of the 1986 Chernobyl nuclear power plant accident, in which a violent explosion at the plant in the Ukraine (formerly the U.S.S.R.) caused the release of large quantities of radioactive substance into the atmosphere (as discussed in Chapter 8). Their analysis revealed three views of the Soviets as stereotypical social villains. First, news reports portrayed the Soviets as "*low tech bumblers*" in stories that focused on such things as the flawed design of the nuclear power plant and the Soviet's inability to solve the many problems caused by the accident. A second stereotypical portrayal was of the Soviets as *unconcerned about human life*. Reports focused on the slow evacuation from the area of the disaster site and the unwillingness of the Soviet authorities to accept help from other countries. The third stereotype was of the Soviets as *deceptive and secretive*. CBS news anchor Dan Rather, for example, said, "The U.S. said Soviet failure to be up front about Chernobyl raises new questions about whether the Soviets can be trusted on arms control."[20]

These stereotypical portrayals were in keeping with the tenor of the times, near the end of the Cold War, when the U.S. public view of the Soviet Union as the "Evil Empire" was almost uncontested. Nevertheless, casting the Soviets as the villains in the drama had several implications for the U.S. public.

The portrayal of Soviets as technologically inept implies that U.S. engineers can design and build safer nuclear power plants; that this kind of accident could not happen in the United States. The portrayal of Soviet authorities as deceptive and unconcerned with human life tacitly suggests that U.S. authorities value human life more than Soviet authorities do, and that they are more truthful with the public. These implied assumptions deflected reflexive considerations of the United States' own vulnerability to this kind of accident. They likewise failed to raise questions about the highly secretive nature of nuclear research and development that for many years has left Americans out of the information/decision loop with regard to the production and use of nuclear technologies. Rather than promoting public dialogue about such things as the safety of our own nuclear power plants and the adequacy of our own evacuation procedures in the event of an accident, the message was sent that such an accident could only happen to the "bumbling" Soviets.

But perhaps an even more important implication of the dramatic portrayal of the Soviets as villains is the fundamental error of attribution that blames individual people or institutions (in this case the Soviets and Soviet authorities) for societal problems. The accident at Chernobyl was framed as resulting from inept, uncaring, secretive people rather than as a collective societal decision to assume the risks and benefits of nuclear power. Placing responsibility for the accident on selected villains deflects attention from the need for an open public dialogue about these risks and benefits.

Selection of Sources

One of the most important factors in determining how a story is framed is the selection of sources—those people who are interviewed, cited, or quoted in the story. It stands to reason that, to a large extent, what gets said is a function of who gets interviewed. The sources on which journalists rely have a strong influence on the framing of the story.

News is framed, to a large degree, by the sources who have the most access to it. No matter how credible or reliable the sources, they almost always have a vested interest in how the story is presented. Because government and official spokespersons, speaking for institutional sources such as government agencies, politicians, the courts, police, and fire officials, comprise the majority of sources used in environmental stories, they exercise political and social power by influencing the way the story is framed. Thus, they often become the primary definers of key issues while other voices are rendered socially silent.[21]

There are many reasons for the predominance of these sources in the news. They tend to be viewed as credible and knowledgeable sources of information. They are readily available and easy to identify. In cases where public danger is involved, such as nuclear disasters, toxic spills, or dangerous fires, official sources have control over access to the site or to informed personnel such as police, firefighters, or agency representatives.

The privileged position of public officials stands in sharp contrast to that of environmental sources, who tend to be local citizens or members of ad hoc advocacy groups. They are more difficult to identify and contact, and may lack the credibility and media savvy of government or other official spokespersons.

Likewise, scientists are seldom used as the dominant news source. Exceptions occur in cases involving highly complex science or technology that necessitate a specific expertise (as in the case of the Three Mile Island accident discussed in

Connections

Drinking Upstream: Online News Sources

Political commentator and author Jim Hightower offers a piece of advice for news consumers and cowboys:

> A bit of wisdom from cowboys of yore: "Always drink upstream from the herd." This is—and always has been—sound advice for swallowing journalism, too. The conventional media overwhelmingly impart the message of officialdom, of the economic powers, of the status quo . . . of the herd. Consume at your own risk.*

"Drinking upstream" has never been easier. Technology has revolutionized environmental news reporting as well as the news industry in general. The Internet has increased the speed, reach, and comprehensiveness of available news to the public. News content is no longer the uniquely privileged domain of professional gatekeepers. But perhaps the biggest change brought about by the Internet news revolution is the transformation of the relationship between news providers and their audiences. Weblogs (or blogs) have changed the traditional closed sender-receiver model of news distribution to a "conversation" model, in which news audiences actively participate in reporting and interpreting news events.

Just as with traditional news sources, the environmental news consumer would be well advised to use critical judgment before swallowing the "upstream news." Not all news providers hold to the same journalistic and editorial fact-checking standards that the more traditional news outlets do. It is also good to keep in mind that many online environmental news providers are advocacy groups with obvious environmental or anti-environmental agendas. Nevertheless, many environmental news organizations have established track records of responsible, accurate reporting, where you can go to find expanded coverage of environmental stories and issues that are largely ignored by mainstream media. Here are a few of my favorite online environmental news sources and publications:

Conservation Magazine: www.conservationmagazine.org

Ecology and Society: www.ecologyandsociety.org

E Magazine: www.emagazine.com

Our Planet (United Nations Environmental Program): www.ourplanet.com

Planet (Sierra Club): www.sierraclub.org/planet

Sierra: www.sierramagazine.org

*Jim Hightower, "Foreword," in Jeff Cohen and Norman Solomon, *Through the Media Looking Glass: Decoding Bias and Blather in the News* (Monroe, ME: Common Courage, 1995), ix.

Chapter 8). For several reasons, scientists tend to receive little attention in news reports. Science, by its very nature, does not fit neatly into the predictable patterns of news coverage and often frustrates the reporter's need for fast, succinct explanations. Science is uncertain, and scientists are trained by profession to question objectively and interpret findings cautiously. The scientists' reticence as sources is also a function of the rigors of scientific inquiry, which often demands long-term investigation under controlled conditions before conclusions are drawn and findings are published or reported to the press.

In addition, science is often highly complex and remote from the personal experience of most people. The language used to discuss scientific evidence is mystifying to the lay person, and reporters often lack the specialized knowledge and technical expertise to adequately translate it. William Burrows, a former reporter for the *New York Times, Washington Post,* and *Wall Street Journal,* goes so far as to suggest that "Most ordinary reporters would practically cross the street to avoid running into an expert since they consider scientists to be unemotional, uncommunicative, unintelligible creatures who are apt to use differential equations and logarithms against them the way Yankee pitchers use fastballs and breaking curves."[22]

Further compounding the journalist's dilemma with regard to science reporting is the problem of dueling experts. Oftentimes in environmental matters, each side in the argument produces its own independent experts. As political theorist Maurice Goldsmith states, "Many have come to feel that for every Ph.D. there is an equal and opposite Ph.D."[23]

An extreme example of dueling experts is detailed by Ross Gelbspan in his book *The Heat Is On,* in which he describes the use of research funded by the coal and petroleum industry to raise doubts about global warming science.[24] He discusses a campaign sponsored by the coal industry, in which a handful of scientists were sent around the country to do media interviews. Their messages were crafted to undermine public confidence in global warming science, often relying on research that was flawed or discredited, and not published in peer-reviewed scientific journals.

The characteristics of science—its uncertainty, long-term focus, and complexity—frustrate the journalist's need to be succinct and to meet deadline pressures, and goes against the journalistic tendency towards social drama. As a result, news coverage of environmental events often fails to provide adequate detail, context, or interpretation. As Wilkins and Patterson suggest, "In the end, the audience is entertained by the hazard without being informed about it."[25]

The Practice of "Balance"

The notion of "balance" or getting "both sides" of the story has long been the journalistic standard for "fair," "objective," "unbiased" reporting. Yet, as if environmental reporters didn't already face enough challenges, the practice of balance can itself be a problem.

Journalistic canons stress objectivity and fairness and preclude journalists from taking sides on a controversial issue. The appearance of advocacy on the part of a reporter can negatively impact perceptions of the reporter's credibility and alienate readers or viewers. Thus, reporters often rely on the routine of balancing—that practice of giving "both sides" equal time on a level playing field. Unfortunately, this journalistic tradition often creates a misleading appearance of "objectivity" and "fairness."

One problem of the routine practice of balancing is what Conrad Smith terms **bipolar myopia,** the notion of "both sides" as if there were only two clearly defined perspectives. Environmental issues are complex and often involve multiple perspectives and varying shades of grey. As Smith suggests, "in stories that involve complex scientific or technical concepts, journalism's traditional bipolar myopia is more likely to provide melodrama than enlightenment; more likely to obscure the truth than to reveal it."[26]

An example of bipolar myopia could be seen in coverage of the fires that burned nearly one-quarter of the Bitterroot National Forest (about 370,000 acres) in the summer of 2000. The sources used in this coverage tended to fall in one of two camps. Those in the first camp recognized the inevitability and the need for forest-thinning fires and criticized forest management fire suppression policies. Those in the second camp placed blame for the fires on environmentalists for preventing logging that would thin the overgrown forests as a way of managing fires.

Wildfire management is a highly complex issue. Many factors must be taken into consideration in coming to informed decisions about when to suppress and when not to suppress fire. Issues such as human safety, the fire dangers posed by logging, alternative methods of forest thinning, when and where to do prescribed burns, and so forth, comprise multiple "sides" to this story that were obscured by the media's attention to only the two opposing sides.

Another way in which the balance canon can be misleading is by creating the impression that there are two equal sides to the story when, in fact, the evidence may point overwhelmingly in one direction—in other words, giving balanced coverage to an unbalanced issue. Giving equal time to both sides may amplify the view of only a small minority.

The reporting of global warming has been extensively criticized for creating the appearance of widespread uncertainty and disagreement among scientists, when in reality, there is overwhelming consensus among the scientific community, despite some lingering uncertainties due to the highly complex nature of the models. Science historian Naomi Oreskes reviewed over nine hundred articles published in refereed science journals between 1993 and 2003 in order to quantify the level of consensus among scientists. She found that "remarkably, none of these papers disagreed with the consensus position."[27] Despite the high degree of consensus among scientists, the practice of balance in news reporting has created the misleading idea that the science is still unsettled and uncertain, although there is evidence that this divergence between newspaper coverage and science has declined in the U.S.[28]

Ross Gelbspan, a Pulitzer Prize winner and longtime reporter for the *Washington Post* and the *Boston Globe,* levels a resounding critique of U.S. press coverage of global warming (with the "singular exception" of the reporting by Andrew Revkin from the *New York Times*). He attributes journalists' "deplorable job of disseminating information" to their relatively unquestioning acceptance of "the campaign of disinformation perpetrated by big coal and big oil."[29] As Gelbspan states, "For many years, the press accorded the same weight to the 'skeptics' as it did to the mainstream scientists. This was done in the name of journalistic balance. In fact, it was journalistic laziness."[30] Because the science is complex and often intimidating for reporters, they tend to rely on information subsidies produced by well-funded campaigns with known ties to the fossil fuel industry.[31]

An experiment conducted by environmental communication scholars Julia B. Corbett and Jessica Durfee found that news reporting does, in fact, have an impact on readers' assessment of the certainty or uncertainty of global warming. They found that when a paragraph that presented the viewpoints of scientists who disagreed with the scientific findings was inserted into the news story, the study participants rated the certainty about the findings on global warming to be significantly lower than the control group who read the article in which the paragraph was not inserted. They found that introducing dissenting opinions into a subject where science is largely in agreement accentuates the uncertainty rather than the scientific consensus. As a result, they said, "media coverage has not communicated the graveness of the phenomenon and the negative consequences for daily life."[32]

In the case of global warming, adhering to the journalistic norm of balance has created biased coverage and perpetuated the myth of uncertainty. Maxwell T. Boykoff and Jules M. Boykoff suggest that this bias, when "hidden behind the veil of journalistic balance, creates both discursive and real political space for the U.S. government to shirk responsibility and delay action regarding global warming."[33]

As mentioned earlier, environmental news reporting is a tough beat, and one of the most difficult dilemmas is the notion of balance. An informed, engaged public requires the fair presentation of multiple, credible perspectives of any given issue. Nevertheless, when balance is treated as the routine activity of getting "both sides" of the story, it is often more misleading than helpful, more confusing than empowering.

Concluding and Looking Ahead

The previous discussion has highlighted just some of the challenges of environmental news reporting. Due to limited broadcast minutes and column inches, the coverage is sometimes meager and often limited to reports of catastrophes or discrete events, with little discussion of the context in which the events occurred. Because news is a commercial enterprise, the environmental story tends to be told in ways that make for an entertaining drama, often employing stereotypical characterizations of villains, heroes, and victims. The principal sources tend to be limited to the relatively few who have access to journalists, which leads to an overdependence on official sources. Bipolar myopia can obscure the multiple perspectives of complex issues, and the practice of balance can create a sense of widespread uncertainty even though the consensus may be overwhelming.

While reporters could undoubtedly do a better job, making these changes in news gathering practices would require expanded information gathering time, resources, and column inches or news minutes—luxuries which may not be afforded to many environmental journalists. Reporters must also curb the impulse to become "greens with press passes."[34] The ethical canons of the profession demand a certain level of agnosticism and objective detachment. Yet, as environmental reporter Bud Ward points out, in the case of global warming, "Reporters need not be, and most dare not be 'greens with press passes' for society to 'get it' on the pressing science and implications surrounding climate change."[35] The strength of the science will speak for itself.

Ultimately, responsibility falls on the news consumer to seek out multiple venues of information and to view news critically as it is presented, with an understanding of the multiple challenges inherent in environmental news reporting. As news consumers, it is in our best interest to recognize that news coverage has limitations and biases resulting from constraints that are often beyond reporters' control.

It is easy to recognize the role of news organizations in shaping our perceptions about the natural world. Other forms of popular media operate more clandestinely but are extraordinarily powerful, nonetheless. One of the most ubiquitous and

inescapable sites of meaning-making is advertising. The following chapter looks at advertising as a powerful and pervasive cultural force that bombards us with entertaining, attractive, state of the art, multi-million-dollar messages about humans' relationship to the natural world—a relationship that is fundamentally unsustainable.

Discussion Questions and Exercises

Note: For the following discussion questions, these indexes and databases will be useful in locating newspaper articles: *Lexis/Nexis, ABI/Inform,* and *National Newspaper Index.*

1. Examine several news reports about an environmental disaster to see whether the reporters used any of the journalistic treatments discussed in the chapter. Report your findings:
   a. Does the story display the characteristics of social drama villains ("low tech bumblers," who were "unconcerned about human life," and "deceptive and secretive")?
   b. Do other villainous characteristics emerge besides those listed above?
   c. Do the reports tend to make fundamental attribution errors?
   d. Do the stories demonstrate Smith's notion of bipolar myopia?

2. Find three articles about a particular environmental issue covered in newspapers within the last year. Identify and list the stakeholders or experts who are mentioned or interviewed in the story. Do your findings support Miller and Parnell Riechert's claims about who is likely to be used as a source and who is likely to be left out?

3. Explain how our society's demand for entertainment affects environmental journalism.

4. Gelbspan, a critic of environmental reporting, mentions only one reporter who is exempt from his critique—Andrew Revkin from the *New York Times.* Find several articles written by Revkin and discuss why you think he is exempt from the critique. Do you agree or disagree with Gelbspan's assessment? You may want to check out Revkin's Dot Earth blog (http://dotearth.blogs.nytimes.com).

Suggested Readings

Jeff Cohen and Norman Solomon. *Through the Media Looking Glass: Decoding Bias and Blather in the News.* Monroe, ME: Common Courage, 1995.

Ross Gelbspan. *Boiling Point: How Politicians, Big Oil and Coal, Journalists, and Activists Have Fueled the Climate Crisis—And What We Can Do to Avert Disaster.* New York: Basic Books, 2004.

Norman Solomon and Jeff Cohen. *The Wizards of Media Oz: Behind the Curtain of Mainstream News.* Monroe, ME: Common Courage, 1997.

Additional Resources

The *Environment Writer* is a newsletter for journalists that publishes ten issues yearly with free online access (www.environmentwriter.org).

FAIR (Fairness and Accuracy in Reporting) is a national media watchdog group (www.fair.org).

The Society of Environmental Journalists publishes the *SEJournal,* a quarterly journal with free online access (www.sej.org).

Notes

1. Mark Meister and Phyllis M. Japp, *Enviropop: Studies in Environmental Rhetoric and Popular Culture* (Westport, CT: Praeger, 2002), 3.
2. For a detailed historical overview of environmental news reporting see Sharon M. Friedman, "And the Beat Goes On: The Third Decade of Environmental Journalism," *Environmental Communication Yearbook* 1 (2004): 175–187.
3. Friedman, "And the Beat Goes On," 176.
4. Anders Hansen, *The Mass Media and Environmental Issues* (London: Leicester University Press, 1993).
5. William Gamson and Andre Modigliani, "Media Discourse and Public Opinion on Nuclear Power: A Constructionist Approach," *American Journal of Sociology* 95 (1989): 1–10.
6. Conrad Smith, *Media and Apocalypse: News Coverage of the Yellowstone Forest Fires, Exxon Valdez Oil Spill, and Loma Prieta Earthquake* (Westport, CT: Greenwood, 1992).
7. Smith, *Media and Apocalypse,* 67.
8. Smith, *Media and Apocalypse,* 53.
9. Cited in Smith, *Media and Apocalypse,* 94.
10. Mark Miller and Bonnie Parnell Riechert, "Interest Group Strategies and Journalistic Norms: News Media Framing of Environmental Issues," in *Environmental Risks and the Media,* eds. S. Allan, B. Adam, and C. Carter (New York: Routledge, 2000).
11. Miller and Parnell Riechert, "Interest Group Strategies," 52.
12. Gamson and Modigliani, "Media Discourse and Public Opinion."
13. Holly Stocking and Jennifer Pease Leonard, "The Greening of the Media," *Columbia Journalism Review* 29 (1990): 42.
14. Kathleen H. Jamieson and Karlyn K. Campbell, *The Interplay of Influence: Advertising, Politics, and the Mass Media,* 4th ed. (Belmont, CA: Wadsworth, 1997).
15. Kris M. Wilson, "Communicating Climate Change through the Media: Predictions, Politics and Perceptions of Risk," in *Environmental Risks and the Media,* eds. S. Allan, B. Adams, and C. Carter (New York: Routledge, 2000), 207.
16. Wilson, "Communicating Climate Change," 206.
17. R. W. Kates, "Success, Strain, and Surprise," *Issues in Science and Technology* 2 (1985): 46–58.
18. Robert Manoff and Michael Schudson, *Reading the News* (New York: Pantheon, 1986), 6.
19. Lee Wilkins and Phillip Patterson, "Risk Analysis and the Construction of News," *Journal of Communication* 37 (1987): 83.
20. Cited in Wilkins & Patterson, "Risk Analysis," 87.
21. Miller and Parnell Riechert, "Interest Group Strategies."
22. William Burrows, "Science Meets the Press: Bad Chemistry," *Sciences,* April 1980, 15.
23. Maurice Goldsmith, *The Science Critic: A Critical Analysis of the Popular Presentation of Science* (New York: Routledge & Kegan Paul, 1987), 17.
24. Ross Gelbspan, *The Heat Is On: The High Stakes Battle over Earth's Threatened Climate* (Reading, MA: Addison-Wesley, 1997).
25. Wilkins and Patterson, "Risk Analysis," 13.
26. Smith, *Media and Apocalypse,* 179.
27. Naomi Oreskes, "The Scientific Consensus on Climate Change," *Science* 306 (December 3, 2004): 1686.
28. M. T. Boykoff, "Flogging a Dead Norm? Newspaper Coverage of Anthropogenic Climate Change in the United States and the United Kingdom from 2003 to 2006," *Area* 39, December 2007, 470–481.
29. Ross Gelbspan, *Boiling Point: How Politicians, Big Oil and Coal, Journalists, and Activists Have Fueled the Climate Crisis—and What We Can Do to Avert Disaster* (New York: Basic Books, 2004), 72.
30. Gelbspan, *Boiling Point,* 72–73.

31. See Gelbspan, *Boiling Point;* L. Antilla, "Climate Skepticism: US Newspaper Coverage of the Science of Climate Change," *Global Climate Change* 15 (2005): 338–352; D. Demeritt, "The Construction of Global Warming and the Politics of Science," *Annals of the Association of American Geographers* 91 (2001): 307–337; Maxwell T. Boykoff and Jules M. Boykoff, "Balance as Bias: Global Warming and the US Prestige Press," *Global Environmental Change* 14 (2004): 125–126.

32. Julia B. Corbett and Jessica L. Durfee, "Testing Public (Un)certainty of Science Media Representations of Global Warming," *Science Communication* 26 (December 2004): 144.

33. Boykoff and Boykoff, "Balance as Bias," 134.

34. Bud Ward, "The Effects of Climate Change on Journalism as We Know It," *SE Journal* 17 (2007): 20.

35. Ward, "The Effects of Climate Change," 20.

Chapter 10

Green Advertising and the Green Consumer

Each day, we are exposed to approximately three thousand advertisements,[1] promising happiness, success, popularity, peace, prosperity, self-fulfillment, and whiter, healthier teeth—and all for the mere purchase of a product. Advertisements pop up on our computer screens, fill up our mailboxes, and confront us from T-shirts, billboards, and city buses. Their jingles and slogans are widely shared symbols of our culture. No matter how asinine and irritating they may be, you can't leave home without them and they're everywhere you want to go.

Billions of dollars are spent each year on marketing consumer products. Corporate America has put the best and the brightest to work to figure out ways to get us to buy all those things we really don't need. One thing they have discovered is that green is gold. It seems that nature can sell just about anything to anybody.

This chapter begins with a discussion of green marketing and the various types of green claims, then goes on to take a critical look at how nature is represented in advertising and the messages that these ads send about humans' relationship to the natural world. It concludes by asking you to consider the contradictions underlying the very notion of green consumerism and the implications of green consumerism as a form of environmental advocacy.

Identifying and Targeting the Green Consumer

The 1980s saw the emergence of widespread green advertising as corporate America capitalized on the lucrative market of green consumers. Products conspicuously labeled as "environmentally friendly," "recyclable," "biodegradable," or any number of other eco-friendly descriptors were targeted for those people who were concerned about environmental issues.

A number of market researchers have identified and profiled green consumers. For example, the market research polling firm of RoperASW publishes the Green Gauge Report, which provides poll data about green consumer attitudes and behaviors.[2] It identifies five distinct segments of consumers, based on environment-friendly behaviors. The first is the "true blue greens," who tend to be environmental activists and leaders. The "greenback greens" don't have the time or inclination to be activists and leaders, but are most likely to buy green products. The third segment of green consumers is the "sprouts," environmental fence-sitters who may be pro-environmental on some issues and not on others. The "grousers" are uninvolved and uninterested in environmental issues. They tend to believe that the problem is too big for them to solve. The last group, the "basic browns," are the least involved. They tend to be uninterested in or even hostile toward environmental reforms.

Another classification system is based on consumer motivations. Green marketing consultant Jacqueline Ottman identified three segments. The first is the "planet passionates," who are motivated by concern for preserving the planet. The second group, which Ottman calls "health fanatics," are motivated by concern for the preservation of personal health. "Animal lovers" make up the third group. As the name suggests, people who fall into this category are motivated by concern for the preservation and fair treatment of animals.[3] These are just two of the many classification systems that have emerged to identify and target this attractive market segment.

Along with the increase in green marketing came increased concern about the veracity of green product claims. Many environmental catchwords or phrases, such as "environmentally safe," "biodegradable," "recyclable," "compostable" and "ozone friendly," are highly ambiguous and subject to multiple interpretations. These terms operate within a grey area that media scholar Daniel J. Boorstin terms the **advertising penumbra,**[4] where claims are not exactly false and yet not exactly true either. For example, the advertiser making the claim that its product is biodegradable is not really telling us much. After all, the pyramids are biodegradable.

Mass media scholar Dennis Hayes identified four techniques that marketers use to take advantage of the green consumer market.[5] The first he terms "ecopornography," which is simply a lie. The second is to tell a "narrow truth" designed to mislead. Some use the third technique, which is to donate to some environmental cause for every purchase made. This is often a comparatively small and painless sacrifice on the part of the producer but serves as an effective public relations tool. The fourth technique is honesty—some do, in fact, make genuine claims about genuine efforts toward environmental responsibility. The obvious problem with techniques one, two, and three (if the donation is, in fact, more public relations than philanthropy) is that claims that lie or mislead can tarnish the credibility of those product producers who promote genuinely green products and services.

Suspicions about product claims received widespread public attention in 1989, when the state attorneys general in ten states filed suit against Mobile, the maker of *Hefty* trash bags, and American Enviro Products, the parent company of *Bunnies Plus* disposable diapers, for their misleading claims about the photo-degradable plastics used in their products. Photo-degradable plastics, if exposed to sunlight, will degrade to plastic dust in about a year—a far shorter time than it would take most other kinds of plastic to degrade. However, using Haye's classifications, this claim would fall under the heading of "telling a narrow truth designed to mislead." Although it is true that photo-degradable plastics do disintegrate faster than other plastics when exposed to sunlight, in sanitary landfills which, by law, must be covered, these plastics are no more degradable than any other bag or diaper.

As increasing suspicion began to erode consumer confidence, the Federal Trade Commission (FTC) issued the "Guide for the Use of Environmental Marketing Claims" in 1992. This document provides advertisers with specific guidelines for complying with the Federal Trade Commission Act, which prohibits unfair or deceptive advertising claims. These guidelines have helped to curtail the use of false or misleading terms in product advertising, yet the consumer must still be wary and read the fine print. If, for example, the label says "recycled," the label must tell you what percentage of the product or package is made of recycled materials, unless it consists 100 percent of recycled materials. Labels that use words such as "environment-friendly" or that display environmental seals are fundamentally meaningless unless additional information is supplied, specifically detailing why the product is environment-friendly and the nature of the organization that awarded the seal.

By the late 1990s the green ad boom had largely run its course. The number of green marketing messages had dropped significantly. Marketing strategies had taken a decidedly anti-green turn. Marketers began launching a whole new class of disposable products, such as disposable plastic food storage containers and disposable dusters and cleaning rags. Automobile manufacturers set in motion an aggressive and highly successful industry-wide push to sell larger, less fuel-efficient vehicles, such as pickup trucks and sports utility vehicles.

Today, with increasing awareness of and concern about global warming, the number of products advertised as "green" is again on the rise. A marked increase in corporate green-image advertising is also coming from the energy and transportation sectors. Such ads position a company as a caring corporate citizen and tout its proactive stance on protecting the environment.

Advertisers take various approaches when they invoke nature to sell products. In some ads, the connection between nature and the product advertised is explicitly stated; in others, the connection is more subtly implied. The following section examines different types of green ads, with examples of each, to demonstrate the way in which products or producers are marketed to the environmentally concerned consumer.

Types of Green Advertising

Marketing scholars Subhabrata Banerjee, Charles S. Gulas, and Easwar Iyer define green advertising as any ad that meets one or more of the following criteria: (1) it "promotes a green lifestyle, with or without highlighting a product or service;" (2) it "explicitly or implicitly addresses the relationship between a product or service and the biophysical environment;" and (3) it "presents a corporate image of environmental responsibility." Each of these criteria will be examined in greater detail in the following sections.[6]

Ads That Promote a Green Lifestyle

The Rechargeable Battery Recycling Corporation (RBRC) offers an example of *an ad that promotes a green lifestyle*. The RBRC is a nonprofit organization that promotes recycling portable rechargeable batteries. In one ad, the viewer is drawn to a picture of a pileated woodpecker perched on top of a rechargeable drill battery and a smiling Richard Karn ("Al" from TV's *Home Improvement*) in the bottom right-hand corner. The copy asks the reader to guess what a pileated woodpecker and a cordless drill battery have in common? The answer is, "When you recycle your rechargeable batteries, you preserve his environment and ours." Another RBRC ad is shown in Figure 10.1. Although these ads do not specifically highlight a product or service, they do list the major retail stores where you can drop off used batteries.

Another way of promoting a green lifestyle is to encourage the consumer to purchase the advertiser's eco-friendly product. Ford offers an example in its ad for the Ford Escape, a gas/electric SUV, which shows a picture of an old-growth redwood forest. Superimposed on the pristine view are the words "Finally, a vehicle that can take you to the very places you are helping to preserve." As you turn the page you find a picture of the vehicle and copy that tells you of its fuel efficiency and lower emissions, "which means that this SUV, by nature, is kinder and gentler on nature." Thus a "kinder, gentler" lifestyle, according to this ad, is one that uses less gas and emits fewer pollutants while plowing across the delicate forest floor. The obvious paradox of driving through "the very places you are helping to preserve" apparently was not a matter of concern for the ad designers.

Figure 10.1
Promoting a Green Lifestyle

Advertisers routinely claim that their products or services promote a greener lifestyle. Although recycling batteries may seem to be a very small lifestyle change, it can actually make a big difference. Call2Recycle is a program of the Rechargeable Battery Recycling Corporation, a nonprofit organization that promotes recycling the rechargeable batteries that power many of our electronic devices, such as cell phones, laptop computers, digital cameras, and electric razors. On average, consumers use six wireless products a day and replace their cell phones every eighteen to twenty-four months. Most of the discarded batteries and phones end up in landfills, despite laws in some states that prohibit their disposal in the solid waste stream because they release toxic metals such as mercury, lead, and cadmium.

Call2Recycle, Rechargeable Battery Recycling Corporation

Ads That Address the Relationship between a Product and Nature

The ad for the Ford Escape also serves as an example of the second category of green advertising: *ads that address the relationship between a product and the biophysical environment.* In these ads, the message conveyed is that by purchasing the product, the consumer will be rewarded with a close and personal relationship with nature. Marketers of sports utility vehicles (SUVs) offer a particularly rich source of examples of this kind of advertising message. Through the purchase of a Ford Escape you will be rewarded with an escape to the places you are helping to preserve. With a Jeep Grand Cherokee, the adventurous can "Climb Mountains. Traverse Rivers." As an added benefit, "with its 330-hp 5.7 liter HEMI V8 that's more powerful than anything in its class," you can also "Taunt Sports Cars." Not only will you find escape and adventure, you will do it in style and comfort. The Lexus GX470 ad tells you to "Relive the Journeys of the Pioneers. Except for that Braving the Elements and Incredible Hardships Part."

It's not just SUVs that reward you with nature. Nature has been used to sell everything from bath soap to lawn fertilizer, from whiskey to granola bars. Ads for Nature Valley granola bars picture hikers in various settings of earthly paradise such as beside mountain lakes, in pristine forests, or on spectacular rock formations.

Where Does Your Food Come From?

The Best Tasting Food
Ripens Close to Home.

Buy Fresh. Buy Local.

foodroutes.org

Figure 10.2
Promoting a Closer
Relationship to Nature

Advertising claims that promise a closer relationship with nature are often misleading or oversimplified. Yet some organizations, such as FoodRoutes Conservancy, really do deliver on their advertising claims. The fruits and vegetables in your grocery store's produce section traveled an average of thirteen hundred miles and spent up to fourteen days in transit. A closer relationship with your local tomato and its grower actually does give you "the best tasting food" along with healthier and more sustainable eating habits.

FoodRoutes Conservancy

The ad copy tells you to "Let Nature Valley take you wherever you want to go." It is "the energy bar nature intended." For the mere purchase of an energy bar, the rewards of nature are there for the taking—just as nature intended.

In the previous advertising examples, the relationship between the product and nature is either explicitly stated or more subtly implied. SUVs and granola bars take you to nature. However, the most common use of nature in advertisements relies on a more indirect form of implied relationship—nature as backdrop. In these ads, the product is superimposed against a backdrop of nature in the form of animals, a sparkling river, a forest, and so forth. Products that may have little or no connection to the scenic nature depicted are tacitly associated with nature, thus transforming their meanings. When the ad appropriates symbols of nature, the product is no longer just a bar of soap, but a shower under a mountain waterfall; not just a room freshener, but a field of wildflowers; not just dryer sheets, but a mountain breeze. When we purchase these products, we can experience the beauty and joy of nature without ever having to leave home.

If we critically analyze the implied messages of ads that use nature as a backdrop, the absurdity of the claims is readily apparent. The power in these ads lies in the fact that we rarely do examine them critically. On an almost subliminal level, the values that we hold for nature become associated with the product. We value mountain waterfalls, so we value the soap that has a mountain-waterfall association attached to it.

These ads present a highly anthropocentric and narcissistic view of humans' relationship to the natural world. Like the product it comes with, nature is constructed as something to be consumed for enjoyment, adventure, comfort, and convenience. Although nature itself is not for sale, in purchasing the product, you purchase the relationship with nature the product provides for you. Drawing on the words of the old Prudential Insurance slogan, environmental communication scholar Julia B. Corbett tells us, "we can indeed own a piece of the rock—if we have the right vehicle and the right shoe to get us there, and the right lip balm and hand-held Global Positioning System to keep us safe when we are out there."[7]

Ads That Present a Corporate Image of Environmental Responsibility

The third kind of green ads are *ads that present a corporate image of environmental responsibility*. One example is an ad in *Better Homes and Gardens* magazine. The Dawn (dishwashing liquid made by Proctor and Gamble) logo is displayed along with the words in large letters, "SAVING WILDLIFE FOR OVER 20 YEARS." Smaller print below reads, "Wildlife experts choose Dawn because it's effective on grease while being gentle on skin. To help, visit saveaduck.com." When you go to this web site you find out that "Dawn dishwashing liquid has proudly donated thousand of gallons of Dawn detergent to help clean birds and wildlife affected by oil spills." Once again, you don't have to look deep to find the paradox of a major producer of petroleum-based products advertising its generosity in donating a small portion of one of its products to the victims of oil transportation accidents. The irony is further deepened when you learn that Proctor and Gamble has been boycotted by animal rights groups on behalf of the animals it uses to test products.

The Dawn example represents what is commonly referred to as **greenwash,** defined by the *Oxford English Dictionary* as "disinformation disseminated by an organization so as to present an environmentally responsible public image." It is in the interest of the corporation to foster a public image of environmental responsibility, especially those corporations that have been the subject of high profile attacks because of environmental accidents or polluting practices. Often, however, the green public image is more public relations than substance.

CorpWatch,[8] an organization that monitors and exposes corporate practices involving issues such as human rights, environmental justice, labor rights, and industrial pollution, describes some of the advertising techniques used to promote the green corporate image. One is *to impress you with environmental projects*. For example, a glossy ad for Shell Corporation in the *National Geographic* magazine asks the viewer, "What do we really need in today's energy-hungry world?" The answer: "More gardens." The copy tells of Shell's support of the Flower Garden Banks National Marine Sanctuary, a spectacular bank of coral and sponges in the Gulf of Mexico. This is undoubtedly a worthy project. However, the corporation's commitment to preserving these reefs is put into question in light of the fact that the direct funding for this project is a mere $5000 per year while the cost of advertising in *National Geographic* is in the six-figure range.[9]

Another advertising technique used to promote a green corporate image is *to distract attention from a destructive product or products by focusing on an eco-friendly product*. A General Motors ad states that "Someone should bring environmentally conscious technologies to environmentally sensitive locations. Which is why the National Park Service is celebrating the delivery of 18 shuttle buses to Yosemite National Park that are powered by GM's advanced hybrid technology." The ad copy goes on to extol the environmental virtues of these hybrid buses in terms of reducing engine noise and emissions, and ends by saying "That's how we approach the environment at GM." Ironically, GM also approaches the environment by manufacturing and aggressively marketing vehicles such as the Chevy Trailblazer, the Cherokee Suburban, the Cadillac Escalade, and the Hummer, which average from eleven to sixteen miles per gallon in city driving.[10] Vehicle for vehicle, GM is the auto industry's worst emitter of smog-forming pollutants and second worst (only behind Ford) in producing heat-trapping emissions.[11] Many of these vehicles are among the seven thousand vehicles that enter the park each day during the busy tourist season. If GM truly feels that "someone should bring environmentally conscious technologies" to Yosemite, it apparently feels it should be someone else where passenger vehicles are concerned.

Skepticism of green corporate images is warranted as the advertising penumbra is cast over dazed and cynical consumers, who are left wondering whether any truly green products or product producers actually exist. Greenwash and misleading product labels do more than simply misrepresent corporate interests. They actually work to inhibit the genuine greening of corporate America. *Greenlife*, an advocacy organization that gathers and disseminates information about sustainable consumption, explains that "Endowed with bigger marketing and public relations budgets, greenwashers shut the door on genuinely green business struggling to get a foothold in the marketplace."[12] In addition, greenwash "lures investors who link environmental performance with profitable financial performance, and misleads policy makers charged with designing and enforcing environmental regulation."[13] Greenwash also impacts the consumer. The burden of finding out which businesses are making a good faith effort to be genuinely green and which products are environment-friendly is left to the beleaguered and often confused would-be-green consumer.

Advertising professionals are highly adept at identifying consumer needs or desires, stimulating those needs or desires, and then offering a product or service as a means of satisfying them. Yet, consumers aren't dopes. If one were to examine the implied claims in many ads, the absurdity would be readily apparent—use this air freshener and your living room will be magically transformed into a fresh, mountain meadow.

In analyzing the logical fallacies of the ad, one misses the symbolic sleight-of-hand that takes place right before our eyes. Rhetorical scholar John D. Ramage explains it like this: "It would be as if a literary critic, a terminally Serious One, decided to devote all his time and energy to lecturing lovers about the egregious logical fallacies in love poetry."[14] Just as in poetry, it is not the logic that works on the consumer mind, it is the values attached to the images and words of the ad that are then projected onto the product—values that may, in fact, have nothing to do with the product being advertised. To draw on the words of Ramage once again, "Words instantaneously animate objects within a magical space where one image transfers meaning to another merely by their proximity to one another."[15]

Nature is particularly "magical" in advertising because of the multiple values its images invoke—escape from boredom, adventure, serenity, peace, danger, savagery, and so on. Green marketers lead consumers down a product-lined path to a fantasy world of nature on sale.

The Fantasy World of Nature
According to Green Ads

Advertising situates humans and nature in a relationship in which nature is viewed almost solely as a resource, with no intrinsic value beyond its use to humans for recreation, comfort, or convenience. This utilitarian view of nature is constructed through symbolic representations of nature that are often misleading and more closely resemble a world of fantasy than the real world of nature. The following discussion looks at four commonly employed images of nature and the implications of these fantasy constructions.

Nature Is Sublime

Advertisers call on the **convention of the sublime,** a literary and artistic convention that, as environmental communication scholar Christine L. Oravec suggests, "acts as a screen or a projection of human preferences upon the natural scene."[16] It is a paradise on earth that has no mosquitoes, ticks, poison ivy, or dirt. Even SUVs driving through creek beds show no signs of mud. This world of nature has not been blemished by the marks of human intervention—the forests have not been logged, the meadows have not been overgrazed, and the rivers have not been diverted for irrigation. There is nothing in the Edenic, sublime portrayal of nature to suggest that pristine nature is anything but commonplace, or that there is any cause for concern or action.

Nature Is "Out There"

Nature in advertising is almost always portrayed as someplace "out there" and rarely as part of our everyday lives. With the exception of ads for such things as lawn fertilizers and allergy medications, nature is never in our own backyards, towns, or cities. As communication scholar Diane S. Hope states, "Nothing in these ads indicates that the natural world is always with us, where we live and work, in the polluted river down the road, in the diminishing green spaces of our cities, in the toxic mix of chemicals in our back yards."[17] This narrow view of nature serves to preclude concern for local ecologies, and masks the connection between what we do in our everyday lives and the impact it has on the natural world. According to green marketers, nature will always be someplace "out there," preserved in all of its pristine beauty, no matter what kind of production and consumption we practice "right here."

Nature Is for Personal Consumption

Another fantasy image that is commonly used in advertising portrays nature as ours for consumption on the personal level. Nothing in these ads suggests that the consumer may be trespassing or may not have the right to be there. The idea of individual ownership of nature is less than subtly articulated in the KIA ad for the midsize Sorento. A multiple-choice question is given for the reader's consideration with boxes to check the correct answer: "You can drive off a paved highway: (a) If traffic is congested; (b) When instructed to do so by a patrolman; (c) If it's a two-lane highway; or (d) Whenever you damn well please, thanks to the available Torque-On-Demand 4WD and the standard 3.5-liter V6." Although the viewer is not actually given the correct answer, response "d" is highlighted as the obvious best answer. You pass the test by recognizing that nature is yours for personal consumption anywhere and anytime you please—if you own the right vehicle.

Nature Is Indestructible

Advertising sends the message that our personal consumption of nature will not harm it—that driving through a creek bed or hiking on a mountain ridge will in no way blemish the pristine scenery. Ads ignore the fact that human recreational use of nature inevitably has an impact. Obviously, some recreational uses are more disruptive than others. One motorized vehicle can do more harm in one day than a Boy Scout Troop will do in a year of careful hiking and packing out. Yet green ads make no distinction between low-impact and high-impact recreation, nor are consumers encouraged to tread softly and carefully in their nature outings.

These four commonly used fantasy constructions of nature are deceptive, and misleading, with ultimately harmful consequences. Nature is depicted as sublime, problem-free, indestructible, somewhere-out-there, and, as the ad tells us, ours for personal use and enjoyment whenever we "damn well please." This highly anthropocentric view of nature fails to recognize any intrinsic value in nature aside from its use for human enjoyment or comfort. It ignores the fact that few wilderness areas remain and masks the destruction on much of our federal lands from grazing, mining, logging, and road building. The ads overlook the impact that such things as industrial wastes, smokestacks, and chemical fertilizers have on the natural world that we see in the ads. Furthermore, when nature is depicted as "the big out there," the value of nature in our own backyards and communities is overlooked, implying that it is only the "out there" that we need to be concerned about.

Images of nature are manipulated to evoke emotions and appeal to human values because the bottom line is that "green sells." Green products are marketed to help save the planet even though their planet-saving potential may be, to say the least, miniscule. Corporations market themselves as green corporate citizens even though their "green advocacy" may be highly questionable and the values that we place on nature are used to sell products that aren't even vaguely green. The green consumer who truly wishes to make responsible purchasing choices is often left feeling manipulated, misled, and confused.

The Green Consumer

Distinguishing the green from the not-so-green products can be complicated and confusing. A truly green choice would require a **cradle to grave audit** of the product's entire lifespan, including an assessment of the amount of energy used to produce the product, how much pollution was created in its production, how far and by what means the product was transported, the "greenness" of the other products made by the company and its subsidiaries, and the impact of the product's final disposal.

If a person were to really take all this seriously, a trip to the grocery store would require months of research before even entering the store, and at the end of the shopping trip, the cart would have very few items. And after all that, you have to decide what kind of bag to bring them home in. The production of plastic bags requires less energy and has fewer environmental impacts than does the production of paper bags, but almost all recycling centers take paper bags while few accept plastic bags. The obvious solution to the dilemma is to bring your plastic or

Connections

Walmart Going Green?

Companies are beginning to realize that adopting green strategies is more than window dressing to entice consumers. In the face of an image crisis that was keeping customers away, Walmart, the world's largest retail chain, has adopted an ambitious green agenda. In October 2005, the CEO of Wal-Mart Stores, Inc., the parent company, announced three new corporate goals: to rely on 100 percent renewable energy; to limit waste through recycling and packaging reduction; and to sell "environmentally friendly," "sustainable" products, including compact fluorescent light bulbs, for which Walmart has set a goal to sell one hundred million a year. The retailer has also become the world's largest supplier of organic foods.

What began as a defensive strategy has become a plus on the corporate balance sheet. Walmart has trimmed its electricity bill by 17 percent since 2002 and will save $2.4 million annually from using less packaging on house-brand toys alone.

No matter what its motivations, the greening of Walmart has far-reaching environmental impacts. Consider, for example, that its 2002 sales of $245 billion would make it number thirty-one on the list of the world's largest economies—ahead of Saudi Arabia, Switzerland, and Austria. Its U.S. stores sales record for a single day ($1.4 billion on November 29, 2002) is larger than the annual gross domestic product of Monaco, Greenland, or Belize. With an army of sixty-five thousand suppliers, Walmart's massive clout has a massive impact on the supply chain. For example, Walmart's commitment to sell fish only from certified sustainable fisheries has brought an about-face in the industry as suppliers hasten to meet sustainability standards.

New green corporate image notwithstanding, Walmart faces an uphill battle on the image front. To meet its wholesale prices, its many vendors subcontract with overseas agents for goods manufactured in unregulated and often very poor working conditions. Likewise, its domestic labor practices and its subversion of local businesses have been the target of widespread public criticism. Although its new green-image makeover may not entirely win over Walmart skeptics, even hard-core skeptics will recognize its potential for promoting sustainable practices among suppliers and other global giants.

Source: John Carey, "Big Strides to become the Jolly Green Giant," *Business Week*, January 29, 2007, 57.

paper grocery bags back to the store and use them again or to use canvas or net bags to carry your groceries.

Determining the "true greenness" of a product is a complicated, time-consuming process. There are product watch groups and published green guides to help with this, but it is still a difficult and time-consuming task. Many consumers lack the time or incentives to do an exhaustive search of the products they buy. Thus, along with the burden of informed, responsible green purchasing comes the burden of guilt for our inevitable failure to be "truly green" consumers. And if that's not enough to make us feel guilty, then consider all the things we buy that we "want" but don't really "need."

The Consumer "Goat"

A number of writers have criticized the consuming public for their naiveté and their senseless subjugation to the mass hypnosis of advertising.[18] Toby Smith, in her influential book *The Myth of Green Marketing: Tending Our Goats at the Edge of Apocalypse*, describes and questions this "manipulation thesis":

> these writers assert that individuals (except for themselves, it seems) exhibit a catalogue of unflattering traits. We are easily influenced, self-centered, insecure, incapable of making an independent judgment, egotistical, self-aggrandizing, and uninterested in the consequences of our actions. In short, *individuals are like goats—they are attracted to shiny objects and they will consume anything.* (italics added)[19]

Smith objects to this kind of consumer characterization and suggests that "moralizing and lamenting the fickle character of the human race (mostly women) is not explanatory, prescriptive, or inspiring."[20] Consumers are exhorted to be informed and to make reasonable, independent decisions. Yet, as independent decision makers, we come to vastly different conclusions about what is "reasonable," what is "necessary," and what is merely playing into our desire for fashion, novelty, or status. Is deodorant, for example, a necessity or a luxury in your life?

Smith points out that we come to our decisions about what is reasonable consumer behavior from within the ideological universe of a consumer society. "The question then is not why cannot the stupid consumer see the obvious nonsense of consumerism, but how is the individual *making sense* of it."[21] Rather than casting blame on the consumer, one needs to understand how the reality of what makes sense—what is reasonable, good, right, natural—is constructed and maintained within the hegemony of a capitalistic/consumer framework—a framework that places the green consumer in a situation of irreconcilable contradictions.

The Paradox of Green Consumerism

Corporations have a vested interest in insuring that consumers consume. Our system of industrial capitalism measures success by growth. This growth-oriented ethic is legitimized and reinforced by ideologies and institutions that support its hegemonic structures. The myth of the "American dream" is based on the individual's success in literally and figuratively buying into its supporting structures and ideologies and, in so doing, achieving the good life. Progress, innovation, development, and new and better technologies are all considered to be right, good, and normal. Challenges to these expansionist ideals are interpreted as antiprogressive, Luddite, elitist, unscientific, and "unfortunate but correctable."[22] Yet, the growth-oriented, expansionistic ethic is ultimately unsustainable, because the resources upon which it depends are finite.

For a privileged few, the "good life" of consumption comes at a tremendous social and environmental cost. Consumption is inherently anti-green. Hence, green consumption is inherently oxymoronic. Green consumerism serves to reinforce the practices necessary for the continued existence of the hegemony-driven, unsustainable status quo. As media scholar William Kilbourne puts it, "Advocating green consumption is advocating more consumption, more technology, more economic growth, all considered anathema to the ecological position." Thus, if viewed from a truly green position, "the only green product is one that is not produced."[23]

Green marketers ask the consumer to choose between a nondegradable and a degradable garbage bag, but they never ask the consumer to choose between a garbage bag and no garbage bag at all. Environmental economists Christopher Plant and David H. Albert explain, "The whole idea that we could possibly do without most of these goods is never mentioned, because no one stands to make additional profit from not producing things: the alternative lies outside of the market and subsequently receives no attention."[24]

Some critics even go so far as to suggest that recycling as a form of environmental advocacy is antithetical to a truly green position. "After all," explains environmental communication scholar Julia B. Corbett, "the message of recycling is not to reduce or avoid consumption, but essentially to consume something again."[25] Environmental and political writer Kirkpatrick Sale suggests that we view recycling not as an answer to our waste problems but "as a confession that the system of packaging and production in this society is out of control."[26] He likens recycling centers to hospitals, as a last chance effort to deal with an ill that never should have been created in the first place.

Critics of consumerism do not suggest that we just stop consuming the products of industrial capitalism. Indeed, few of us would be able to survive without them. Nor do most of them suggest that green consumerism is total bunk, that we should ignore it altogether and not even attempt to be responsible consumers. The reason for the critique is to bring to light the assumptions that drive green consumerism—assumptions that paradoxically also ground the environmental problems we face.

When our environmental problems are attributed to irresponsible, goat-like consumers, then the solution likewise must come from the consumers in the form of individual purchasing choices. Yet our patterns of consumption are shaped in ways that, in reality, give us few choices. As environmental writer Brian Tokar explains, "[Green consumerism] is based on the myth that environmental problems are largely the result of individual consumer choices, neglecting all of the ways in which these choices are shaped and constrained by decisions made in corporate board rooms well beyond the reach of public scrutiny."[27]

Focusing on consumers as the cause and cure of the problem ignores the production side of the equation and fails to challenge the role of industry and the corporate board room. "Seen in this context," says environmental communication scholar John W. Delicath, "green consumerism represents not individual consciousness-raising, but industry bullet dodging."[28] Green consumerism not only deflects attention from industry, it allows industry to define and limit the nature of environmental activism to the very practices that encourage unsustainable resource use.

Green marketers tell us to consume our way out of our environmental problems, and suggest that their products are not only good for the environment, but good for the purchaser as well. We can purchase photo-degradable diapers and still have the most leak-free diaper on the shelves. We can purchase an environmentally friendly vehicle and still have all of the amenities of a luxury vehicle. As Kermit the Frog points out in an ad for the Ford Escape hybrid, "I guess it *is* easy being green." Little or no sacrifice is required in this exercise of virtue.

One of the biggest criticisms of consumerism-as-environmental-advocacy is that it lulls consumers into a false sense of complacency by suggesting that our environmental problems can be solved by relatively sacrifice-free, wise consumption. Green consumer discourse fails to address the deeper problems, the harder choices, and the need for significant changes. Kirkpatrick Sale puts it like this:

What I find truly pernicious about such solutions is that they get people thinking they are actually making a difference and doing their part to halt the destruction of the earth: "There, I've taken all the bottles to the recycling center and used my string bag at the grocery store; I guess that will take care of global warming."[29]

Sale goes on to say that this kind of message misleads consumers by failing to acknowledge the "very hard truths, hard choices, and hard actions" that are required of individuals. But more importantly, it diverts attention from the "larger forces of society—corporate and governmental—where true power and true destructiveness lie."[30]

One of the things that make advertising such a powerful cultural force is the **myth of immunity.** We tend to believe that advertising does not influence our buying decisions and to dismiss its impact on our attitudes and beliefs.[31] Although a particular ad may not influence us to go out and buy that particular product, the perpetual assault of advertising impacts all of us in one way or another.

Advertising does not work in a vacuum. It exists as part of a culture whose ideologies and institutions of control serve to reinforce and maintain the hegemonic chokehold of a consumption-driven system. The success of the system, suggests Plant and Albert, lies in "its ability to draw everything into its cold embrace, to reduce all value to dollar values, and to co-opt even its harshest critics."[32] Even many environmental groups have succumbed to its pressure by selling T-shirts, calendars, and coffee mugs in order to gain the attention of a consumer society. Environmental writers Lisa A. Benton and John R. Short discuss the inherent contradiction in the commercialization of environmentalism and urge us to "remember that when we purchase merchandise, even environmental merchandise, we condone a set of ideologies (about the positive attributes of mass production and mass consumption) that are part of the dominant technological metadiscourse."[33] Rather than challenging an unsustainable status quo, green marketers offer a simple solution to our environmental problems. Yet, it is obvious that we cannot consume our way out of overflowing landfills, disappearing species, or a warming planet. Real solutions are not for sale at your local shopping mall or grocery store.

Concluding and Looking Ahead

This chapter has presented a harshly critical perspective on green advertising, green consumerism, and the corporate machine that drives and promotes our unsustainable consumer practices. Although this critique of the manipulations of corporate America is in many cases warranted, placing all the blame on powerful corporate evildoers is a cartoon depiction of a complex problem. We are, in many ways, "goat-like" consumers. As environmental writer Curtis White explains, "Something in the very fabric of our daily life is deeply anti-nature as well as anti-human. It inhabits not just bad-guy CEOs at Monsanto and Weyerhaeuser but nearly every working American, environmentalists included."[34]

I would encourage you to make a good faith effort towards green consumption with the understanding that every small act helps, but without losing sight of the fact that it is a very small act indeed when placed in the larger context of the problems we face. When advocacy is limited to the act of purchasing, its pro-environmental impact is marginal at best. Yet, as environmental writer Toby Smith points out, there is no one best way to clean up the environment: "As an isolated activity, green consumerism as it was (and is) promoted probably has no effect on cleaning up the ecosystem; but neither will any other single factor . . . . The causes are multiple and so must be the approaches to change."[35]

Cultural studies scholar Chris Barker aptly describes contemporary consumer culture as "a wasteland—a culture with a black hole of meaninglessness at its heart—that more and more of everything will not solve, for this particular monster feeds off precisely that desire."[36] Addressing our environmental problems requires finding new and creative ways of living, involving significant changes on the individual level as well as political and social actions to transform the institutions and practices that feed our voracious consumer culture. It's not easy being green, but for our efforts we will be a healthier, happier society living on a healthier, happier planet.

Because of its ubiquity, advertising is one of the most influential sites of meaning construction, but many other cultural influences also contribute to our view of nature and humans' place in it. The following chapter will take you on a tour of a few of these consumer-monster feeding sites.

Discussion Questions and Exercises

1. The chapter discusses several categories of green consumer markets ("true greens," "planet passionates," etc.). Which of these best fits your own consumer profile? Which one is the least descriptive? Explain your answers.

2. The chapter discusses four commonly used images of nature: nature as sublime, nature as "out there," nature for personal consumption, and nature as indestructible. Find an ad that uses one or more of these themes. Discuss how it uses the images and the message the ad sends about humans' relationship to nature.

3. Do you agree with Sale, who suggests that the green consumer solution diverts people from the hard truth by leading them to believe that they have done their part and no more should be required of them? Explain your answer.

Suggested Readings

Sharon Beder. *Free Market Missionaries: The Corporate Manipulation of Community Values*. London: Earthscan, 2006.

Julia B. Corbett, "A Faint Green Sell: Advertising and the Natural World;" Diane S. Hope, "Environment as Consumer Icon in Advertising Fantasy;" and Richard K. Olsen, "Living Above It All: The Liminal Fantasy of Sports Utility Vehicle Advertisements." In Mark Meister and Phyllis M. Japp (Eds.), *Enviropop: Studies in Environmental Rhetoric and Popular Culture*. Westport, CT: Praeger, 2002.

Toby M. Smith. *The Myth of Green Marketing: Tending Our Goats at the Edge of Apocalypse*. Toronto: University of Toronto Press, 1998.

Brian Tokar. *Earth for Sale: Reclaiming Ecology in the Age of Corporate Greenwash*. Boston: South End, 1997.

Notes

1. J. B. Twitchell, *Adcult USA: The Triumph of Advertising in American Culture* (New York: Columbia University Press, 1996).
2. RoperASW, "Green Gauge Report 2002: Americans' Perspective on Environmental Issues: Yes . . . But," 2002, http://www.roperasw.com (accessed July 30, 2005).
3. Jacqueline Ottman, "Know Thy Target," 2003, http://www.greenmarketing.com/articles/IB_03nov.html (accessed July 30, 2005).

4. Daniel J. Boorstin, "The Rhetoric of Democracy," in *American Mass Media,* eds. R. Atwan, B. Orton, and W. Vesterman (New York: Random House, 1982).

5. Dennis Hayes, "Feeling Green about 'Green,'" *Advertising Age* 62 (1991): 46–54.

6. Subhabrata Banerjee, Charles S. Gulas, and Easwar Iyer, "Shades of Green: A Multidimensional Analysis of Environmental Advertising," *Journal of Advertising* 24 (1995): 21–31.

7. Julia B. Corbett, "A Faint Green Sell: Advertising and the Natural World," in *Enviropop: Studies in Environmental Rhetoric and Popular Culture,* eds. M. Meister and P. M. Japp (Westport, CT: Praeger, 2002), 157.

8. http://www.corpwatch.org

9. Greenlife, "Don't be Fooled: America's Ten Worst Greenwashers," 2005, http://www.thegreenlife.org/dontbefooled.html (accessed July 30, 2005).

10. U.S. Environmental Protection Agency, "Green Vehicle Guide," http://epa.gov/greenvehicles (accessed July 30, 2005).

11. Greenlife, "Don't be Fooled."

12. Greenlife, "Don't be Fooled," 2.

13. Greenlife, "Don't be Fooled," 3.

14. John D. Ramage, *Rhetoric: A User's Guide* (New York: Pearson Education, 2006), 199.

15. Ramage, *Rhetoric,* 199.

16. Christine L. Oravec, "To Stand Outside Oneself: The Sublime in the Discourse of Natural Scenery," in *The Symbolic Earth: Discourse and the Creation of the Environment,* eds. J. G. Cantrill and C. L. Oravec (Lexington: University Press of Kentucky, 1996), 59.

17. Diane S. Hope, "Environment as Consumer Icon in Advertising Fantasy," in *Enviropop: Studies in Environmental Rhetoric and Popular Culture,* eds. M. Meister and P. M. Japp (Westport, CT: Praeger, 2002), 168.

18. See, for example, M. Mellor, *Breaking the Boundaries: Toward a Feminist Green Socialism* (London: Virago, 1992); S. Irvine and A. Ponton, *A Green Manifesto: Politics for a Green Future* (London: Optima, 1988); S. Irvine, *Beyond Green Consumerism* (London: Friends of the Earth, 1989).

19. Toby Smith, *The Myth of Green Marketing: Tending Our Goats at the Edge of Apocalypse* (Toronto: University of Toronto Press, 1998), 14.

20. Smith, *The Myth of Green Marketing,* 114.

21. Smith, *The Myth of Green Marketing,* 116.

22. Smith, *The Myth of Green Marketing,* 7.

23. William Kilbourne, "Green Advertising: Salvation or Oxymoron?" *Journal of Advertising* 24 (1995): 16.

24. Christopher Plant and David H. Albert, "Green Business in a Gray World: Can It Be Done?" in *Green Business: Hope or Hoax,* eds. C. Plant and J. Plant (Philadelphia: New Society, 1991), 3.

25. Corbett, "A Faint Green Sell," 155.

26. Kirkpatrick Sale, "The Trouble with Earth Day," in *Green Business: Hope or Hoax,* eds. C. Plant and J. Plant (Philadelphia: New Society, 1991), 60.

27. Brian Tokar, *Earth for Sale: Reclaiming Ecology in the Age of Corporate Greenwash* (Boston: South End, 1997), xiv.

28. John W. Delicath, "The Rhetoric of Green Consumerism: A Social Ecological Critique," *Speaker and Gavel* 31 (1994): 15.

29. Sale, "The Trouble with Earth Day," 60.

30. Sale, "The Trouble with Earth Day," 60.

31. S. Alter, "'Influenced by the Ad? Not me,' Most Say," *Advertising Age,* June 10, 1985, 15.

32. Plant and Albert, "Green Business," 2.

33. Lisa A. Benton and John R. Short, *Environmental Discourse and Practice* (Malden, MA: Blackwell, 1999), 203.

34. Curtis White, "The Idols of Environmentalism: Do Environmentalists Conspire against Their Own Interests?" *Orion Magazine,* March/April 2007, http://www.orionmagazine.org (accessed March 20, 2007).

35. Smith, *The Myth of Green,* 7.

36. Chris Barker, *Making Sense of Cultural Studies: Cultural Problems and Critical Debates* (Thousand Oaks, CA: Sage, 2002), 174.

Chapter 11

Popular Culture and the Environment

There is perhaps a no more iconic figure of U.S. pop culture than Homer Simpson. Homer represents all we love to hate and hate to admit about ourselves. We love to hate Homer because of his hedonistic drives, voracious consumerism, ethnocentric arrogance, and naïve susceptibility to media influence. At the same time, we have a perplexing fondness for this bumbling protagonist that stems from more than just his entertainment value and the years of head-shaking, eyeball-rolling enjoyment he has provided. When we laugh at Homer, we laugh at ourselves, begrudgingly recognizing in him the worst in ourselves.

Homer is far more than a product of a production company, a TV network, and its sponsors. Homer is a product of a culture and its fundamental assumptions, beliefs, and core values. As such, Homer offers a means of self-reflexive acknowl-edgement of our own complicity in the dominant social order.[1] We are, after all, products of the same culture that created Homer. As a national icon, Homer not only reflects the culture in which he was created, he also serves to perpetuate and create the core values of the culture.

The term **popular culture** refers to the commercially produced stream of language and images that create cultural meanings that most people know and understand. For instance, if I were to ask you where the happiest place on earth is, you would most likely know that this happens to be Disney World. You can probably tell me what peanut butter "choosy mothers choose," where to go if you feel like "eating good in the neighborhood," and what kind of carbonated cola is "the real thing." These examples are only a small fraction of the almost innumer-able pop culture messages, images, and meanings that have been commercially produced and mass marketed, and that have created widely shared meanings in U.S. culture.

The images and messages come to us from multiple sources or sites of meaning-making—television commercials, magazines, theme parks, greeting cards, and so on. The messages of popular culture are often overlooked as trivial. Yet, the constant bombardment of multiple messages from the multiple sites of popular culture have a profound impact on the way a culture views itself. Popular culture is a window through which to view a culture's values—values that are largely a mani-festation of the messages created through mass-mediated sites of meaning making. Thus, the messages of pop culture both reflect and create the culture's core values.

Among the many and diverse sites of meaning construction, the dominant message is universal: Consume! As environmental communication scholars Mark Meister and Phyllis M. Japp put it, "Popular culture is a world where commodifica-tion reigns, a world in which everything is a product for consumption; everything is for sale in some aspect or another."[2] The natural world is no exception—nature is for sale.

It would be impossible to map exhaustively the multiple and diverse sites of meaning construction within the domain of popular culture. The few sites presented for your consideration in this chapter are offered as a way of bringing to your atten-tion the pervasive influence of popular culture messages and the human/nature relationship they construct.

The chapter calls attention to a number of the rhetorical forms and themes that have been addressed earlier. It demonstrates ways in which these forms and themes can be used to inform our understanding of the human/nature relationship that is constructed through the discursive practices of particular sites of meaning construction. Some of the familiar topics include myth, the sublime, the jeremiad, and green consumption. Some new concepts are also introduced for your consideration, such as the "priest" and the "bard," as well as an interesting look at "meat" and the crossing of the human-nature divide.

The following is a condensed tour of various sites that will take you from your living room to the depths of distant oceans—from the mundane to the exotic. The tour has two purposes. The first is to introduce you to some popular culture sites of meaning-making that you may not have previously considered in this light. The second goal is to find the "true meaning" of nature, as defined through diverse mass-mediated messages.

The tour will stop at the greeting card display at a local store in Anywhere, U.S.A. From there, it takes on a more exotic flavor as we embark on a SeaWorld adventure. Then we will go back home for a relaxing evening in front of the television with the Nature Channel. As a fitting end to a long day of popular culture sightseeing, the tour concludes with a bedtime story by Dr. Seuss. But before we take off, it's always good to check the weather.

Nature According to The Weather Channel (TWC)

As one of its slogans states, "You need us for everything you do." Perhaps this is why The Weather Channel (TWC), a 24-hour cable service broadcast since 1982, is the most popular cable network in the United States. TWC's computer-generated graphics of radar satellite images gives us up-do-date weather conditions and forecasts to help us plan for everything we do. TWC can also supply us with the appropriate map for everything we do, as cultural critic Andrew Ross points out:

> fishing maps, business travel maps, picnic maps, indoor relative humidity maps . . . tanning maps, allergy maps . . . the ominously named 'aches and pains index,' influenza maps, precipitation maps, radar maps, storm history maps, windy travel maps . . . each charting in detail the distribution of daily weather effects on our bodies, and each sponsored in turn by the manufacturer of an appropriate product.[3]

If the product you need is not displayed in sponsor ads, you need only visit the online Weather Channel Store to find the appropriate merchandize for everything you do—clothing, backpacks, rain gauges, lanterns, gardening tools—a virtual shopping mall supplying products for all your weather needs.

TWC's diverse audience reflects the diversity of motives for watching the show. Viewer interest in weather watching stems from social, economic, and entertainment motives. We use weather forecasts to plan our social activities, such as picnics or golf tee times. The forecasts are important to farmers, road departments, construction and utility workers, and so on because of the work-related economic impacts of weather. A portion of the audience is also made up of weather enthusiasts who simply find weather fascinating and entertaining. TWC further enhances its entertainment value with special segments such as "Weather Rewind," a short program of some of the more spectacular weather video footage from around the country, or "The Chase," which features video from intrepid tornado chasers.

Meister examined the rhetoric of TV meteorology as it is displayed on The Weather Channel (TWC) to create a discourse of "weathertainment." Although meteorology is a science, according to Meister, its most prominent function is to relate the natural phenomenon of weather to the everyday lives of viewers. As such, the computer-generated graphics, radar, and satellite images go beyond the science of meteorology and the model-based predictions of where, when, and how much rain will fall or what the wind speeds will be. The entertaining display of "expertise and visual eloquence shape how we view the weather, nature, and those social and economic activities that are historically associated with weather and nature."[4] In other words, televised weather forecasts are a form of rhetoric. One rhetorical act they perform is to "naturalize the social" by placing the discussion of weather (natural) in the context of its impact on human activities (social). Sunshine means plan a pool party. A snowstorm means stock up on groceries.

Meister borrows from rhetorical scholar Thomas M. Lessl the notion of the **bardic voice,** or the cultural storyteller, and the **priestly voice,** or the voice of the expert.[5] He suggests that TV meteorologists, like the bard, must reflect the cultural practices that are relevant to the current social and economic circumstances, but must also speak with the authority of the priest. Empowered by a higher authority, the priest is given elite status which, in the case of the meteorologist, is conferred by scientific expertise. Weather watchers rely on the "priestly counsel" of the on-camera meteorologist to direct their everyday lives.

The meteorologist combines the bardic voices of behind-the-scenes communication specialists who create the visual displays of jet streams, air pressure gradients, and the like with the divine insight of the priest-scientist. Like the priest prophesying about the apocalypse, the on-camera meteorologist warns of impending danger by tracing the path of the storm.

Meister notes that, with all of the satellite technology and weather-enhancing software, the actual atmospheric science of meteorology is given little, if any, airtime. "Science, nature, and specifically the atmosphere of the earth are all relegated to the background as priestly props for aiding the high-tech weather presentation specifically targeted to address how the weather may potentially impact social and economic issues."[6] Nor are ecological conditions related to weather given much on-air consideration. There are no satellite images of greenhouse gas concentrations or retreating ice caps. Rather, the focus is on the business and leisure conditions of the weather.

The ultimate product is an entertainment-based discourse that provides a background for displaying corporate sponsorship and advertising consumer products. As Meister points out:

> Weather features that focus on cold snaps are sponsored by Thermalite Therma Wear or Wigwam Socks; allergy and health features are sponsored by Afrin Nasal Spray; and international weather is sponsored by AT&T. . . . the earth's atmosphere becomes a commodity; effective in so far as it provides an effective background for the sponsorship.[7]

The mass production of expertise, combined with the dramatic visual displays, juxtaposes the natural and the cultural and presents this reconstructed culture/nature as a cultural commodity. Thus, "nature, with all of its priestly and bardic tones to 'ecology,' 'sustainable development,' 'business ecology,' and 'spirituality,' become intrinsic components of how we buy and sell nature."[8]

The importance of weather in our lives, along with the expertise of the priest and the eloquence of the bard, combine to create an entertaining site of meaning-making and an effective billboard for advertisers. Armed with the latest weather conditions, nasal spray, and thermal wear, we are now ready to leave for the next site on our tour of popular culture—the greeting card display. Perhaps there we will find a meaning of nature that goes beyond what to wear or when to plant the tomatoes.

Nature According to Greeting Cards

Nature adorns and gives meaning to our everyday lives in ways that we often over-look or take for granted. Images of snow-capped mountains, brilliantly plumed exotic birds, fields of wildflowers, and cuddly bears decorate our calendars, screen savers, and personalized checks, each image sending a rarely interrogated message about the natural world and humans' place in it.

Nature images are especially popular as the theme or backdrop for greeting cards. Americans spend billions of dollars a year on this commonly accepted form of what communication scholar Diana Rehling refers to as "mass-produced inter-personal communication."[9] Nature, it seems, is the appropriate backdrop for almost any message one cares to send. Expressions of sympathy are superimposed on fields of wildflowers or gently flowing rivers. A pair of swans provide the romantic backdrop for a declaration of undying love. Rugged mountains set the scene for messages of encouragement or congratulations. And because we care enough to send the very best, all these images are cropped, digitally modified, color-enhanced, and touched up to represent nature in its most sublime perfection.

In order to understand the ways of symbolizing nature and the way that nature is used in this particular site of meaning-making, Rehling examined commercial greeting cards made by Hallmark, American Greetings, and Gibson, the three major greeting card companies in the United States. Rehling identifies four common uses of nature in greeting cards: (1) nature is used to set a mood, (2) nature is used to provide a setting for humans, (3) nature is used to give meaning to relationships and occasions, and (4) nature is used to stand in for humans.[10]

Images of nature are used *to set the mood* for the verbal sentiment expressed in the greeting card's message. Rehling points out that nature is particularly useful in setting the tone for messages that relate to religious or spiritual matters. Religion-based holidays are represented by clearly recognizable natural icons—the rabbits among pastel blooms for Easter, red cardinals in the snow-flocked evergreen trees for Christmas. After the death of a loved one, spiritual comfort can be found in a desert flower or the ocean's rolling surf. The "true meaning" of a marriage celebra-tion can be found in the water lilies on a lake. Happiness and fulfillment can be found in turning away from the commercialized, materialistic world and turning to nature. (A moment's reflection will reveal the obvious paradox of sending this message via commercially mass-produced greeting cards.)

Along with setting the mood, nature is used in greeting cards *to provide a setting for humans and human interactions.* A birthday card designed for a father to give to a son shows a solitary man with a backpack and a walking stick standing on the edge of a rock ledge overlooking a green valley far below. The text of the card expresses a father's pride in the son's accomplishments, which, explains Rehling, symbolically links the strength, determination, and courage of the difficult climb up the mountain with the son's other accomplishments. The son has tested himself against the challenge and emerges victorious over the rugged wilderness.

Rehling points out the contrast between this particular image of the rugged nature-conqueror, in whom the father takes great pride, and a card created for a

Celebrate!

Figure 11.1   Nature in Greeting Cards

This greeting card, depicting a happy child romping in a field of wild grasses, uses nature to give form and substance to the meaning of celebration. To celebrate is to turn away from the materialistic world and turn to nature somewhere in the "big out there." The card also gives meaning to nature as a carefully selected, pristine background for celebration (sans grasshoppers and ticks). Such tacit messages ignore the fact that nature is not an Edenic, undefiled, somewhere-out-there, and that its ultimate purpose is not necessarily to serve as a setting for human interactions.

daughter that features a woman in a white dress and a brimmed, beribboned hat sitting amid a field of wild flowers. Genteel flowers scenes are commonly used as settings for women, whereas rugged wilderness provides a commonly used backdrop for men.

Nature also provides the appropriate setting for human interactions. Two silhouetted lovers kiss on the deserted beach. A man and a child fish side by side on the banks of the pond. In like fashion, the interaction gives meaning to the setting and thus defines nature's meaning through the human interactions that take place in it—nature is romantic, nature is comforting, nature is inspirational, and so on.

Just as the meaning of nature is defined by the human interaction, so is the human interaction defined by the natural setting. Nature gives substance and concrete form to the abstract idea of a father's love, an ideal romance, or whatever the featured relationship may be. Thus, nature is used *to give meaning to the relationship, or the special occasion.* Like the oak tree that provides strength and protection, so too does the father to whom the card is given. A couple's perfect relationship is reflected in the perfectly pristine mountain lake, and so on.

The creators of greeting cards often use nature *to stand in for humans.* A bear playing with a cub, for example, might be used to represent a human parent-child relationship. The relationship of the animals is thus personified—the bear/cub relationship is likened to the human mother/child relationship. Another way in which greeting cards personify animals is to place wildlife in human settings. Animals are pictured in hats, trousers, and aprons; as playing poker around a kitchen table or lounging on the couch. These anthropomorphic constructions project human characteristics onto the animal, often depicting them as cute, humorous, or cuddly, and ignoring their wildness and ferocity.

As Rehling points out, for many of us, encounters with the commodified version of nature outnumber our encounters with actual wilderness. Yet, it is a misleading version in that the images of nature used in greeting cards are carefully selected, cropped, framed, and digitally enhanced, with only the most idealistic depictions making the cut for mass production. The less-than-sublime landscapes, along with nature's weeds, ticks, thorns, and toads, are conspicuously absent from this sublime version of nature.

Rehling discusses several implications that accompany these idealized constructions of nature. One is that *the natural world is in perfect order and therefore not in need of protection or concern.* One sees no evidence of logging, grazing, or other scars of human encroachment. As discussed in the previous chapter, the sublime construction of nature suggests, among other things, that pristine nature is commonplace, so there is no need for concern. Another implication of the commodified version of nature is that *it constructs a value dichotomy separating that which we should concern ourselves with protecting (mountains, streams, and bears) and that which, by virtue of omission, we should not value (marshes, toads, and worms).* Yet, in the complex web of ecosystem interaction, the not-quite-so-sublime elements play vital roles and deserve concern and protection.

There are also implications regarding the substitution of animal images for humans. *When animals are used to represent human relationships, the roles that are implied in the relationship become "naturalized."* "Nature," in this sense, is that which is "natural," "the norm," and beyond human choice or debate. When gender roles, for example, are naturalized (when we see Mamma Bear in an apron, serving the porridge), the roles are perceived to be the norm or what is unquestionably right because it is the "natural" way. In "genderizing" nature, gender roles are likewise naturalized.

Furthermore, *when nature is used to represent a relationship or occasion, the character of the relationship or the occasion is also naturalized*—made to seem normal, right, beyond debate. Yet, like the natural settings represented, they are impossibly perfect relationships. The inherent message is that this is what your relationship or holiday gathering should be like; if it is not, it must be inferior and in some way "unnatural." Greeting cards, then, can promote unrealistic expectations of nature, as well as unrealistic expectations of humans' relationship to other humans and to the natural world.

When we purchase a nature-inspired greeting card, we are not obviously purchasing "real nature" (except for the natural resources that were consumed in the card's production, packaging, transporting, marketing, mailing, and so on). We are purchasing corporate-mediated meanings of nature, meanings that profoundly direct the way we view and treat the natural world. To find "real nature," we must go to SeaWorld—the next stop on our tour of pop culture sites.

Nature According to SeaWorld

SeaWorld parks, owned and operated by the world's largest brewer, Anheuser-Busch, offer close encounters with nature, inviting visitors to "touch the magic." The central themes of these parks are marine animals and nature exhibits with

Figure 11.2
Shamu, the Killer Whale

Since Sea World first began training orcas in the mid 1960s, public perceptions of these magnificent and highly intelligent creatures have been transformed from "killer whale" to "lovable pet" status. Both representations are misleading. Orcas are not actually whales: they are believed to be the largest species of dolphin. And although there are no documented cases of orcas attacking humans in the wild, they are not harmless pets. Captive orcas have attacked handlers and caused several human deaths at marine parks, making this a rather perilous perch for Shamu's co-star.

Image Copyright Mike Liu, 2010
Used under license from Shutterstock.com

Shamu, the trained killer whale, starring as the featured creature and the registered trademark of the parks. There are currently about twenty-one Shamus (orcas) in captivity in SeaWorld's various facilities and parks around the country.

The estimated 11.35 million annual visitors to SeaWorld navigate the globe, taking in some of its most spectacular sites along the way—an Arctic ice floe inhabited by penguins, a shark-infested tropical reef, and the creatures who haunt the eerie remains of sunken ships in the Bermuda Triangle, to name a few. Visitors are treated to unobstructed views of nature that one would rarely see in the real world, where habitat protects and hides, rather than displays, its inhabitants. Among the most popular exhibits are pools holding dolphins, rays, skates, and sea stars, where visitors are invited to actually "touch the magic," as the park's promotional theme promises.

The star of the show is Shamu, the trained orca. Orca whales were first held in captivity and developed as an entertainment resource by SeaWorld's founders in the mid-1960s. They are now the featured attraction at all four SeaWorld parks. Crowds watch in amazed wonder as Shamu launches the trainer off its snout and performs various other tricks-for-treats that emphasize how very intelligent and human-like orcas are.

Along with a close encounter with nature, visitors can purchase a host of other SeaWorld-themed commodities: T-shirts, stuffed animals, storybooks, nature books,

Connections

Field Notes
from a Whale Watcher
Watching Whale Watchers
Watch Whales

This time, the adult rises higher than before, flipping the baby forward tail almost over head. I gasp, delighted with what I've just witnessed only a few meters away. . . . I look for someone to tell, but don't find anyone who seems to have seen it. So, I say quietly to whomever is around, "Did anyone see that baby just do a flip over the adult?" No answer to a question that wasn't really aimed at anyone. But I immediately feel this speaking on my part reduced some power of the experience.

This is a brief excerpt from more than one thousand pages of field notes written by environmental communication scholar Tema Milstein over the course of four years as a participant-observer on a marine monitoring boat in the coastal waters between Washington state and British Columbia. The monitoring boat's mission was to keep watch on the whale-watch industry and educate private boaters about whale-watch guidelines. Milstein observed the whale watchers on sea and on land in order to gain an understanding about the ways in which the human-nature relationship is mediated through both human and whale communication.

Milstein discusses how human perceptions of whales have undergone a major shift in the past 50 years—"transformed from dangerous villains targeted by military bombing practices and fishing industry bullets, to entertainers captured to perform

postcards, and numerous other souvenirs whose producers hold licensing agreements with Anheuser-Busch. For a refreshing break from all the shopping and sightseeing, hospitality centers offer free beer-tasting to weary and thirsty adults.

Communication scholar Susan G. Davis explored the constructed meanings of nature and humans' place in it as delivered to mass audiences by SeaWorld designers and promoters. According to Davis, Anheuser-Busch exemplifies the ways in which "definitions of nature and the solutions to its problems are now massively authored by the private sphere of conglomerate, corporate culture."[11] Nature, as defined by Anheuser-Busch, is called into service of both profit and public relations, creating revenue along with a positive public view of the corporation by calling attention to the conservation, reclamation, and education programs it sponsors. Nature theme parks, says Davis, "show corporations like Anheuser-Busch rising to the conservation occasion with spontaneous good will."[12]

Anheuser-Busch emphasizes its involvement with research on marine mammals, including its successful efforts to foster orca reproduction in captivity, its animal rescue and rehabilitation efforts, and its education programs in public schools and at the parks. By associating itself and its products with education, conservation, and animal research and rescue, Anheuser-Busch promotes itself as an environmentally concerned and socially responsible corporate citizen. Customers have the for paying marine park audiences, to environmental icons sought out in the wild and heeded as the pulse of oceanic health."

So whose rhetoric was responsible for transforming perceptions of whales from target practice to iconic status? One influential forum for the rhetorical reshaping of perceptions of whales, suggests Milstein, is the marine parks and aquariums, where "the mass public came close to whales for the first time. . . . Instead of fearing or hating the whales, people began to find that they could relate to these whales and care about them." Ironically, the capturing of whales, although highly traumatizing and devastating to whale populations, may also have created a forum for whales to speak on behalf of their wild relatives. Milstein cautions, however, that the messages of the captive orcas are "highly mediated by the corporate entertainment industry" and that "these commercially appealing representations are not reflective of orca realities or wild orca–human relations."

Perhaps an even more influential rhetorical forum for transforming public perceptions about orcas has been the growing popularity of the whale-watch tourism industry and the profound impact that the physical presence of whales in the wild has on the whale watchers. "The whales in many ways speak for themselves," says Milstein, and with an eloquence that often leaves the human partners in the dialogue speechless or frustrated by the limitations of language-mediated communication. Watching the whale watchers watch whales reveals the profoundly transformative power of this kind of human/nature dialogue and its potential for creating public support for the preservation, and even restoration, of whale populations in the wild.

Source: Tema Milstein, "When Whales 'Speak for Themselves': Communication as a Mediating Force in Wildlife Tourism," *Environmental Communication: A Journal of Nature and Culture* 2 (2008): 173–192.

good feeling of knowing that with the price of a ticket, they too, are collaborating in these worthwhile efforts. As a line from one show states, "Just by being here, you're showing that you care."

In short, Anheuser-Busch has effectively crafted nature into a profitable commercial enterprise that also serves to market the corporation as socially and environmentally responsible, creating a vision of nature and its future that promotes the interests of corporate America. SeaWorld's mass-produced corporate version of nature, much like the messages of the corporate-sponsored green advertising campaigns discussed in the previous chapter (nature is the sublime, indestructible "out there," for personal consumption), defines a fundamentally unsustainable human/nature relationship driven by consumption while paradoxically defining itself as a socially responsible defender and protector of nature.

Davis suggests that SeaWorld represents more than just one small piece of popular culture's mass-produced corporate definition of nature. She suggests that it represents "a new kind of institution," in that it attempts to "occupy the cultural space and functions" of nonprofit, publicly funded institutions of research and education, such as aquariums and natural history museums.[13] SeaWorld's privately produced, profit-driven version of nature "displaces or hides other kinds of connections or contacts that need to be made."[14] "Try to imagine," says Davis, "a theme park mounting a thoughtful exhibit on ocean pollution,"[15] or even more unimaginable, exhibits showing the environmental impacts of beer manufacturing or nature theme parks. The green marketing version of nature obscures a long history of industrial pollution and resource depletion, and ignores alternative forms of activism that are not primarily driven by a profit motive. The "new kind of institution" recasts nature and the solutions to its problems as something that can be left up to the "spontaneous good will" of corporations such as Anheuser-Busch.

It's not that Anheuser-Busch or other producers of commercial "nature" enterprises shouldn't conduct research or engage in conservation or animal rescue activities. Indeed, corporate pro-environmental activity is not undermined or negated just because it is also used as a marketing device. But as Davis suggests, "not all entertainment should be commercial and education should not be collapsed into public relations and a ruthless drive for corporate profits."[16] She calls on us to create and support alternative sites of education, research, and entertainment, where the definition of nature is a product of a wide range of images and information that are not as driven by the tyranny of the bottom line.

So far, our quest for the "true meaning of nature" has taken us to several thought-provoking and wallet-lightening sites of meaning construction. By now it should be quite apparent that nature, according to mainstream popular culture, is a commodity attractively displayed on store shelves, exhibited in aquariums, or presented as computer-generated graphics of satellite images. These mass-marketed messages maintain a comfortable, business-as-usual, human-nature relationship, in which humans are consumers and nature is that which is consumed. Yet, the powerful messages of pop culture can also be used to challenge the status quo and offer alternative, more sustainable ways of looking at humans' relationship to the natural world.

Put away your credit cards and we'll head back home for a look at one sight of alternative meaning construction that resides right in your own living room, in the form of the television nature documentary. Nature documentaries have gained widespread audiences with the emergence of cable channels such as the Discovery Channel, Animal Planet, and the National Geographic Channel. The following takes a look at one such nature documentary that sends an alternative, albeit unsettling, message about humans' relationship to the nature world.

Nature According to *Grizzly Man*

At the 2005 Sundance Film Festival, the film *Grizzly Man,* directed by Werner Herzog, received broad critical acclaim and a number of prestigious awards, launching the documentary into mainstream media exposure with repeated airings on Discovery and Animal Planet. The film explores more than one hundred hours of video footage shot by Timothy Treadwell over the thirteen summers he spent living with and studying the grizzly bears in the Katmai National Park and Preserve on the Alaskan Peninsula.

As a self-described "eco-warrior" and "bear whisperer," Treadwell produced spectacular video footage of the bears as part of his efforts to protect the bears and their natural habitat from human encroachment and destruction. His videos document the daring proximity to the animals that he was able to routinely negotiate. Nick Jans, in his book *The Grizzly Maze,* expresses the astonishment that many felt at the relationship that Treadwell established with the bears: "Not only did they not attack, but they seemed to give a collective ursine shrug and accept him as a somewhat odd-smelling and harmless hanger-on."[17]

During the winter months, Treadwell returned to his home in Malibu, where he spent his time working with Grizzly People, a nonprofit organization he founded,[18] and taking his love of bears to schools, where his passion and bear antics made him a hit with children and teachers. After the 1997 release of his book, *Among Grizzlies: Living with Wild Bears,*[19] Treadwell gained celebrity status with appearances on shows such as *The Late Show with David Letterman.*

Herzog's film, however, takes the viewer beyond a historical review of the life and work of a dedicated eco-warrior and presents a disquieting and thought-provoking look at the nature/culture divide and what it means for humans to step beyond the protective boundaries of culture. I have used the terms "unsettling" and "disquieting" because Treadwell, unfortunately, died a hideous and "grizzly" death, meted out by the wildness he was attempting to save. In October 2003, Treadwell and his girlfriend, Amy Huguenard, were killed and partially eaten by a one-thousand-pound grizzly.

Environmental communication scholar Julie K. Schutten explores the imaginary and arbitrary line between "wild nature" and "culture" and the implications of deconstructing that line when the predator becomes the prey. "This reversal," suggests Schutten, "may trouble some viewers because humans do not get eaten—they eat. Treadwell's life and death, as portrayed in the film, can work to jar the status quo by interrupting the nature/culture dualism."[20] In our human-ordered world, it is humans (as subject) who turn animals into meat (or objects). "If animals make humans into meat," says Schutten, "then the hierarchy of human over animal and culture over nature is threatened."[21]

It was evident from the buzz in the blogosphere that a number of viewers were, in fact, troubled by the message. Schutten gives a number of examples from the blog discourse of resistance to the deconstruction of the human/nature relationship. Treadwell was characterized as "eccentric," "mentally ill," or "crazy," by people claiming that he "got what he deserved" or that he was practicing an "antihuman eco-religion."

Although many bloggers and critical reviewers applauded Treadwell's desire to protect the bears, many felt that he went too far—that he violated the "boundaries" when he attempted to establish a close relationship with the bears. Werner Herzog, the film's producer and narrator, expresses this sentiment when he tells his audience, "I discovered a film of human ecstasies and darkest inner turmoil. As if there was a desire in him to leave the confinements of his humanness and bond with the bears. Treadwell reached out, seeking a primordial encounter. But in doing so, he crossed an invisible line."[22]

One could easily draw the conclusion that the line between wild nature and culture is, in fact, not so imaginary or arbitrary, and that we only fool ourselves in thinking otherwise. Yet, a closer reading reveals that the message may not be that simple and may not, in fact, reinforce the human/culture divide, but may actually serve to "interrupt" or challenge it.

In the triumph of bear over human, the comfortable notion of human invulnerability and superiority is shattered along with the rationale that justifies humans' mastery over nature. The manner in which Treadwell died is a jarring reversal of the subject-object human/nature relationship and compels us to consider what it is like to be the dominated rather than the dominator. In so doing, it forces us to give at least a fleeing thought to the moral implications of our own arrogance and indifference—an uncomfortable, disquieting introspection. Schutten observes that it seems as if "we can stomach humans-killing-humans better than other animals-killing-humans because it keeps humans at the top of the hierarchy."[23]

Numerous environmental writers and philosophers have called for an environmental ethic that challenges the dualistic framework that places humans over animals and culture over nature (as discussed in greater depth in the discussion of radical environmental philosophies in Chapter 5). Aldo Leopold, for example, calls for a land ethic that "changes the role of homo sapiens from conqueror of the land-community to plain member and citizen of it."[24] From this perspective, humans are not separate from or superior to nature, but part of nature.

As members of a shared community, humans are vulnerable to the same ecosystem strains and stresses as the nonhuman inhabitants who share it. Schutten draws attention to our mutual vulnerability by pointing out that Treadwell's risk of being killed by the bears was heightened by human-caused stressors on the ecosystem. During the summer that he was killed, the berry crop, on which bears depend through the long Alaskan winters, had failed due to changing weather patterns in a warming Alaska. As a result, an above-average number of bears came to the water to feed on salmon, which led to more aggression among the bears as they competed for food.

Although Treadwell's case is an extreme example, it serves to demonstrate how the line between culture and nature becomes increasingly blurred as both humans and nonhumans come to recognize our shared vulnerability to a stressed ecological system. The stark realization that we are part of and not separate from nature, and that we are, as ecofeminist Karen J. Warren observes, "both the eaters and the eaten,"[25] is brought into focus. The fluid and arbitrary line between nature and culture is erased in the recognition that humans and nonhumans are members and citizens of a shared biotic community.

We've almost concluded our tour of pop culture sites of meaning-making. *Grizzly Man* offers a distinctly different, and far less comforting, view of the "meaning of nature" than the packaged, air-brushed, or simulated versions displayed at the previous sites on the tour. Because lingering images of the film's version of nature may put you off your popcorn or disturb your sleep, a fitting end to our long day of searching for the "meaning of nature" is a bedtime story by the award-winning children's author and environmental prophet, Dr. Seuss.

Nature According to Dr. Seuss

For over seven decades, Dr. Seuss (the pen name for Theodor Geisel) has touched the hearts of countless children with his rhyming narratives, wacky wordsmithing, and uniquely zany characters. At the time of his death in 1991, Geisel had authored forty-seven books with over two hundred million copies sold. Today he remains one of the best-selling and best-loved children's authors.[26]

Published in 1971, *The Lorax* emerged along with the growing awareness and concern generated by the environmental movement. The popularity of this cautionary tale has propelled its characters far beyond the pages of an entertaining bedtime story to what is described by environmental communication scholar Dylan Wolfe as "iconic status in the environmental canon."[27] It is arguably Seuss's most controversial work, having been banned in some school libraries because of its less-than-subtle criticism of the logging industry. Geisel admitted that the book stemmed from a very deep-seated anger about the growing environmental problems and was intended as "propaganda with a plot."[28]

The Lorax is narrated by the Once-ler who tells the story of an idyllic land of the "Truffula Trees" where "Brown Bar-ba-loots" frisked, "Humming-Fish" hummed, and "Swomee-Swans" sang—that is, until the Once-ler arrived in his covered wagon and began chopping down the Truffula Trees. You see, the tree's silken tufts were just what he needed to make "Thneeds" ("A Thneed's a Fine-Something-That-All-People-Need!").

From the stump of the first felled tree emerges the Lorax, a mysterious character who has come to "speak for the trees, for the trees have no tongues." Ignoring the Lorax's repeated warnings, the Once-ler continues to voraciously cut down the Truffula Trees to feed the commercial success of his Thneed-making business. As the trees disappear, the skies fill with "smogulous smoke," and the pond becomes polluted with the factory's "leftover goo," the Lorax is forced to send the Bar-ba-loots, the Humming-Fish, and the Swomee-Swans away to find a more hospitable landscape, for they can no longer survive in the polluted surroundings. Even the Once-ler's family abandons him once the trees disappear and the factory closes. Sadly, the Lorax, too, takes leave of the place by mysteriously ascending to the sky, leaving behind one final message spelled out in a pile of rocks for the Once-ler to ponder: "UNLESS."

For many years, the Once-ler remains secluded in his desolate surroundings to ponder the meaning of the mysterious message until one day, a curious boy appears at the Once-ler's door and asks to hear the story of how the Lorax was lifted away. In the retelling of the story, the Once-ler, at long last, realizes what the Lorax meant: "UNLESS someone like you cares a whole awful lot, nothing is going to get better. It's not." He gives the boy the last Truffula Seed and tells him to grow a forest and protect it so that the Lorax and his friends may come back.

Wolfe examined how *The Lorax* functions as a rhetorical text to challenge the hegemonic ideologies that celebrate entrepreneurship, technology, and industrial growth. Among other things, he looked at Geisel's use of the jeremiadic form and myth to create his message of opposition.[29]

Wolfe demonstrates how the story functions as an ecological jeremiad. (The jeremiad as a rhetorical form is discussed in Chapter 7). The inhabitants of a chosen land have been expelled because they have broken the covenant. In this case, an ecological covenant has been broken, causing the inhabitants to flee the plagues and famines of the once-bountiful land. The prophet in the story, rather than speaking for an angry god, has been ordained to speak on behalf of the trees. Like the prophet Jeremiah who scolds the Israelites, the Lorax rebukes the Once-ler for his covenant-defying behavior. And in keeping with the jeremiadic form, the Lorax offers a redemptive possibility through a single Truffula seed placed into the hands of one small boy.

In addition to Geisel's use of the jeremiadic form, Wolfe points out the strong influence of myth, with many of the themes of the frontier myth figuring dominantly in the narrative. (The frontier myth is discussed in Chapter 5.) Wolfe calls attention to the Once-ler's arrival in what looks like a covered wagon—"as much a mythic symbol of the frontier's Oregon Trail as the Once-ler's subsequent pioneer activity of laying claim and settling the wildness about him."[30] As in the frontier myth, the wilderness is conquered, and nature's bounty, through hard work and technological innovations (such as the "Super-Axe-Hacker" that Once-ler invented), brings prosperity to the Once-ler.

Unlike most popular retellings of the frontier myth, Geisel quickly moves the narrative from the pioneer settlement and harvesting of the wilderness to a narrative of industrial greed and the pollution and environmental degradation that inevitably accompany unchecked industrial expansion. The "collision of ecology and the American myth," explains Wolfe, "produces the jeremiadic evils . . . . Through simple cause and effect relationships, the prophetic Lorax ties the historic American myth to the breaking of the divine ecological covenant."[31] As such, the story functions as opposition rhetoric that challenges rather than celebrates the ideologies embedded in the mythic narratives.

As with a number of Geisel's more controversial books with strong political overtones (including *The Butter Battle Book* and *Yertle the Turtle*), *The Lorax* has been criticized for using children's literature as a medium for propagandizing about highly complex and multifaceted issues. When constructed within the genre of children's literature, the issues are necessarily oversimplified and reduced to condensed, good versus evil, cause and effect relationships. The narrative's allegorical representation of the logging industry, as driven by greed to produce products we don't need, casts all loggers and the commercial products of the industry in a negative light and fails to bring to the reader's attention that even children's books are products of the timber industry.

In response to Geisel's highly unflattering portrayal of the logging industry, the National Wood Flooring Manufacturers Association funded the writing and production of *The Truax*. This children's book, modeled after Dr. Seuss's style of rhyming and colorful characters, offers a logging-friendly counter to *The Lorax*.[32]

Other critics of *The Lorax* have argued that the story's ending, which places the responsibility of restoring the future in the hands of one small boy, sends a message of the individualization of responsibility and deflects attention from the collective social, political, and economic changes that are required.[33] Thus, in the end, *The Lorax* fails to direct attention to or challenge the ideologies of contemporary industrial capitalism and consumerism. Nevertheless, even Geisel's critics recognize the creative genius of a narrative that resonates with adults and children alike, creating an enduring and endearing environmental prophet. And, as Wolfe states, "A prophet, it seems, turned out to be one thing the environmental movement needed."[34] Geisel provided to the emerging public discourse of environmental concern "a powerful preachment calling for a renewed covenant with nature; a mythic challenge to the ideologically-driven retelling of American history; and a simple, colorful, charismatic prophet."[35]

Here we end our tour of selected popular culture sites of meaning construction in our quest to find the "true meaning of nature." By now, you have probably realized that multiple meanings of nature emerge through multiple sites and media. You have probably also realized that, as William Cronon states, "nature is not nearly so natural as it seems." Once we acknowledge "the deeply troubling truth that we can never know firsthand the world 'out there'—the 'nature' we seek to understand and protect—but instead must encounter the world through the lenses of our own ideas and imaginings,"[36] then we must also acknowledge the importance of critically examining the nature of the constructed realities we view through those lenses. We can choose to see the world in different ways through different lenses and, to draw on the words of Cronon once again, "it is surely worth pondering what would happen if we did."[37]

Concluding and Looking Ahead

The rhetorical critic may seem to play the unenviable role of a sanctimonious Jeremiah, perpetually engrossed in nitpicking, nagging, and condemning—one who, in the words of Winston Churchill, "has all the virtues I dislike and none of the vices I admire." How, one might ask, can the rhetorical critic enjoy anything when everything is subject to intense critical scrutiny and censure? I am compelled to confess that, as one who engages in the academic exercise of rhetorical criticism, I nevertheless send greeting cards at the drop of an occasion, I have purchased my fair share of "Save-the-Whales" boxer shorts and anatomically correct inflatable penguins, and I was as enthralled with the magic of SeaWorld as any six-year-old who ever came through the turnstiles. These contradictions may seem hypocritical, but the fact is that even the most curmudgeonly critic cannot drop out of culture, nor does this chapter intend to convey that directive. Rather, the rhetorical critic challenges you to become alert and contemplative consumers, to become close readers and interpreters of the pervasive and persistent messages of popular culture, to become engaged in the conversation, and to imagine the possibilities of a different way of seeing the world.

There are multiple ways we can change our learned behaviors and shift away from the lifestyle of consumption relentlessly promoted through popular culture. But ultimately, change must happen not only on the individual level, but in multiple arenas—educational, corporate, legal, and legislative. The following chapters direct your attention from citizens as consumers to citizens as activists, and to their role in influencing changes in the policies and practices of our institutions of control.

The still-unfolding drama of environmental history is infused with the voices of those who opted to exercise their rights as citizens in a democracy and to take on the difficult and often frustrating work of bringing about change. The next chapter begins with a discussion of the National Environmental Policy Act that gave a voice to citizen stakeholders. It also explores other significant pieces of legislation that have particular relevance for the citizen activist.

Discussion Questions and Exercises

1. This chapter has looked at only a few of the many sites of popular culture where meaning is mass-produced and distributed. What are some other sites? What kind of human/nature relationship is constructed within these sites?

2. Explain how weather forecasts are a form of rhetoric and how they serve to "naturalize the social."

3. Many messages of pop culture remain obscured until brought to light through critical examination. Even a humorous cartoon, like the one on page 94, can send messages that are not necessarily intended by its creator, but nevertheless convey particular messages about the natural world and humans' place in it. Now that you have examined multiple forms of rhetoric and sites of meaning construction, go back to this cartoon and analyze its message by answering the following questions:
   a. What wild bear characteristics are obscured in the anthropomorphized depiction?
   b. What human characteristics are naturalized?
   c. What does the cartoon imply about human encroachment and impact on wilderness areas?
   d. Do you think this cartoon could inadvertently encourage some people to feed the real bears in real wilderness parks? Why or why not?
   e. How might the messages in this cartoon ultimately be harmful to both bears and to humans?

Suggested Readings

William Cronon (Ed.). *Uncommon Ground: Toward Reinventing Nature*. New York: Norton, 1995.

Neil Evernden. *The Social Construction of Nature*. Baltimore: Johns Hopkins University Press, 1992.

Mark Meister and Phyllis M. Japp (Eds.). *Enviropop: Studies in Environmental Rhetoric and Popular Culture*. Westport, CT: Praeger, 2002.

Notes

1. Anne Marie Todd, "Prime-Time Subversion: The Environmental Rhetoric of *The Simpsons*," in *Enviropop: Studies in Environmental Rhetoric and Popular Culture*, eds. M. Meister and P. M. Japp (Westport, CT: Praeger, 2002), 63.

2. Mark Meister and Phyllis M. Japp, eds., *Enviropop: Studies in Environmental Rhetoric and Popular Culture* (Westport, CT: Praeger, 2002), 7.

3. Andrew Ross. *Strange Weather: Culture, Science, and Technology in the Age of Limits* (London: Verso, 1991), 242.

4. Mark Meister, "Meteorology and the Rhetoric of Nature's Cultural Display," *Quarterly Journal of Speech* 87 (2001): 419.

5. Thomas M. Lessl, "The Priestly Voice," *Quarterly Journal of Speech* 75 (1989): 183–197.

6. Meister, "Meteorology," 420.

7. Meister, "Meteorology," 423–424.

8. Meister, "Meteorology," 426.

9. Diana L. Rehling, "When Hallmark Calls upon Nature: Images of Nature in Greeting Cards," in *Enviropop: Studies in Environmental Rhetoric and Popular Culture,* eds. M. Meister and P. M. Japp (Westport, CT: Praeger, 2002), 14.

10. Rehling, "When Hallmark Calls."

11. Susan G. Davis, "Touch the Magic," in *Uncommon Ground: Toward Reinventing Nature,* ed. W. Cronon (New York: Norton, 1995), 217.

12. Davis, "Touch the Magic," 215.

13. Davis, "Touch the Magic," 207.

14. Davis, "Touch the Magic," 216.

15. Davis, "Touch the Magic," 217.

16. Davis, "Touch the Magic," 217.

17. Nick Jans, *The Grizzly Maze* (New York: Penguin, 2005), 12.

18. http://www.grizzypeople.com

19. T. Treadwell and J. Palovak, *Among Grizzlies: Living with Wild Bears* (New York: Ballantine, 1997).

20. Julie K. Schutten, "Chewing on the Grizzly Man: Getting to the Meat of the Matter," *Environmental Communication: A Journal of Nature and Culture* 2 (2008): 209.

21. Schutten, "Chewing," 204.

22. Werner Herzog (Director/Narrator), *Grizzly Man* [DVD]. United States: Lions Gate Films and Discovery Docs.

23. Schutten, "Chewing," 205–206.

24. Aldo Leopold, *A Sand County Almanac: And Sketches Here and There* (Oxford, UK: Oxford University Press, 1949/1977), 204. By permission of Oxford University Press, Inc.

25. Karen J. Warren, *Ecofeminist Philosophy: A Western Perspective on What It Is and Why It Matters* (New York: Rowman & Littlefield, 2000).

26. http://www.catinthehat.org/history.htm

27. Dylan Wolfe, "The Ecological Jeremiad, the American Myth, and the Vivid Force of Color in Dr. Seuss's *The Lorax*," *Environmental Communication: A Journal of Nature and Culture* 2 (2008): 21.

28. Cited in E. Moje and W. R. Shyu, "Oh, the Places You've Taken Us: The *Reading Teacher's* Tribute to Dr. Seuss," in *Of Sneetches and Whos and the Good Dr. Seuss: Essays on the Writings and Life of Theodor Geisel,* ed. T. Fensch (Jefferson, NC: McFarland, 1997), 196.

29. Wolfe, "The Ecological Jeremiad."

30. Wolfe, "The Ecological Jeremiad," 13.

31. Wolfe, "The Ecological Jeremiad," 14.

32. T. Birkett, *The Truax,* 1994. http://www.nofma.org/Portals/0/Publications/TRUAX.pdf (accessed March 13, 2008).

33. L. Lebduska, "Rethinking Human Need: Seuss's *The Lorax,*" *Children's Literature Association Quarterly* 19 (1994–95): 170–176; N. op de Beeck, "Speaking for the Trees: Environmental Ethics in the Rhetoric and Production of Picture Books," *Children's Literature Association Quarterly* 30 (2005): 265–287.

34. Wolfe, "The Ecological Jeremiad," 20.

35. Wolfe, "The Ecological Jeremiad," 20.

36. William Cronon, *Uncommon Ground: Toward Reinventing Nature* (New York: Norton, 1995), 25.

37. Cronon, *Uncommon Ground,* 34.

Part V

Public Participation
and Environmental Advocacy

Chapter 12
Public Participation in Environmental Decision-Making

Writer and historian Wallace Stegner, a self-described national park addict, once wrote: "Let me bear testimony, as the Mormons say, and acknowledge the debt I owe to a federal bureau for more than sixty years of physical and spiritual refreshment, and for the reassurance it gives me that despite all its faults, democracy is still the worst form of government except for all the others."[1] A key component in the functioning of a democracy is the right of citizens to participate in their own governance. History has repeatedly demonstrated the advantages of a free and open society. Still, multiple and opposing voices can make democratic decision-making a messy and unwieldy undertaking.

One of the most difficult jobs of the federal land managers, such as those who manage the national parks that Wallace Stegner so loved, is reconciling the many voices and interests that have a place at the decision-making table. The United States Park Service oversees the nation's network of 391 areas set aside by Congress for protection, including more than 100 national historic parks and sites, 74 national monuments, 58 national parks, and 28 national memorials, along with national preserves, seashores, parkways, battlefields, and so on. Established in 1916 with the passage of the National Park System Organic Act, the Park Service is charged with an almost impossible task—"to preserve, protect, and share the legacies of this land."[2] The mandate to "share" our national parks with millions of visitors each year places tremendous stress on the natural systems of the parks and creates significant challenges for park managers who must also "protect" and "preserve" the parks.

Other federal land management agencies, such as the United States Forest Service and the United States Bureau of Land Management, are responsible for carrying out resource management directives that are often conflicting or incompatible. Though these agencies are charged by law to regulate the "multiple uses" of federal lands, competing interests for these uses inevitably collide. Federal land managers often find themselves caught in the middle of highly charged conflicts among environmentalists, ranchers, miners, loggers, recreational users, and private citizens who are profoundly impacted by land use decisions.

Although democracy can sometimes get ugly, we, the citizens, own the public lands, and it only makes sense that we, the citizens, should have a say in the decisions about how the land is used and managed. Yet, until 1970 no real effort was made to inform the public of federal land use decisions, nor was there any structural mechanism in place for giving citizens an active role in the decision making process. In 1970, a new law provided just such a mechanism for informing the public about projects that might be harmful to the environment and for establishing procedures for incorporating public comment into the decision-making process.

The National Environmental Policy Act (NEPA) and Public Participation

Since its signing into law by President Richard Nixon on January 1, 1970, the **National Environmental Policy Act (NEPA)** has done much to merit Senator Henry "Scoop" Jackson's characterization of it then as "the most important and far-reaching environmental and conservation measure ever enacted by Congress."[3] In a piece of legislation barely three pages long, NEPA set forth the requirements for examining the impacts of a major action on both the natural and human environment before deciding whether that action should be approved. Major actions include everything from gravel mining on federal lands to constructing highways and dams.

NEPA also provided the framework for incorporating human values and community-based input into the decision-making process, thus giving a voice to those who must bear the economic, social, and environmental consequences of government policy and land use decisions. For the first time, government agencies were required to prepare an environmental analysis that integrated input from the stakeholders, state and local governments, and Native American tribes when considering a major land use proposal. **Stakeholders** are those who have a stake in the outcome of the decision or who will be affected by the agency's decision.

One of NEPA's defining innovations was its emphasis on including the public as consultants in federal agency decisions. Prior to NEPA, the public had little opportunity to engage in dialog concerning the social, economic, and environmental costs and benefits of an agency's land use decision. Nor was there much recourse to challenge these decisions once they were made.

The past four decades have seen dramatic changes in the role of the public in environmental decision-making. Public involvement has become a requirement in nearly every program in which federal funds are used. Other federal laws enacted after NEPA followed suit in mandating public participation in agency decision-making. For example, the **Comprehensive Environmental Response, Compensation, and Liability Act** of 1980 (CERCLA, also known as "Superfund") provides for public participation in the decisions about the cleanup of hazardous waste sites. Similarly, the **Resource Conservation and Recovery Act** of 1976 (RCRA) calls for public participation in the permit processes for waste treatment, storage, and disposal.

NEPA applies only to federal agencies and to activities and programs supported by federal funds. It does not cover state managed and supported projects. However, most states have adopted their own state environmental policy guidelines, sometimes referred to as **State Environmental Policy Acts (SEPAs)** or **little NEPAs.** Many municipal agencies have implemented similar public participation procedures for their land use decisions. The public is now involved in many deliberations, including building freeways and off-road vehicle parks, developing national parks and entertainment theme parks, and constructing dams and big box retail stores. In short, NEPA paved the way on local, state, and national levels for giving citizens a voice in the decisions that impact the natural and human environments.

Gathering public input is not always required, as, for example, in the case of routine management practices such as thinning brush or maintaining hiking trails in forests. Nor is it always appropriate, as in the case of emergency management scenarios such as forest fires or floods. However, when it is appropriate, it offers many advantages. Public participation creates a sense of citizen involvement and responsibility; it strengthens the sense of community among stakeholders; it increases trust; it can lead to long-term working relationships with the agency; and it can diminish the likelihood of costly and lengthy appeals and litigation. But perhaps most important, public participation processes lead to better environmental

Figure 12.1   National Park Ranger

National park rangers have a tough job: they are tasked to preserve and protect the park's natural resources and, at the same time, share them with millions of people who visit our national parks each year. One way of reconciling these incompatible goals is through interpretive programs that foster stewardship of the resources and meaningful connections to the park for visitors such as these schoolchildren.

National Park Service

decisions. Including a diverse range of people gives decision makers a broad range of knowledge, local wisdom, and experiences from which to draw.

Several methods for incorporating public participation in decision processes have been developed. The most common is the public meeting, where citizens are invited to express their concerns in person or through written comments. Other participation methods include citizen review panels and advisory boards in which selected community members closely interact with agency decision makers over an extended period of time. For example, the citizen advisory board chartered by the Department of Energy at Los Alamos National Laboratory to make recommendations about radioactive waste management and cleanup has been in place for over ten years.

The following section explains the process that federal land managers use for assessing a land use proposal, gathering public input, and making a decision about whether to approve a proposed land use. Because NEPA established the blueprint for almost all public participation procedures, the discussion focuses on the NEPA process. Other law-mandated processes, such as those for CERCLA and RCRA, as well as most state and municipal processes, operate under the same general guidelines, although each has its own specific directives.

Steps to the NEPA Process

Figure 12.2 will help in following the process steps and decision options within the NEPA process as it is discussed. The process begins with a **notice of intent** informing the public of a particular land use proposal that is being considered. This land use might be a logging company asking the Forest Service for a logging permit or a city asking to build an off-road vehicle park on land managed by the Bureau of Land Management. Once the notice of intent has been served, NEPA requires the federal agency to prepare a statement of the environmental impacts of the proposed action, an **Environmental Assessment (EA).** For instance, if the proposed action is a lease for oil drilling on federal lands, the environmental impacts discussed in the EA might include the effects on local vegetation, wildlife, air quality, and so on.

The **Council on Environmental Quality (CEQ),** the agency responsible for overseeing implementation of the NEPA process, recommends that the EA document be no longer than ten to fifteen pages, exclusive of appendices. If, upon completion of the EA, it is determined that the proposed action will result in no significant adverse impacts, the agency will issue a **Finding of No Significant Impact (FONSI)** and the proposed action can be approved.

An alternative form of the FONSI is the **Mitigative Alternative to a Finding of No Significant Impact,** often referred to as a **Mitigative FONSI.** If the environmental assessment reveals the likelihood of adverse environmental impacts, the agency can make changes in the proposed action or include measures that will mitigate or lessen the impacts of the proposed action. For example, if the assessment determines that a proposed off-road vehicle park would create too much soil erosion on some of the hills in the proposed park, the agency might declare some of the hills off limits or include restrictions on the size of off-road vehicles (ORVs) that can be used in the park, and conclude the NEPA process by issuing a Mitigative FONSI. This document, in effect, says that while the agency believes there will be negative impacts to the environment as a result of the proposed action, the changes made and the mitigation measures added to the proposal will eliminate or lessen these impacts enough so that the proposed action can proceed.

If, however, the EA concludes that the impacts may be so significant that a few modifications to the plan (as in the mitigative FONSI) will not fix the problems, the proposed action must be put through a more detailed and stringent analysis called an **Environmental Impact Statement (EIS).** The EIS often ends up as a document that is hundreds of pages long. The individuals who prepare the document are usually experts from a variety of fields—biologists, hydrologists, engineers, archeologists—who work as a team to identify and examine the possible environmental impacts of the proposed action.

If, at the outset of the decision-making process, the agency believes that the proposed land use action will have significant environmental impacts or that the action will be highly controversial, it may dispense with the EA and go directly into the more rigorous EIS process. Because the EIS is a detailed, long, and costly process, the agency may instead decide on the **No Action Alternative,** which simply means that the agency decides not to approve any version of the proposed action.

Once the EA or EIS is completed, the agency determines whether to approve the proposed action. Even if the EIS determines there will be significant environmental impacts from the proposed action, the agency decision makers may still

Basic NEPA

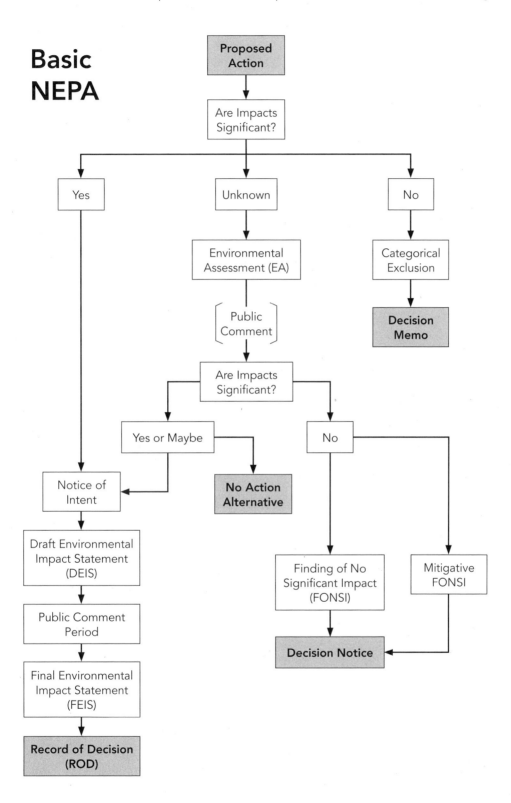

Figure 12.2   Steps to NEPA

decide to approve it if they feel the need for the action warrants its approval. For example, the assessment might show that the off-road vehicle park would have significant environmental impacts, but that the benefits from the park (such as decreased illegal ORV use on other nearby lands or the need for the park's ORV safety training programs) outweigh the negative impacts.

Affected parties have the right to appeal the agency's decision through administrative processes in which a review board decides the appeals. The appeal may also end up in litigation in the courts. In either forum, appeals are time-consuming and costly, and can delay the decision for years. Most appeals resulting from NEPA have dealt primarily with inadequacy of the EA or the EIS. The preparation of a less stringent Environmental Assessment (EA) rather than a full Environmental Impact Statement (EIS) is the most common source of conflict under NEPA.[4] In these cases, citizens challenge the decision because they feel that the agency has not done enough to determine the degree and scope of the real impacts that a full-fledged study, as called for in an EIS, would reveal.

Problems with the Implementation of NEPA

The most common form of gathering citizen input is the public hearing, in which citizen stakeholders are invited to ask questions and express their concerns about a proposed action. There is almost universal consensus among those who have examined or participated in these traditional forums that they are among the least effective of all methods of involving the public. Other forums, such as citizen advisory boards, review panels, and other forms of collaborative processes (discussed later in this chapter) are generally more effective means of involving citizens in the decision-making process.

An extensive study conducted in 1997 by the Council on Environmental Quality (CEQ) found several problems with traditional public hearings. The following is a list of frequently stated observations and concerns:

- Citizens felt that they were treated as adversaries rather than welcome participants.
- Citizens felt that they were invited too late to discuss an already well-developed project.
- Citizens felt that their input was not reflected in changes to the proposal.
- Citizens felt overwhelmed by the resources available to agencies and proponents of the action or project.

The study concluded that "substantial opportunities exist to improve the effectiveness and efficiency of the NEPA process."[5]

On the other side of the table, decision authorities are often faced with an antagonistic public that seems unwilling to consider any compromises or alternatives. Indeed, public forums can be highly contentious and often devolve into angry shouting matches among competing interests. It is easy to understand why agency officials may perceive that citizen groups' tactics are overly dramatized and hysterical or that their concerns or demands are simply delaying tactics. Yet, the angry, "overly emotional," "hysterical" citizen behavior may also be due to the nature of the process. Traditional forms of public participation often lead to a frustrated, disillusioned, skeptical, and angry public and, in turn, to costly legal or administrative appeals.

Those protesting an action may even find themselves charged with a **SLAPP suit,** an acronym that stands for "strategic litigation against public participation," a lawsuit in which a corporation or developer sues an individual or a nonprofit organization for interference with its business interests. If, for instance, a local neighborhood association organized a strong opposition to an oil company's bid to drill on public land near the community, the oil company might file a SLAPP suit against the neighborhood association for interfering with its business interests.

Although few SLAPP suits actually win in court, the threat of a financially and emotionally draining court battle can have a chilling effect and effectively silence citizen activists. Many states have anti–SLAPP suit statutes that protect citizens' First Amendment rights against the intimidation of SLAPP suits.

There are many problems with implementing NEPA directives, as well as room to improve the effectiveness and efficiency of public participation forums in environmental decision-making. In an effort to understand the underlying causes of the problems, environmental communication scholar Susan L. Senecah drew on her extensive experience of working with government agencies and on numerous case studies that have explored the problems and pitfalls of public processes. She concluded that the problems revealed in almost all of the cases can be attributed to a single factor—lack of trust. "Trust," observes Senecah, "is overwhelmingly the most commonly identified missing or present element in ineffective or effective processes. It seems that all effective process elements, or the antithesis of ineffective process elements, ultimately support the creation, enhancement, or maintenance of trust."[6]

Building Trust through the Trinity of Voice: Access, Standing, and Influence

Senecah offers a theoretical tool with which to better understand the "practices of trust" in public participation processes through what she terms the **Trinity of Voice.** According to Senecah, the three elements of voice—*access, standing,* and *influence*—must be present in order to build and maintain trust among agencies and stakeholders and to support an open and responsive decision-making process.

Access

Access, an element of building and maintaining trust, refers to giving participants sufficient and fair opportunity to express their opinions and concerns. There should be a sense of safety that allows people to express opinions without fear of reprisal or ridicule. There should be an understanding that their opinions and concerns will be given full and fair consideration. Access also includes readily available information and technical assistance for citizen stakeholders.

Several practices can inhibit citizen access. Dates and times of public hearings, advertised in the legal notice sections of newspapers, are often overlooked. Many hearings are held at times and places that are not readily accessible or convenient for those interested in participating. Strict procedural rules at the hearings may also inhibit public access. For example, a person wishing to express a concern may be given a very limited time to speak, in order to accommodate others who may also wish to express a concern. In addition, the public nature of the hearings—the presence of a microphone and an audience—will inevitably inhibit some from voicing their concerns.[7]

Standing

The second element necessary for building and maintaining trust is **standing,** described by Senecah as the "civic legitimacy, the respect, the esteem, and the consideration that all stakeholders' perspectives should be given."[8] Access and standing must go hand in hand. Merely allowing someone access to express an opinion is meaningless if that opinion is not listened to with respect, courtesy, and at least a degree of empathy. (I once observed a public meeting in which one of the agency officials actually fell asleep during the public comments.)

One aspect of standing that has been extensively examined by environmental communication researchers is that accorded to the voice of "science and expertise" as opposed to the voice of the "layperson." As discussed in Chapter 8, opinions based on scientific "facts" tend to be given more standing in decision processes than are the values expressed by the layperson. Important values such as aesthetics, community vision, identity, and sense of place sometimes carry little weight in the deliberation process.

While experts are granted superior standing, the structural format of the public hearing, with its procedural guidelines for determining who gets to speak, when, and for how long, does little to enhance the standing given to the public. Stakeholders are often left with a sense of powerlessness and the feeling that their needs, concerns, and deeply held values don't count.

Influence

The third element necessary for gaining and maintaining trust is **influence,** which involves a willingness on the part of the decision-making agency to openly and thoughtfully weigh stakeholders' concerns, ideas, and wishes before making the decision. The agency decision makers must make a good-faith effort to relinquish preconceived notions about what decision should be made and consider all alternatives carefully. Influence does not mean that citizens' preferences are adopted in a plan that is entirely favorable to their own point of view. Rather, it means that, in a fair and open process, all concerns were carefully considered.

In the absence of access, standing, and influence, the process becomes merely a "compliance hoop" through which an agency must jump before going ahead with a planned action. In a process sometimes referred to as the "decide, announce, defend" strategy,[9] an agency decides what to do, announces it to the public, and then uses the assessment process to defend its decision. The compliance hoop model undermines the intent of NEPA through its failure to use public participation as a means to better decision-making and by using the NEPA process as merely an instrument to validate *a priori* decisions. A great deal of time, money, and resources are spent creating EA or EIS documents and holding public meetings that have little effect on the ultimate outcome of the decision or lead to only minor concessions to citizen concerns. The following case study demonstrates what this "compliance-hoop" model of public participation can look like.

A Case of the Compliance-Hoop Public Participation Model

In this case, the local citizens were concerned about the impacts of a proposed gravel mining operation on Bureau of Land Management (BLM) land immediately adjacent to several residential neighborhoods. The proposed mine generated tremendous opposition at the public meetings that BLM held as part of the NEPA process.

Local residents expressed concerns about the mine's impacts on the fragile desert terrain of the area and on the creek that runs through the mine site, an important watershed area. Many also expressed concern for the preservation of the documented archeological sites in the area and the nesting habitat of Great Horned Owls and other birds. Still others expressed concerns about the tremendous amount of water required for mining operations; the impacts of dust, noise, and truck traffic; and the safety, health, and quality of life of the surrounding communities.

Despite the numerous concerns expressed at the public meetings and in over five hundred letters from local residents, the mine was allowed to go forward with only a few superficial concessions, in the form of a Mitigative FONSI. The meager concessions included increasing the mine's distance from the creek by twenty-five feet, limiting the mine's operations to eleven hours a day instead of twelve as originally proposed, the relocation of two rare cactuses, and setting the back-up alarms on operating equipment to the minimum required volume.

In light of the multiple impacts and community concerns, there was a general feeling among community members that these superficial concessions demonstrated little public standing and influence. Not surprisingly, several administrative appeals followed, as well as a court battle in which a small, local, nonprofit organization took on the federal government (BLM) and the multinational gravel mining corporation. It took five years for the appeals to be settled (all of them in BLM's favor) and no further concessions were granted to community members.[10]

Before jumping to the conclusion that the public input process is just a waste of everyone's time, we should note that in some cases the process has been highly successful (read on) and public input has had considerable influence on decisions. In addition, it is often difficult to determine the degree of influence that the public has had on the agency decision-makers: what appears to be little influence may, in fact, be considerable.[11]

Traditional versus Innovative Public Participation Practices

There are numerous approaches for implementing public input processes. Gregg B. Walker and Steven Daniels, through extensive research and consulting work with government agencies and other organizations, have observed many different forms of public participation processes. They distinguish between two fundamental types of public participation approaches that an agency can take. Traditional approaches, such as the public hearings in the gravel mine case discussed above, tend to be consultative in nature. **Consultative approaches,** while providing citizens with the opportunity to express their concerns, offer no guarantees that their input will have any meaningful influence. Their degree of influence depends on the benevolent indulgence of the decision authority.

Collaborative approaches, on the other hand, give participants more authority and influence. All parties actually work together to review the issues and make the decision. As Walker explains, agencies share the power and the decision responsibility by providing opportunities "for parties to work together assertively in order to make meaningful progress in the management of controversial and conflict-laden policy situations."[12] Collaborative processes usually take the form of citizen advisory boards or review panels, in which a select group of stakeholders have been appointed to the board by the agency. These boards take a highly active and often long-term role in decisions concerning a particular site.

Collaborative processes offer the promise for greatly enhanced public voice, standing, and influence, but they may not always be feasible or appropriate. There are times when the agency cannot or should not relinquish decision authority. For example, land use restrictions because of endangered species or wetlands areas will necessarily inhibit the possibility of collaboration in land use decisions. In addition, collaborative processes generally take more time and resources than do traditional public participation processes. When decisions must be made within a limited time frame and with limited resources, it may not be possible to implement a truly collaborative process.

When they are feasible, collaborative processes tend to be more effective and successful than consultative approaches, but there are still plenty of opportunities for such processes to fail. The following case study examines two citizen advisory panels and illustrates what can go right (the yin) and what can go wrong (the yang) with collaborative processes.

The Yin and Yang of Participation Processes

Environmental communication scholar Stephen P. Depoe did a comparative analysis of two vastly different outcomes from two citizen review panels that were created to address the cleanup of the radioactive contamination at a former uranium processing plant in southwest Ohio.[13] One group, the Fernald Citizen Task Force (FCTF), was organized for the purpose of providing input and making recommendations to the Department of Energy (DOE) regarding the cleanup of the contaminated area. The other group, the Fernald Health Effects Subcommittee (FHES), was established by the Center for Disease Control (CDC). The members of this group interacted with the scientists and technical experts to examine the data from environmental health studies and to make recommendations to the CDC about dealing with the health threats.

The two groups, both working on Fernald issues but with different government agencies, provided a unique opportunity to compare and contrast what Depoe describes as "the spectacular success of the Fernald Citizens Task Force" with the experiences of the Fernald Health Effects Subcommittee, which, he concluded, "represented just about everything that could go wrong with a citizen advisory panel."[14] He compared the two groups across a four-point evaluation grid and found profoundly different group dynamics across all four criteria.

Depoe's analysis revealed that the two groups differed significantly with regard to the first evaluation criterion: *the involvement of citizens representing diverse perspectives*. The FCTF was made up of a diverse group of stakeholders, representing a wide range of interests and perspectives. Among its fourteen members, all of whom were local residents, were citizen activists, health professionals, local business owners, teachers, and local government officials. The FHES, however, was made up mostly of doctors and health care professionals; less than half of the members were from the immediate Fernald area.

The two groups likewise differed with regard to the second evaluation criterion: *access to information and resources*. The members of the FCTF were provided with direct access to information resources and Fernald personnel, as well as an independent technical support consultant. In contrast, information was provided to the FHES through "long, ponderous presentations of technical information made by government officials and experts."[15] The CDC made little effort to adapt the highly technical information to make it more understandable for the committee members.

The third criterion, *the frequency of the groups' face-to-face discussions,* also revealed marked differences between the two groups. The FCTF met monthly, usually on Saturday mornings, for about three hours, at a nearby facility that was convenient for the members. Group members also met with their assigned subgroups and in several informal social gatherings. As Depoe says, "stable membership and regular meetings allowed task force members to develop relationships, discover common values, and influence each other."[16] The FHES, in contrast, met with the CDC quarterly outside of the Fernald area, causing hardships for some group members and for community members who wished to attend the meetings.

The groups also differed with regards to the fourth criterion: *the equitable distribution of power.* The FCTF used a democratic model with equal voting power, and set its own agenda and work plan. The group made efforts to include the broader community by opening all of its meetings to the public, holding workshops and presentations, and allowing citizens to help define the issues and question experts. The FHES, in contrast, held few votes, since most of the meeting time was taken up with informational presentations. Meeting agendas were determined by the group's chair and the CDC representatives. The group did little to encourage participation from the community. The written comments received from community members were largely ignored.

It is probably not surprising that the results of the two groups' efforts were very different. The FCTF was able to significantly influence the DOE's decisions, resulting in cleanup efforts that met with broad community approval. Even after its initial charter was completed, the group continued to work with local environmental and historic preservation organizations to formulate post-cleanup plans for turning the site into a community asset. In contrast, the influence of the FHES appeared to be minimal at best. The CDC ultimately decided that further health studies were not required, nor was the FHES. The group was terminated despite dissent from group members and community residents.

Many significant changes in environmental policies and practices have come about through the efforts of ordinary citizens who have been given access, standing, and influence through participatory practices. Although the process may not always run smoothly, participation in environmental decisions is an important part of the functioning of a democracy. Public participation offers a means of gathering relevant insight and knowledge from diverse groups of people, ultimately leading to better and more acceptable decisions.

Essential to effective citizen participation is access to information, which has been greatly advanced by a number of right-to-know laws, as well as by communication technologies that have created fingertip access to information that, for early environmental activists, was either too difficult and costly to obtain, or simply not available. The following sections examine some significant pieces of legislation that have greatly enhanced citizen access to information and the ability of citizen activists to influence change.

Freedom of Information, Sunshine, and the Right to Know

Signed into law by President Lyndon B. Johnson on July 4th, 1966, the **Freedom of Information Act (FOIA)** permits any person to request and obtain a federal agency's records, including meeting transcripts, documents, letters, photographs, and tapes. It does not apply, however, to information that is protected from disclosure by the FOIA's nine statutory exemptions, nor does it require Congress or the courts to supply information upon request. Upon receiving a request for information under the FOIA, the agency is required to act promptly unless "exceptional circumstances" require extra information processing time. The law, as it was initially articulated, gave agencies a great deal of freedom in the interpretation of "exceptional circumstances" and allowed them to charge exorbitant prices for the requested information. In response to these and other implementation problems, Congress adopted several amendments in 1986, including time limits for processing information (usually within ten to thirty days) as well as specifications for the kinds of fees that can be charged. Commercial users are required to pay for agency services related to finding, reviewing, and duplicating materials, but private citizens, news media, and educational institutions pay only duplication fees.

These amendments have helped close some loopholes, but the backlog for information requests has often made it difficult for agencies to comply with the time limits. It is not uncommon, for example, to wait months or even a year before receiving information requested from the Federal Bureau of Investigation.[17] Despite the problems with its implementation, the law has greatly expanded the information available to citizens and has made getting information much easier than it was prior to FOIA.

Another significant amendment to the FOIA was the **Electronic Freedom of Information Act (E-FOIA),** which President Bill Clinton signed into law in 1996. This amendment requires federal agencies to post key records online and to provide indexes and guidance for online users. Although this law increased the accessibility of information and decreased the backlog for processing information requests, an audit of 150 federal agencies' web sites, conducted by the National Security Archive, found that many agencies had not fully complied with E-FOIA requirements.[18]

The audit report, released in 2007, revealed that only one in five federal agencies posted all four categories of information that the law specifically required, and only one in three agencies provided the required indexes of records. The audit also found that several agencies' contact information was either not available or incorrect. One fax number given for sending FOIA requests, for example, was actually the phone number of a maternity ward at a military base.

The audit also found agencies that provided excellent FOIA web sites. Among the "E-Stars" were the U.S. Department of Education and the National Aeronautics and Space Administration. Among the "E-Delinquents" identified in the report were the Air Force, Immigration and Customs Enforcement, and Veterans Affairs.

Acquiring information under the FOIA sometimes takes time, patience, and dogged determination. Additional obstacles were put in place to increase national security in the wake of the terrorist attacks of September 11, 2001. Despite the delays, restrictions, and exemptions that can undermine the intent of the FOIA, the act has done much to increase the transparency and accountability of government agencies and to inform citizen activists and reporters on the environmental beat.

Another major leap toward public access to information came in 1976, when Congress enacted **The Government in the Sunshine Act.** Most often referred to as **The Sunshine Act,** this legislation requires all government agencies that are subject to the FOIA to provide public notice of their meetings and to open their meetings to the public. It also allows citizens to obtain records of the meetings through the

Federal Register. There are exemptions to public access to meetings, but agencies must keep transcripts of all meetings and a citizen can petition the courts for access to the transcripts of closed meetings.

Another piece of legislation that has been a tremendous assistance to citizen activists came about in response to the 1984 tragedy in Bhopal, India, in which thousands of people were killed by the accidental release of toxic chemicals from a Union Carbide facility. The death toll, by some estimates, was over 20,000, with an additional 120,000 people suffering injuries or long-term health impairments.[19] **The Emergency Planning and Right to Know Act,** enacted in 1986, requires facilities that use hazardous chemicals above a certain threshold limit to report the use of the chemicals to the EPA and to notify local agencies of the potential chemical hazards present in their communities. It also requires state and local authorities to prepare responses to emergencies created by chemical releases.

One particularly useful resource for citizen activists is the **Toxic Release Inventory (TRI),** a national database of toxic chemical emissions. The Emergency Planning and Right to Know Act requires the EPA to compile this database, which has proven to be a valuable information tool for bringing to light the chemical hazards and toxic pollutants from industrial plants. One can access information about the chemical hazards in any given community through the EPA's TRI Explorer (www.epa.gov/triexplorer) or through Scorecard, sponsored by Green Media Toolshed (www.scorecard.org).

The information available to citizens as a result of the NEPA, the FOIA, the Sunshine Act, and the Emergency Planning and Right to Know Act has enhanced government accountability and transparency, and also helped to level the information field for citizen groups, environmental organizations, and community activists.

Citizen participation has been a defining characteristic of the political landscape and the catalyst for many environmental protection measures we currently have in place. Nevertheless, environmental activists operate in the rugged terrain of an ever-changing political landscape. The journey has been one of peaks and valleys, as competing demands for diminishing natural resources have threatened the hard-fought gains of environmental activists. The following discussion offers a brief historical summary of the remarkable journey of the still-evolving environmental movement.

The Citizen Activist in a Changing Political Landscape

Environmental activism has a long, vibrant, multifaceted history. At the end of this chapter you will find a list of books from authors who have taken on the task of compiling the environmental movements' rich and remarkable history. An annotated timeline of selected significant milestones leading up to the first Earth Day and beyond is also included at the end of this book. As you look over the timeline, you will notice that most of the significant environmental protection measures came about in the years immediately prior to, and in the decade following, the first Earth Day in 1970. The response to the publication of Rachel Carson's *Silent Spring* in 1962 is often cited as the catalyst for the mass mobilization of the modern environmental movement.

The early successes of the movement in the 1970s gave rise to the formidable challenges of the 1980s. Referred to by environmental historian Benjamin Kline

Figure 12.3   United Nations Climate Summit in Copenhagen

Twelve years after international talks produced the Kyoto Protocol, leaders from around the world met in Copenhagen at the United Nations climate summit in December 2009. This historic event, billed as the most important meeting of our times, was the first time that representatives of all leading economies of the world assembled to take action on climate change. The talks were contentious and chaotic, and failed to produce a binding agreement, despite years of preparations and prior negotiations. The world was nevertheless heartened by United States President Barack Obama's pledge to join the global fight.

Larry Downing/REUTERS

as the decade of "conservative backlash,"[20] this era suffered significant setbacks to the environmental protection advancements made in the previous decade. President Ronald Reagan dismantled, rolled back, or repealed many environmental protection measures and placed notoriously anti-environmental appointees in key environmental positions (as discussed in Chapter 6).

During this period, the environmental movement enjoyed a period of backlash-against-the-backlash, as environmental organizations saw an unprecedented surge in memberships. Kline reports that in 1965, the ten largest mainstream environmental groups had a combined membership of less than 500,000 and a combined annual budget of less than $10 million. By 1990, those numbers had jumped to 7.2 million members and a combined annual budget of $514 million. Yet, many believed that the environmental movement had lost sight of its grassroots heritage and had become more comfortable with lobbying and litigation than with mobilizing citizen action. As Kline put it, the environmental movement "had become diluted by its own popularity, becoming trendy and corporate rather than aggressive, as it had been in the proactive days of the 1970s."[21]

The 1990s could perhaps best be described as a decade of environmental identity crisis, as mainstream organizations struggled to reinvigorate an ambivalent public in the face of continuing anti-environmental initiatives. Although some encouraging advances were made, especially on the global stage (such as the historic Earth Summit in Rio de Janeiro in 1992 and the multination Kyoto Protocol agreement in 1997), the environmental movement, in many ways, remained in the quagmire of an identity crisis while facing an unprecedented ambush of environmental protections in the new millennium. Many believe that the George W. Bush administration (2001–2008) outdid even the Reagan administration in dismantling environmental protections. It had become increasingly imperative for the environmental movement to articulate a direction and a vision capable of inspiring a new generation of environmental activists and leaders.

As the twenty-first century unfolds, environmentalists are cautiously optimistic that a more sustainable vision has begun to emerge. The election of Barack Obama to the United States presidency in 2008 ushered in an administration committed to developing alternative energy sources, reinstating and strengthening environmental protections, and passing climate change legislation. Obama's efforts toward reaching an international climate agreement have given global impetus to this formidable but crucial endeavor.

The "New" Green Movement: Environmental Activism in the New Millennium

How will environmental historians characterize the first decade of the twenty-first century? The trends of an era are usually crystallized in retrospect. When historians take stock of the first decade of the new millennium, they will most likely remark on the slow but clearly visible awakening of the American public to the crisis of climate change. As lawmakers advance and retreat in their attempts to pass national climate and energy legislation, a "new" green movement is taking shape at the grassroots level, with churches, local communities, and non-profit organizations leading the way.

The "new" green movement is characterized by several emerging trends. One is the growing emphasis on green consumerism as a way to live a greener life. As in the 1980s, consumers (at least those who can afford it) are demanding greener products. Producers are catering to the demands with product lines such as Home Depot's Eco Options and Patagonia's outdoor wear, which include a range of eco-friendly products for the green consumer. The burgeoning popularity of farmers' markets and community gardens have tapped into consumers' desire for more eco-friendly food sources.

Recognizing that averting large-scale environmental catastrophe will require more than just greener shopping choices, the green consumer trend has extended beyond the retail shelves, with a growing demand for green home energy, green home design, and green community planning. Many municipalities have implemented incentives in the form of rebates and tax credits for certified green-building businesses and energy efficient homes.

Another emerging trend in the "new" green movement places emphasis on reducing the consumption of goods and services and moving toward lifestyles of moderation. Advocates of this approach to greening the planet ask us to re-examine our "misplaced allegiance" to consumerism as the path to happiness and look instead to the things that money can't buy. Environmental lawyer and advocate James Gustave Speth, in his book *Bridge at the Edge of the World,* summarizes the multiple messages of these wise-up-and-scale-down advocates:

> They say to us: Confront consumption. Practice sufficiency. Work less. Reclaim your time—it's all you have. Turn off technology. Join No Shopping Day. Buy Nothing. No Logo. Practice mindfulness and playfulness. Live in the natural world; let nature nurture. Create social environments where overconsumption is viewed as silly, wasteful, ostentatious. Create commercial-free zones. Buy local. Eat slow food. Simplify your life. Shed possessions. Downshift. Create a local currency. Build consumer-owned cooperatives. Take back America.[22]

In short, these campaigns ask us to take stock of our ecological footprints and recognize just how much of what we consume we can comfortably do without. They point out that the "sacrifices" we make are, in many ways, more liberating than constraining and ultimately more satisfying than the relentless struggle for more and more goods and services.

Concluding and Looking Ahead

This chapter has taken a broad look at the important and challenging role of citizen activists in a democratic society. The discussion has covered citizen participation in the management of public lands and in other environmental decisions, as well as some of the major legislation that has greatly expanded access, standing, and influence for citizen activists. The chapter has also looked briefly at the dynamic and ever-changing political terrain that has influenced the spectacular successes as well as the dismal failures of environmental activists.

This brief overview of the trends in environmental activism is far from complete. It overlooks many of the fronts in the battle to save the planet. There are many shades of green in addition to the grassroots greens that have been highlighted in this chapter—green lobbyists inside the Washington, D.C., beltway, green litigators in courtrooms, green leaders in corporate boardrooms, and the elected greens in all levels of government. We owe a large debt of gratitude to all those who took to the streets, the public hearings, the courtrooms, and the boardrooms to speak on behalf of the environment. However serious the problems we currently face, they would be much worse today if it were not for the successes of those who came before us.

The activists and organizations of the early environmental movement and today have directed their efforts toward the protection of nonhuman nature—wilderness, biological diversity, species habitat, and so forth. They have tended to assume a separation between "things environmental" with which environmentalists concern themselves and "things social" that are left up to human rights or social justice activists, often ignoring the ways in which the exploitation of nature and the exploitation of humans mutually reinforce one another.

Today a growing and dynamic movement challenges this view of environmentalism. It has redefined "environment" to include concerns not just about the nature "out there," but about the nature in our own backyards, as well as the real threats faced every day by those who are most impacted by environmental pollutants. From its grassroots beginning in the early 1980s, the environmental justice movement has emerged to become a powerful voice in local, national, and global political landscape and drawn the world's attention to the close relationship between ecological justice and human justice.

Discussion Questions and Exercises

1. This chapter has focused largely on the problems and frustrations that citizen activists face and has given far less attention to federal land managers who are often placed in the difficult position of having to mediate among multiple competing voices when making land use decisions. Interview someone from one of our federal land management agencies to get a candid, firsthand account of how he or she views the NEPA process.

2. Visit the online FOIA Reading Room of a government agency and examine some of the frequently requested records. Give a report on what you found and evaluate the web site's accessibility and user-friendliness.

3. Go to Scorecard (www.scorecard.org) and find out about the chemical hazards in or near your community. Report on what you find.

Suggested Readings

Steven E. Daniels, and Gregg B. Walker. *Working through Environmental Conflict: The Collaborative Learning Approach.* Westport, CT: Praeger, (2001).

Stephen P. Depoe, John W. Delicath, and Marie-France Aepli Elsenbeer, (Eds.). *Communication and Public Participation in Environmental Decision Making.* Albany: State University of New York Press, 2004.

Recommended Readings on the History of the Environmental Movement.

Robert Gottlieb. *Forcing the Spring: The Transformation of the American Environmental Movement.* Washington, DC: Island, 1993.

Paul Hawken. *Blessed Unrest: How the Largest Movement in the World Came into Being, and Why No One Saw It Coming.* New York: Viking, 2007.

Samuel P. Hays. *A History of Environmental Politics since 1945.* Pittsburgh: University of Pittsburgh Press, 2000.

Benjamin Kline. *First Along the River: A Brief History of the U.S. Environmental Movement.* 2nd ed. San Francisco: Acada, 2000.

Phillip Shabecoff. *A Fierce Green Fire: The American Environmental Movement.* Washington, DC: Island, 2003.

Louis S. Warren (Ed.). *American Environmental History.* Malden, MA: Blackwell, 2003.

Notes

1. Wallace Stegner, *Marking the Sparrow's Fall: Wallace Stegner's American West* (New York: Henry Holt, 1998), 135.
2. http://www.nps.gov
3. *National Environmental Policy Act of 1969, Congressional Record* 115 (1969).
4. Council on Environmental Quality, *The National Environmental Policy Act: A Study of its Effectiveness after Twenty-Five Years* (Washington, DC: Government Printing Office, 1997).
5. Council on Environmental Quality, *The National Environmental Policy Act,* 35.
6. Susan L. Senecah, "The Process Trinity of Voice, Standing, and Influence: The Role of Practical Theory in Planning and Evaluating the Effectiveness of Environmental Participatory Processes," in *Communication and Public Participation in Environmental Decision Making,* eds. S. P. Depoe, J. W. Delicath, and M. Aepli Elsenbeer (Albany: State University of New York Press, 2004), 20–21.

7. B. Ceckoway, "The Politics of Public Hearings," *Journal of Applied Behavioral Science* 17 (1981): 566–582.

8. Senecah, "The Process Trinity," 24.

9. T. F. Yosie and T. D. Herbst, "Using Stakeholder Processes in Environmental Decision-Making: An Evaluation of Lessons Learned, Key Issues, and Future Challenges," 1998, http://www.riskworld.com/Nreports/1998stakehold/html (accessed April 10, 1999).

10. Judith Hendry, "Decide, Announce, Defend: Turning the NEPA Process into an Advocacy Tool Rather Than a Decision Making Tool," in *Communication and Public Participation in Environmental Decision Making,* eds. S. P. Depoe, J. W. Delicath, and M. Aepli Elsenbeer (Albany: State University of New York Press, 2004), 99–112.

11. Craig Waddell, "Saving the Great Lakes: Public Participation in Environmental Policy," in *Green Culture: Environmental Rhetoric in Contemporary America,* eds. C. G. Herndl and S. C. Brown (Madison: University of Wisconsin Press, 1996), 141–165.

12. Gregg B. Walker, "The Roadless Initiative as National Policy: Is Public Participation an Oxymoron?" in *Communication and Public Participation in Environmental Decision Making,* eds. S. P. Depoe, J. W. Delicath, and M. Aepli Elsenbeer (Albany: State University of New York Press, 2004), 123.

13. Stephen P. Depoe, "Public Involvement: Civic Discovery and the Formation of Environmental Policy: A Comparative Analysis of the Fernald Citizens Task Force and the Fernald Health Effects Sub Committee," in *Communication and Public Participation in Environmental Decision Making,* eds. S. P. Depoe, J. W. Delicath, and M. Aepli Elsenbeer (Albany: State University of New York Press, 2004), 157–173.

14. Depoe, "Public Involvement," 171.

15. Depoe, "Public Involvement," 164.

16. Depoe, "Public Involvement," 166.

17. Thomas L. Tedford and Dale A. Herbeck, *Freedom of Speech in the United States,* 6th ed. (State College, PA: Strata, 2009).

18. K. Adair and C. Nielsen, "File Not Found," The National Security Archive, George Washington University, 2007, http://www.gwu.edu/~nsarchiv/NSAEBB/NSAEBB216/index.htm (accessed March 19, 2007).

19. International Campaign for Justice in Bhopal, "What Happened in Bhopal?" http://www.bhopal.org/whathappened.html (accessed July 7, 2007).

20. Benjamin Kline, *First Along the River: A Brief History of the U.S. Environmental Movement,* 2nd ed. (San Francisco: Acada, 2000).

21. Kline, *First Along the River,* 109.

22. James Gustave Speth, *The Bridge at the Edge of the World: Capitalism, the Environment, and Crossing from Crisis to Sustainability* (New Haven. CT: Yale University Press, 2008), 163.

Chapter 13

From the Ground Up: The Environmental Justice Movement

The humanoid, pizza-obsessed Teenage Mutant Ninja Turtles mutated into superheroes after coming into contact with toxic ooze. Peter Parker transformed into Spiderman with superhuman abilities after being bitten by an irradiated spider at a science demonstration. These fantasy characters and many other fictitious superheroes or supervillains with toxic-induced abnormalities (X-Men, the Joker, the Hulk, Ant Man, and so forth) reflect what environmental communication scholar Phaedra C. Pezzullo suggests is our culture's "love-hate feelings about the toxic chemical industry."[1] On the one hand, says Pezzullo, toxins represent "humanity out of control" and the evil forces against whom the superheroes fight to save the planet and its ordinary humans. On the other hand, toxins endow these characters with extraordinary physical and mental capabilities, allowing us to vicariously transcend our human limitations.

While these toxic transformations make for entertaining characters, it doesn't take a lot of "spider sense" to know that in real life, exposure to toxic environmental pollutants can have serious health effects. Among them are cancer, heart disease, respiratory ailments, neurological damage, birth defects, miscarriages, and sterility. For real people, living with the real threats, in real places, there are no warrior turtles or super spiders to save the planet, and voices of the would-be heroes are often silenced or ignored. Polluted communities and the silencing of those who unjustly bear a disproportionate share of the toxic consequences are the driving concerns for the environmental justice movement.

Environmental Justice

Environmental justice, a growing area of study and activism, has brought attention to what human ecologist Robert R. Higgins describes as "the cultural perception of minority communities as *appropriately polluted spaces*."[2] These "sacrifice zones,"[3] as environmental justice activist Robert D. Bullard calls them, are located far away from and out of view of the centers of power. The beginning of the grassroots environmental justice movement is commonly attributed to activists in Warren County, North Carolina, where, in 1982, a protest was staged to block the import of more than seven thousand truckloads of PCB-contaminated soil to a local landfill.[4] Hundreds of citizens from this rural area, mostly African-Americans, gathered to meet the toxic shipments. Many protestors lay down across the road to block the trucks. More than five hundred people were arrested during this six-week campaign.

Although the protestors failed to halt the shipments to the landfill (it would be another two decades before the site was finally cleaned up), this landmark case drew national attention to the inequitable distribution of human-made environmental hazards in low-income and minority communities. Since then, the movement has gained momentum and influence and has empowered many who were previously silenced or ignored.

Several key achievements mark the movement's rise to national prominence and give testimony to the effectiveness of grassroots organizing. The first of these occurred in October of 1991, when the First National People of Color Environmental Leadership Summit convened in Washington, D.C., bringing together community activists and leaders from across the United States. At this historic gathering, summit delegates adopted the "Principles of Environmental Justice," creating a unified vision and shaping the future of the nascent movement.

Another pivotal moment in the environmental justice movement's development came in the form of an executive order signed by President Bill Clinton in 1994. The **Environmental Justice Executive Order 12898** directed federal agencies to develop strategies for identifying and addressing environmental justice issues. It also established the National Environmental Justice Advisory Council (NEJAC) within the Environmental Protection Agency.

These achievements promoted a political framework for environmental justice issues and placed them on the political agenda. Although the George W. Bush administration dealt a serious blow to the movement's political momentum, environmental justice issues appeared on the national radar once again with the 2008 election of President Barack Obama and the appointment of Lisa Jackson, a dedicated environmental justice proponent, to head the Environmental Protection Agency. Increased funding for environmental justice programs and the appointment of senior advisors to oversee them indicated the EPA's commitment to addressing environmental justice issues.

Environmental Racism

Environmental racism is defined by Robert D. Bullard, one of the leading voices of the movement, as "practices or policies that disparately impact (whether intended or unintended) people of color and exclude people of color from decision-making boards and commissions."[5] Claims of race-based inequities or "environmental racism" have been leveled against corporate polluters, developers, and the government.

The rationale for the disproportionate distribution of environmental hazards is clearly spelled out in the now infamous report produced in 1984 by Cerrell and Associates, a private consulting firm hired by the California Waste Management Board. The report provided a profile of neighborhoods most likely to organize effective resistance to hazardous waste facilities, and cautioned its client not to site waste disposal in those areas. The obvious inference is to place the unwanted facilities where residents lack the resources to resist effectively. The report states:

> All socioeconomic groupings tend to resent the nearby citing of major
> facilities, but middle and upper socioeconomic strata possess better
> resources to effectuate their opposition. Middle and higher socioeconomic
> strata neighborhoods should not fall within the one-mile and five-mile
> radius of the proposed site.[6]

A 1987 study entitled *Toxic Waste and Race in the United States,* sponsored by the Commission for Racial Justice of the United Church of Christ, provided the first comprehensive study of environmental racism. The study found that three out of five African-Americans live in communities with toxic waste sites. A 1994 update of the study found that ethnic and racial minorities were 47 percent more likely than European-Americans to live near hazardous facilities.[7]

Not only do minorities bear a disproportionate share of environmental hazards, there is evidence that government protection against pollution is also distributed inequitably. A 1992 study published in the *National Law Journal* reported that

Connections

Toxic Tours as Advocacy Rhetoric

Areas of hazardous pollution tend to be tucked away and out of site for those who live on the proverbial "other-side-of-the-tracks," leaving the fortunate blissfully unaware of the hazards. Toxic tours are organized by environmental justice groups for a variety of audiences, including politicians, government officials, reporters, and academics. Local tour guides provide information and direct tourists to view the toxic sites and polluting industries in the neighborhood. The tours also provide opportunities for visitors to hear residents' firsthand accounts of their struggles and to learn about the health effects of living in a toxic neighborhood.

Environmental communication scholar Phaedra C. Pezzullo suggests that activists who organize these tours "have begun to articulate a powerful mode of rhetorical invention that should not be taken for granted." Toxic tours, says Pezzullo, serve as a means of communicating the "presence" of these often invisible hazards by "narrow[ing] the distance, literally and figuratively, between those who live, work, and play elsewhere and those who live, work, and play within these contaminated communities." By bringing together the two different worlds, "these tours collapse the false separation between production and waste, wealth and poverty, and privilege and race, to illustrate how these spheres are dependent on and, thus, obligated to each other."

The sights, sounds, and smells of the polluted neighborhood offer a powerful critique of the dominant discourses of toxic waste through personal encounters with the contaminated community and its residents. As Pezzullo states, "Toxics are rearticulated as 'real.'" The clotheslines and swing sets under looming smokestacks tell a poignant story of the injustice of "who benefits from, and who pays for, toxic industries."

Source: Phaedra C. Pezzullo, "Toxic Tours: Communicating the 'Presence' of Chemical Contamination," in *Communication and Public Participation in Environmental Decision Making*, eds. S. P. Depoe, J. W. Delicath, and M. Aepli Elsenbeer (Albany, NY: State University of New York Press, 2004).

government agencies treat polluters in predominantly minority neighborhoods less severely than those in predominantly white neighborhoods. The authors of the report calculated that in areas with predominantly white populations, the amount levied for penalties for violations of the Resource Conservation and Recovery Act (RCRA) was about five times the amount levied in areas with predominantly minority populations. The study also showed that Superfund (CERCLA) cleanup programs take longer and are less thorough in minority neighborhoods than in white neighborhoods.[8]

Some people, while recognizing that unequal distributions exist, argue that the disproportionate demographics in hazardous facilities siting is a function of the housing market rather than a function of race. In other words, the comparatively cheap real estate that was attractive to the owners of the hazardous facility is also attractive to people of low income, encouraging them to move to or remain in the area where hazardous facilities have been located.[9]

In a similar vein, others have suggested that the disproportionate presence of hazardous facilities in minority communities is due to the fact that these facilities tend to be concentrated near industrial labor pools. An important question under-lying both of these claims is which came first, the people or the hazardous facility? Did the owners of the hazardous facility target the area for siting because of its minority population, or did the minority population move in after the facility was sited because of the resulting lowered property values or the proximity of the facility for the employees? The answer to this question has important legal impli-cations. Targeting a community of color as a "sacrifice zone" is clearly racist and against the law. However, there is no legal claim for environmental racism if people of color choose to move to areas near hazardous sites.[10] Obviously, the notion of "choice" touches on broader issues of institutional racism that go far beyond the boundaries of any particular facility siting case. Institutional racism involves far-reaching social, political, and economic causes of the disparities that often severely limit choices for people of color.

Environmental justice scholars Paul Mohai and Robin Saha argue that much of the uncertainty in predicting factors of hazardous facility siting (such as race, market forces, and labor pool) results from problems with traditional methods for assessing demographic disparities in the distribution of hazards. Most studies have utilized geographical units such as counties, zip codes, or census tracts to represent proximity to a hazardous facility. The predefined units, however, are not neces-sarily the best means of determining actual distance from the hazard. One could, for example, live in the zip code area of a hazardous waste facility but still be a considerable distance from it.

In an impressive study, Mohai and Saha reassessed national data on 608 haz-ardous waste treatment, storage, and disposal facilities, using actual distance-based methods. They found that when distance-based data were collected, the racial and economic disparities are much larger than shown in previous studies. They con-cluded that racial disparities in the distribution of environmental hazards "are not solely a function of labor force or other socio-economic characteristics."[11] Race is a significant predictor of the citing of hazardous facilities. Other race-related factors, such as discrimination in housing and job markets, constrain individual choices of residential locations and must also be taken into consideration in explaining this disparity.[12] Regardless of the explanation one adopts to explain the siting of hazardous facilities, serious inequities for minority and low-income communities cannot be denied.

The following sections discuss some of the many areas of concern for environ-mental justice activists. Although the previous discussion has focused primarily on racial justice, the movement is committed to justice for all peoples whose voices have been silenced or ignored. In a sense, this movement could be called the "rhetorical justice movement," as the problems addressed all have in common the rhetorical disadvantages that result from racial, social, and political inequalities. Environmental communication scholars Jennifer A. Peeples and Kevin M. DeLuca explain the situation:

> Opposing some of the most powerful corporate and government organizations in the United States, lacking the power to get public and/or private help for their cause without evidentiary backing to their claims, lacking the education to perform the studies themselves, lacking the funds to enlist help from outside organizations, and knowing that every day they are continuing to be contaminated and potentially killed by what exists in their community, members of Environmental Justice face an appalling rhetorical situation.[13]

Figure 13.1   Great Louisiana Toxics March

Residents of the area called "Cancer Alley," living under a cloud of toxic pollutants, joined with environmental groups in an eighty-mile protest march. The Great Louisiana Toxics March began on November 11, 1988, in Devil's Swamp near Baton Rouge, one of the most polluted Superfund sites in the United States. The march ended nine days later with a rally in New Orleans.

©Sam Kittner / kittner.com

Cancer Alley: A Case Study of Environmental Injustice

One of the most notorious and well-documented areas of environmental injustice is Cancer Alley, an 85-mile industrial corridor along the Mississippi River between Baton Rouge and New Orleans. This area is home to more than 125 companies that produce one-quarter of the nation's petrochemicals, including fertilizers, gasoline, paints, plastics, and synthetic fibers. It contains more than 500 hazardous waste sites. Home to a large minority population, it has been a microcosm of activism for the environmental justice movement.

Cancer Alley gained notoriety in 1988, when area residents organized the first Great Louisiana Toxics March to bring attention to the industrial pollution and the resulting health effects in the area. The ten-day march from Baton Rouge to New Orleans drew hundreds of people who joined for an hour or a day as the march came through their communities. Since then, according to science and technology professor Barbara L. Allen, "landmark battles have been won and lost on this marshy turf of the lower Mississippi River."[14]

As discussed in Chapter 1, names play an important role in mediating the reality of the things they represent. In her book, *Uneasy Alchemy: Citizens and Experts in Louisiana's Chemical Corridor Disputes,* Allen summarizes the reality of this industrial landscape for those who have named it "Cancer Alley."

Many residents fear the very place they call home. The anguished townspeople tell stories of illness and disaster. One resident claims that no one over the age of fifty lives in his neighborhood. Another talks of the number of cases of sarconosis, a rare lung disease, in her community . . . . [Another] tells of a woman burned to death in a vinyl chloride fire in her own front yard.[15]

One resident suggests that the name "Cancer Alley" fails to adequately represent the range and number of fatal illnesses that she sees in her community, and instead calls it "Death Alley."

The government, on the other hand, refers to the region as the "Industrial Corridor," and company representatives call it the "Chemical Corridor," terms that privilege the discourse of economics and industry by their representations of the area as a base of production. Allen claims that one can readily identify people's affiliations simply by what they call it. She goes on to say that dialogue between residents and industry representatives is often frustrating because "they speak of different landscapes in different languages, with different intentions."[16]

The history of environmental justice activism in the corridor is long and well-documented. We could choose from a multitude of citizen protests, public hearings, or legal battles as representative case studies of the difficulties faced by citizen activists. A common thread is the rhetorical disadvantages that citizens face when they wish to be heard by regulatory agencies. Yet the decisions made by these agencies have far-ranging implications for the citizens who must live in the toxic communities.

The language of government and industry tends to privilege technical and economic discourse, whereas the language of the community residents is grounded in their everyday experiences. Oftentimes, the regulatory agencies and the polluting industries afford little credence or consideration to the citizen narratives about what it is like to actually live with the contaminated landscape. As Allen explains, government and industry "segregate public input into technical and nontechnical or relevant and irrelevant."[17] The "relevant" discourse tends to be framed in terms of "maximum pounds of emissions releases of unpronounceable chemical compounds. None of their discourse sounds remotely familiar to residents who call the same landscape 'home.'"[18]

Drawing on the legacy of classical rhetoric, environmental communication scholar Robert Cox discusses the notion of "decorum" or "propriety," which calls on the rhetor to adapt "appropriate" ways of speaking to the audience or occasion. He cites the classical Roman orator Cicero's observation about "How inappropriate it would be . . . to use mean and meager language when referring to the majesty of the Roman people."[19] In contemporary times, the concept of decorum still holds an important place in public forums. Unfortunately, in environmental regulatory forums, decorum or appropriate ways of speaking often serve to restrict citizens' ability to participate in a meaningful way.

The appropriate way of speaking is usually not defined by a set of formal rules, but by tacit expectations of the regulatory agency regarding what is considered appropriate or legitimate testimony in a hearing. Judgments about a speaker's testimony are based on expectations about the kind of evidence a speaker should use and the degree of knowledge or expertise a speaker should possess. It is often technical rationality that is judged appropriate, while cultural rationality is given little credence in regulatory forums.

Cox tells the story of Rose Marie Agustine, from a neighborhood on the south side of Tucson, Arizona, where the residents' water wells had been contaminated by leaching toxics from nearby industrial plants. When she and her neighbors tried to get county officials to listen to their concerns about health problems in the neighborhood, one official called them "hysterical Hispanic housewives." Agustine had made the mistake of failing to abide by the standard of decorum that places authority on the rhetoric of toxicology and epidemiology, rather than on the evidence of her own body and her personal experience of living in the toxic community. The Environmental Protection Agency would later confirm the toxicity of the water and its health risks, and list the area as a Superfund priority site.

Unfortunately, dismissing citizen voices as "indecorous" is not unusual—especially for women who are often viewed as simply hysterical or overemotional "housewives." And ironically, it is often this dismissal that has led women to step out of their comfort zones as mothers and housewives to take on leadership roles in environmental justice cases. Women have been the driving force of the environmental justice movement and hold the majority of leadership positions with local environmental justice groups.[20] As environmental justice scholar Giovanna di Choro explains, "The identity and experience of being a 'mother' and the outrage at watching local corporations and government officials exhibiting total disregard for the lives of their children, have significantly motivated many women to become politically active."[21]

Environmental communication scholars Jennifer A. Peeples and Kevin M. DeLuca examined ways in which the feminine rhetorical style of "militant mothers" in environmental justice cases has been used to challenge the polluting practices that have threatened their homes and families. The traditional feminine characteristics of caring, empathy, and nurturance are manifested in discourse in which personal experiences and anecdotal evidence are the primary modes of proof. Added to the feminine style of the women activists is the "maternal militancy" of protective mothers, making their rhetoric a combination of confrontational protectiveness and confirming nurturance.

This style of rhetoric, though often dismissed in forums where technical rationality is privileged, can to unite and empower a constituency by constructing truth not as scientific "fact," but as "based on personal experiences as mothers and through the knowledge gained from the community and their bodies."[22] Thus, their rhetorical style affirms and empowers mothers and housewives to speak their own truth even when their claims are dismissed by "experts." The indecorous outrage of militant mothers has mobilized community campaigns to clean up contaminated areas, to stop polluting practices of industries, or to stop toxic sites from being built in their neighborhoods.

The previous discussion of the environmental justice movement has focused on issues pertaining to the inequitable distribution of hazardous facilities in urban areas, but activists have also challenged many other environmental injustices. The following section moves from the urban to the rural, with a look at the plight of farm workers.

Environmental Justice and Farm Workers

Another issue that environmental justice advocates have challenged is the health risks that exposure to agricultural pesticides pose to our nation's farm workers. Dr. Marion Moses, an expert in pesticide-related health problems, describes some of the immediate and long-range health effects of pesticide exposure: "Acute effects range from rashes, chemical burns, and other skin problems to systemic poisoning, which can lead to nausea, vomiting, and even death. Chronic effects can include cancer, sterility, spontaneous abortion, stillbirth, birth defects, and a variety of neuropathological and neurobehavioral disorders."[23]

Labor-intensive crops such as fruits and vegetables require large numbers of seasonal farm workers for hand-cultivating and harvesting the crops. Dependence on cheap labor often leads to the exploitation of minority workers, many of whom are imported from Mexico. A national survey of U.S. agricultural workers reported that 90 percent of all farm workers are Hispanic (77 percent are from Mexico), with an average educational grade level of 6.9 years.[24]

Several factors contribute to the rhetorical disadvantages that migrant farm workers face, one of which is a lack of standing in regulatory forums. As discussed in the previous chapter, standing refers to "the civic legitimacy, the respect, and the esteem and consideration that all stakeholders' perspectives should be given."[25] Their lack of standing stems from a fundamental lack of regulatory protections.

Farm workers are excluded from worker safety protections guaranteed by the 1970 Occupational Safety and Health Act (OSHA). Likewise, they are intentionally excluded from the Fair Labor Standards Act, which governs child labor and minimum wage standards, and the National Labor Relations Act, which guarantees the right to form collective bargaining unions. They are denied the protection of Worker's Compensation Insurance and rarely receive health benefits from employers. Many states do not require that running water and toilets be installed in migrants' housing. And, with parental consent, children as young as twelve years of age can work in the fields. In short, national and state policies do little to protect farm workers from the devastating health effects of pesticides and poor working conditions.

In addition to lacking regulatory protections, farm workers are at a rhetorical disadvantage that stems from their unwillingness to seek protection from authorities. The EPA estimates that twenty thousand to three hundred thousand acute pesticide poisonings occur each year among farm workers. The wide disparity in estimated numbers is due, in large part, to strong disincentives for both workers and employers to report pesticide-related illnesses. Workers fear the loss of income and employers fear the loss of perishable crops if workers must be removed from the field.

Further perpetuating the powerlessness of farm workers are the powerful forces of industry and consumers. As environmental communication scholar Emily Plec points out, the influence that the multibillion-dollar pesticide manufacturing industry has with regulatory agencies and lawmakers, as well as consumer practices which privilege the shiny apple to the one with a worm hole in it, "practically insure that chemical pesticides will be one of the primary solutions to which farmers turn to address their needs."[26]

Before grabbing the flawless apple or tomato from the produce bins, we would do well to consider our role as consumers in perpetuating the exploitation of farm workers. Environmental communication scholar Jean P. Retzinger reminds us that protecting farm workers is in our own best interest as well as theirs:

> Our bodies are linked as well to the bodies of those farm workers who make our eating possible. The health of one is inextricably tied to the health of all. We can and should eat our vegetables. But doing so will constitute a "healthy

choice" only if we purchase fruits and vegetables grown and harvested by farm workers laboring in safe, healthy, and sustainable environments.[27]

The inequitable distribution of hazardous sites and the plight of minority farm workers are just two examples of the wide range of issues that environmental justice advocates have taken up. Another area of concern for environmental justice activists has to do with Native Americans and the environmental degradation of Indian lands.

Environmental Justice and Indigenous Peoples

The nation's 287 Indian reservations, from Florida to Alaska, are among the most environmentally degraded and exploited lands in the rural United States. Because the Bureau of Indian Affairs issues the permits on Indian lands for waste disposal, mining, and so forth, the U.S. Environmental Protection Agency has no role in monitoring or regulating environmental protection standards. Big industries find this freedom from environmental controls alluring and will pay high dividends for the use of reservation lands. It should be noted, however, that in many cases, tribal sovereignty has been invoked to impose even higher standards than the EPA would require. Nevertheless, because of the many problems Native Americans face—high unemployment rates, substandard housing, lack of health care, to name a few— many tribal leaders find themselves in a survival mode and are willing to accept landfills, incinerators, mines, and dams in return for money and jobs.

Native Americans often face the same rhetorical disadvantages as those faced by farm workers or the residents of Cancer Alley and other polluted urban areas. The disadvantages stem from the tendency by regulatory agencies to privilege technical rationality over cultural rationality, thus restricting those not versed in the "appropriate" language from meaningful participation in regulatory hearings. Native Americans are likewise up against power imbalances and social inequalities that affect their ability to influence agency decision makers.

Church Rock, New Mexico, in the Navajo Nation, is a case in point. Church Rock is a rural community of Dine Navajo families, many of whom eke out a meager living herding cattle, sheep, and goats along the Rio Puerco. (*Rio* is the Spanish word for "river.") For many years, tribal leaders leased uranium mining rights to several companies, including the United Nuclear Corporation (UNC). UNC's mining process involves extracting uranium from ore (usually sandstone) by grinding the ore into fine sand and leaching it with sulfuric acid. In the process, 99.9 percent of the ore that is mined is left over as waste, or "tailings," that retain 85 percent of the ore's original radioactivity. In addition to creating the huge piles of radioactive tailings, the milling process leaves behind large amounts of acid milling liquids called "liquor," which contain radioactive isotopes that have been leached out in the milling process. The liquor is held in ponds so the liquids can evaporate. The leftover solids are then stored as radioactive waste.

In their 1982 book *Killing Our Own,*[28] Harvey Wasserman and Norman Solomon detail the events and the ensuing Congressional hearings of what is believed to be the largest release of radioactive liquid in United States history. In the early morning hours of July 16, 1979, the dam holding the liquor at the Church Rock UNC mine gave way, sending ninety million gallons of the contaminated liquid into the Rio Puerco, destroying the water supply for numerous Navajo communities, and carrying the toxic metals many miles downstream. The subsequent hearings

Connections

Environmental Justice and Environmentalism: Friends or Foes?

In the early 1990s, environmental justice activists gained national media attention for their harsh criticism of the nation's largest environmental organizations, accusing them of racism in their hiring and environmental policies, and chastising them for their indifference to the plight of communities of color, both at home and abroad. Environmental justice advocates, exasperated by mainstream environmentalists' limited focus on the preservation of wilderness areas and the protection of endangered species, had called on them to take into account the link between social justice issues and environmental issues. Since then, several environmental organizations, including Greenpeace, the Sierra Club, and the World Wildlife Fund, have broadened their agendas to include environmental justice projects and campaigns.

While many applaud environmental groups' adoption of social justice issues, others are not as enthusiastic about the alliance. Environmental communication scholar, Kevin DeLuca, for example, suggests that the Sierra Club's incorporation of an environmental justice agenda "represents a retreat from speaking for the trees to once again speaking for people, just like everyone else."

Recognizing that the push to save wildlife and wilderness can sometimes involve "brutal choices," DeLuca nevertheless takes a firm stand:

> If we put people first, we will stand by and watch as the last rhino horn, the last tiger penis, and the last seahorse are ground up and consumed. . . . we will stand by and watch as a poor villager eradicates the last clouded leopard in a futile attempt to eradicate poverty.

DeLuca goes on to argue that putting wilderness first does not mean abandoning humans—that in attending to wilderness issues, we do, in fact, attend to human issues. He calls for environmental justice activists and environmentalists to form alliances when it makes strategic sense to do so, but to retain their distinct identities and goals.

Source: Kevin M. DeLuca, "A Wilderness Environmentalism Manifesto: Contesting the Infinite Self-Absorption of Humans," in *Environmental Justice and Environmentalism: The Social Justice Challenge to the Environmental Movement*, eds. R. Sandler and P. C. Pezzullo (Cambridge, MA: MIT Press, 2007).

and investigations revealed multiple problems with the dam's structure and operation that made its failure almost inevitable. In the ensuing Congressional hearings, Frank Paul, a Navajo Tribal Counsel member, explained the situation this way:

> Somehow United Nuclear Corporation was permitted to locate a tailings pond and a dam on an unstable geologic formation. Somehow UNC was allowed to build an unsafe tailings dam not in conformance to its own design criteria. Somehow UNC was permitted to inadequately deal with warning cracks that had appeared over two years prior to the date the dam failed. Somehow UNC was permitted to continue a temporary dam for six months beyond its design life. . . . Somehow UNC was permitted to deal with the spill by doing almost nothing.[29]

Three months after the spill, company representatives reported to the House Committee hearings that their cleanup efforts, along with natural effects such as wind and rain, had "largely restored normal conditions to the area."[30] The mine and mill were back in operation in less than five months with only minor changes made to the design of the dam, despite widespread community opposition.

The inadequacy of UNC's response to the accident and the powerlessness of the affected Navajo communities to do anything about it is poignantly symbolized by a local resident who stated that "the UNC put up signs saying 'contaminated wash, keep out.' But our cows, sheep, and horses can't read. Most of us can't read, write, or speak English."[31]

The Church Rock area is now an EPA-designated superfund site. Uranium-contaminated soil and water are believed to contribute to an organ cancer rate among Navajo teenagers that is seventeen times the national average.[32] The full extent of the health impacts will probably never be known, not only because the residents of Church Rock faced all the barriers to statistically verifying health effects that were pointed out in the discussion of epidemiology in Chapter 8, but also because of one even more daunting confounding variable—the enduring nature of the threat. Thorium 230, just one of several isotopes leached out in the uranium milling process, has a half-life of eighty thousand years. How does one calculate the effects of a hazard for eighty thousand years into the future?

Over 60 percent of all known uranium deposits in the United States are on Native American lands extending over large areas of Arizona, Colorado, New Mexico, South Dakota, Utah, and Wyoming.[33] The advent of the nuclear industry and the subsequent milling, mining, and enrichment on Native American lands have resulted in what environmental justice advocates Ward Churchill and Winona LaDuke have termed "radioactive colonialism."[34] Native American communities, like other lands colonized by an imposing outside power, are drawn into the operations of powerful nuclear energy industry and must then depend on that industry and its experts to protect their lands and health. When industry protections fail, Native Americans must then rely on government regulatory agencies to redress the problem—agencies that tend to place greater authority on technical rationality than on the experiences and values of those who must live with the consequences. Many Native Americans living in affected communities lack sufficient material resources, ready access to expert resources, and the kind of knowledge that is required to understand the complexities of nuclear technologies and the epidemiological impacts of radiation. They find themselves rhetorically disadvantaged and unable to participate equally with industry resources and experts in regulatory forums.

The case studies we have discussed represent only a few of the issues that environmental justice activists and scholars have addressed. I hope these cases have helped shed some light on the environmental and the rhetorical inequities that people of color face in the United States.

Environmental Justice Abroad

The role of economic globalization and transnational corporations in perpetuating environmental injustice is another area of concern for environmental justice advocates. International trade agreements such as the General Agreement on Tariffs and Trade (GATT) and the North American Free Trade Agreement (NAFTA) foster economic globalization and increasingly permeable national borders. The **World Trade Organization (WTO),** which came into existence in 1994 as a result of the "Uruguay Round" of global trade negotiations (replacing GATT), oversees the implementation and enforcement of the rules of world trade. In a document over twenty-six thousand pages long, member nations granted the WTO significant powers as an international trade-governing body to enforce its rules, including the ability to levy stiff penalties against member nations that violate the rules.

While many hailed the creation of WTO as a step toward global cooperation and economic prosperity, critics charge that the organization enhances corporate power at the expense of human rights and environmental protections. Although international trade agreements support economic expansion, environmental protections and labor standards are often viewed as trade barriers that are illegal under the rules of these agreements because they add costs to production or diminish sales. The WTO tribunal can levy stiff penalties against a member state for such trade barriers.

The much-publicized case of the United States embargo on Mexican tuna illustrates how trade rules can create obstacles to environmental protections. The United States prohibited Mexican tuna imports because the nets used to catch the tuna also caught a large number of dolphins, thus violating the U.S. Marine Mammal Protection Act. In 1991, a WTO dispute resolution panel ruled that the U.S. was imposing a trade barrier that was illegal under GATT. While the United States has the right to enforce environmental laws within its own jurisdictional boundaries, the panel reasoned, it does not have the right to impose its environmental laws and values on the rest of the world.

One of the strongest criticisms leveled against international trade agreements is that the behind-the-scenes decision-making practices of powerful, unelected tribunals exclude those who ultimately must bear the largest share of the impacts. This lack of transparency offers freedom from accountability for the global institutions, rendering local citizens powerless to protect themselves through any form of democratic governance or representation. Vandana Shiva, a physicist, ecologist, and human rights activist, sums up this major criticism of the WTO:

> In reality, free trade has vastly expanded the freedom and powers of transnational corporations to trade and invest in most countries of the world, while significantly reducing the powers of national governments to restrict their operations. . . . Free trade is not free. . . . In essence, GATT cripples the democratic institutions of individual countries—local councils, regional governments, and parliaments—leaving them unable to carry out the will of their citizens.[35]

The protests outside the 1999 WTO ministerial meeting in Seattle brought world attention to the secrecy and lack of accountability of the powerful, unelected decision makers. The start of the meeting was delayed as an estimated fifty thousand protestors from across the country and the world blocked the streets surrounding the meeting site, chanting slogans such as "Whose streets? Our streets! Whose world? Our world!" and "This is what democracy looks like."

The protests brought together an unprecedented alliance of environmental groups, human rights organizations, antisweatshop activists, labor unions, and farmers, all united in their concern about the domination of the world economy by a few hundred giant transnational corporations. Protestors scaled flagpoles, construction cranes, and interstate overpasses to unfurl anti-WTO banners. Longshoremen from San Diego to Anchorage staged a one-day strike. Seattle taxi drivers took the afternoon off as a show of solidarity for the protestors. In imitation of the Boston

Tea Party that helped to spark the American Revolution, the United Steelworkers of America rallied on Seattle's waterfront and dumped fake Chinese steel into the harbor. Their banner read, "No Globalization without Representation."

The sheer number of protestors and the image events they staged drew a great deal of media attention to the multiple issues surrounding economic globalization. But perhaps the message that drew the most attention was the one sent unintentionally as the Seattle police, state troopers, and the National Guard faced down the protestors with pepper spray, tear gas, and rubber pellets. The harsh treatment of the protestors served to further highlight some of the deepest concerns of the protestors—the diminishing rights of individuals and democratic institutions.

Protest groups now routinely gather to protest the meetings of the WTO and of other powerful international economic brokers such as the World Bank, the International Monetary Fund (IMF), and the G-8 summits. Although the WTO is making strides (albeit small and halting strides) toward stronger environmental and worker protections, many restraints created by international trade agreements still limit the environmental and worker protection policies that participating nations can enforce without costly sanctions for the trade barriers those policies create.

In the wake of global economic expansion fueled by international trade agreements, the human and environmental impacts of industrial development have become a major concern for environmental justice advocates. One area of particular concern is the border between the United States and Mexico. Cheap labor and lax environmental protection controls attract manufacturers to free trade zones along the border. Companies from the United States and other countries import manufacturing equipment and materials duty-free into Mexico and export the finished product back to the home country. Over forty-five hundred foreign companies operate ***maquiladoras*** (manufacturing for export industries) along the border, assembling everything from clothing and toys to auto parts and electronics. Nearly one million people, the majority of whom are women, work in the *maquiladoras* for as little as twenty-eight to forty-five dollars a week, in conditions where occupational safety and health protections are lax and numerous violations of workers' basic rights systematically occur.[36]

There are also serious environmental problems associated with the toxic waste produced in *maquiladoras*. Despite an agreement between the United States and Mexico that the toxic waste produced by U.S. companies in the *maquiladoras* is to be returned to the U.S., there is evidence that in many cases toxic wastes are stored on the production sites along the border or simply dumped into local waterways and sewer systems, creating health hazards for workers and residents who live in or near these industrial zones.[37]

The U.S./Mexican border is only one of a rapidly growing number of free trade zones or areas where multinational manufacturing is carried out on a large scale. Others include China's Kwang Chow Province, Guatemala, El Salvador, Nicaragua, Honduras, Indonesia, Singapore, Thailand, and the Philippines. With increasing economic globalization, the list is rapidly expanding.

The previous discussion represents only a sample of a multitude of concerns that have been taken up by environmental justice activists, whose efforts, in the face of seemingly insurmountable obstacles and unbeatable odds, have gained worldwide attention and improved the lives of many at home and abroad.[38]

Regardless of whether injustice resides in Louisiana's Cancer Alley or in sweatshops around the world, in our own backyards or on distant shores, it impacts us all. The human environment and the natural environment are inextricably linked.

As environmental justice scholar and activist Robert D. Bullard has remarked, "social inequality and imbalances of power are at the heart of environmental degradation, resource depletion, pollution, and even overpopulation. The environmental crisis can simply not be solved effectively without social justice."[39] Addressing one requires addressing the other as well. Perhaps no other problem brings this point home more clearly than global warming.

The Injustice of Global Warming

Shishmaref is an Inupiat village on an island five miles off the coast of the Seward Peninsula in Alaska. This small island (about a quarter mile across and two and one-half miles long), has been inhabited for centuries by the Inupiat. Almost all the village's 591 residents, like many native villagers in Alaska, live off subsistence hunting.

Traditionally the seal hunting season began as the spring thaw was underway, when the men of Shishmaref would drive out over the ice in dog sleds or snowmobiles. In the early 1990s, hunters began to notice that the sea ice was beginning to form later in the fall and to break up earlier in the spring. The men have switched to using boats for the hunts because by the time the seals arrive in the spring, it is no longer safe to drive out on the ice.

At its highest point, the village of Shishmaref is only twenty-two feet above sea level. When the sea ice layer formed earlier in the fall, it protected the village from sea storm surges. The ice kept the water from being churned up by the wind—much like a tarp over a swimming pool. Without this protective covering, storm surges have begun to scour away the land and the houses. In 2002, recognizing that the already dire situation would only get worse, the residents voted to move the entire village to the mainland.[40] It appears that the inhabitants of Shishmaref are the first climate change refugees.

On the opposite side of the globe, the small island country of Tuvalu and its neighboring island states are also threatened by storm surges linked to global warming and rising sea levels. Tuvalu, which consists of nine small islands, is one of five sovereign atoll countries. Tuvalu gained the world's attention in 2001 when news emerged that it had begun preparing for the foreseeable time when it will no longer be habitable. Tuvalu negotiated a deal with New Zealand (after being rejected by Australia) whereby a number of Tuvalu's some ten thousand citizens would be allowed to move to New Zealand each year over the next thirty to fifty years and given immigration status as "ecological refugees."

In some ways, the Inupiat of Shishmaref and the citizens of Tuvalu may be the fortunate among the doomed. For them, the warnings hit early and hard, convincing them of the need to make preparations for future survival. Around one-half of the world's population lives in coastal areas threatened by rising sea levels. If predictions hold, Bangladesh alone stands to lose one-fifth of its land to rising sea levels, creating twenty million ecological refugees.[41]

Nor are rising sea levels the only cause for concern. More frequent and extreme droughts are likely to impact cities' ability to provide adequate water. As farms fail in a warming world, it is predicted that famine will create fifty million ecological refugees in Africa alone. The spread of tropical diseases will increase as they become viable further from the equator and as increased flooding from tropical storms multiplies the outbreaks of waterborne diseases.

It would seem as if global warming were an equal opportunity destroyer, but as environmental writer Ross Gelbspan explains, "Climate change hits poor countries

Figure 13.2   Polar Bear Protestor

Progress toward an international climate agreement has been hard won. This polar bear dummy reclines in the main hall at the United Nations climate change conference in Poznań, Poland, convened in December 2008. This conference was part of the preliminary planning efforts for a new climate treaty to be crafted in Copenhagen, Denmark, in December 2009 to replace the flawed 1997 Kyoto Protocol. The weary bear has work left to do, since no binding agreement was reached in Copenhagen.

Kacper Pempel/REUTERS

the hardest—not because nature discriminates against the poor but because poor countries cannot afford the kinds of infrastructure needed to buffer its impacts."[42] The developing nations of the world have heavily subsidized the wealth of industrialized nations. There are serious questions left unanswered as to how we can repay that ecological debt.[43]

Concluding: The Global Commons

Garrett Hardin's well-known essay, "The Tragedy of the Commons" (included in the appendix of this book), discusses the logic behind individuals pursuing their own short term goals at the expense of the greater community, and ultimately, their own long-term interests. "Picture a pasture open to all," says Hardin. Because it is in the herdsman's own best interest to maximize his gain, "The only sensible course [for the herdsman] to pursue is to add another animal to his herd. And another."[44] While the herdsman receives all the benefits from adding more animals, the negative effects of overgrazing are shared by all the herdsmen. Thus, in personalizing the profits while socializing the costs, he enjoys 100 percent of the benefits, while having to bear only a percentage of the costs. Ultimately, the commons will fail for all and "therein," says Hardin, "is the tragedy. Each man is locked into a system that compels him to increase his herd without limit—in a world that is limited. . . . Freedom in a commons brings ruin to all."[45]

The logic of the commons has created a global crisis for all. In a global economy driven by fossil fuels, our atmospheric commons are failing and we are now faced with the costs that all will share. However, unlike the costs shared equally by Hardin's hypothetical herdsmen, the costs of global warming will be born disproportionately by the world's poorest populations, those who can least afford to deal with them.

Policy makers tend to view problems in an economic framework—the costs of climate change impacts versus the costs of addressing the problem. Yet, at its core, climate change is not primarily an economic issue, or even an environmental issue. It is a moral issue, and addressing the problem in a timely and responsible fashion is a moral imperative that will require a coordinated global effort. And it is this globally shared responsibility that offers a ray of hope in the grim forecast. A collaborative global response to climate change could very well be the catalyst for uniting our fractured world into a more prosperous, equitable, and peaceful global community.

We created our world through symbols, and we can change it through symbols. The transition from our current self-destructive practices to a sustainable future will require a compelling and unifying narrative that reconstructs our human/nature relationship, from one that is characterized by dominance and exploitation to one that recognizes that all of nature, both human and nonhuman, shares a unitary, fragile planet. This was the message, spoken to the United Nations delegates by Oren Lyons of the Onondaga Nation, and with which I will leave you:

> I do not see a delegation for the four-footed. I see no seat for eagles. We forget and we consider ourselves superior, but we are after all a mere part of the creation. And we stand between the mountain and the ant, somewhere and there only, as part and parcel of the Creation.[46]

Discussion Questions and Exercises

1. Read Garrett Hardin's classic essay, "The Tragedy of the Commons" (included in the appendix). Explain what you think he means by his statement, "Freedom in a commons brings ruin to all."

2. Do you agree or disagree with Kevin DeLuca's argument that if environmental groups take on social justice issues, they will retreat from "speaking for the trees to once again speaking for people, just like everyone else"? Explain your answer.

3. Many "militant mothers" have taken on the role of environmental justice activists and have brought about significant changes, sometimes against overwhelming odds. Some of these women are Mother Jones, Louis Gibbs, Winona LaDuke, Wangari Maathai, and Erin Brockovich. Do some research on one of these women (or find a militant mother of your own to research) and report what you find.

Suggested Readings

Barbara L. Allen. *Uneasy Alchemy: Citizens and Experts in Louisiana's Chemical Corridor Disputes*. Cambridge, MA: MIT Press, 2003.

J. Robert Cox. "'Free Trade' and the Eclipse of Civil Society: Barriers to Transparency and Public Participation in NAFTA and the Free Trade Area of the Americas," In S. P. Depoe, J. W. Delicath, and M. Aepli Elsenbeer (Eds.), *Communication and Public Participation in Environmental Decision Making*. Albany: State University of New York Press, 2004, 201–219.

Phaedra C. Pezzullo. "Touring 'Cancer Alley,' Louisiana: Performance of Community and Memory for Environmental Justice," *Text and Performance Quarterly* 23 (2003): 226–252.

Ronald Sandler and Phaedra C. Pezzullo (Eds.) *Environmental Justice and Environmentalism: The Social Justice Challenge to the Environmental Movement.* Cambridge, MA: MIT Press, 2007.

Andrew Simms. *Ecological Debt: The Health of the Planet and the Wealth of Nations.* London: Pluto, 2005.

Notes

1. Phaedra C. Pezzullo, *Toxic Tours: Rhetorics of Pollution, Travel, and Environmental Justice* (Tuscaloosa: University of Alabama Press, 2007), 61.

2. Robert R. Higgins, "Race, Pollution, and the Mastery of Nature," *Environmental Ethics* 16 (1994): 252–264.

3. Robert D. Bullard, ed., *Confronting Environmental Racism: Voices from the Grassroots* (Boston: South End, 1993).

4. See, for example, J. Agyeman, B. Doppelt, K. Lynn, and H. Hatic, "The Climate Justice Link: Communicating Risk with Low Income and Minority Audiences," in *Creating a Climate for Change,* eds. S. C. Moser and L. Dilling (Cambridge, MA: Cambridge University Press, 2007); R. D. Bullard and B. H. Wright, "Environmentalism and the Politics of Equity: Emergent Trends in the Black Community," *Midwestern Review of Sociology* 12 (1987): 21–37; J. S. Dryzek, *The Politics of the Earth: Environmental Discourses,* 2nd ed. (New York: Oxford University Press, 2005).

5. Robert D. Bullard, "Residential Segregation and Urban Quality of Life," in *Environmental Justice: Issues, Policies, and Solutions,* ed. B. Bryant (Washington, DC: Island, 1995), 77.

6. Cerrell & Associates, Inc., "Political Difficulties Facing Waste-to-Energy Conversion Plant Siting" (Los Angeles: California Waste Management Board, 1984).

7. B. Goldman and L. Fitton, "Toxic Waste and Race Revisited," (Washington, DC: Center for Policy Alternatives, 1994).

8. M. Lavelle and M. Coyle, "Unequal Protection: The Racial Divide in Environmental Law," *National Law Journal,* September 21, 1992, S1–S6.

9. V. Been, "Locally Undesirable Land Uses in Minority Neighborhoods: Disproportionate Siting or Market Dynamics?" *The Yale Law Journal* 103 (1994): 1383–1422.

10. Been, "Locally Undesirable Land Uses."

11. Paul Mohai and Robin Saha, "Reassessing Racial and Socioeconomic Disparities in Environmental Justice Research," *Demography* 43 (2006): 395.

12. L. W. Cole and S. R. Foster, *From the Ground Up: Environmental Racism and the Rise of the Environmental Justice Movement* (New York: New York University Press, 2001).

13. Jennifer A. Peeples and Kevin M. DeLuca, "The Truth of the Matter: Motherhood, Community, and Environmental Justice," *Women's Studies in Communication* 29 (2006): 61.

14. Barbara L. Allen, *Uneasy Alchemy: Citizens and Experts in Louisiana's Chemical Corridor Disputes* (Cambridge, MA: MIT Press, 2003).

15. Allen, *Uneasy Alchemy,* 27.

16. Allen, *Uneasy Alchemy,* 35.

17. Allen, *Uneasy Alchemy,* 35.

18. Allen, *Uneasy Alchemy,* 36.

19. Robert Cox, "Reclaiming the 'Indecorous' Voice: Public Participation by Low-Income Communities in Environmental Decision-Making," in *Proceedings of the Fifth Biennial Conference on Communication and Environment,* eds. C. Brant Short and Dayle Hardy-Short (Flagstaff, AZ: 1999), 21–31.

20. H. Epstein, "Ghetto Miasma: Enough to Make You Sick?" *The New York Times,* October 12, 1995, Sec. 6, 75.

21. Giovanna di Choro, "Defining Environmental Justice: Women's Voices and Grassroots Politics," *Socialists Review* 22 (1992): 113.

22. Peeples and DeLuca, "The Truth of the Matter," 62.

23. Marion Moses, "Farmworkers and Pesticides," in *Confronting Environmental Racism: Voices from the Grassroots,* ed. R. D. Bullard (Boston: South End, 1993), 166.

24. R. Das, A. Steege, S. Baron, J. Beckman, X. Vergara, P. Sutton, and R. Harrison, "Pesticide Illness among Farmworkers in the United States and California," 2002, http://www.dhs.ca.gov/ohb/AGInjury/soeh0702.pdf (accessed October 10, 2007).

25. Susan L. Senecah, "The Process Trinity of Voice, Standing, and Influence: The Role of Practical Theory in Planning and Evaluating the Effectiveness of Environmental Participatory Processes," in *Communication and Public Participation in Environmental Decision Making,* eds. S. P. Depoe, J. W. Delicath, & M. Aepli Elsenbeer (Albany: State University of New York Press, 2004), 24.

26. Emily Plec, "Poisoning a People, Poisoning a Planet," in *Proceedings of the 8th Biennial Conference on Communication and Environment,* eds. L. S. Volkening, D. Wolfe, E. Plec, W. Griswold, and K. DeLuca (Jekyll Island, GA: 2005), 83.

27. Jean P. Retzinger, "The Embodied Rhetoric of 'Health' from Farm Fields to Salad Bowls," in *Proceedings of the 8th Biennial Conference on Communication and Environment,* eds. L. S. Volkening, D. Wolfe, E. Plec, W. Griswold, and K. DeLuca (Jekyll Island, GA: 2005), 112.

28. Harvey Wasserman and Norman Solomon, *Killing Our Own: The Disaster of America's Experience with Atomic Radiation* (New York: Dell, 1982).

29. Cited in Wasserman and Solomon, *Killing Our Own,* 18.

30. Cited in Wasserman and Solomon, *Killing Our Own,* 120.

31. Cited in Wasserman and Solomon, *Killing Our Own,* 151.

32. B. Bryant and P. Mohai, "The Michigan Conference: A Turning Point," *EPA Journal* 18 (March/April, 1992): 9–10.

33. Ward Churchill and Winona LaDuke, "Native America: The Political Economy of Radioactive Colonialism," *Critical Sociology* 13 (1986): 51–78.

34. Churchill and LaDuke, "Native America."

35. Vandana Shiva, *Biopiracy: The Plunder of Nature and Knowledge* (Boston: South End, 1997), 113.

36. *Comité Fronterizo de Obreras* (CFO-Border Committee Women Workers) "Six Years after NAFTA: A View from inside the *Maquiladoras.*" http://www.cfmaquiladoras.org/seistlc.en.html (accessed March 24, 2007).

37. J. Clapp, "Distancing of Waste: Overconsumption in a Global Economy," in *Confronting Consumption,* eds. T. Princen, M. Maniates, and K. Conca (Cambridge, MA: MIT Press, 2002), 155–176.

38. For a comprehensive analysis of the antisweatshop movement in Central America, see R. Armbruster-Sandoval, *Globalization and Cross-Border Labor Solidarity in the Americas: The Anti-Sweatshop Movement and the Struggle for Social Justice* (New York: Routledge, 2005).

39. Bullard, *Confronting Environmental Racism,* 23.

40. Elizabeth Kolbert, *Field Notes from a Catastrophe: Man, Nature, and Climate Change* (New York: Bloomsbury, 2006).

41. World Disasters Report, 2001 (International Federation of the Red Cross and Red Crescent Societies, Geneva, 2001).

42. Ross Gelbspan, *Boiling Point: How Politicians, Big Oil and Coal, Journalists, and Activists Have Fueled the Climate Crisis—and What We Can Do to Avert Disaster* (New York: Basic Books, 2004), 145.

43. Andrew Simms, *Ecological Debt: The Health of the Planet and the Wealth of Nations* (London: Pluto, 2005).

44. Garrett Hardin, "The Tragedy of the Commons," *Science,* 1968, 1244.
45. Hardin, "The Tragedy of the Commons."
46. Cited in A. Harvey, ed., *The Essential Mystics: Selections from the World's Greatest Wisdom Traditions* (San Francisco: HarperSanFrancisco, 1996), 14–15.

Appendix: Additional Readings

Henry David Thoreau
A Winter Walk
(1843)

The wind has gently murmured through the blinds, or puffed with feathery softness against the windows, and occasionally sighed like a summer zephyr lifting the leaves along, the livelong night. The meadow-mouse has slept in his snug gallery in the sod, the owl has sat in a hollow tree in the depth of the swamp, the rabbit, the squirrel, and the fox have all been housed. The watch-dog has lain quiet on the hearth, and the cattle have stood silent in their stalls. The earth itself has slept, as it were its first, not its last sleep, save when some street-sign or wood-house door has faintly creaked upon its hinge, cheering forlorn nature at her midnight work, —the only sound awake twixt Venus and Mars, —advertising us of a remote inward warmth, a divine cheer and fellowship, where gods are met together, but where it is very bleak for men to stand. But while the earth has slumbered, all the air has been alive with feathery flakes descending, as if some northern Ceres reigned, showering her silvery grain over all the fields.

We sleep, and at length awake to the still reality of a winter morning. The snow lies warm as cotton or down upon the window-sill; the broadened sash and frosted panes admit a dim and private light, which enhances the snug cheer within. The stillness of the morning is impressive. The floor creaks under our feet as we move toward the window to look abroad through some clear space over the fields. We see the roofs stand under their snow burden. From the eaves and fences hang stalactites of snow, and in the yard stand stalagmites covering some concealed core. The trees and shrubs rear white arms to the sky on every side; and where were walls and fences, we see fantastic forms stretching in frolic gambols across the dusky landscape, as if nature had strewn her fresh designs over the fields by night as models for man's art.

Silently we unlatch the door, letting the drift fall in, and step abroad to face the cutting air. Already the stars have lost some of their sparkle, and a dull, leaden mist skirts the horizon. A lurid brazen light in the east proclaims the approach of day, while the western landscape is dim and spectral still, and clothed in a sombre Tartarian light, like the shadowy realms. They are Infernal sounds only that you hear, —the crowing of cocks, the barking of dogs, the chopping of wood, the lowing of kine, all seem to come from Pluto's barn-yard and beyond the Styx, —not for any melancholy they suggest, but their twilight bustle is too solemn and mysterious for earth. The recent tracks of the fox or otter, in the yard, remind us that each hour of the night is crowded with events, and the primeval nature is still working and making tracks in the snow. Opening the gate, we tread briskly along the lone country road, crunching the dry and crisped snow under our feet, or aroused by the sharp clear creak of the wood-sled, just starting for the distant market, from the early farmer's door, where it has lain the summer long, dreaming amid the chips and stubble; while far through the drifts and powdered windows we see the farmer's early candle, like a paled star, emitting a lonely beam, as if

First Published in *The Dial* (October 1843), 211–226.
Reprinted in *Thoreau's Writings: Excursions and Poems* (New York: Houghton and Mifflin, 1906), pp. 163–183.

some severe virtue were at its matins there. And one by one the smokes begin to ascend from the chimneys amidst the trees and snows.

. . . .

The sun at length rises through the distant woods, as if with the faint clashing swinging sound of cymbals, melting the air with his beams, and with such rapid steps the morning travels, that already his rays are gilding the distant western mountains. Meanwhile we step hastily along through the powdery snow, warmed by an inward heat, enjoying an Indian summer still, in the increased glow of thought and feeling. Probably if our lives were more conformed to nature, we should not need to defend ourselves against her heats and colds, but find her our constant nurse and friend, as do plants and quadrupeds. If our bodies were fed with pure and simple elements, and not with a stimulating and heating diet, they would afford no more pasture for cold than a leafless twig, but thrive like the trees, which find even winter genial to their expansion.

The wonderful purity of nature at this season is a most pleasing fact. Every decayed stump and moss-grown stone and rail, and the dead leaves of autumn, are concealed by a clean napkin of snow. In the bare fields and tinkling woods, see what virtue survives. In the coldest and bleakest places, the warmest charities still maintain a foothold. A cold and searching wind drives away all contagion, and nothing can withstand it but what has a virtue in it; and accordingly, whatever we meet with in cold and bleak places, as the tops of mountains, we respect for a sort of sturdy innocence, a Puritan toughness. All things beside seem to be called in for shelter, and what stays out must be part of the original frame of the universe, and of such valor as God himself. It is invigorating to breathe the cleansed air. Its greater fineness and purity are visible to the eye, and we would fain stay out long and late, that the gales may sigh through us, too, as through the leafless trees, and fit us for the winter, —as if we hoped so to borrow some pure and steadfast virtue, which will stead us in all seasons.

. . . .

Nature confounds her summer distinctions at this season. The heavens seem to be nearer the earth. The elements are less reserved and distinct. Water turns to ice, rain to snow. The day is but a Scandinavian night. The winter is an arctic summer.

How much more living is the life that is in nature, the furred life which still survives the stinging nights, and, from amidst fields and woods covered with frost and snow, sees the sun rise.

> "The foodless wilds
> Pour forth their brown inhabitants."

The gray squirrel and rabbit are brisk and playful in the remote glens, even on the morning of the cold Friday. Here is our Lapland and Labrador, and for our Esquimaux and Knistenaux, Dog-ribbed Indians, Novazemblaites, and Spitzbergeners, are there not the ice-cutter and wood-chopper, the fox, muskrat, and mink?

Still, in the midst of the arctic day, we may trace the summer to its retreats, and sympathize with some contemporary life. Stretched over the brooks, in the midst of the frost-bound meadows, we may observe the submarine cottages of the caddice worms, the larvae of the Plicipennes. Their small cylindrical cases built around themselves, composed of flags, sticks, grass, and withered leaves, shells, and pebbles, in form and color like the wrecks which strew the bottom, —now drifting along over the pebbly bottom, now whirling in tiny eddies and dashing down steep falls, or sweeping rapidly along with the current, or else swaying to and fro at the end of some grass-blade or root. Anon they will leave their sunken habitations, and, crawling up the stems of plants, or to the surface, like gnats, as perfect insects henceforth, flutter over the surface of the water, or sacrifice their short lives in the flame of our candles at evening. Down yonder little glen the shrubs are drooping under their burden, and the red alder-berries contrast with the white ground. Here are the marks of a myriad feet which have already been abroad. The sun rises as proudly over such a glen, as over the valley of the Seine or the Tiber, and it seems the residence of a pure and self-subsistent valor, such as they never witnessed, — which never knew defeat nor fear. Here reign the simplicity and purity of a primitive age, and a health and hope far remote from towns and cities. Standing quite alone, far in the forest, while the wind is shaking down snow from the trees, and leaving the only human tracks behind us, we find our reflections of a richer variety than the life of cities. The chicadee and nuthatch are more inspiring society than statesmen and philosophers, and we shall return to these last, as to more vulgar companions. In this lonely glen, with its brook draining the slopes, its creased ice and crystals of all hues, where the spruces and hemlocks stand up on either side, and the rush and sere wild oats in the rivulet itself, our lives are more serene and worthy to contemplate.

. . . .

But now, while we have loitered, the clouds have gathered again, and a few straggling snow-flakes are beginning to descend. Faster and faster they fall, shutting out the distant objects from sight. The snow falls on every wood and field, and no crevice is forgotten; by the river and the pond, on the hill and in the valley. Quadrupeds are confined to their coverts, and the birds sit upon their perches this peaceful hour. There is not so much sound as in fair weather, but silently and gradually every slope, and the gray walls and fences, and the polished ice, and the sere leaves, which were not buried before, are concealed, and the tracks of men and beasts are lost. With so little effort does nature reassert her rule and blot out the traces of men. Hear how Homer has described the same. "The snow-flakes fall thick and fast on a winter's day. The winds are lulled, and the snow falls incessant, covering the tops of the mountains, and the hills, and the plains where the lotus-tree grows, and the cultivated fields, and they are falling by the inlets and shores of the foaming sea, but are silently dissolved by the waves." The snow levels all things, and infolds them deeper in the bosom of nature, as, in the slow summer, vegetation creeps up to the entablature of the temple, and the turrets of the castle, and helps her to prevail over art.

The surly night-wind rustles through the wood, and warns us to retrace our steps, while the sun goes down behind the thickening storm, and birds seek their roosts, and cattle their stalls.

> "Drooping the lab'rer ox
> Stands covered o'er with snow, and *now* demands
> The fruit of all his toil."

Though winter is represented in the almanac as an old man, facing the wind and sleet, and drawing his cloak about him, we rather think of him as a merry woodchopper, and warm-blooded youth, as blithe as summer. The unexplored grandeur of the storm keeps up the spirits of the traveller. It does not trifle with us, but has a sweet earnestness. In winter we lead a more inward life. Our hearts are warm and cheery, like cottages under drifts, whose windows and doors are half concealed, but from whose chimneys the smoke cheerfully ascends. The imprisoning drifts increase the sense of comfort which the house affords, and in the coldest days we are content to sit over the hearth and see the sky through the chimney top, enjoying the quiet and serene life that may be had in a warm corner by the chimney side, or feeling our pulse by listening to the low of cattle in the street, or the sound of the flail in distant barns all the long afternoon. No doubt a skilful physician could determine our health by observing how these simple and natural sounds affected us. We enjoy now, not an oriental, but a boreal leisure, around warm stoves and fireplaces, and watch the shadow of motes in the sunbeams.

Sometimes our fate grows too homely and familiarly serious ever to be cruel. Consider how for three months the human destiny is wrapped in furs. The good Hebrew Revelation takes no cognizance of all this cheerful snow. Is there no religion for the temperate and frigid zones? We know of no scripture which records the pure benignity of the gods on a New England winter night. Their praises have never been sung, only their wrath deprecated. The best scripture, after all, records but a meagre faith. Its saints live reserved and austere. Let a brave devout man spend the year in the woods of Maine or Labrador, and see if the Hebrew Scriptures speak adequately to his condition and experience, from the setting in of winter to the breaking up of the ice.

Now commences the long winter evening around the farmer's hearth, when the thoughts of the indwellers travel far abroad, and men are by nature and necessity charitable and liberal to all creatures. Now is the happy resistance to cold, when the farmer reaps his reward, and thinks of his preparedness for winter, and, through the glittering panes, sees with equanimity "the mansion of the northern bear," for now the storm is over,

> "The full ethereal round,
> Infinite worlds disclosing to the view,
> Shines out intensely keen; and all one cope
> Of starry glitter glows from pole to pole."

John Muir
excerpts from
The Wild Parks and Forest Reservations of the West
(1901)

The most extensive, least spoiled, and most unspoilable of the gardens of the continent are the vast tundras of Alaska. In summer they extend smooth, even, undulating, continuous beds of flowers and leaves from about lat. 62° to the shores of the Arctic Ocean; and in winter sheets of snowflowers make all the country shine, one mass of white radiance like a star. Nor are these Arctic plant people the pitiful frost-pinched unfortunates they are guessed to be by those who have never seen them. Though lowly in stature, keeping near the frozen ground as if loving it, they are bright and cheery, and speak Nature's love as plainly as their big relatives of the South. Tenderly happed and tucked in beneath downy snow to sleep through the long, white winter, they make haste to bloom in the spring without trying to grow tall, though some rise high enough to ripple and wave in the wind, and display masses of color—yellow, purple, and blue—so rich that they look like beds of rainbows, and are visible miles and miles away. . . .

As early as June one may find the showy Geum glaciale in flower, and the dwarf willows putting forth myriads of fuzzy catkins, to be followed quickly, especially on the dryer ground, by mertensia, eritrichium, polemonium, oxytropis, astragalus, lathyrus, lupinus, myosotis, dodecatheon, arnica, chrysanthemum, nardosmia, saussurea, senecio, erigeron, matrecaria, caltha, valeriana, stellaria, Tofieldia, polygonum, papaver, phlox, lychnis, cheiranthus, Linnæa, and a host of drabas, saxifrages, and heathworts, with bright stars and bells in glorious profusion, particularly Cassiope, Andromeda, ledum, pyrola, and vaccinium—Cassiope the most abundant and beautiful of them all. Many grasses also grow here, and wave fine purple spikes and panicles over the other flowers—poa, aira, calamagrostis, alopecurus, trisetum, elymus, festuca, glyceria, etc. Even ferns are found thus far north, carefully and comfortably unrolling their precious fronds—aspidium, cystopteris, and woodsia, all growing on a sumptuous bed of mosses and lichens; not the scaly lichens seen on rails and trees and fallen logs to the southward, but massive, round-headed, finely colored plants like corals, wonderfully beautiful, worth going round the world to see. I should like to mention all the plant friends I found in a summer's wanderings in this cool reserve, but I fear few would care to read their names, although everybody, I am sure, would love them could they see them blooming and rejoicing at home.

On my last visit to the region about Kotzebue Sound, near the middle of September, 1881, the weather was so fine and mellow that it suggested the Indian summer of the Eastern States. The winds were hushed, the tundra glowed in creamy golden sunshine, and the colors of the ripe foliage of the heathworts, willows, and birch—red, purple, and yellow, in pure bright tones—were enriched with those of berries which were scattered everywhere, as if they had been showered from the clouds like hail. When I was back a mile or two from the shore, reveling in this color-glory, and thinking how fine it would be could I cut a square of the tundra sod of conventional picture size, frame it, and hang it among the paintings on my

From John Muir, "The Wild Parks and Forest Reservations of the West," in *Our National Parks* (Boston and New York: The Riverside Press, Houghton Mifflin, 1901).

study walls at home, saying to myself, "Such a Nature painting taken at random from any part of the thousand-mile bog would make the other pictures look dim and coarse," I heard merry shouting, and, looking round, saw a band of Eskimos—men, women, and children, loose and hairy like wild animals—running towards me. I could not guess at first what they were seeking, for they seldom leave the shore; but soon they told me, as they threw themselves down, sprawling and laughing, on the mellow bog, and began to feast on the berries. A lively picture they made, and a pleasant one, as they frightened the whirring ptarmigans, and surprised their oily stomachs with the beautiful acid berries of many kinds, and filled sealskin bags with them to carry away for festive days in winter.

Nowhere else on my travels have I seen so much warmblooded, rejoicing life as in this grand Arctic reservation, by so many regarded as desolate. Not only are there whales in abundance along the shores, and innumerable seals, walruses, and white bears, but on the tundras great herds of fat reindeer and wild sheep, foxes, hares, mice, piping marmots, and birds. Perhaps more birds are born here than in any other region of equal extent on the continent. Not only do strong-winged hawks, eagles, and water-fowl, to whom the length of the continent is merely a pleasant excursion, come up here every summer in great numbers, but also many short-winged warblers, thrushes, and finches, repairing hither to rear their young in safety, reinforce the plant bloom with their plumage, and sweeten the wilderness with song; flying all the way, some of them, from Florida, Mexico, and Central America. In coming north they are coming home, for they were born here, and they go south only to spend the winter months, as New Englanders go to Florida. Sweet-voiced troubadours, they sing in orange groves and vine-clad magnolia woods in winter, in thickets of dwarf birch and alder in summer, and sing and chatter more or less all the way back and forth, keeping the whole country glad. Oftentimes, in New England, just as the last snow-patches are melting and the sap in the maples begins to flow, the blessed wanderers may be heard about orchards and the edges of fields where they have stopped to glean a scanty meal, not tarrying long, knowing they have far to go. Tracing the footsteps of spring, they arrive in their tundra homes in June or July, and set out on their return journey in September, or as soon as their families are able to fly well.

This is Nature's own reservation, and every lover of wilderness will rejoice with me that by kindly frost it is so well defended.

Aldo Leopold
Thinking Like a Mountain
(1949)

A deep chesty bawl echoes from rimrock to rimrock, rolls down the mountain, and fades into the far blackness of the night. It is an outburst of wild defiant sorrow, and of contempt for all the adversities of the world. Every living thing (and perhaps many a dead one as well) pays heed to that call. To the deer it is a reminder of the way of all flesh, to the pine a forecast of midnight scuffles and of blood upon the snow, to the coyote a promise of gleanings to come, to the cowman a threat of red ink at the bank, to the hunter a challenge of fang against bullet. Yet behind these obvious and immediate hopes and fears there lies a deeper meaning, known only to the mountain itself. Only the mountain has lived long enough to listen objectively to the howl of a wolf.

Those unable to decipher the hidden meaning know nevertheless that it is there, for it is felt in all wolf country, and distinguishes that country from all other land. It tingles in the spine of all who hear wolves by night, or who scan their tracks by day. Even without sight or sound of wolf, it is implicit in a hundred small events: the midnight whinny of a pack horse, the rattle of rolling rocks, the bound of a fleeing deer, the way shadows lie under the spruces. Only the ineducable tyro can fail to sense the presence or absence of wolves, or the fact that mountains have a secret opinion about them.

My own conviction on this score dates from the day I saw a wolf die. We were eating lunch on a high rimrock, at the foot of which a turbulent river elbowed its way. We saw what we thought was a doe fording the torrent, her breast awash in white water. When she climbed the bank toward us and shook out her tail, we realized our error: it was a wolf. A half-dozen others, evidently grown pups, sprang from the willows and all joined in a welcoming melee of wagging tails and playful maulings. What was literally a pile of wolves writhed and tumbled in the center of an open flat at the foot of our rimrock.

In those days we had never heard of passing up a chance to kill a wolf. In a second we were pumping lead into the pack, but with more excitement than accuracy: how to aim a steep downhill shot is always confusing. When our rifles were empty, the old wolf was down, and a pup was dragging a leg into impassable slide-rocks.

We reached the old wolf in time to watch a fierce green fire dying in her eyes. I realized then, and have known ever since, that there was something new to me in those eyes—something known only to her and to the mountain. I was young then, and full of trigger-itch; I thought that because fewer wolves meant more deer, that no wolves would mean hunters' paradise. But after seeing the green fire die, I sensed that neither the wolf nor the mountain agreed with such a view.

Since then I have lived to see state after state extirpate its wolves. I have watched the face of many a newly wolfless mountain, and seen the south-facing slopes wrinkle with a maze of new deer trails. I have seen every edible bush and seedling browsed, first to anaemic desuetude, and then to death. I have seen every edible

Aldo Leopold, "Thinking Like a Mountain," in *A Sand County Almanac: With Essays on Conservation from Round River* (New York: Oxford University Press, 1949). By permission of Oxford University Press, Inc.

tree defoliated to the height of a saddlehorn. Such a mountain looks as if someone had given God a new pruning shears, and forbidden Him all other exercise. In the end the starved bones of the hoped-for deer herd, dead of its own too-much, bleach with the bones of the dead sage, or molder under the high-lined junipers.

I now suspect that just as a deer herd lives in mortal fear of its wolves, so does a mountain live in mortal fear of its deer. And perhaps with better cause, for while a buck pulled down by wolves can be replaced in two or three years, a range pulled down by too many deer may fail of replacement in as many decades. So also with cows. The cowman who cleans his range of wolves does not realize that he is taking over the wolf's job of trimming the herd to fit the range. He has not learned to think like a mountain. Hence we have dustbowls, and rivers washing the future into the sea.

We all strive for safety, prosperity, comfort, long life, and dullness. The deer strives with his supple legs, the cowman with trap and poison, the statesman with pen, the most of us with machines, votes, and dollars, but it all comes to the same thing: peace in our time. A measure of success in this is all well enough, and perhaps is a requisite to objective thinking, but too much safety seems to yield only danger in the long run. Perhaps this is behind Thoreau's dictum: In wildness is the salvation of the world. Perhaps this is the hidden meaning in the howl of the wolf, long known among mountains, but seldom perceived among men.

Rachel Carson
A Fable for Tomorrow
(1962)

There was once a town in the heart of America where all life seemed to live in harmony with its surroundings. The town lay in the midst of a checkerboard of prosperous farms, with fields of grain and hillsides of orchards where, in spring, white clouds of bloom drifted above the green fields. In autumn, oak and maple and birch set up a blaze of color that flamed and flickered across a backdrop of pines. Then foxes barked in the hills and deer silently crossed the fields, half hidden in the mists of the fall mornings.

Along the roads, laurel, viburnum and alder, great ferns and wildflowers delighted the traveler's eye through much of the year. Even in winter the roadsides were places of beauty, where countless birds came to feed on the berries and on the seed heads of the dried weeds rising above the snow. The countryside was, in fact, famous for the abundance and variety of its bird life, and when the flood of migrants was pouring through in spring and fall people traveled from great distances to observe them. Others came to fish the streams, which flowed clear and cold out of the hills and contained shady pools where trout lay. So it had been from the days many years ago when the first settlers raised their houses, sank their wells, and built their barns.

Then a strange blight crept over the area and everything began to change. Some evil spell had settled on the community: mysterious maladies swept the flocks of chickens; the cattle and sheep sickened and died. Everywhere was a shadow of death. The farmers spoke of much illness among their families. In the town the doctors had become more and more puzzled by new kinds of sickness appearing among their patients. There had been several sudden and unexplained deaths, not only among adults but even among children, who would be stricken suddenly while at play and die within a few hours.

There was a strange stillness. The birds, for example—where had they gone? Many people spoke of them, puzzled and disturbed. The feeding stations in the backyards were deserted. The few birds seen anywhere were moribund; they trembled violently and could not fly. It was a spring without voices. On the mornings that had once throbbed with the dawn chorus of robins, catbirds, doves, jays, wrens, and scores of other bird voices there was now no sound; only silence lay over the fields and woods and marsh.

On the farms the hens brooded, but no chicks hatched. The farmers complained that they were unable to raise any pigs—the litters were small and the young survived only a few days. The apple trees were coming into bloom but no bees droned among the blossoms, so there was no pollination and there would be no fruit.

The roadsides, once so attractive, were now lined with browned and withered vegetation as though swept by fire. These, too, were silent, deserted by all living things. Even the streams were now lifeless. Anglers no longer visited them, for all the fish had died.

In the gutters under the eaves and between the shingles of the roofs, a white granular powder still showed a few patches; some weeks before it had fallen like snow upon the roofs and the lawns, the fields and streams.

No witchcraft, no enemy action had silenced the rebirth of new life in this stricken world. The people had done it themselves.

This town does not actually exist, but it might easily have a thousand counterparts in America or elsewhere in the world. I know of no community that has experienced all the misfortunes I describe. Yet every one of these disasters has actually happened somewhere, and many real communities have already suffered a substantial number of them. A grim specter has crept upon us almost unnoticed, and this imagined tragedy may easily become a stark reality we all shall know.

What has already silenced the voices of spring in countless towns in America? This book is an attempt to explain.

Garrett Hardin
The Tragedy of the Commons
(1968)

At the end of a thoughtful article on the future of nuclear war, J. B. Wiesner and H. F. York concluded that: "both sides in the arms race are . . . . confronted by the dilemma of steadily increasing military power and steadily decreasing national security. *It is our considered professional judgement that this dilemma has no technical solution.* If the great powers continue to look for solutions in the area of science and technology only, the result will be to worsen the situation."

I would like to focus your attention not on the subject of the article (national security in a nuclear world) but on the kind of conclusion they reached, namely that there is no technical solution to the problem. An implicit and almost universal assumption of discussions published in professional and semipopular scientific journals is that the problem under discussion has a technical solution. A technical solution may be defined as one that requires a change only in the techniques of the natural sciences, demanding little or nothing in the way of change in human values or ideas of morality.

In our day (though not in earlier times) technical solutions are always welcome. Because of previous failures in prophecy, it takes courage to assert that a desired technical solution is not possible. Wiesner and York exhibited this courage; publishing in a science journal, they insisted that the solution to the problem was not to be found in the natural sciences. They cautiously qualified their statement with the phrase, "it is our considered professional judgment . . . ." Whether they were right or not is not the concern of the present article. Rather, the concern here is with the important concept of a class of human problems which can be called "no technical solution problems," and more specifically, with the identification and discussion of one of these.

It is easy to show that the class is not a null class. Recall the game of tick-tack-toe. Consider the problem. "How can I win the game of tick-tack-toe?" It is well known that I cannot, if I assume (in keeping with the conventions of game theory) that my opponent understands the game perfectly. Put another way, there is no "technical solution" to the problem. I can win only by giving a radical meaning to the word "win." I can hit my opponent over the head; or I can falsify the records. Every way in which I "win" involves, in some sense, an abandonment of the game, as we intuitively understand it. (I can also, of course, openly abandon the game— refuse to play it. This is what most adults do.)

The class of "no technical solution problems" has members. My thesis is that the "popular problem," as conventionally conceived, is a member of this class. How it is conventionally conceived needs some comment. It is fair to say that most people who anguish over the population problem are trying to find a way to avoid the evils of overpopulation without relinquishing any of the privileges they now enjoy. They think that farming the seas or developing new strains of wheat will solve the problem—technologically. I try to show here that the solution they seek cannot be found. The population problem cannot be solved in a technical way, any more than can the problem of winning the game of tick-tack-toe.

From Garrett Hardin, "The Tragedy of the Commons," *Science* 162 (1968): 1243–48.
Reprinted with permission from AAAS.

What Shall We Maximize?

Population, as Malthus said, naturally tends to grow "geometrically" or, as we would now say, exponentially. In a finite world this means that the per-capita share of the world's goods must decrease. Is ours a finite world?

A fair defense can be put forward for the view that the world is infinite; or that we do not know that it is not. But, in terms of the practical problems that we must face in the next few generations with the foreseeable technology, it is clear that we will greatly increase human misery if we do not, during the immediate future, assume that the world available to the terrestrial human population is finite. "Space" is no escape.

A finite world can support only a finite population; therefore, population growth must eventually equal zero. (The case of perpetual wide fluctuations above and below zero is a trivial variant that need not be discussed.) When this condition is met, what will be the situation of mankind? Specifically, can Bentham's goal of "the greatest good for the greatest number" be realized?

No—for two reasons, each sufficient by itself. The first is a theoretical one. It is not mathematically possible to maximize for two (or more) variables at the same time. This was clearly stated by von Neumann and Morgenstern, but the principle is implicit in the theory of partial differential equations, dating back at least to D'Alembert (1717–1783).

The second reason springs directly from biological facts. To live, any organism must have a source of energy (for example, food). This energy is utilized for two purposes: mere maintenance and work. For man, maintenance of life requires about 1600 kilocalories a day ("maintenance calories"). Anything that he does over and above merely staying alive will be defined as work, and is supported by "work calories" which he takes in. Work calories are used not only for what we call work in common speech; they are also required for all forms of enjoyment, from swimming and automobile racing to playing music and writing poetry. If our goal is to maximize population it is obvious what we must do: We must make the work calories per person approach as close to zero as possible. No gourmet meals, no vacations, no sports, no music, no literature, no art. . . .

. . . .

I think that everyone will grant, without argument or proof, that maximizing population does not maximize goods. Bentham's goal is impossible.

In reaching this conclusion I have made the usual assumption that it is the acquisition of energy that is the problem. The appearance of atomic energy has led some to question this assumption. However, given an infinite source of energy, population growth still produces an inescapable problem. The problem of the acquisition of energy is replaced by the problem of its dissipation, as J. H. Fremlin has so wittily shown. The arithmetic signs in the analysis are, as it were, reversed; but Bentham's goal is unobtainable.

The optimum population is, then, less than the maximum. The difficulty of defining the optimum is enormous; so far as I know, no one has seriously tackled this problem. Reaching an acceptable and stable solution will surely require more than one generation of hard analytical work—and much persuasion.

We want the maximum good per person; but what is good? To one person it is wilderness, to another it is ski lodges for thousands. To one it is estuaries to nourish ducks for hunters to shoot; to another it is factory land. Comparing one good with another is, we usually say, impossible because goods are incommensurable. Incommensurables cannot be compared.

Theoretically this may be true; but in real life incommensurables are commensurable. Only a criterion of judgment and a system of weighting are needed. In nature the criterion is survival. Is it better for a species to be small and hideable, or large and powerful? Natural selection commensurates the incommensurables. The compromise achieved depends on a natural weighting of the values of the variables.

Man must imitate this process. There is no doubt that in fact he already does, but unconsciously. It is when the hidden decisions are made explicit that the arguments begin. The problem for the years ahead is to work out an acceptable theory of weighting. Synergistic effects, nonlinear variation, and difficulties in discounting the future make the intellectual problem difficult, but not (in principle) insoluble.

Has any cultural group solved this practical problem at the present time, even on an intuitive level? One simple fact proves that none has: there is no prosperous population in the world today that has, and has had for some time, a growth rate of zero. Any people that has intuitively identified its optimum point will soon reach it, after which its growth rate becomes and remains zero.

Of course, a positive growth rate might be taken as evidence that a population is below its optimum. However, by any reasonable standards, the most rapidly growing populations on earth today are (in general) the most miserable. This association (which need not be invariable) casts doubt on the optimistic assumption that the positive growth rate of a population is evidence that it has yet to reach its optimum.

We can make little progress in working toward optimum population size until we explicitly exorcise the spirit of Adam Smith in the field of practical demography. In economic affairs, *The Wealth of Nations* (1776) popularized the "invisible hand," the idea that an individual who "intends only his own gain," is, as it were, "led by an invisible hand to promote . . . the public interest." Adam Smith did not assert that this was invariably true, and perhaps neither did any of his followers. But he contributed to a dominant tendency of thought that has ever since interfered with positive action based on rational analysis, namely, the tendency to assume that decisions reached individually will, in fact, be the best decisions for an entire society. If this assumption is correct it justifies the continuance of our present policy of *laissez faire* in reproduction. If it is correct we can assume that men will control their individual fecundity so as to produce the optimum population. If the assumption is not correct, we need to reexamine our individual freedoms to see which ones are defensible.

Tragedy of Freedom in a Commons

The rebuttal to the invisible hand in population control is to be found in a scenario first sketched in a little-known pamphlet in 1833 by a mathematical amateur named William Forster Lloyd (1794–1852). We may well call it "the tragedy of the commons," using the word "tragedy" as the philosopher Whitehead used it. "The essence of dramatic tragedy is not unhappiness. It resides in the solemnity of the remorseless working of things." He then goes on to say, "This inevitableness of destiny can only be illustrated in terms of human life by incidents which in fact involve unhappiness. For it is only by them that the futility of escape can be made evident in the drama."

The tragedy of the commons develops in this way. Picture a pasture open to all. It is to be expected that each herdsman will try to keep as many cattle as possible on the commons. Such an arrangement may work reasonably satisfactorily for centuries because tribal wars, poaching, and disease keep the numbers of both man and beast well below the carrying capacity of the land. Finally, however, comes the day of reckoning, that is, the day when the long-desired goal of social stability becomes a reality. At this point, the inherent logic of the commons remorselessly generates tragedy.

As a rational being, each herdsman seeks to maximize his gain. Explicitly or implicitly, more or less consciously, he asks, "What is the utility *to me* of adding one more animal to my herd?" This utility has one negative and one positive component.

1. The positive component is a function of the increment of one animal. Since the herdsman receives all the proceeds from the sale of the additional animal, the positive utility is nearly +1.

2. The negative component is a function of the additional overgrazing created by one more animal. Since, however, the effects of overgrazing are shared by all the herdsmen, the negative utility for any particular decision-making herdsman is only a fraction of -1.

Adding together the component partial utilities, the rational herdsman concludes that the only sensible course for him to pursue is to add another animal to his herd. And another. . . . But this is the conclusion reached by each and every rational herdsman sharing a commons. Therein is the tragedy. Each man is locked into a system that compels him to increase his herd without limit—in a world that is limited. Ruin is the destination toward which all men rush, each pursuing his own best interest in a society that believes in the freedom of the commons. Freedom in a commons brings ruin to all.

Some would say that this is a platitude. Would that it were! In a sense, it was learned thousands of years ago, but natural selection favors the forces of psychological denial. The individual benefits as an individual from his ability to deny the truth even though society as a whole, of which he is a part, suffers. Education can counteract the natural tendency to do the wrong thing, but the inexorable succession of generations requires that the basis for this knowledge be constantly refreshed.

A simple incident that occurred a few years ago in Leominster, Massachusetts, shows how perishable the knowledge is. During the Christmas shopping season the parking meters downtown were covered with plastic bags that bore tags reading: "Do not open until after Christmas. Free parking courtesy of the mayor and city council." In other words, facing the prospect of an increased demand for already scarce space, the city fathers reinstituted the system of the commons. (Cynically, we suspect that they gained more votes than they lost by this retrogressive act.)

In an approximate way, the logic of the commons has been understood for a long time, perhaps since the discovery of agriculture or the invention of private property in real estate. But it is understood mostly only in special cases which are not sufficiently generalized. Even at this late date, cattlemen leasing national land on the Western ranges demonstrate no more than an ambivalent understanding, in constantly pressuring federal authorities to increase the head count to the point where overgrazing produces erosion and weed-dominance. Likewise, the oceans of the world continue to suffer from the survival of the philosophy of the commons. Maritime nations still respond automatically to the shibboleth of the "freedom of the seas." Professing to believe in the "inexhaustible resources of the oceans," they bring species after species of fish and whales closer to extinction.

The National Parks present another instance of the working out of the tragedy of the commons. At present, they are open to all, without limit. The parks themselves are limited in extent—there is only one Yosemite Valley—whereas population seems to grow without limit. The values that visitors seek in the parks are steadily eroded. Plainly, we must soon cease to treat the parks as commons or they will be of no value to anyone.

What shall we do? We have several options. We might sell them off as private property. We might keep them as public property, but allocate the right to enter them. The allocation might be on the basis of wealth, by the use of an auction system. It might be on the basis of merit, as defined by some agreed-upon standards. It might be by lottery. Or it might be on a first-come, first-served basis, administered to long queues. These, I think, are all objectionable. But we must choose—or acquiesce in the destruction of the commons that we call our National Parks.

Selected Bibliography

Abbey, E. *The Monkeywrench Gang*. New York: Avon, 1973.

Agyeman, J., B. Doppelt, K. Lynn, and H. Hatic, "The Climate Justice Link: Communicating Risk with Low Income and Minority Audiences." In *Creating a Climate for Change,* edited by S. C. Moser and L. Dilling, 119–138. Cambridge, MA: Cambridge University Press, 2007.

Alders, H. "Towards Biodiversity in Politics." In *Biodiversity and Global Change,* edited by O. T. Solbrig, H. M. van Emden, and P. G. W. J. van Oordt, 9–12. Oxon, UK: CAB International, 1994.

Allen, B. L. *Uneasy Alchemy: Citizens and Experts in Louisiana's Chemical Corridor Disputes.* Cambridge, MA: MIT Press, 2003.

Anderson, T. L., and D. R. Leal. *Free Market Environmentalism.* Boulder, CO: Westview, 1991.

Anthony, C. "Foreword." In *The Struggle for Ecological Democracy: Environmental Justice Movements in the U.S.,* edited by D. Faber, i–iv. New York: Guilford, 1998.

Antilla, L. "Climate Skepticism: US Newspaper Coverage of the Science of Climate Change." *Global Climate Change* 15 (2005): 338–352.

Armbruster-Sandoval, R. *Globalization and Cross-Border Labor Solidarity in the Americas: The Anti-Sweatshop Movement and the Struggle for Social Justice.* New York: Routledge, 2005.

Arnold, R. "Overcoming Ideology." In *A Wolf in the Garden: The Land Rights Movement and the New Environmental Debate,* eds. Phillip D. Brick and R. McGregor Cawley, 15–26. Lanham, MD: Rowman & Littlefield, 1996.

Bailey, R. *Eco-Scam: The False Prophets of Ecological Apocalypse.* New York: St. Martin's, 1993.

Banerjee, S., C. S. Gulas, and E. Iyer. "Shades of Green: A Multidimensional Analysis of Environmental Advertising." *Journal of Advertising* 24 (1995): 21–31.

Barker, C. *Making Sense of Cultural Studies: Cultural Problems and Critical Debates.* Thousand Oaks, CA: Sage, 2002.

Bast, J. L., P. J. Hill, and R. Rue, *Eco-Sanity: A Common Sense Guide to Environmentalism.* Lanham, MD: Madison, 1994.

Beauregard, R. A. *When America Became Suburban.* Minneapolis: University of Minnesota Press, 2006.

Becher, A. *Biodiversity: A Reference Handbook.* Santa Barbara, CA: ABC-CLIO, 1998.

Beck, U. "Risk Society and the Provident State." Translated by M. Chalmers. In *Risk, Environment, and Modernity: Towards a New Ecology,* edited by S. Lash, B. Szerszynski, and B. Wynne, 27–43. Thousand Oaks, CA: Sage, 1996.

Beder, S. *Free Market Missionaries: The Corporate Manipulation of Community Values.* London: Earthscan, 2006.

Been, V. "Locally Undesirable Land Uses in Minority Neighborhoods: Disproportionate Siting or Market Dynamics?" *The Yale Law Journal* 103 (1994): 1383–1422.

Benton, L. A., and J. R. Short. *Environmental Discourse and Practice.* Malden, MA: Blackwell, 1999.

Berry, T. *The Great Work: Our Way into the Future.* New York: Bell Tower, 1999.

Berry, W. *The Unsettling of America.* San Francisco: Sierra Club Books, 1977.

Berry, W. *The Gift of Good Land: Further Essays Cultural and Agricultural.* San Francisco: North Point, 1981.

Berry, W. *Creative Energy: Bearing Witness for the Earth.* San Francisco: Sierra Club Books, 1988.

Bolch, B., and H. Lyons, *Apocalypse Not: Science, Economics, and Environmentalism.* Washington, DC: Cato Institute, 1993.

Bookchin, M. *Post-Scarcity Anarchism.* Berkeley, CA: Ramparts, 1971.

Bookchin, M. *Our Synthetic Environment.* New York: Knopf, 1974.

Bookchin, M. "Social Ecology versus Deep Ecology." *Socialist Review* 18 (1988): 28.

Bookchin, M. "Death of a Small Planet." *Progressive,* August 1989, 19–23.

Bookchin, M. "What is Social Ecology?" In *Environmental Philosophy: From Animal Rights to Radical Ecology,* edited by M. E. Zimmerman, J. B. Callicott, G. Sessions, K. J. Warren, and J. Clark, 354–373. Englewood Cliffs, NJ: Prentice Hall, 1993.

Boorstin, D. "The Rhetoric of Democracy." In *American Mass Media,* edited by R. Atwan, B. Orton, and W. Vesterman, 45–51. New York: Random House, 1982.

Bormann, E. "Symbolic Convergence Theory: A Communication Formulation." *Journal of Communication* 35 (1985): 128–138.

Bostrom, A., and D. Lashoff. "Weather or Climate Change?" in *Creating a Climate for Change,* edited by S. C. Moser and L. Dilling, 31–43. Cambridge, MA: Cambridge University Press, 2007.

Boykoff, M. T. "Flogging a Dead Norm? Newspaper Coverage of Anthropogenic Climate Change in the United States and the United Kingdom from 2003 to 2006." *Area* 39 (December 2007): 470–481.

Boykoff, M. T., and J. M Boykoff. "Balance as Bias: Global Warming and the US Prestige Press." *Global Environmental Change* 14 (2004): 125–126.

Bradford, G. "Toward a Deep Social Ecology." In *Environmental Philosophy: From Animal Rights to Radical Ecology,* edited by M. E. Zimmerman, J. B. Callicott, G. Sessions, K. J. Warren, and J. Clark, 418–437. Englewood Cliffs, NJ: Prentice Hall, 1993.

Brick, P. "Determined Opposition: The Wise Use Movement Challenges Environmentalism." In *Landmark Essays on Rhetoric and the Environment,* edited by C. Waddell, 195–208. Mahwah, NJ: Erlbaum, 1998.

Bright, C. *Life out of Bounds.* New York: Norton, 1998.

Bright, C. "Anticipating Environmental 'Surprise.'" In *State of the World 2000: Worldwatch Institute Report on Progress toward a Sustainable Society,* edited by L. R. Brown, C. Flavin, and H. French, 22–38. New York: Norton, 2000.

Brion, D. J. *Essential Industry and the NIMBY Phenomenon.* New York: Quorum, 1991.

Brook, E. J. "Atmospheric Science: Tiny Bubbles Tell All." *Science* 310 (November 25, 2005): 1285–1287.

Brummett, B. *Rhetoric in Popular Culture.* New York: St. Martin's, 1994.

Bruner, M., and M. Oeschlaeger, "Rhetoric, Environmentalism, and Environmental Ethics." In *Landmark Essays on Rhetoric and the Environment,* edited by C. Wadell, 209–225. Mahwah, NJ: Erlbaum, 1998.

Bryant, B., ed. *Environmental Justice: Issues, Policies, and Solutions.* Washington DC: Island, 1995.

Bryant, B., and P. Mohai, "The Michigan Conference: A Turning Point." *EPA Journal* 18 (March/April 1992): 9–10.

Bryant, D., L. Burke, J. W. McManus, and M. Spalding. *Reefs at Risk: A Map-Based Indicator of Threats to the World's Coral Reefs.* Washington, DC: World Resources Institute, 1998.

Bryant, D., D. Nielson, and L. Tangley. *The Last Frontier Forests: Ecosystems and Economies on the Edge.* Washington, DC: World Resources Institute, 1997.

Bryson, B. *The Mother Tongue: English and How it Got that Way.* New York: Avon, 1990.

Bsumek, P. "The Idea of Rhetoric in the Field of Environmental Communication: Reflecting on 'Ways of Knowing' in Our Own Field and Advancing a Theory of Rhetorical Realism." In *Proceedings of the Seventh Biennial Conference on Communication and Environment,* edited by G. B. Walker and W. J. Kinsella, 236–246. Sublimity, OR: July 2003.

Bullard, R. D., ed. *Confronting Environmental Racism: Voices from the Grassroots.* Boston: South End, 1993.

Bullard, R. D. "Residential Segregation and Urban Quality of Life." In *Environmental Justice: Issues, Policies, and Solutions,* edited by B. Bryant, 76–85. Washington, DC: Island, 1995.

Bullard, R. D., and B. H. Wright. "Environmentalism and the Politics of Equity: Emergent Trends in the Black Community." *Midwestern Review of Sociology* 12 (1987): 21–37.

Bullis, C. "Retalking Environmental Discourse from Feminist Perspectives: The Radical Potential of Ecofeminism." In *The Symbolic Earth: Discourse and the Creation of the Environment,* edited by J. G. Cantrill and C. Oravec, 123–148. Lexington: University Press of Kentucky, 1996.

Burke, K. *A Grammar of Motives.* New York: Prentice Hall, 1945.

Burke, K. *The Philosophy of Literary Form: Studies in Symbolic Action.* New York: Vintage, 1957/1973.

Burke, K. *Language as Symbolic Action: Essays on Life, Literature, and Method.* Berkeley: University of California Press, 1966.

Burrows, W. "Science Meets the Press: Bad Chemistry." *Sciences,* April 1980, 15–19.

Cahn, M. A. *Environmental Deceptions.* Albany: State University of New York Press, 1995.

Callahan, T. "Trees and Volcanoes Cause Smog! More Myths from the 'Wise Use' Movement." *The Humanist,* January/February 1996, 29–34.

Callenbach, E. *Ecotopia.* Berkeley: Banyan Tree, 1975.

Cantrill, J. G., and C. L. Oravec, eds. *The Symbolic Earth: Discourse and the Creation of the Environment.* Lexington: University Press of Kentucky, 1996.

Capra, F. *The Web of Life: A New Scientific Understanding of Living Systems.* New York: Anchor, 1996.

Carson, R. *Silent Spring.* New York: Fawcett, 1962.

Check, T. "Re-thinking the Irreparable." Paper presented at the Annual Convention of the National Communication Association, Chicago, IL, November 1999.

Churchill, W., and W. LaDuke. "Native America: The Political Economy of Radioactive Colonialism." *Critical Sociology* 13 (1986): 51–78.

Clapp, J. "Distancing of Waste: Over Consumption in a Global Economy." In *Confronting Consumption,* edited by T. Princen, M. Maniates, and K. Conca, 155–176. Cambridge, MA: MIT Press, 2002.

Cohen, J., and N. Solomon. *Through the Media Looking Glass: Decoding Bias and Blather in the News.* Monroe, ME: Common Courage, 1995.

Cohen, J. E. *How Many People Can the Earth Support?* New York: Norton, 1995.

Cole, L. W., and S. R. Foster. *From the Ground Up: Environmental Racism and the Rise of the Environmental Justice Movement.* New York: New York University Press, 2001.

Commoner, B. *The Closing Circle: Man, Nature, and Technology.* New York: Knopf, 1971.

Coontz, S. *The Way We Never Were: American Families and the Nostalgia Trap.* New York: Basic Books, 1992.

Corbett, J. B. "A Faint Green Sell: Advertising and the Natural World." In *Enviropop: Studies in Environmental Rhetoric and Popular Culture,* edited by M. Meister and P. M. Japp, 141–160. Westport, CT: Praeger, 2002.

Corbett, J. B., and J. L. Durfee. "Testing Public (Un)certainty of Science Media Representations of Global Warming." *Science Communication* 26 (December 2004): 129–159.

Cox, J. R. "The Die is Cast: Topical and Ontological Dimensions of a *Locus* of the Irreparable." *Quarterly Journal of Speech* 68 (1982): 227–239.

Cox, J. R. "Reclaiming the 'Indecorous' Voice: Public Participation by Low-Income Communities in Environmental Decision-Making." *Proceedings of the Fifth Biennial Conference on Communication and Environment,* edited by C. B. Short and D. Hardy-Short, 21–31. Flagstaff, AZ: July 1999.

Cox, J. R. "Free Trade and the Eclipse of Civil Society: Barriers to Transparency and Public Participation in NAFTA and the Free Trade Area of the Americas." In *Communication and Public Participation in Environmental Decision Making,* edited by S. P. Depoe, J. W. Delicath, and M. Aepli Elsenbeer, 201–219. Albany: State University of New York Press, 2004.

Cox, J. R. *Environmental Communication and the Public Sphere.* Thousand Oaks, CA: Sage, 2006.

Cronon, W., ed. *Uncommon Ground: Toward Reinventing Nature.* New York: Norton, 1995.

Daily, G. C., ed. *Nature's Services: Societal Dependence on Natural Ecosystems.* Washington, DC: Island, 1997.

Dance, F. E. X. "Swift, Slow, Sweet, Sour, Adazzle, Dim: What Makes Human Communication Human." *Western Journal of Speech Communication* 44 (1980): 60–63.

Daniels, S. E., and G. B. Walker. *Working through Environmental Conflict: The Collaborative Learning Approach.* Westport, CT: Praeger, 2001.

Davis, Devra. *When Smoke Ran Like Fire: Tales of Environmental Deception and the Battle against Pollution.* New York: Basic Books, 2002.

Davis, S. G. "Touch the Magic." In *Uncommon Ground: Toward Reinventing Nature,* edited by W. Cronon, 204–217. New York: Norton, 1995.

de Geus, M. *Ecological Utopias: Envisioning the Sustainable Society.* Utrecht, Netherlands: International, 1999.

de Geus, M. *The End of Over-Consumption: Towards a Lifestyle of Moderation and Self-Restraint.* Utrecht, Netherlands: International, 2003.

de Saussure, F. *Course in General Linguistics.* Edited by C. Bally and A. Sechehaye. London: Peter Owen, 1960.

Dear, M. "Understanding and Overcoming the NIMBY Syndrome." *Journal of the American Planning Association* 58 (1992): 288–301.

Delicath, J. W. "In Search of Ecotopia: 'Radical Environmentalism' and the Possibilities of Utopian Rhetorics." In *Earthtalk: Communication Empowerment for Environmental Action,* edited by S. A. Muir and T. L. Veenendall, 153–169. Westport, CT: Praeger, 1996.

DeLoach, M., M. S. Bruner, and J. S. Gossett. "An Analysis of the 'Tree-Hugger' Label." In *Enviropop: Studies in Environmental Rhetoric and Popular Culture,* edited by M. Meister and P. M. Japp, 95–110. Westport, CT: Praeger, 2002.

DeLuca, K. M. *Image Politics: The New Rhetoric of Environmental Activism.* New York: Guilford, 1999.

DeLuca, K. M. "A Wilderness Environmentalism Manifesto: Contesting the Infinite Self-Absorption of Humans." In *Environmental Justice and Environmentalism: The Social Justice Challenge to the Environmental Movement,* edited by R. Sandler and P. C. Pezzullo, 27–55. Cambridge, MA: MIT Press, 2007.

DeLuca, K. M., and A. T. Demo. "Imaging Nature: Watkins, Yosemite, and the Birth of Environmentalism." *Critical Studies in Media Communication* 17 (2000): 241–261.

Demeritt, D. "The Construction of Global Warming and the Politics of Science." *Annals of the Association of American Geographers* 91 (2001): 307–337.

Deming, A. H., and L. E. Savoy, eds. *The Colors of Nature: Culture, Identity, and the Natural World.* Minneapolis, MN: Milkweed, 2002.

Depoe, S. P. "Public Involvement: Civic Discovery and the Formation of Environmental Policy: A Comparative Analysis of the Fernald Citizens Task Force and the Fernald Health Effects Sub Committee." In *Communication and Public Participation in Environmental Decision Making,* edited by S. P. Depoe, J. W. Delicath, and M. Aepli Elsenbeer, 157–173. Albany: State University of New York Press, 2004.

Depoe, S. P., J. W. Delicath, and M. Aepli Elsenbeer, eds. *Communication and Public Participation in Environmental Decision Making.* Albany: State University of New York Press, 2004.

Derrida, J. *Of Grammatology.* Baltimore: Johns Hopkins University Press, 1976.

Devall, B., and G. Sessions, *Deep Ecology.* Salt Lake City, UT: Peregrine, 1985.

di Choro, G. "Defining Environmental Justice: Women's Voices and Grassroots Politics." *Socialists Review* 22 (1992): 93–131.

Dickerson, J. "Utopian and Dystopian Master Narratives in a Posthuman World." Paper presented at the 2005 International Communication Association Annual Meeting, New York, May 26–30, 2005.

Dowie, M. *Losing Ground: American Environmentalism at the Close of the Twentieth Century.* Cambridge, MA: MIT Press, 1995.

Dryzek, J. S. *The Politics of the Earth: Environmental Discourses,* 2nd ed. New York: Oxford University Press, 2005.

Ehrlich, P. R. *The Population Bomb.* New York: Ballantine, 1968.

Eisenberg, E. *The Ecology of Eden.* New York: Knopf, 1998.

Emerson, R. W. "Nature." In *The Great New Wilderness Debate,* edited by J. B. Callicott and M. P. Nelson, 28–30. Athens: University of Georgia Press, 1836/1998.

Erwin, T. L. "The Tropical Forest Canopy: The Heart of Biotic Diversity." In *Biodiversity,* edited by E. O. Wilson, 123–129. Washington, DC: National Academy, 1988.

Estes, J. A., M. T. Tinker, T. M. Williams, and D. F. Doak, "Killer Whale Predation on Sea Otters Linking Oceanic and Near Shore Ecosystems." *Science* 282 (October 16, 1998): 473–476.

Evernden, N. *The Social Creation of Nature.* Baltimore: Johns Hopkins University Press, 1992.

Faber, D. "A More 'Productive' Environmental Justice Politics: Movement Alliances in Massachusetts for Clean Production and Regional Equity." In *Environmental Justice and Environmentalism: The Social Justice Challenge to the Environmental Movement,* edited by R. Sandler and P. C. Pezzullo, 135–164. Cambridge, MA: MIT Press, 2007.

Farrell, T. B., and G. T. Goodnight. "Accidental Rhetoric: The Root Metaphors of Three Mile Island." *Communication Monographs* 48 (1981): 271–300.

Fisher, W. R. "Narration as a Human Communication Paradigm: The Case of Public Moral Argument." *Communication Monographs* 51 (1984): 1–22.

Fisher, W. R. *Human Communication as Narration: Toward a Philosophy of Reason, Value, and Action.* Columbia: University of South Carolina Press, 1987.

Flannery, T. *The Weather Makers: How Man Is Changing the Climate and What It Means for Life on Earth.* New York: Atlantic Monthly Press, 2005.

Foreman, D. *Ecodefense: A Field Guide to Monkeywrenching.* Tucson, AZ: Ned Ludd, 1985.

Foreman, D. *Rewilding North America: A Vision for Conservation in the 21st Century.* Washington, DC: Island, 2004.

Foss, S. K. *Rhetorical Criticism: Exploration and Practice,* 2nd ed. Prospect Heights, IL: Waveland, 1996.

Foss, S. K., K. A. Foss, and R. Trapp. *Contemporary Perspectives on Rhetoric,* 3rd ed. Prospect Heights, IL: Waveland, 2002.

Foucault, M. *The Archeology of Knowledge and the Discourse on Language,* translated by A. M. Sheridan Smith. New York: Pantheon, 1972.

Friedman, S. M. "And the Beat Goes On: The Third Decade of Environmental Journalism." *Environmental Communication Yearbook* 1 (2004): 175–187.

Fromm, H. "Full-Stomach Wilderness and the Suburban Esthetic." In *Holding Common Ground,* edited by P. Lindholdt and D. Knowles, 36–40. Spokane: Eastern Washington University Press, 2005.

Gamson, W. A., and A. Modigliani. "Media Discourse and Public Opinion on Nuclear Power: A Constructionist Approach." *American Journal of Sociology* 95 (1989): 1–10.

Gelbspan, R. *The Heat Is On: The High Stakes Battle over Earth's Threatened Climate.* Reading, MA: Addison-Wesley, 1997.

Gelbspan, R. *Boiling Point: How Politicians, Big Oil and Coal, Journalists, and Activists Have Fueled the Climate Crisis—and What We Can Do to Avert Disaster.* New York: Basic Books, 2004.

Gill, A. *Rhetoric and Human Understanding.* Prospect Heights, IL: Waveland, 1994.

Goffman, E. *The Presentation of Self in Everyday Life.* Garden City, NY: Doubleday, 1959.

Goldman, B., and L. Fitton. *Toxic Waste and Race Revisited.* Washington, DC: Center for Policy Alternatives, 1994.

Goldsmith, M. *The Science Critic: A Critical Analysis of the Popular Presentation of Science.* New York: Routledge and Kegan Paul, 1987.

Gore, A. *An Inconvenient Truth: The Planetary Emergence of Global Warming and What We Can Do About It.* New York: Rodale, 2006.

Gottlieb, R. *Forcing the Spring: The Transformation of the American Environmental Movement.* Washington, DC: Island, 1993.

Gray, J. "Trail Mix: A Sojourn on the Muddy Divide between Nature and Culture." *Text and Performance Quarterly* 30 (2010), in press.

Gregg, R. B. "The Ego Function of the Rhetoric of Protest." Reprinted in *Readings on the Rhetoric of Social Protest,* edited by C. E. Morris III and S. H. Browne, 45–60. State College, PA: Strata, 2001.

Grossberg, L. *We Gotta Get Out of This Place: Popular Conservatism and Postmodern Culture.* New York: Routledge, 1992.

Hansen, A. *The Mass Media and Environmental Issues.* London: Leicester University Press, 1993.

Hardin, G. "The Tragedy of the Commons." *Science* 162 (1968): 1243–1248.

Hardin, G. *Living within Limits: Ecology, Economics, and Population Taboos.* New York: Oxford University Press, 1993.

Hardin, G., and J. Baden, eds. *Managing the Commons.* San Francisco: Freeman, 1977.

Hardy-Short, D. C., and C. B. Short. "'Now Our Million Dollar View Is Gone': Rhetorical Presentation of the Wildland-Urban Interface during the 2000 Montana Bitterroot Fires." In *Proceedings from the Seventh Biennial Conference on Communication and the Environment,* edited by G. B. Walker and W. J. Kinsella, 247–257. Sublimity, OR: July 2003.

Hauser, G. A. *Introduction to Rhetorical Theory.* Prospect Heights, IL: Waveland, 1986.

Hawken, P. *Blessed Unrest: How the Largest Movement in the World Came into Being, and Why No One Saw It Coming.* New York: Viking, 2007.

Hayakawa, S. I. *Language in Thought and Action.* 4th ed. New York: Harcourt Brace Jovanovich, 1978.

Hays, S. P. *A History of Environmental Politics since 1945.* Pittsburgh: University of Pittsburgh Press, 2000.

Hellenbach, T. O. "The Future of Monkeywrenching." In *Ecodefense: A Field Guide to Monkeywrenching,* 2nd ed., edited by D. Foreman & B. Haywood, 18–23. Tucson, AZ: Ned Ludd, 1987.

Heller, L. K. "The Rhetoric of Ecotage: Earth First! and the Language of Violence." *Speaker and Gavel* 31 (1994): 50–65.

Henberg, M. "Wilderness, Myth, and American Character." *The Key Reporter* 59 (Spring, 1994): 7–11.

Hendry, J. "Decide, Announce, Defend: Turning the NEPA Process into an Advocacy Tool Rather Than a Decision Making Tool." In *Communication and Public Participation in Environmental Decision Making,* edited by S. P. Depoe, J. W. Delicath, and M. Aepli Elsenbeer, 99–112. Albany: State University of New York Press, 2004.

Hendry, J. "Mystery, Paradox, and Occupational Psychosis in the Stewardship Discourse of Nuclear Weapons." Paper presented at the National Communication Association Convention, Boston, November 2005.

Hendry, J. "Public Discourse and the Rhetorical Construction of the Technospecter." *Environmental Communication: A Journal of Nature and Culture* 2 (2008): 302–319.

Higgins, R. R. "Race, Pollution, and the Mastery of Nature." *Environmental Ethics* 16 (1994): 251–264.

Hintz, C., and E. Ostry, eds. *Utopian and Dystopian: Writing for Children and Young Adults.* New York: Routledge, 2003.

Hope, D. S. "Environment as Consumer Icon in Advertising Fantasy." In *Enviropop: Studies in Rhetoric and Popular Culture,* edited by M. Meister and P. M. Japp, 161–174. Westport, CT: Praeger, 2002.

Hunter, J. R. *Simple Things Won't Save the Earth*. Austin: University of Texas Press, 1997.

Irvine, S. *Beyond Green Consumerism*. London: Friends of the Earth, 1989.

Irvine, S., and A. Ponton. *A Green Manifesto: Politics for a Green Future*. London: Optima, 1988.

Jamieson, K. H., and K. K. Campbell. *The Interplay of Influence: Advertising, Politics, and the Mass Media,* 4th ed. Belmont, CA: Wadsworth, 1997.

Jans, N. *The Grizzly Maze*. New York: Penguin, 2005.

Javna, J. *50 Simple Things You Can Do to Save the Earth*. Berkeley, CA: Earth Works, 1989.

Javna, J., S. Javna, and J. Javna. *50 Simple Things You Can Do to Save the Earth: Completely New and Updated for the 21st Century*. New York: Hyperion, 2008.

Kassman, K. *Envisioning Ecotopia: The U.S. Green Movement and the Politics of Radical Social Change*. Westport, CT: Praeger, 1997.

Kates, R. W. "Success, Strain, and Surprise." *Issues in Science and Technology* 2 (1985): 46–58.

Katz, S. B., and C. R. Miller. "The Low-Level Radioactive Waste Siting Controversy in North Carolina: Toward a Rhetorical Model of Risk Communication." In *Green Culture: Environmental Rhetoric in Contemporary America,* edited by C. G. Herndl and S. C. Brown, 110–140. Madison: University of Wisconsin Press, 1996.

Kilbourne, W. E. "Green Advertising: Salvation or Oxymoron?" *Journal of Advertising* XXIV (1995): 7–19.

Killingsworth, M. J., and J. S. Palmer. *Ecospeak: Rhetoric and Environmental Politics in America*. Carbondale: Southern Illinois University Press, 1992.

Killingsworth, M. J., and J. S. Palmer. "Millennial Ecology: The Apocalyptic Narrative from *Silent Spring* to Global Warming." In *Green Culture: Environmental Rhetoric in Contemporary America,* edited by C. G. Herndl and S. C. Brown, 21–45. Madison: University of Wisconsin Press, 1996.

King, A. A. *Power and Communication*. Prospect Heights, IL: Waveland, 1987.

Kingsolver, B. *Animal, Vegetable, Miracle: A Year of Food Life*. New York: Harper Perennial, 2007.

Kinsella, W. J. "Public Expertise: A Foundation for Citizen Participation in Energy and Environmental Decisions." In *Communication and Public Participation in Environmental Decision Making,* edited by S. P. Depoe, J. W. Delicath, and M. A. Elsenbeer, 83–95. Albany: State University of New York Press, 2004.

Kinsella, W. J. "One Hundred Years of Nuclear Discourse: Four Master Themes and Their Implications for Environmental Communication." In *Environmental Communication Yearbook* 2, edited by S. Senecah, 49–72. Mahwah, NJ: Erlbaum, 2005.

Kline, B. *First Along the River: A Brief History of the U. S. Environmental Movement,* 2nd ed. San Francisco: Acada, 2000.

Kolbert, E. *Field Notes from a Catastrophe: Man, Nature, and Climate Change*. New York: Bloomsbury, 2006.

Korzybski, A. *Science and Sanity: An Introduction to Non-Aristotelian Systems and General Semantics*. Lakeville, CT: International Non-Aristotelian Library, 1958.

Lake, R. W. "Rethinking NIMBY." *Journal of the American Planning Association* 59 (1993): 87–93.

Lange, J. I. "Refusal to Compromise: The Case of Earth First!" *Western Journal of Speech Communication* 54 (1990): 473–494.

Lange, J. I. "The Logic of Competing Information Campaigns: Conflict over Old Growth and the Spotted Owl." *Communication Monographs* 60 (1993): 239–257.

Langer, S. *Philosophy in a New Key.* New York: New American Library, 1951.

Lavelle, M., and M. Coyle. "Unequal Protection: The Racial Divide in Environmental Law." *National Law Journal* (September 21, 1992): S1–S6.

Lebduska, L. "Rethinking Human Need: Seuss's *The Lorax*." *Children's Literature Association Quarterly* 19 (1994–95): 170–176.

Lee, M. F. "Violence and the Environment: The Case of Earth First!" *Terrorism and Political Violence* 7 (1995): 109–128.

Leopold, A. "Wilderness as a Form of Land Use." In *The Great New Wilderness Debate*, edited by J. B. Callicott and M. B. Nelson, 75–84. Athens: University of Georgia Press, 1925/1998.

Leopold, A. *A Sand County Almanac: And Sketches Here and There.* Oxford, UK: Oxford University Press, 1949/1977.

Lessl, T. M. "The Priestly Voice." *Quarterly Journal of Speech* 75 (1989): 183–197.

Lewis, M. *Green Delusions: An Environmentalist's Critique of Radical Environmentalism.* Durham, NC: Duke University Press, 1992.

Lewis, T. A. "Cloaked in a Wise Disguise." *National Wildlife,* October/November 1992, 4–9.

Limbaugh, R. *The Way Things Ought to Be.* New York: Simon and Schuster, 1992.

Liptak, K. *Saving Our Wetlands and Their Wildlife.* New York: Franklin Watts, 1991.

Little, C. E. *The Dying of the Trees: The Pandemic in American Forests.* New York: Viking, 1995.

Lovelock, J. *Gaia: A New Look at Life on Earth.* Oxford, UK: Oxford University Press, 1979.

Lovelock, J. *The Vanishing Face of Gaia: A Final Warning.* London: Allen Lane, 2009.

Lynch, B. D. "The Garden and the Sea: U.S. Latino Environmental Discourses and Mainstream Environmentalism." *Social Problems* 40 (1993): 108–124.

Lyotard, J. F. *The Postmodern Condition: A Report on Knowledge.* Manchester, UK: University of Manchester Press, 1984.

Manoff, R. K., and M. Schudson, eds. *Reading the News.* New York: Pantheon, 1986.

Martin, D. "The Joining of Human, Earth, and Spirit." In *Earth and Spirit: The Spiritual Dimensions of the Environmental Crisis,* edited by F. Hull, 43–57. New York: Continuum, 1993.

McGee, M. C. "The 'Ideograph': A Link between Rhetoric and Ideology." *Quarterly Journal of Speech* 66 (1980): 1–16.

McKibben, B. *The End of Nature.* New York: Random House, 1989.

McKibben, B. "A Deeper Shade of Green." *National Geographic,* August 2006, 33–41.

Meister, M. "Meteorology and the Rhetoric of Nature's Cultural Display." *Quarterly Journal of Speech* 87 (2001): 415–428.

Meister, M., and P. M. Japp. "Sustainable Development and the Global Economy." *Communication Research* 25 (1998): 399–421.

Meister, M., and P. M. Japp, eds. *Enviropop: Studies in Environmental Rhetoric and Popular Culture.* Westport, CT: Praeger, 2002.

Mellor, M. *Breaking the Boundaries: Toward a Feminist Green Socialism.* London: Virago, 1992.

Merchant, C. *The Death of Nature.* New York: Harper and Row, 1980.

Merwin, W. S. *The Lice.* New York: Atheneum, 1967.

Miller, A. S. *Gaia Connections: An Introduction to Ecology, Ecoethics, and Economics,* 2nd ed. New York: Rowman and Littlefield, 2003.

Miller, M. M., and B. Parnell Riechert. "Interest Group Strategies and Journalistic Norms: News Media's Framing of Environmental Issues." In *Environmental Risks and the Media,* edited by S. Allan, B. Adam, and C. Carter, 45–54. New York: Routledge, 2000.

Milstein, T. "When Whales 'Speak for Themselves': Communication as a Mediating Force in Wildlife Tourism." *Environmental Communication: A Journal of Nature and Culture* 2 (2008): 173–192.

Mohai, P., and R. Saha. "Reassessing Racial and Socioeconomic Disparities in Environmental Justice Research." *Demography* 43 (2006): 383–399.

Moje, E., and W. R. Shyu. "Oh, the Places You've Taken Us: The *Reading Teacher'*s Tribute to Dr. Seuss." In *Of Sneetches and Whos and the Good Dr. Seuss: Essays on the Writings and Life of Theodor Geisel,* edited by T. Fensch. Jefferson, NC: McFarland, 1997.

Moses, M. "Farmworkers and Pesticides." In *Confronting Environmental Racism: Voices from the Grassroots,* edited by R. D. Bullard, 161–178. Boston: South End, 1993.

Muir, J. "Selections from *Our National Parks.*" In *The Great New Wilderness Debate,* edited by J. B. Callicott and M. B. Nelson, 48–62. Athens: University of Georgia Press, 1901/1998.

Muir, J. *The Yosemite.* New York: Century, 1912.

Muir, J. "Man's Place in the Universe." In *A Thousand-Mile Walk to the Gulf,* edited by W. F. Badè. New York: Houghton Mifflin, 1916.

Muir, S. A. "Cultural and Critical Grammars of the Apocalypse: Strategies for a New Millennium." In *Proceedings of the 4th Biennial Conference on Communication and Environment,* edited by S. L. Senecah, 28–36. Cazenovia, NY: July 1997.

Murphy, P. C. *What a Book Can Do: The Publication and Reception of Silent Spring.* Boston: University of Massachusetts Press, 2005.

Naess, A. "The Deep Ecological Movement: Some Philosophical Aspects." *Philosophical Inquiry* 8 (1986): 10–31.

Naess, A. *Ecology, Community, and Lifestyle.* Cambridge, UK: Cambridge University Press, 1989.

Naess, A. "Simple in Means, Rich in Ends: An Interview with Arne Naess by Stephen Bodian." In *Environmental Philosophy: From Animal Rights to Radical Ecology,* edited by M. E. Zimmerman, J. B. Callicott, G. Sessions, K. J. Warren, and J. Clark, 182–192. Englewood Cliffs, NJ: Prentice Hall, 1993. This interview was originally published in 1982 by *The Ten Directions,* Los Angeles Zen Center.

Nash, R. *Wilderness and the American Mind.* New Haven, CT: Yale University Press, 1967.

Nash, R. *The American Environment: Readings in the History of Conservation.* London: Addison-Wesley, 1968.

National Research Council. *Understanding Risk: Informing Decisions in a Democratic Society.* Washington, DC: National Academy Press, 1996.

National Research Council. *Abrupt Climate Change: Inevitable Surprises.* Washington, DC: National Academy Press, 2002.

Nelson, G. *Beyond Earth Day: Fulfilling the Promise.* Madison: University of Wisconsin Press, 2002.

Ogden, C. K., and I. A. Richards. *The Meaning of Meaning,* 8th ed. New York: Harcourt, Brace, & World, 1946.

Oliver, M. *White Pine.* New York: Harcourt Brace, 1994.

Olsen, R. K., Jr. "Living Above It All: The Liminal Fantasy of Sports Utility Vehicle Advertisements." In *Enviropop: Studies in Environmental Rhetoric and Popular Culture,* edited by M. Meister and P. M. Japp, 175–196. Westport, CT: Praeger, 2002.

Opie, J., and N. Elliot. "Tracking the Elusive Jeremiad: The Rhetorical Character of American Environmental Discourse." In *The Symbolic Earth: Discourse and Our Creation of the Environment,* edited by J. G. Cantrill and C. L. Oravec, 9–37. Lexington: University of Kentucky Press, 1996.

Oravec, C. L. "Conservationism vs. Preservationism: The 'Public Interest' in the Hetch Hetchy Controversy." *Quarterly Journal of Speech* 70 (1984): 444–458.

Oravec, C. L. "To Stand Outside Oneself: The Sublime in the Discourse of Natural Scenery." In *The Symbolic Earth: Discourse and the Creation of the Environment,* edited by J. G. Cantrill and C. L. Oravec, 58–75. Lexington: University Press of Kentucky, 1996.

Oreskes, N. "The Scientific Consensus on Climate Change." *Science* 306 (December 3, 2004): 1686.

O'Sullivan, J. "The Great Nation of Futurity." *The United States Democratic Review* 6 (1839): 426–430.

Ott, B. L., and E. Aoki. "Popular Imagination and Identity Politics: Reading the Future in 'Star Trek: The Next Generation,'" *Western Journal of Communication* 65 (2001): 392–415.

Pacala, S., and R. Socolow. "Stabilization Wedges: Solving the Climate Problem for the Next 50 Years with Current Technologies." *Science* 305 (August 13, 2004): 968–972.

Paystrup, P. "Plastics as a 'Natural Resource': Perspective by Incongruity for an Industry in Crisis." In *The Symbolic Earth,* edited by J. G. Cantrill and C. L. Oravec, 176–197. Lexington: University Press of Kentucky, 1996.

Peeples, J. A. "Aggressive Mimicry: The Rhetoric of Wise Use and the Environmental Movement." *The Environmental Communication Yearbook* 2 (2005): 1–17.

Peeples, J. A., and K. M. DeLuca. "The Truth of the Matter: Motherhood, Community, and Environmental Justice." *Women's Studies in Communication* 29 (2006): 59–87.

Perelman, C., and L. Olbrechts-Tyteca. *The New Rhetoric: A Treatise on Argumentation,* translated by J. Wilkinson and P. Weaver. Notre Dame, IN: University of Notre Dame Press, 1971.

Peterson, T. R. *Sharing the Earth: The Rhetoric of Sustainable Development.* Columbia: University of South Carolina Press, 1997.

Peterson, T. R., and C. C. Horton. "Rooted in the Soil: How Understanding the Perspectives of Landowners Can Enhance the Management of Environmental Disputes." In *Landmark Essays on Rhetoric and the Environment,* edited by C. Waddell, 165–194. Mahwah, NJ: Erlbaum, 1998.

Pezzullo, P. C. "Performing Critical Interruptions: Rhetorical Invention and Narratives of the Environmental Justice Movement." *Western Journal of Communication* 64 (2001): 1–25.

Pezzullo, P. C. "Touring 'Cancer Alley,' Louisiana: Performance of Community and Memory for Environmental Justice." *Text and Performance Quarterly* 23 (2003): 226–252.

Pezzullo, P. C. "Toxic Tours: Communicating the 'Presence' of Chemical Contamination." In *Communication and Public Participation in Environmental Decision Making,* edited by S. P. Depoe, J. W. Delicath, and M. A. Elsenbeer, 235–254. Albany: State University of New York Press, 2004.

Pezzullo, P. C. *Toxic Tours: Rhetorics of Pollution, Travel, and Environmental Justice.* Tuscaloosa: University of Alabama Press, 2007.

Plant, C., and D. H. Albert. "Green Business in a Gray World: Can It be Done?" In *Green Business: Hope or Hoax,* edited by C. Plant and J. Plant, 1–8. Philadelphia: New Society, 1991.

Plec, E. "Poisoning a People, Poisoning a Planet." *Proceedings of the 8th Biennial Conference on Communication and Environment,* edited by L. S. Volkening, D. Wolfe, E. Plec, W. Griswold, and K. DeLuca, 82–91. Jekyll Island, GA: July 2005.

Plough, A., and S. Krimsky. "The Emergence of Risk Communication Studies: Social and Political Context." *Science, Technology, and Human Values* 12 (1987): 4–10.

Plumwood, V. "Nature, Self, and Gender: Feminism, Environmental Philosophy, and the Critique of Rationalism." *Hypathia* VI, No. 1 (Spring 1991): 3–27.

Plumwood, V. *Feminism and the Mastery of Nature.* New York: Routledge, 1993.

Proctor, J. D. "Whose Nature? The Contested Moral Terrain of Ancient Forests." In *Uncommon Ground: Toward Reinventing Nature,* edited by W. Cronon, 269–297. New York: Norton, 1995.

Ramage, J. D. *Rhetoric: A User's Guide.* New York: Pearson Education, 2006.

Ramos, T. "Wise Use in the West: The Case of Northwest Timber Industry." In *Let the People Judge,* edited by J. D. Echeverria and R. B. Eby, 82–118. Washington, DC: Island, 1995.

Ray, D. L., and L. R. Guzzo. *Environmental Overkill: Whatever Happened to Common Sense?* New York: Harper Perennial, 1994.

Rehling, D. L. "When Hallmark Calls upon Nature: Images of Nature in Greeting Cards." In *Enviropop: Studies in Environmental Rhetoric and Popular Culture,* edited by M. Meister and P. M. Japp, 13–30. Westport, CT: Praeger, 2002.

Retzinger, J. P. "The Embodied Rhetoric of 'Health' from Farm Fields to Salad Bowls." In *Proceedings of the 8th Biennial Conference on Communication and Environment,* edited by L. S. Volkening, D. Wolfe, E. Plec, W. Griswold, and K. DeLuca, 104–112. Jekyll Island, GA: July 2005.

Rifkin, J., Ed. *The Green Lifestyle Handbook: 1001 Ways You Can Heal the Earth.* New York: Henry Holt, 1990.

Roelofs, J. "Charles Fourier: Proto-Red-Green." In *Minding Nature: The Philosophers of Ecology,* edited by D. Macauley, 43–58. New York: Guilford, 1996.

Ross, A. *Strange Weather: Culture, Science, and Technology in the Age of Limits.* London: Verso, 1991.

Rossi, P. *Francis Bacon: From Magic to Science.* London: Routledge and Kegan Paul, 1968.

Roush, J. "Freedom and Responsibility: What We Can Learn from the Wise Use Movement." In *Let the People Judge,* edited by J. D. Echeverria and R. B. Eby, 1–10. Washington, DC: Island, 1995.

Rowland, R. C. "On Mythical Criticism." *Communication Studies* 41 (1990): 106–116.

Sagan, C. *The Pale Blue Dot: A Vision of the Human Future in Space.* New York: Random House, 1994.

Salleh, A. "Living with Nature: Reciprocity or Control?" In *Ethics of Environmental Development,* eds. J. Ronald Engle and Joan Gibb Engle (Tucson: University of Arizona Press, 1990). 245–253.

Sandler, R., and P. C. Pezzullo, eds. *Environmental Justice and Environmentalism: The Social Justice Challenge to the Environmental Movement.* Cambridge, MA: MIT Press, 2007.

Sattell, S. "Framing the Monarchs: A Study of the Monarch Butterfly Controversy and Its Role in the U.S. Debate on Genetically Engineered Crops." In *Proceedings of the Sixth Biennial Conference on Communication and Environment,* edited by M. Aepli, J. W. Delicath, and S. P. Depoe, 121–140. Cincinnati, OH: July 2001.

Schiappa, E. "The Rhetoric of Nukespeak." *Communication Monographs* 56 (1989): 253–272.

Schutten, J. K. "Chewing on the Grizzly Man: Getting to the Meat of the Matter." *Environmental Communication: A Journal of Nature and Culture* 2 (2008): 193–211.

Schwarze, S. "Environmental Melodrama." *Quarterly Journal of Speech* 92 (2006): 239–261.

Senecah, S. L. "The Sacredness of Natural Places: How a Big Canyon Became a Grand Icon." In *Proceedings from the Conference on the Discourse of Environmental Advocacy,* edited by C. L. Oravec and J. G. Cantrill, 203–223. Salt Lake City: University of Utah Humanities Center, July 1992.

Senecah, S. L. "The Process Trinity of Voice, Standing, and Influence: The Role of Practical Theory in Planning and Evaluating the Effectiveness of Environmental Participatory Processes." In *Communication and Public Participation in Environmental Decision Making,* edited by S. P. Depoe, J. W. Delicath, and M. Aepli Elsenbeer, 13–33. Albany: State University of New York Press, 2004.

Sessions, G. "Deep Ecology: Introduction." In *Environmental Philosophy: From Animal Rights to Radical Ecology,* edited by M. E. Zimmerman, J. B. Callicott, G. Sessions, K. J. Warren, and J. Clark, 161–170. Englewood Cliffs, NJ: Prentice Hall, 1993.

Seton, E. T. *Wild Animals I Have Known.* New York: Scribners, 1898.

Shabecoff, P. *A Fierce Green Fire: The American Environmental Movement.* Washington, DC: Island, 2003.

Shanahan, J., and K. McComas. *Nature Stories: Depictions of the Environment and Their Effects.* Cresskill, NJ: Hampton, 1999.

Shellenberger, M., and T. Nordhaus. *Break Through: From the Death of Environmentalism to the Politics of Possibility.* Boston: Houghton Mifflin, 2007.

Shiva, V. *Biopiracy: The Plunder of Nature and Knowledge.* Boston: South End, 1997.

Short, B. "Earth First! and the Rhetoric of Moral Confrontation." *Communication Studies* 42 (1991): 172–188.

Shotter, J. *Cultural Politics of Everyday Life: Social Constructionism, Rhetoric, and Knowing of the Third Kind.* Toronto: University of Toronto Press, 1993.

Simms, A. *Ecological Debt: The Health of the Planet and the Wealth of Nations.* London: Pluto, 2005.

Smith, C. *Media and Apocalypse: News Coverage of the Yellowstone Forest Fires, Exxon Valdez Oil Spill, and Loma Prieta Earthquake.* Westport, CT: Greenwood, 1992.

Smith, T. M. *The Myth of Green Marketing: Tending Our Goats at the Edge of Apocalypse.* Toronto: University of Toronto Press, 1998.

Snow, D. A., and R. D. Benford. "Master Frames and Cycles of Protest." In *Frontiers in Social Movement Theory,* edited by A. D. Morris and C. McClurg Mueller, 133–155. New Haven, CT: Yale University Press, 1992.

Snyder, G. *The Practice of the Wild: Essays.* San Francisco: North Point, 1990.

Snyder, G. *Turtle Island.* New York: New Directions, 1974.

Solomon, N., and J. Cohen. *The Wizards of Media Oz: Behind the Curtain of Mainstream News.* Monroe, ME: Common Courage, 1997.

Speth, J. G. *The Bridge at the Edge of the World: Capitalism, the Environment, and Crossing from Crisis to Sustainability.* New Haven. CT: Yale University Press, 2008.

Spirn, A. W. "Constructing Nature: The Legacy of Frederick Law Olmsted." In *Uncommon Ground: Toward Reinventing Nature,* edited by W. Cronon, 91–113. New York: Norton, 1995.

Stegner, W., ed. *This Is Dinosaur: Echo Park Country and its Magic Rivers.* New York: Knopf, 1955.

Stegner, W. *Marking the Sparrow's Fall: Wallace Stegner's American West.* New York: Henry Holt, 1998.

Stewart, C. J., A. S. Smith, and R. E. Denton, Jr. *Persuasion and Social Movements,* 4th ed. Prospect Heights, IL: Waveland, 2001.

Stocking, H., and J. P. Leonard. "The Greening of the Media." *Columbia Journalism Review* 29 (1990): 37–44.

Szasz, A. *Shopping Our Way to Safety: How We Changed from Protecting the Environment to Protecting Ourselves.* Minneapolis: University of Minnesota Press, 2007.

Taylor, B. C., and J. Hendry. "Insisting on Persisting: The Nuclear Rhetoric of 'Stockpile Stewardship.'" *Rhetoric and Public Affairs* 11 (2008): 303–334.

Tedford, T. L., and D. A. Herbeck. *Freedom of Speech in the United States,* 6th ed. State College, PA: Strata, 2009.

Thiele, L. P. *Environmentalism for a New Millennium: A Challenge of Coevolution.* New York: Oxford University Press, 1999.

Thompson, R. "Emerson, Divinity, and Rhetoric in Transcendentalist Nature Writing and Twentieth-Century Ecopoetry." In *Ecopoetry: A Critical Introduction,* edited by S. Bryson, 29–38. Salt Lake City: University of Utah Press, 2002.

Thoreau, H. D. *Huckleberries.* Iowa City: Windhover Press, University of Iowa, 1971.

Thoreau, H. D. "Walking." In *The Great New Wilderness Debate,* edited by J. B. Callicott and M. P. Nelson, 31–41. Athens: University of Georgia Press, (1862/1998).

Todd, A. M. "Prime-Time Subversion: The Environmental Rhetoric of *The Simpsons.*" In *Enviropop: Studies in Environmental Rhetoric and Popular Culture,* edited by M. Meister and P. M. Japp, 63–80. Westport, CT: Praeger, 2002.

Tokar, B. *Earth for Sale: Reclaiming Ecology in the Age of Corporate Greenwash,* Boston: South End, 1997.

Treadwell, T., and J. Palovak. *Among Grizzlies: Living with Wild Bears*. New York: Ballantine, 1997.

Turner, F. J. *The Frontier in American History*. New York: Henry Holt, 1947.

Twain, M. *Extracts from Adam's Diary. A Short Story by Mark Twain*. New York: Harper, 1904.

Twitchell, J. B. *Adcult USA: The Triumph of Advertising in American Culture*. New York: Columbia University Press, 1996.

Vygotsky, L. S. *Mind in Society: The Development of Higher Psychological Processes*, edited by M. Cole, V. John-Steiner, S. Scribner, and E. Souberman. Cambridge, MA: Harvard University Press, 1978.

Waddell, C. "Saving the Great Lakes: Public Participation in Environmental Policy." In *Green Culture: Environmental Rhetoric in Contemporary America*, edited by C. G. Herndl and S. C. Brown, 141–165. Madison: University of Wisconsin Press, 1996.

Waddell, C., ed. *Landmark Essays on Rhetoric and the Environment*. Mahwah, NJ: Erlbaum, 1998.

Walker, G. B. "The Roadless Initiative as National Policy: Is Public Participation an Oxymoron?" In *Communication and Public Participation in Environmental Decision Making*, edited by S. P. Depoe, J. W. Delicath, and M. Aepli Elsenbeer, 113–135. Albany: State University of New York Press, 2004.

Ward, B. "The Effects of Climate Change on Journalism As We Know It." *SE Journal* 17 (2007): 6, 20.

Warren, K. J. "The Power and Promise of Ecological Feminism." *Environmental Ethics* 12 (1990): 125–144.

Warren, K. J. "Ecofeminism." In *Environmental Philosophy: From Animal Rights to Radical Ecology*, edited by M. E. Zimmerman, J. B. Callicott, G. Sessions, K. J. Warren, and J. Clark, 253–265. Englewood Cliffs, NJ: Prentice Hall, 1993.

Warren, K. J. *Ecofeminist Philosophy: A Western Perspective on What It Is and Why It Matters*. New York: Rowman and Littlefield, 2000.

Warren, L. S., ed. *American Environmental History*. Malden, MA: Blackwell, 2003.

Wasserman, S., and N. Solomon. *Killing Our Own: The Disaster of America's Experience with Atomic Radiation*. New York: Dell, 1982.

Weart, S. R. *The Discovery of Global Warming*. Cambridge, MA: Harvard University Press, 2003.

Weaver, R. *Language is Sermonic: Richard M. Weaver on the Nature of Rhetoric*. edited by R. L. Johannesen, R. Strickland, and R. T. Eubanks. Baton Rouge: Louisiana State University Press, 1970.

Weiner, N. *The Human Use of Human Beings: Cybernetics and Society*, 2nd ed. Garden City, NY: Doubleday, 1954.

West, E. "A Longer, Grimmer, but More Interesting Story." In *Trails: Toward a New Western History*, edited by P. Nelson Limerick, C. A. Milner II, and C. E. Rankin, 103–111. Lawrence: University Press of Kansas, 1991.

White, L., Jr. "The Historical Roots of Our Ecological Crisis." In *Western Man and Environmental Ethics*, edited by I. G. Barbour, 18–30. Reading, MA: Addison-Wesley, 1973.

Whybrow, P. C. *American Mania: When More is Not Enough*. New York: Norton, 2005.

Wilkins, L., and P. Patterson. "Risk Analysis and the Construction of News." *Journal of Communication* 37 (1987): 80–92.

Willard, B. "Mythic Arcadia: Reading the Landscapes of Conservation Communities." In *Proceedings of the 7th Biennial Conference on Communication and Environment,* edited by G. B. Walker and W. J. Kinsella, 202–208. Silver Falls State Park, OR: July 2003.

Wilson, E. O. *The Diversity of Life.* New York: Norton, 1993.

Wilson, E. O. *The Creation: An Appeal to Save Life on Earth.* New York: Norton, 2006.

Wilson, K. M. "Communicating Climate Change through the Media: Predictions, Politics and Perceptions of Risk." In *Environmental Risks and the Media,* edited by S. Allan, B. Adams, and C. Carter, 201–217. New York: Routledge, 2000.

Wolfe, D. "The Ecological Jeremiad, the American Myth, and the Vivid Force of Color in Dr. Seuss's *The Lorax.*" *Environmental Communication: A Journal of Nature and Culture* 2 (2008): 3–24.

Worm, B., E. B. Barbier, N. Beaumont, J. E. Duffy, C. Folke, B. S. Halpern, J. B. C. Jackson, H. K. Lotze, F. Micheli, S. R. Palumbi, E. Sala, K. A. Selkoe, J. J. Stachowicz, and R. Watson, "Impacts of Biodiversity Loss on Ocean Ecosystem Services," *Science* 314 (November 3, 2006): 787–790.

Worster, D. "Beyond the Agrarian Myth." In *Trails: Toward a New Western History,* edited by P. N. Limerick, C. A. Milner II, and C. E. Rankin. Lawrence: University of Kansas Press, 1991.

Zakin, S. *Coyotes and Town Dogs: Earth First! and the Environmental Movement.* Tucson: University of Arizona Press, 2002.

Zimmerman, M. E., J. B. Callicott, G. Sessions, K. J. Warren, and J. Clark, eds. *Environmental Philosophies: From Animal Rights to Radical Ecology.* Englewood Cliffs, NJ: Prentice Hall, 1993.

Timeline: Environmental Milestones

The following is an annotated timeline of notable events and significant pieces of legislation spurred by the modern environmental movement in the United States. Although far from all-inclusive, the entries on this timeline represent important breakthroughs and accomplishments in the long and ongoing struggle for environmental protections.

1962 *Silent Spring*, by Rachel Carson

Many believe that because of its impact on the public consciousness, *Silent Spring* was the catalyst for the modern environmental movement. As a result of the fallout from this book, new laws were passed restricting the sale and use of agricultural chemicals.

1964 Wilderness Act

This legislation was passed to protect wilderness areas and set up processes for future preservation of wilderness lands.

1966 Freedom of Information Act (FOIA)

FOIA permits any person to request and obtain a federal agency's records, including meeting transcripts, documents, letters, photographs, tapes, and so forth. Some information is protected from disclosure, for reasons such as national security exemptions. The FOIA was amended in 1986 to close several disclosure loopholes that undermined citizens' ability to obtain information.

1966 National Wildlife Refuge System Administration Act

This act provided directives for the establishment and management of areas for wildlife protection and conservation.

1968 Wild and Scenic Rivers Act

This legislation provided for the protection and preservation (in free-flowing condition) of rivers that are significant because of their scenic, recreational, fish and wildlife, geologic, cultural, or historic features.

1969 The National Environmental Policy Act

Believed by many to be the most significant piece of environmental legislation ever passed, the law requires federal land managers to assess environmental impacts before going ahead with a planned action such as logging or mining on federal lands. It also requires federal agencies to involve citizen stakeholders in their land-use decision processes.

1970 First Earth Day

April 22, 1970, the first Earth Day, was a coast-to-coast event in which 20 million people took part in rallies, events, or clean-up projects across the country. This remains the largest single-day demonstration in United States history. An estimated 125,000 people rallied in Washington, D.C., to call attention to environmental problems.

1970   Clean Air Act

This act regulated smog-causing pollutants and directed the EPA to establish air quality standards. Originally enacted in 1963, the 1970 version expanded protections to include such things as smokestack scrubbers, catalytic converters on automobiles, and removing lead from gasoline. A 1990 amendment added additional pollutants to regulation standards and established emissions trading permits.

1970   Environmental Protection Agency (EPA)

The EPA was established by executive order to serve as an independent agency in the executive branch, to coordinate government action on behalf of the environment.

1972   Clean Water Act

Originally called the Federal Water Pollution Control Act, this legislation regulated the release of pollutants into waterways and mandated the restoration of polluted waters. (Significant amendments were added in 1977.)

1972   Federal Insecticide, Fungicide, and Rodenticide Act (FIFRA)

This act mandates that EPA regulate the sale and use of pesticides and provides EPA with the corresponding oversight authority. Originally passed in 1947, the law was fundamentally rewritten in 1972 and has undergone numerous amendments throughout the course of its history.

1972   Marine Mammal Protection Act (MMPA)

This act prohibits the taking of marine mammals in United States waters as well as importing of marine mammals and marine mammal products into the U.S. All marine mammals (with some exemptions) are protected under MMPA.

1972   Marine Protection, Research, and Sanctuaries Act (MPRSA)

Also known as the **Ocean Dumping Act,** this act prohibits dumping materials into U.S. territorial ocean waters that would negatively impact, degrade, or endanger the marine environment or human health.

1973   Endangered Species Act

This historic piece of legislation mandated federal agencies to list all species in danger of extinction and to develop plans for their recovery, including the protection of critical habitat for endangered species.

1974   Safe Drinking Water Act (SDWA)

The primary federal law that ensures the quality of drinking water in the U.S., this law authorized the EPA to set water quality standards and oversee water suppliers' implementation of these standards on the local and state level.

1976   Resource Conservation and Recovery Act (RCRA)

This act regulates the disposal of solid and hazardous wastes. RCRA bans all open dumping and mandates controls over the treatment, storage, and disposal of hazardous waste.

1976   Toxic Substances Control Act (TSCA or TOSCA)

This act authorized the EPA to obtain the data necessary for assessing chemicals and to regulate the production and use of dangerous chemicals.

1976   The Government in the Sunshine Act

Most often referred to as **The Sunshine Act,** this legislation requires all government agencies that are subject to the FOIA (1966) to provide public notice of their meetings and to open their meetings to the public. It also allows citizens to obtain records of their meetings through the Federal Register. There are, however, certain exemptions from disclosure.

1977   Soil and Water Conservation Act

This act established soil and water conservation programs to assist landowners and land users, at their request, to conserve and protect soil and water on private and nonfederal lands.

1978   National Parks and Recreation Act

This act nearly tripled the amount of land set aside as wilderness in national parks, by adding fifteen new parks to the National Park system.

1980   Comprehensive Environmental Response, Compensation, and Liability Act (CERCLA)

More commonly known as the **Superfund Act,** this legislation authorized the EPA to hold responsible parties liable for remediation of hazardous wastes. It also created a "superfund" to be used by the EPA to help fund the cleanup of designated sites.

1986   Emergency Planning and Community Right-to-Know Act

This act required facilities to report their use of hazardous chemicals and authorized the EPA to create the Toxic Release Inventory (TRI), a nationwide database of toxic chemical emissions. It also required local and state agencies to prepare responses to emergencies caused by chemical releases.

1987   The Montreal Accord on Ozone

Also called the **Montreal Protocol,** this agreement, signed by the United States and twenty-three other nations of the world, promised to phase out the production of ozone-destroying chlorofluorocarbons (CFCs).

1988   Intergovernmental Panel on Climate Change (IPCC)

This collaboration of scientists was established by the World Meteorological Organization and the United Nations Environment Programme to examine the available research on climate change and make assessment reports, the first of which was issued in 1990.

1990   First Assessment Report (FAR) of the IPCC

The first report of the IPCC verified claims that atmospheric CO_2 concentrations resulting from human activities were substantially increasing. They predicted that under the business-as-usual scenario, global mean temperatures would increase .3° C per decade. A supplement to this report, published in 1992, confirmed the major conclusions of the 1990 report.

1990   Pollution Prevention Act

This Act established the national policy to reduce pollution at its source, in order to reduce the need for waste disposal and management.

1992   Earth Summit in Rio de Janeiro

This historic United Nations conference brought world leaders together in Brazil to discuss plans for addressing global sustainability. A significant outcome of the meeting was *Agenda 21,* a document outlining sustainable development practices. The summit reconvenes every five years to assess progress towards Agenda 21 goals.

1994   Environmental Justice Executive Order 12898

Signed by President Bill Clinton, this order directed federal agencies to develop strategies for identifying and addressing environmental justice issues. It also established the National Environmental Justice Advisory Council within the EPA.

1995   Second Assessment Report (SAR) of the IPCC

The Intergovernmental Panel on Climate Change confirmed that greenhouse gas concentrations in the atmosphere had continued to increase at a pace consistent with the predictions of the first report in 1990. The panel also reported significant progress in distinguishing between natural and human-caused influences on climate, as well as increased confidence in the models predicting future climate change, although many uncertainties remain.

1996   Electronic Freedom of Information Act (E-FOIA)

An amendment to the 1966 Freedom of Information Act (FOIA), the legislation requires federal agencies to post key records online (with certain exemptions) and provide indexes and guidance for online users.

1997   The Kyoto Protocol

Formally called the **Kyoto Protocol to the United Nations Framework Convention on Climate Change,** this agreement commits participating industrialized countries to cut CO_2 emissions. Conspicuously absent from the signatories were the United States, Australia, and Russia, although Russia ratified it in 2004. The accord went into effect in 2005, when it was finally ratified by the required number of nations—the United States and Australia still not among them. The United States had officially withdrawn in 2001.

2001   Third Assessment Report (TAR) of the IPCC

The IPCC reports that confidence in the ability of models to predict climate change has continued to increase, and that there is now strong evidence that most of the warming that has occurred over the past fifty years is attributable to human activities.

2007   Fourth Assessment Report (AR4) of the IPCC

This is by far the most sobering report released so far. Its language is considerably stronger than the guarded language of the previous reports. "The warming of the climate system is unequivocal," says the report. It predicts that world temperatures could rise between 1.1° C and 6.4° C (2.0° F and 11.5° F) during the twenty-first century and that sea levels will probably rise 18 to 59 centimeters (7.8 to 23.22 inches). The report also states that atmospheric CO_2 concentrations now exceed any in the past 650,000 years. It gives a sobering summary of the likely future impacts of climate change and reports that we are already committed to a 1.5° C (2.7° F) increase in warming, even if we were to immediately halt all CO_2 emissions.

2007   Nobel Peace Prize Awarded to Al Gore and the IPCC

This prestigious recognition was awarded to the Intergovernmental Panel on Climate Change and former United States vice president Al Gore, placing the world spotlight on the science of global warming and the importance of communicating the need for action.

2009   Copenhagen Climate Change Conference (COP15)

World leaders assembled in Copenhagen, Denmark, to craft a new global agreement to replace the 1997 Kyoto Protocol. Although no binding agreement was produced from the talks, the historic meeting signaled a global recognition of the urgency of the problem of climate change and showed a willingness on the part of the United States and China (the world's two largest emitters of CO_2) to take leadership roles in reaching an international agreement.

Credits and Acknowledgments

Grateful acknowledgment is made for permission to use the following:

Excerpts on pages 5, 7, 206–208, and 212, from *Uncommon Ground: Toward Reinventing Nature,* ed. William Cronon (New York: Norton, 1995). Reprinted by permission of W. W. Norton & Company, Inc.

"The Climate Change Solution in Wedges," textbox on page 27 adapted from Stephen Pacala and Robert Socolow, "Stabilization Wedges: Solving the Climate Problem for the Next 50 Years with Current Technologies," *Science* 305 (August 13, 2004): 968–972. Reprinted with permission from AAAS.

Excerpt on page 65 from BIG YELLOW TAXI. Words and Music by JONI MITCHELL. © 1970 (Renewed) CRAZY CROW MUSIC. All Rights Administered by SONY/ATV MUSIC PUBLISHING. All Rights Reserved.

Excerpts on pages 84, 92–93, and 103 from Kevin M. DeLuca, *Image Politics: The New Rhetoric of Environmental Activism* (New York: Guilford, 1999). Reprinted by permission of The Guilford Press.

"New Arcadia or Suburban Sprawl?" textbox on page 91, adapted from Barb Willard "Mythic Arcadia: Reading the Landscapes of Conservation Communities," in *Proceedings of the 7th Biennial Conference on Communication and Environment,* eds. G. B. Walker and W. J. Kinsella (Silver Falls State Park, OR, July 2003). Used by permission of Barbara E. Willard.

Excerpt from Gary Snyder on page 95. Copyright © 2003 by Gary Snyder from *The Practice of the Wild: Essays.* Reprinted by permission of Counterpoint.

Excerpt on page 95 from "For A Coming Extinction" by W. S. Merwin. Copyright ©1967 by W. S. Merwin, reprinted with permission of The Wylie Agency LLC.

Excerpts on page 102 from the Earth First! website, www.EarthFirst.org. Used by permission of Earth First!

Wombat quote in "Rhetoric of Unification: Words of Wombat Wisdom," textbox on page 116, accessed at www.global-mindshift.org/memes/wombat.swf. Used by permission of Global Mindshift Foundation.

Excerpts from National Resource Defense Council mailings on pages 128 and 129. Reprinted by permission of Natural Resources Defense Council, Inc.

Discussion of the rhetoric of the irreparable appeals on pages 128 and 129 adapted from Terence Check, "Re-thinking the Irreparable." (Paper presented at the Annual Convention of the National Communication Association, Chicago, IL, 1999.) Used by permission of Terence Check.

Excerpts on pages 132–133 from Global Scenario Group, *Great Transition.* Reprinted by permission of the Tellus Institute.

Excerpts on pages 194 and 195 from Kirkpatrick Sale, "The Trouble with Earth Day," in *Green Business: Hope or Hoax,* eds. C. Plant and J. Plant (Philadelphia: New Society Publishers, 1991). Reprinted by permission of New Society Publishers.

Excerpts on pages 210 and 211: From THE LORAX by Dr. Seuss, copyright ® and copyright © by Dr. Seuss Enterprises, L.P. 1971, renewed 1999. Used by permission of Random House Children's Books, a division of Random House, Inc.

Excerpts on pages 240 and 243 from Jennifer A. Peeples and Kevin M. DeLuca, "The Truth of the Matter: Motherhood, Community and Environmental Justice," *Women's Studies in Communication* 29 (2006). Reprinted by permission of *Women's Studies in Communication.*

Credits for figures appear in the figure captions.

Credits for Additional Readings appear on the first pages of the respective readings.

Index